An Unusual C. V.
(or latter day tales of a grandfather, with apologies
to Sir Walter Scott)
The first half at least! (1932 - 1959)

Foreword and Introduction by
Professor Angus MacKay

Copyright 2010

Second paperback edition published in Great Britain
December 2012
by
Bronte Media Services

First paperback edition published
July 2010

All rights reserved
No part of this publication may be reproduced, stored in a retrieval system or transmitted in any form or by any means: electronic, mechanical, photocopying, recording or otherwise without the prior permission of the publisher.

ISBN: 9781906349141

Foreword

by Professor A.V.P. Mackay

I feel the pulse before I hear the unmistakable exhaust note as the exquisite silver open top Jaguar XK120 sweeps up the drive to my house. Out hops Bob, surely too spritely for his more than three score years and ten, chin and shoulders slightly forward – as always, seeking, purposeful and genial. He has come to enquire, with patience and some embarrassment, about the progress with this foreword. Rightly so; the narrative that follows is so unusual and compelling, it has been a very hard act to precede.

The stated purpose of the book is to record, for his children, the 'first half' of the life and times of this remarkable man. However, it is also essentially the story of a man and his car, a loving, respectful and constant relationship that has now lasted nearly 60 years. What follows will reward the reader with immediate enjoyment, but its value is more than that. It provides an important record of post-war colonial life through the eyes of a participant whose frankness can at times seem almost offensive, but which is always compelling. The question of the active ingredients to the man inevitably presses for an answer. He was born in East London within the sound of Bow Bells, of a Cuban-born English mother and a Scottish father who was a successful City rubber trader. Rich genetic diversity came from both parents – French, German and Irish lineage on his mother's side, aptitude for the colourful and adventurous seems evident in his Victorian forebears; for example maternal grandfather pioneered the building of railways in Mexico, South America and Cuba. This advantageous genetic endowment must have helped him to hit the ground running and so make the best use of his strict Christian upbringing, Grammar and Public schooling, and early hair-raising escapades. From schooldays he seems to have personified the Scouting attributes of loyalty, kindness and thrift, mixed with an ample dose of hunger for adventure and a disregard for personal safety if it conflicted with his considered purpose at the time. Nature and nurture of course interact continually, and in Bob's case the net result has been a fearless, tenacious, yet morally driven persona.

Still in his teens, at an age when most young men would be pondering what to do with their lives, he had trained in the international rubber market, gone like his father before him into the rubber trade in Malaya, and already been 'noticed', apparently by the British Secret Service as an asset to be exploited.

This was in the early 1950's when Malaya was the target of communist avarice, a theatre in which overt war was taking place albeit given no higher status than an 'emergency' by the post Churchillian government of the day. Alongside his official rather Gentleman Jim occupation and lifestyle, he became engaged with considerable relish in clandestine armed conflict with the communist insurgents, a member of a small special forces outfit, partly comprising remnants of Force 136 that had conducted a guerrilla campaign against the Japanese following the fall of Singapore. Admiration for Churchill emerges clearly and nostalgically throughout this account, as does hatred of both the practice and theory of communism. Descriptions of the hardships and naked violence of jungle conflict come interspersed with anecdotes of the social high life and fleeting romances – none perhaps more striking than the incredible Connie, the beautiful jive champion of South East Asia, who proved herself equally talented with a Webley 38 revolver as she and Bob fought off a roadside ambush. Five communist terrorists were killed and the only recorded injury to the other side was a broken fingernail sustained by Connie as she pulled the pin from a grenade. The Jaguar XK that had been bought new and shipped from Coventry to Singapore, and although not featuring in that particular action, was destined to play a lead role in many of this man's remarkable life events. In a later encounter, near Bentong, man and Jaguar were driving, characteristically at a round 100 miles per hour, when both were hit by bullets. Clearly rather irritated, Bob screeched to a halt, reversed furiously, and quickly dispatched the assailant. Bob's wounds have healed but the XK retains the evidence to this day as two concealed holes in its aluminium skin.

A brief sojourn was to be spent back home in the British Isles, where this far from ordinary life continued, inevitably, to be sprinkled with colour and high risk exploits. Encounters with Diana Dors at Pinewood and a certain spirited Princess at the yacht club on the Isle of Wight were all par for the course, as was another of Bob's skirmishes with death as a passenger in a high speed car crash. Assigned to a new trading company in Djakarta, he returned to South East Asia, to be reunited with his faithful Jaguar, and where his 'other job' this time was to assess the extent of communist activity along the Indonesian side of the border with British North Borneo. It is during this period that we read an account of personal hardship, danger and bravery in the tropical jungle that must equal any in published fiction or history. Bear in mind this was a very young man, whose exploits by the time he reached 20 would have been enough to fill any normal person's memoirs, but he soon embarked on a completely new series of adventures and achievements – now in the air as well as on land.

Having been smitten with the excitement of flying while out East, he developed his largely self-taught knowledge and skills to become Chief Engineer for Short Aviation, based at Lossiemouth, servicing and flying de-commissioned Mosquitos. His admiration for the Rolls Royce Merlin engine grew to equal that for Sir Winston Churchill. Typical of the man, white knuckle experiences continued to feature, this time above the unsuspecting inhabitants of Morayshire. The Mosquito connection then took him to Canada where he and his then wife, and XK, started yet another new life, and a family. It is here that Bob indulges perhaps more fully in his accounts of the joy of driving his car to the limit, initially to some resentment from the local Motor Club, to be replaced by astonishment and finally awe. Two gems come to mind from this period, both illustrating particular facets of his character. The first is his sympathy for the underdog, expressed in this instance by his offer to drive the modest car of a habitual loser in the local rallies and the butt of undeserved derision. Dramatic victory was the outcome, made all the more savoury by the defeat of one particularly conceited rival. The second is his single-minded perseverance with the challenge of the moment. This time competing in the trusty XK in the British Empire Motor Club's International Winter Rally. Having driven for 68 hours in Arctic temperatures, fallen through the ice of a frozen lake, to be pulled out by wire ropes attached to the same bumper irons that pulled Mosquitos from hangers at Lossiemouth, man and car went on to win the Silver Rosebowl. The car trade then progressively became the focus of Bob's fortunes in Canada, and this persisted after his return to England in 1959 where he became involved in top level race car preparation. Before leaving Canada he had been introduced to a remarkably innovative carburettor known as the Fish, a development that was to feature large in later years. It was clearly with little regret that he left Canada; "the only thing I brought back apart from Fish and family, was the XK".

The concluding period of this 'first half' is spent in his now native and beloved Argyll. Taking a breather? Not a bit of it. The Fish carburettor is evolved and widely applied and acclaimed, and the Argyll Turbo GT was created in a former laundry building in Lochgilphead. This bespoke supercar, once described as "Scotland's Bristol" and the star of the very last Kelvin Hall Scottish Motor Show in the year of its launch in 1983, was designed, developed and produced with no government finance, only Bob's tenacity and his sound engineering knowledge, aeronautical background and competition experience.

The glimpses that I have tried to give the reader into the narrative that follows are no more than that. The full story is as riveting and remarkable as any that might have emerged from the pen of Ian Fleming. It is told in a no-nonsense style, and one which is endearing in its occasional admission that the precise sequence of events as they unfold may reflect more on the way memories emerge than on calendar accuracy. However, the veracity is unquestioned. The author pulls no punches in his disdain for the politically correct, his contempt for the contemporary obsession with health and safety, and even for certain nations and cultures of which he has had distasteful experience. All expressed with a conviction and validity that can only come form having been there, done that. Whether a second half of this curriculum vitae will be written remains to be seen. The XK has been treated to a new coat but is otherwise largely as it left Brown's Lane in early 1951 (apart from the bullet holes), a fact that is as remarkable and, sadly, as anachronistic as the spirit of its proud companion.

We salute you Tuan XK Bob.

ANGUS V.P. MACKAY

Educated at George Heriot's School and the Universities of Edinburgh and Cambridge. Bachelor of Science, Bachelor of Medicine, Bachelor of Surgery (Edin), Master of Arts, Doctor of Philosopy (Cantab), Fellow of the Royal College of Physicians of Edinburgh, Fellow of the Royal College of Psychiatrists, Teacher in Psychiatry, Fellow of the Royal Society of Medicine.

Awarded O.B.E. for services to medicine.

Currently Professor of Psychological Medicine, University of Glasgow, Chairman of the Research Advisory Committee of the Sackler Institute of Psychobiology, Member of the Board of the Medicines and Healthcare Products Regulatory Agency (UK), Member of the Mental Health Tribunal of Scotland.

Previously Medical Research Council Research Fellow in Edinburgh and Cambridge; Senior Clinical Scientist, MRC Neurochemical Pharmachology Unit, Cambridge; Lector in Pharmacology, Trinity College, Cambridge; Consultant Psychiatrist, Physician Superintendent and Clinical Director, Argyll and Dumbarton Mental Health Services; Member of the Committee on Safety of Medicines; Chairman of the Health Technology Board of Scotland, Chairman of the Secretary of State's Independent Scrutiny Panel. Chair or Member of various national bodies concerned with medical and neuroscientific research, mental health service standards and delivery, medical professional distinction awards, and the licensing and regulation of medicines in the UK and Europe. Invited lecturer in the UK, continental Europe and the USA.

Author/co-author of some ninety publications on neurochemistry, neuropharmacology and mental health services.

Sport: rowing - Captain of Boats, George Heriot's; University of Edinburgh First Eight; Churchill College Cambridge First Eight and Coxless Pair.

Hobbies: rowing, sailing, rhododenrons, Jaguar cars.

Contents

1.	The early years	1
2.	The formative years	8
3.	Veggie time	12
4.	Uncle C	14
5.	Scouting	16
6.	First jumps	19
7.	First flights	20
8.	Commercial training	21
9.	Enter the outside world	25
10.	Singapore	29
11.	Up country	37
12.	Finally to work	39
13.	Action man!	41
14.	Theft?	44
15.	Port Swettenham	56
16.	Enter Connie	58
17.	Politics and incompetent policies..	69
18.	Conspirators	72
19.	First Sortie	73
20.	The Melshams	77
21.	Petaling	80
22.	Mc.G. tech.	93
23.	Innovative jungle clothing.	97
24.	Jungle Equipment	99
25.	Salt, the fallacy of?	102
26.	Jumping	104
27.	Enter Geoff 'B'	106
28.	Hash House Harriers	109
29.	Frank's mobile	111
30.	No go area?	113
31.	XK120 wounded!	116
32.	Airborne	121
33.	Damp squibs	123
34.	Hills	125
35.	Swamps	127
36.	A fine Policeman.	132
37.	Islands	136

38.	The influence of cars	...	...	...	143
39.	Air recces	...	...	...	155
40.	Epic Flight	...	...	...	157
41.	Impending sadness	...	...	...	165
42.	Templer, the General and the man...		...		169
43.	Singapore, some thoughts...		...	...	172
44.	Racial prejudice?	...	...	...	174
45.	Underway (finally)	...	...	...	182
46.	Cultural shocks?	...	...	...	183
47.	Egypt again!	...	...	...	184
48.	Eulogy for a dog	...	...	...	187
49.	Setback? (or just a delay)..		...	...	194
50.	Gainfully employed again		...	...	203
51.	The nefarious element!	...	...	...	205
52.	The journey back East	...	...	...	206
53.	Djakarta	...	...	...	210
54.	Nonnie	...	...	...	214
55.	Commerce again!	...	...	...	219
56.	A sad faux pas	...	...	...	223
57.	Surabaya	...	...	...	225
58.	Smallie	...	...	...	228
59.	Kim Ling Lee	...	...	...	231
60.	Borneo-one	...	...	...	239
61.	B.2. (wild man of-B?)	...	...	...	246
62.	En route	...	...	...	250
63.	W. Borneo, itself	...	...	...	253
64.	Up river	...	...	...	256
65.	Even further!	...	...	...	258
66.	The other tack	...	...	...	260
67.	Decisions, decisions	...	...	...	262
68.	Very alone	...	...	...	264
69.	A new home	...	...	...	266
70.	Found them!	...	...	...	267
71.	Typical commies	...	...	...	269
72.	My good turn	...	...	...	270
73.	New friends?	...	...	...	272
74.	The lion's den?	...	...	...	274
75.	Bingo!	...	...	...	275
76.	Double bingo!	...	...	...	278

77.	Friends, again	... ...	281
78.	Disaster?	... ...	283
79.	Needs must!	... ...	284
80.	Water baby	... ...	287
81.	Not funny	... ...	289
82.	9-10 & out!	... ...	291
83.	Brain into gear	... ...	293
84.	Disaster, almost	... ...	297
85.	Escape, Stage 1 completed	... ...	302
86.	Escape, Stage 2 completed	... ...	306
87.	Palembang	... ...	308
88.	Djakarta, at last	... ...	309
89.	Sick again	... ...	318
90.	Bali	... ...	320
91.	Post Bali	... ...	326
92.	Homeward bound	... ...	327
93.	Home?	... ...	329
94.	Prue., in person	... ...	331
95.	Unemployed?	... ...	333
96.	Out of…comes life!	... ...	335
97.	Mosquito reunion	... ...	336
98.	Lossiemouth	... ...	341
99.	Instant promotion	... ...	343
100.	Skulduggery?	... ...	345
101.	Fun Mossies	... ...	347
102.	M. in Law trouble already!	... ...	350
103.	Penn, a third rate pilot	... ...	351
104.	A salient lesson	... ...	355
105.	Penn, the regular thief.. ...	... ...	356
106.	To marry or ?	... ...	358
107.	Enter Peter Nock, pilot extrordinaire	...	361
108.	..and Penn the liar	... ...	362
109.	Another con. man (boy) ...	... ...	363
110.	More Peter N.	... ...	364
111.	Another Israeli!	... ...	367
112.	Musings	... ...	369
113.	Lossie. madness?	... ...	371
114.	Entering the valley of D.........	... ...	374
115.	Postscript	... ...	378

116.	Some further technicalities	...	...	...	380
117.	More musings	...	...	...	382
118.	Some neighbourly and local activities		...		384
119.	The hated Paisley bit!	...	...	...	387
120.	Relief, Lossie again	...	...	...	391
121.	Naval clangers	...	...	...	394
122.	Personal flying & clangers?	...	...	...	396
123.	Learning experience	...	...	...	399
124.	Specialised Mossies	...	...	...	401
125.	To some a gamble?	...	...	...	403
126.	Put your money ...	...	...	...	406
127.	Hopes dashed	...	...	...	408
128.	Self employed!?	...	...	...	409
129.	The other Lossie	...	...	...	410
129a	Lossie, confirmed *June 2005*		...	...	413
130.	Off to a new life	...	...	...	418
131.	Work, Canadian style!	...	...	...	421
132.	Transition?	...	...	...	424
133.	Motor sport?	...	...	...	427
134.	Up a gear?	...	...	...	430
135.	The writing on the wall?	...	...	...	433
136.	Americans cheat, too!	...	...	...	434
137.	Gerry Bisson, the ongoing friendship		...		437
138.	Spartans, a growing unease	...	...	...	439
139.	At large with Spartans	...	...	...	442
140.	American security!	...	...	...	446
141.	Police matters!	...	...	...	448
142.	Justice?	...	...	...	453
143.	More nonsense	...	...	...	455
144.	That winter rally!	...	...	...	458
145.	A bit of flying	...	...	...	470
146.	Carling Avenue	...	...	...	473
147.	Financial matters	...	...	...	479
148.	Exit Spartans	...	...	...	483
149.	Eric Liebman	...	...	...	488
150.	Ice racing fun	...	...	...	490
151.	Inferior Merlins	...	...	...	494
152.	Selling cars	...	...	...	496
153.	Moving house	...	...	...	499

154.	French idiosyncrasies	...	...	...	501
155.	The ever-growing business	...	...	503
156.	The showroom	...	...	...	505
157.	Second thoughts	...	...	...	508
158.	UK Home sweet home? ...	...	...	510
159.	A wise decision?	...	...	...	513
160.	Forward to the past!	...	...	...	514

Author's Notes

This screed was never originally thought of as a potential 'book', but was written as a series of notes and stories for present and future family members, plus any interested friends. Hence the often non-sequential pattern or layout, with the words just being put down as some entirely forgotten memories returned. All this has led to a total lack of professional literacy presentation.

However, over a period of time encouraging friends, acquaintances and even accidental meetings and encounters made me realise that it all contained a lot of almost unique information of interest to many others. Featuring a wider interest than my very personal perspectives on colonial history and politics, survival (jungle and otherwise), the flying of some exciting aircraft, race relations, business, health, enterprise and pragmatism, all no doubt tempered by my total; hatred of communism and all it stands for. In other words it covers a sadly lost era of Britishness, which today with the European led nanny state and criminally crazy Health and Safety and Political Correctness regulations would certainly now land me in prison! A lot we should all be concerned about!

I can therefore only hope that any readers will find at least some elements of this now book of interest and an aid to understanding our largely lost historic perspective and place in the world. But perhaps most importantly it will also have the ability to record and give credit to the, so many, unsung heroes and be a reminder that Malaya was the only shooting war in which the evil of the communist threat was beaten and therefore, in part, what our lost Britishness was all about.

1. The early years

While I am in no way trying to excuse or justify my character and behaviour faults, it may possibly explain them! I therefore ask you not to decide whether they are right or wrong but either 'justified or understandable'.

First I was blessed with two very good and understanding parents but who had very strict ideas on what was right and wrong. They in turn had had slightly fanatical religious upbringings, which they both agreed would not be foisted onto their children. In my father's case back in Windygates, Fife, it was the Church of Scotland which thought he should be severely punished if he either rode a bike or read a novel on a Sunday. My mother came from a Catholic background and had been partly educated in a Convent. They both agreed that their children would not be 'christened' and would be free to make our own choices in due course. This in retrospect ensured that we would be distinct individuals as we were the only kids that were not 'christened', both in the neighbourhood and at our schools. One got used to, and possibly even a little proud, to be different. We grew up knowing full well that we were distinct individuals and not just part of a flock of dumb sheep. Perhaps the one exception to this was my parent's total horror and intolerance towards blasphemy. Their sound teaching of this evil remains with me to this day. I still cringe both mentally and physically in reaction to it, similar to my reaction to the sight of two disgusting perverts kissing on TV or in a film!

My father, one Robert McLaren Henderson was the second son in a family of five children. Three boys and two girls. His father's name was George and he was the local Justice of the Peace and the third largest employer in the area, after the coal mines and Haig Whiskey, as in "don't be vague, ask for Haig" and their world famous dimple bottles. The family firm of George Henderson were general contractors and constructors and appeared to be largely self sufficient in as much as they seemed to make most things they required, and then go off into often remote areas to install whatever was required.

The Hendersons are a sept of the Clan Gunn. Grandfather George Henderson came from a Scottish east coast and Borders area branch. No doubt descended from a long line of raping and pillaging Vikings with the original name of Hendrickson! And since there were vague family stories about one of the ancestors being hung for sheep stealing the family may well have been part of the Scottish headache to the English, namely the infamous Border Reivers.

My father's mother, Janet McLaren came from the central and inland areas of Perthshire in what might be described as the foothills of the Highlands of Scotland. The McLarens are one of the few matriarchal Scottish clans (descended from mermaids would you believe?) and judging by my grandmother's demeanour it remained in the blood! She could be described as a potentially fearsome galleon in full sail! She was a mother hen with the full authoritative manner of a handsome cockerel, domestically she certainly ruled the roost. The centre of the McLaren clan lands were traditionally around Loch Voil and Balquhidder in Strathyre. They were not Catholics or Jacobites but due to the often almost fanatical clan loyalty they fought at Culloden with the Stewarts of Appin due to a matrimonial connection! Of all the clans fighting and dying there, the McLarens must have suffered the greatest proportion of clan losses of any. If you go to the Balquhiddir church yard today you will see many McLaren graves interspersed with those of McGregors reflecting generations of murderous feuds. Unfortunately for the McLarens there were many more McGregors, so many more of them survived! This combined and disproportionate loss seems to have been more than made up in quality and ability, if you now count the remarkable success of the McLarens widespread around the world in so many fields including public service, commerce, engineering, science and academia.

My mother's family name was Walter so we can assume that there was some German blood involved. Her name was Stella and she was the youngest of six, four brothers and an older sister who owned and ran the English School in the middle of Mexico City for at least a couple of generations. My mother's father was a real Victorian, internationally acknowledged, pioneering railway builder and engineer and judging by the family lifestyle must have been very successful. He was involved in opening up and building railways in Mexico, Central America, Cuba and finally Columbia where my mother spent her first years. Family tradition has it that grandmother

Walter, who died a couple of years before I was born, had traces of French and Irish blood in her as well. I, Robert McLaren Henderson Junior turned up on June 12th 1932 born at home on one of the so called 'Royal Roads' in Forest Gate, in those days a very pleasant area of East London. The address being 89 Claremont Road, which is supposedly within the range of Bow Bells, which in turn makes me by an accident of birth, a London cockney. So I am a bit of an international mongrel but still predominately Scottish.

The first recallable milestone in my young life was starting proper school at the age of 3.1/2 years old, a full two years younger than the next nearest age group. This age gap was to stay with me in one form or another until I was well into my twenties or more. I don't think I was particularly precocious but was more than happy to try and keep up with the older children and I was not overawed in any way. By the time I was seven, about the time of the outbreak of World War Two, I received the overall school prize for French - the book *A Tale of Two Cities,* which may indicate the level of intellect the school authorities thought I had reached? Early on it had appeared that my reading ability was remarkable, until it was discovered that I was reading from the wrong page entirely and convincingly from memory. I could hardly read at all! I was not cheating, at the age of four I thought that was reading. I was becoming a big strapping lad and often a full head taller than my peers which often led to my being singled out for discipline even when I was not actually the guilty one.

There was at least one occasion when it turned out to be an advantage though. A group of us were throwing snowballs at the odd passing car. When one of the car victims stopped and the driver got out all the other culprits ran away leaving me to face his wrath. A very tall man confronted me with obvious annoyance and demanded to know who had done it. I think to his surprise, I owned up and apologised. This coupled with the fact that all the rest had hastily departed, leaving me to take the blame, somehow impressed him. I received a strong lecture about the dangers involved and a demand to know my name and where I lived.

The next day my parents received a very nice phone call about me and an invitation for me to call at the gentleman's house about half a mile away. This I did and was invited in by a woman and given some hot chocolate and digestive biscuits. Shortly after the tall man came in and introduced himself. He was a Dr. French and he told me that since I had been so frank and honest with him over the snowball incident, it should be recognised and rewarded. He took me out to his garage and showed me the most splendid toboggan I had ever seen. It had very professional curved runners, was quite big and very robust in its construction. In return for my honourable(?) behaviour it was to be lent to me every winter, whenever I wished. I was thrilled and became the envy of my more cowardly pals.

It was the first incident outside the family to bring home the 'honesty is the best policy', point so clearly. This being part of the background to our family philosophy of punishment. A given sanction for an offence but then more than doubled, if one lied about it or refused to own up. The lie always being the much more serious matter. This was the same Dr. French that later, during the blitz and when carrying out much the same brave action as my father in dealing with an incendiary bomb, unfortunately nearly lost him his legs when it exploded.

An interesting aside from this period which reflects the changed times, was that my mother went to a lot of trouble and embarrassment to explain to me, aged four, where babies came from. This because she thought that as my younger brother approached birth I might wonder why there was less room to sit on her lap! As you will imagine I was full of this new knowledge and announced all about it at school. The headmistress was not amused, denied it and claimed it was all nonsense. I, of course went home and wanted to know why I had been fed such an untruth? I have since noted that very often children will accept information from outsiders ahead of their own parents. Why? This must have been particularly galling to my mother as, while she was no prude, she had a very sheltered upbringing and had barely known the answer herself a mere six years before when she and my father were first married, she being only twenty at that time and not that long out of a convent!

My brother was born nearly five years after me and named after my mother's closest brother Clifford and after my father's father, George. Possibly the gap in years between my brother and me was partly responsible for us having nothing very much in common, even to this day. Although saying that I am sure if it was ever required, either of us would drop everything and go to the ends of the earth to help the other in any sort of serious emergency. I am sure we share the same fierce family loyalty and indignant sense of right and wrong which in our entirely different type of lives would naturally show in varying ways.

My mother's family as I've already mentioned would be best described as Victorian, adventurous and as archetypal British colonial as they come. My mother, Stella, was born in Cuba while her father was busy pioneering the railway system out there as he did in both Mexico and Columbia. She therefore never spoke a word of English until she came ashore at Liverpool, the day before World War One was declared in 1914. The ship they should have been on, was a few days behind and was sunk by the Germans, so but for fate, neither I, nor any of my family reading this, would even be here! Being a late starter in learning English probably accounted for my mother's unusual command of the language. Possibly because she missed the bad influence of all the silly baby-talk most of us are subjected to. My mother living initially in Havana, Cuba and then in Bogotar and Cartaghena Columbia would only have heard Spanish spoken by the family friends, staff and anyone else she would have come across.

Her family brought back home to the UK a magnificent parrot called Polly (what else). It was her mother's and appeared to dislike men in general. When her mother died, a few years before I was born, my mother was landed with it, as it would attack her father but largely ignored mine, luckily. Some years later, one Sunday afternoon when Polly was allowed out of its cage for a wing stretching session and while my father was sleeping off a good lunch with his arms hanging down at the side of his chair. The wretched parrot strolled over and bit one of his fingers quite badly. The imagination conjures up a *Tom and Jerry* type of leap in the air and a very painful awakening. The parrot was promptly despatched to a remote female cousin out in Essex. Some years later my father was heard, entirely out of character for him, to make the vindictive remarks to the effect that, "perhaps they might forget to take the parrot into the air raid shelter with them and then Hitler's bombing may finally serve a useful purpose!"

When my mother was younger and before she met my father she and her family would regularly take their annual holiday at a farm near Blagdon in Somerset. She, my father and I revisited the Owens farm as a new family when I was about four years old. The Owens had a very nice Collie sheepdog, who would, as was its practice when called, sprint across the field, jump straight over a gate and across the lane into the farm house. On this one occasion, and most unusually, a car was passing and hit the dog. The dog was thought to be fatally injured and the vet was called to put it down. Before he arrived however, the dog produced pups, totally unexpectedly. The vet put the survival down to the pups taking the impact. She fully recovered and so did the pups. My parents immediately then booked one. About two months later our new puppy was collected from Paddington Station, having travelled up in a crate, and brought home. I was in bed with whooping cough at the time so the, now large puppy was brought up to see me. It leapt onto the bed and made a great fuss. It was clearly going to be my dog, but along with the responsibilities of looking after him. He was already a very handsome animal. Half Lassie type Collie and half Chow. He had the Collie colouring and coat but with a shorter, broader nose and of course was a much bigger and broader dog altogether. I have never ever seen one like it since. He deserved to have been a breed of his own. Within only a few months he stood at my shoulder height and we became inseparable.

My father named him Stengah (pronounced Stinger) and developed a special whistle call for him. The name's meaning escaped me for many years, in fact until I went to Malaya myself, where the name was often used to denote a well known drink along with other beverages like a Singapore Sling. It was also used as an alternative description of Eurasians or half-castes, which the dog was. The Malay word for one is satu or abbreviated to sa for short. The word for half is tengah, so, sa-tengah or stengah.

Stinger went everywhere with me, like a mobile guard dog and companion. My parents entirely trusted the combination and I had much more freedom to roam as a result than other kids of my age. We travelled many miles away from home over all the heaths, woodlands, commons and downs. Often away from home most of the day. Stinger would always place himself between me and a road or water. We became known far and wide as the boy with the big dog. He was an amazing animal but had to live outside, like his mother, as he could not breathe properly indoors. One of the very few times he did leave me a few yards away was when he went out onto thin ice and pulled a child out of the water before the adults could get a ladder to effect a rescue themselves from the partly frozen pond. He just shook off the cold water and we continued on our way as if nothing had happened.

Unfortunately Stengah met with a very sad end. He died at about the age of ten from poisoning. With what was thought to be rat poison on some food that a bird had dropped into our garden. That was the only explanation anyone could come up with. A very sad loss. I have had many dogs since but none of them have been half or 'satingah' the dog he was. This was all very formative in my mind and philosophy. The circumstances of his birth taught me that when there is ever a slight sign of life, there is still hope. This was brought home to me by another dog named Rocky, some fifty years later. He had his head run over and squashed, lost most of his blood and was unconscious. He came round much later, totally paralysed but gradually got the use of each leg back over the following months. He had got his name originally, as he was the runt and only survivor of his litter. Never say Die!

2. The formative years

The next memorable epic landmark in my life was the radio announcement of the start of the Second World War by Neville Chamberlain in September 1939. My father called me into the house and told me that, what I would hear, was history and the world would never be the same again. How right he was. After the broadcast he and I had quite a long practical and philosophical discussion as to what it would all mean and the changes that we could expect in all our lives. Some might find it strange when you consider that I was only just turned seven years old at the time. Within a very short time my father had joined the local L.D.V.(Local Defence Volunteers) which later became the Home Guard (Dad's Army and all that). I went along and helped to dig the defence ditches and fill hundreds of sand bags at a suitable spot on our local main road. I marched behind on their parading and after a while even joined in weapon training. Initially they had only two rifles, a few shot guns and some dummy grenades. I learned a lot and later became a good shot even with the heavy 303 Lee Enfield rifle. Bravely not letting on about my badly bruised shoulder! I also became very adept on the Bren Gun crew and at throwing grenades. All of which came in very handy many years later in Malaya. I learned a lot about anti-tank mines, how to handle detonators, sticky bombs, smoke grenades etc.

Well, thanks to the Battle of Britain the Germans did not come but I was already well adjusted to the idea of shooting the first one that dared to come within range of our rather pathetic dugout. I was told that my abilities had been noted and that there were sure to be tasks for me in due course. This, from a Major Bonsor, whose driveway entered the main road at the Home Guard's entrenchment position. More of the Major later. The majority of children were evacuated but my brother and I were not, nor in fact did we dig bomb shelters in the back garden as most of the neighbours did. Except in serious air raids, we all slept in our own beds, then during serious air raids we would sleep under the dining room table, close to the reinforced chimney, which my father very wisely said was always the strongest part of any house.

The air raids night after night did not bother me at all despite the potential horror and terror. This was thanks to the example of the calm and stoic behaviour that my parents always displayed. I was never scared or upset which may well account for my relatively cool (not callous) behaviour in later life during some terrible situations. The worst of the blitz took place when I was still only about ten years old but I still remember it very clearly. The digging out of bodies and bits from the rubble and from crashed aircraft as well. My parents did not like me being involved in such matters, so most times I was a bit economical with the truth, or just being discrete? This may well have been the start of my lifetime obsession, that most information is no one else's business and that most information should be largely restricted to a 'need to know' basis only. The tongue and gossip is one of societies worst enemies. In addition my mother always advised against putting anything in writing, unless it was very clear and absolutely accurate.

The night our house was bombed my brother and I were fast asleep upstairs. My mother and father were sitting listening to the radio during this particular air raid when an incendiary bomb came through the roof, through their bedroom and down into the sitting room to land within about eight feet of them where it burst into flames. My father went straight to it, to try and stifle it (knowing that one in four were explosive) my mother calmly came upstairs to waken us boys. No panic, just instructions to "get dressed quickly and get out". We came downstairs a few minutes later to see our father dragging the burning bomb, all wrapped up in a bear-skin rug, through the hall with a view to chucking it out of the front door. At the last moment it slipped out of the rug and the, by now furiously burning, magnesium bomb flared up to the ceiling. As luck would have it a good neighbour, Mr. Dodd, a local air raid warden arrived with his ubiquitous bucket of sand and a stirrup pump and helped to put it out. After a cup of tea we all went upstairs to bed as if nothing had happened and before the 'all clear' had even sounded.

The next morning we discovered how lucky we had been as there were nearly a dozen of these bombs within our garden boundary, three within only a foot or so of the house! Four hits instead of one, and despite my father's bravery, would certainly have meant our house being burnt to the ground as some neighbours were. Doctor French had, like my father, tried to deal with an incendiary bomb himself by attempting to scoop it into a bucket but it had exploded and he nearly lost his legs! There were many other similar incidents which we all treated as normal, which of course they had become. Some people suffered badly but I think the majority actually gained strength from it all. The Germans had certainly badly miscalculated the strength of the British character, Some would say it was thanks to having a leader like Winston Churchill and often they would be right but in my case it came down through my parents.

Later at grammar school I joined the cadets (under age again I think) and proved that prowess with the heavy Lee Enfield 303 rifle also worked with the much lighter .22 rifles up in the range that was situated in the roof of the school. I scored more 'possibles' than all the others put together. However my scouting activities were my first love and I was a great admirer of Baden Powell. I gained most of the public service badges that lead up to becoming a King's scout but my real passion was for the outdoor badges like Pioneer and Backwoodsman (I was told I was the youngest to gain it) but my real pride was finally gaining the Bushman's Thong, again I was told I was the first one in the district for over fifteen years! It included real cross-country navigation, alone at night using only the stars (I carried a torch and a compass for emergency use only). It took me nearly eight hours, alone in the blackout (no street or house light at all!), muddy, torn, scratched, wet and having fought off a guard dog with my staff before I finally burst through another hedge over an hour ahead of schedule and within a hundred yards of my awaiting examiner, Mr. Coppen who, apart from being the local Deputy District Commissioner for the Scouts, was also head gardener on the Red House estate owned by the aforementioned Major Bonsor. It appeared I was 'noticed' again.

As I arrived at the end of this tough assignment Mr. Coppen mildly said "I think you can assume you've passed but to tell you the truth I did not think it was possible!" Praise indeed and in retrospect that was one of the most satisfying sense of achievement moments of my life. Perhaps even the start of my supreme confidence, trust, and faith that although not actually immortal, people could be almost invincible if they had the belief in themselves and the stamina to go with it. (perhaps a bit precocious for one still in his early teens).

Having made patrol leader in my original scout troop (The 3rd Banstead) I then foresook becoming troop leader to transfer to the Sea Scouts to train on a still active M.T.B. (wartime Motor Torpedo Boat) which enabled some of us to make various nefarious cross channel trips, some to assist in the flushing out of Nazi/Vichy collaborators and criminals. I know that the concept of child soldiers is largely thought of as a modern African or Asian phenomenon but I can assure any reader that it was not so during and immediately after the Second World War. They did a lot more than carry messages!

It was on one of these trips that I developed very serious blood and food poisoning, probably from the food that was cooked communally in not too clean containers which looked suspiciously like dustbins to me! The water supply could not be used for anything internal. Even cleaning teeth required bottled water. I became very ill and the only chance for me was to go into hospital to receive massive regular injections of the new miracle drug - Penicillin. After three weeks of these injections every four hours which took up to twenty minutes to administer, I was discharged as incurable and might have two to three months left! Very character building I can assure you.

3. Veggie time

But as I have since found, on more than one occasion, miracles do happen. At the time I was exceptionally fit, I was junior club champion in both swimming and cycling and later in athletics at school to Victor Laudorum levels. One of my older friends at our local open air swimming pool was one of several film stars that frequented the club, his name was Grant Tyler who had been the star in *Danny Boy*, quite a successful film in its day. He, like me, swam outdoors all year round and he cycled to and from the pool bare-chested, even in the coldest weather. We were, by so called modern standards, much tougher in those days. In my case I was never allowed to get out of a hot bath without a cold shower afterwards (to close the pores, I believe!), regardless of the time of year. My mother was a great believer in the child guru of the time, Truby King, but I have not checked to see if this was one of his advocacies or not. I am sure I probably objected at the time but it certainly stood me in good stead in later life in resisting the cold in general. At boarding school I was one of the Spartans that swam in the sea all year round and frequently, literally broke the ice to swim at various training camps.

An even earlier meeting with a future film star was at Kew when my parents and I were visiting some friends. I spent the afternoon playing with a young girl next door. She was great fun, not at all shy and just a bit younger than me, she was full of confidence but without a sign of precociousness. I liked her instantly and wished that she lived next door to me! Her parents were a fairly well known song and dance act on the West End stage by the name of Andrews. Their daughter was just starting to sing along with them on stage as a family group. She had a voice that impressed me, who normally had absolutely no musical taste at all but even I knew she was very good. She of course went on to be very much more famous than her parents and on the worldwide stage. Her name was Julie Andrews and to this day, I admire her as being entirely unspoilt. Unlike so many 'stars' she appears to be still setting an exceptionally good and impeccable example. Having avoided the almost inevitable sleaze, excesses or corruption that all too often appears to be an unavoidable trademark of modern day show business.

Back to my friend Grant Tyler who was also a strict vegetarian and probably thought of, as most were in those days, as a crank and generally very odd. He invited me to stay with him to convert to a vegetarian diet. I think I rather pooh poohed the idea but I had nothing to loose. My parents were not too sure about it, at all. For the first week or so I was totally starved living entirely on warm water with a touch of lemon. Then, for about two weeks I was promoted to very pure fruit and vegetable juices and then on to a more general vegetarian diet with lots of salad and soya for protein. Within a month the terrible boils and carbuncles started to diminish dramatically. Within three months they went, never to return, leaving me with only the minor scars that I have to this day. The doctors did not (want to) believe it but had no other serious alternative explanation to offer.

My family did not wholly approve and tried very hard to get me to join in the next Christmas dinner, I think it was goose that year. Being pushed, and being me, I resisted. Once over that initial hump of the festive season I never looked back, doubted or felt tempted to eat meat, fish or fowl again, sometimes even prepared to go very hungry instead. My mother conceded my rude health in the following years but always, slightly tongue in cheek, claimed it must have been all the good food she got into me first that sustained me. I in turn would claim that vegetarianism probably saved my life on two later occasions as well, both here and abroad. My strength was not affected at all by the change in diet but there was a noticeable increase in my stamina (partly helped by my obstinate streak as well).

Having earlier been noticed on several occasions I was informed that I could be regarded as a strategic asset in the future, whatever that meant. And how would I feel about allowing my career to be slightly steered in ways that would enable me to use my abilities in the nation's interest, from time to time in an entirely unofficial way? I was then subjected to, what today would be regarded as a very tough physical and psychological assessment. I was given very high ratings on strength, mental and physical stamina, mature judgement, aggressive ability coupled with sheer enthusiasm for constructive action. Good leadership potential coupled with teamwork but not so good at delegation! (these are not my words by the way!).

4. Uncle C

To this day I am not sure who 'spotted' my potential. I have a sneaking suspicion that my Uncle Clifford, the younger of my mother's brothers who was also a proud member of the Artist's Rifles, Territorial Regiment. Some military historians now think they were often the back door into some special forces and other 'off the record' activities. My uncle had given me one of his cap badges which depicts the two Roman gods of Mars,(the god of war) and Minerva (the goddess of intelligence plus arts & crafts). When you stop to think of it, a very good combination depicting the sort of work to be carried out by their members. To this day they must be the least heralded British regiment of all. Probably a good thing bearing in mind that the last thing their activities wanted, would be publicity. This badge I was told to always wear behind my jacket lapel out of sight and only show or produce it under very specific situations. The very few times this arose, it really was an instant and magical key!

There was family talk of me possibly joining the Palestine Police Force or following my father's early career in the Far East. My father having been the second son was expected to go into the Church, the eldest having become an academic and the third and youngest to stay home and take over the family business. Like his elder brother my father was also Dux of his year at school and later, while at Watson's, was picked to play rugby for Scotland but his strict parents would not allow it as it might interfere with his studies. I think that he must have rebelled and took himself off to London where he obtained work in the rubber industry on the trading side for two very famous firms; Harrison and Crossfields and later, McLain Watson. This took him to Singapore, where he also rode a Henderson (no relation) belt driven motorbike and then to Batavia (now Jakarta). On his return to London he became probably the most successful rubber broker ever and of course, back to his rugby! This led to a bit of an injury which in turn led to him meeting my mother which again, in turn means I am here to write all this - a sobering thought!

Several supposed scout camping weekends and others turned into sort of commando sessions without parents knowing. These were very serious and dangerous occasions. I remember well, one session at a site near Poole Harbour where three people were wounded with live ammunition and two drowned in the lake while swimming with too much gear on their backs instead of floating it across and taking their heavy boots off. On this occasion my good friend Tim McAlpine and I were using thick woolly socks over gym shoes which gave the best all round grip for climbing walls, trees and over roofs plus muddy ground and not too heavy to swim in either. The two of us, I think 'gelled' and learnt an awful lot on that fateful course and when, on later occasions, we worked together, the bond of a sort of mutual instinct stood us both in good stead. In practice, a kind of blood brotherhood for over 20 years.

5. Scouting

My personal philosophy by this time was still very much in the mould of the Scout's law and promises and I have to say that I have never changed my mind to this day. The attributes of trusty, loyal, helpful, brotherly, courteous, kind, obedient, smiling, thrifty, pure as the rustling wind. I will make no claim to have done very well with the last one but I have stuck fairly well to the others, I hope. Particularly to the loyalty and trustworthy ones. At school I gained a reputation as one to avoid conflict with because as one boy put it, "once he starts be never gives up, until he wins, whatever the personal cost". This early characteristic did I think stay with me through life. Not because I am not afraid of very much but I have always avoided conflict like the plague but if finally cornered or given no alternative, will as a last resort fight with no holds barred to the bitter end! This has stood me in pretty good stead, be it fighting the hated Communists in Malaya, flying a twin-engined aircraft home on one dodgy, fuel leaking engine or fighting to retain the custody of my children against apparent impossible legal odds. Perhaps the phrase 'tenacity of purpose' maybe appropriate?

For my potential career in commerce it was decided that a public school background would be appropriate, so I left the excellent grammar school and became a boarder, which apart from the athletics, swimming and cycling already mentioned, offered many other useful, often unofficial activities. (I did miss the Rugby though). Like air gun fights on the cliffs and in the bushes. The school failed to stop it any more than they succeeded in making us keep our bikes on the school premises only to be issued during restricted hours (no use to us). We kept them in a garage at a nearby hotel whose owner did not get on with the school authorities very well! This enabled us to sneak out at night and run races and hill climbs by moonlight in the small hours of the morning and then to have the audacity to report the results in the local paper! We did of course use false names. Some used their mother's maiden names. I called myself Gino Bandini.

We became good at picking locks and getting into holiday huts on the cliffs to have feeds and tea etc. We never did any damage and even replaced the methylated spirit and paraffin we may have used for cooking and boiling water for tea. We even tunnelled into the cliff face and came up under a hut and entered that way too. Having a good loyal school attitude, we would not tolerate a bunch of bullies camping near the school one summer who kept picking on some of the our juniors. So we took it upon ourselves to teach them a lesson. Again, in the middle of the night, six of us climbed down the outside drainpipe from the shower room, went and let the tents down with the bullies still inside and dragged them into the cesspit and urine trench while letting off fireworks and making as much noise as possible with bells, klaxon and football rattles. They could never prove who it was but the bullying stopped! The cliffs were frequently out of bounds due to the dangerous wet chalk. There were several serious injuries including one boy who never was well enough to return to school. None of this deterred us from learning the hard way including abseiling down some very dodgy chalk cliffs. When the local village was out of bounds, again we would sneak out at night to go cross-country to avoid roads which might have the odd school master driving home late or even some spoil-sport or tell-tale do-gooder! We would climb over the village baker's back fence and fill up our haversacks with all sorts of cakes and buns to be smuggled back into school and then sold at a considerable profit! The British public school as an institution often has more to do with enterprise of various sorts than mere basic education.

I don't really remember or even know the details of why I left school at least a year early or quite how it all came about. I was placed with a well known international rubber and produce dealer for a full commercial training which included, contracts, shipping, insurance, shipping agency and some marine law. In the evenings I was split between very concentrated courses at the City of London College to augment my commercial ability and Territorial escapades which included learning to jump out of planes at different heights without injury and with different loads and equipment plus some rather dirty and very unsporting methods of dealing with an assailant. Some of which would be a bit messy. On the commercial front I was also given the honour of being the youngest ever to be allowed onto the trading floor of the Rubber Market, in Plantation House, off

Mincing Lane. I also actually traded which theoretically was illegal as I was well under twenty-one years of age.

There was no written contracts at the time, only a 'man's word being his bond'. The actual contract would be drawn up at the end of the day, back at the office from notes. Never while I was there, or in all the many years that my father was there as a dealer and later a broker was there ever a dispute. The millions of pounds that were then involved would be billions today. Honesty, honour and integrity among gentlemen did I hear you say? Yes, it's another world now. It all fitted into my own honest moral code and ethics well and I was very at home in such trusted company and surroundings. By now the Middle East situation was changing very rapidly with the formation of the Nation of Israel, which is a misnomer. It should have been Judah of course, because as all Jews are Israelis but by comparison, very few Israelis are Jews! So there was no obvious long term future with the Palestine Police Force.

6. First jumps

My College work at the City of London college and 'Terri' training made quite a hole in my social life and sporting activities but I still cycled up and down to London every day plus a few miles in the evenings and a couple of hundred at the weekends. Some of my military training continued at the 'Wallops', near Andover which included jumping out of a variety of aircraft after intensive hanger training. This consisted of jumping off a very high scaffolding attached to a cable which in turn was wound round a drum which had a large fan at the other end. The effect was that of a free fall initially until the drum/fan speed had built up to the point where it created some resistance. This slowed ones decent and landing to approximately the sort of speed one would arrive back at ground level in a real parachute jump. "Like jumping off a ten foot wall", I was told! The important lesson was always to land with well bent knees and immediately fall or roll onto one side without cracking the side of your head in the process. Thanks very often, only to the coconut mats and odd mattresses provided until we became more competent.

We were taught how to beat the polygraph or lie detector. This was not just to ensure we became good liars under questioning but to train us not to react hastily or rise to baiting, taunts or insults. Keeping our natural instinctive reactions, impulsive emotions and blood pressure under control. It was also necessary to have plausible answers for family and friends on occasion. We were not to appear obviously reticent or evasive and arouse suspicions. We were taught to carefully change the subject and to chat happily about the usual facetious subjects like football, the weather, cars and women etc. to obviate any impression of secretiveness. Never to react too quickly or over react unless it really was a matter of life and death, then the word to remember was 'lightening'! Plus so many other small but important things, like always march on our heels but switch to the ball of our feet and toes when on activities. Turn toes out when marching but parallel or slightly in, sort of 'pigeon-toed' when on Ops., rather like the North American Indians do.

7. First flights

It was on one of my several visits to the 'Wallops' that I got my first chance of a whiz in an Auster aircraft, used by the army for spotting purposes. Then later in a Miles Magester and onto a Chipmunk in which I managed several hours and numerous circuits and bumps. While up in the Dakota DC3 I was not able to get my own hands on the controls but I did sit up with the pilots to watch every move and experience all the foibles of the machine, if only second hand. When I finally flew one in Singapore it all came very easily. Another regular activity was being dumped, sometimes several hundred miles away, and told to make our own way back by whatever method we could. Be it stealing a bicycle, or even a car, jumping on a goods train or lorry, always making sure we were not caught. Sometimes it would be at night but the most difficult times were, when we were not even allowed to speak to anyone. The idea was of course to encourage enterprise and resourcefulness in what might one day be a hostile and foreign land. We were given money and emergency items sealed up, just in case. Violence was not allowed but we were told that in the real world it may be required but even then it should be avoided if possible as it tends to lead to a trail and brings your existence to light. Any damage was always paid for later. My friend Tim McAlpine finished up late one night in a local jail and it took a phone call to on high and down through the Chief Constable to get him released and any possible charge dropped. Not only was he released like a hot brick but the local police then drove him home in the Police Wolsley, the last 90 miles. He finished getting back first which was not quite the idea of the exercise.

8. *Commercial training*

Commercially I also learnt the skill of grading and selecting sheet rubber, which stood me in very good stead when I finally got to Malaya. It helped to gain the respect and trust of the Chinese dealers and estate managers. This in turn enabled me to get honest market information from these dealers, who I suspect bribed the telephone operators to get some sort of priority calls through. We 'honourable'? Brits who could not engage in such activities were at a distinct disadvantage. We often waited hours to get through to Singapore to get the latest market prices. Some days we might only get two Telexes through and the market could have gone up and down several times in the meantime, with fortunes made or lost! Partly as a result of my, almost non European rapport with the Chinese dealers I was often more successful than my fellow European traders so making my company a lot of money which, of course did not hurt my bonus situation either!

But I get ahead of myself again. One day after I had been working in the London office for several months and had passed through all the appropriate departments a huge man appeared, his raincoat I can only liken to a Bell tent and the lenses of his spectacles as the bottoms of glass bottles. This was our company chairman, one, Sir Walter Fletcher, who I thought I had not met before. This was only true in the sense that I had never spoken to him but I now remembered that he had been one of the silent members present at one of my assessments. Sir Walter was a slightly awesome and distant character who I believe, had been Winston Churchill's right hand man in dealing with covert and dirty aspects of the war in the Far East against the Japanese. I assume that due to his extensive business interests and contacts in the area he would have been the ideal man to organise, run, supply and coordinate Force 136. This was made up of both military and civilians who dodged capture after the disgraceful British surrender of Singapore to the Japanese. They chose to fight on from the Malayan jungle and other areas. They, along with the local Chinese Communist party, were the only real resistance that the Japs. had to contend with for several years. They caused the Japs a lot of problems.

Others joined them in due course to reinforce and supply this remarkably successful guerilla jungle force. Apart from the usual ambushes, sabotage and general psychological warfare they also ran businesses with the Chinese elements of the population and managed to even export rubber and tin to help our war effort! The rubber helped to augment the supplies from Ceylon and elsewhere. Apart from the air drops, submarine and other boats visited to smuggle in men, arms, ammunition and other supplies, then take out any vital produce they could. When I got to Singapore I assumed that it also accounted for several of the company staff being ex 136 members, including one recently appointed (after Toppy's (to be mentioned shortly) return to London), Mr. Lionel Davis who was our overall Managing Director based in Singapore. His nephew, Arthur was to be my immediate boss in Kuala Lumpur when I finally got there.

I have often wondered about the number of men with the names of Davis or Davies that seemed to crop up in such activities. Many readers will remember an actor by the name of Rupert Davies from TV who played the part of *Maigret* in the French police series of the same name. Well his brother, Evan, who could almost pass as his twin also drove an MG TC like mine round Kuala Lumpur in a nonchalant manner. He turned out to have been one of Churchill's bodyguards during the war and had talked Churchill into sending him out to Malaya to act as a sort of a public front and to do a bit of reorganising to the otherwise almost unknown Special Branch. He, however, being a larger than life sort of character often abandoned his office, donned a French looking black beret (a la *Maigret*?) and joined the boys in active C.T. (communist terrorists) hunts. To such an extent that he almost personally hunted down a particularly sadistic C.T. murderer by the name of Goh Peng Tun. Another very effective, larger than life policeman was a Superintendent by the name of Bill Stafford who was known by some as Two Gun Stafford and by the C.T.'s as the Iron Broom. He could appear almost anywhere with any branch of the security forces and usually wearing his incongruous, almost Chinese, black pyjamas plus a black trilby hat! Always armed to the teeth and frequently with more then the two-guns with which he was depicted. His most important personal 'kill' was, at that time the only remaining communist strategist, Lau Yew. Bill Stafford was a real life combination of Clint Eastwood and Bruce Willis.

Still back in London, Sir Walter kindly complimented me on my accomplishments and was sure that I would "do them proud". The other office staff were rather mystified by this as there was nothing in my office work to warrant such comments. They were not to know that the office training was but a necessary and important front. At this time Sir Walter was the Tory (of course) MP for Bury in Lancashire. His brother Charles was also a director of the Company.

A few months or so before I was due to leave for Singapore, a Mr. Topsom, universally know as Toppy and who was the managing director from out there and a London director as well came home with his wife and daughter, a girl whose name was June. We had been childhood pals as a result of the friendship between our respective parents. My first memory of June was, after our two families had been to the London Premier of *Snow White and the Seven Dwarfs*, in 1937, I think, we had all returned to the Topsom flat in a brand new block on the Edgeware Road in West London, running north from Marble Arch at the top of Hyde Park Corner. The memory is vivid because of the absolute panic shown by both our parents when they discovered June and I standing up on the sill at an open window on the fifth floor! We had found a very effective location while playing hide and seek! I had not seen June for a number of years and it was nice to become reacquainted when she came to work for Daddy in the London office. June and I tended to have lunch together and apart from having old times in common, she was able to bring me up to date with life in Singapore. Her mother had frequently let the side down with her drinking and so her father, Toppy, as he was always known, had come to rely more and more on his daughter to act as his hostess at many business functions. So, naturally June had met and knew a great many of the people that I was destined to associate with in due course. It was not initially a full blown boy and girlfriend situation although we got on very well together in general. Our parents, however, thought that we had or should have an 'understanding' and see how it panned out at the end of the three years I was due to be away. I think it was sort of thought of as an unofficial semi engagement. Latterly we saw each other most weekends, alternately at our respective parents homes and then we did write and keep in touch with each other for a while after my departure until a situation arose which I will go into further in due course!

About this same time a chap named Edlin came into the office to meet me having just returned from up country in Malaya, to brief me on conditions generally. Little did I know then that he would cross my path again but indirectly. He, Edlin, having left a nasty and potentially criminal situation behind him in Klang (a place I had never heard of before). A place, that was about to become the centre of my little universe.

Personal portrait
Singapore Christmas 1951

9. Enter the outside world

I was only given a couple of weeks warning and £50 to get myself kitted out for the tropics in Singapore. This was spent at the fashionable, colonial west end shop of Austen Reed. Apart from the usual white shirts, shorts, trousers and cotton socks, I had to obtain a suitable 'shark's skin' white dinner jacket and bow tie. Not really me but if Briton calls and all that! The quality of Austen Reed's clothing was first class, a distinct change from the usual post war utility standards.

I sailed from Southampton on P. & O.'s **Shillong**, a cargo ship, which carried twelve passengers as well. A six weeks journey via Genoa, Port Said, Port Sudan, Aden, Colombo, Penang and on to Singapore. Among the other passengers was a honeymoon couple by the name of Melsham, he was returning to his rubber estate up country in Malaya with his new bride and the largest Great Dane dog I have ever seen! It was huge and lived in a big crate on deck. It was exercised frequently and appeared to have an equally big appetite. Although they already had several guard dogs on the estate in Malaya they thought such an intimidating dog would further discourage the bandits from approaching their perimeter fence but they were also concerned that it may frighten their own security guards! I was to meet the Melshams again, in due course.

The other passengers consisted of an elderly couple, an army officer and his wife, plus a motley collection of bachelors, of which I was one and by far the youngest. I shared my cabin with a dour civil servant type and of course we had absolutely nothing in common. We dressed for dinner each night, so I was well used to wearing my dinner jacket and bow tie long before we reached Singapore. The first port of call was Genoa which is not a particularly attractive city although the hills behind it were. The graveyard had the most imposing of mausoleums I had ever seen, almost a town in its own right. I took tea one afternoon in the almost English, Hotel Columbia(?) where I stole an ashtray as a souvenir. I did, however pay well over the price of the tea! (Eureka! I've since found the stolen ashtray and I was wrong again. The hotel's name in Genova was the Bristol & Palace Hotel).

On my return to the commercial docks late in the evening I was accosted by what I can only describe as the most unattractive, middle-aged woman I had ever seen. Initially I thought she was a homeless beggar but it turned out she was a prostitute. I then and there decided that some men will sleep with anything and in the years that have passed have not changed my mind.

The next port of call was Port Said at the entrance to the Suez Canal. In those days the statue of Ferdinand De Lessops (the French builder) still stood proudly at the entrance to the canal. I think it was torn down during the, so called Suez Crisis, in the fifties. On a recent visit with Fay I found the original plinth but no statue! We went ashore with dire warnings not to venture into the back streets. I met a couple of lads from a Guards Regiment who were heading out to Hong Kong on route to the Korean war on one of the other ships in the harbour. Needless to say we were unwise enough to ignore the warnings and wandered into the back street markets only to be confronted by five locals who were armed with a large sharpened screwdriver, a cross between a kitchen knife and a cleaver, a metal bar and sticks. Their demands were not particularly specific but the gist was! We were cornered and agreed almost instantly that we would go on the offensive. This we did, which clearly caught them off balance. We knocked hell out of them, disarmed some of them, they then ran off like the cowards so many Arabs are. A few minutes later two of them appeared with what we thought to be a local policeman. As we ran off two shots were fired at us from about a hundred yards away. We kept going for about half a mile, zig-zagging through the back streets, heading back towards the other end of the docks.

We found a café and laid low for an hour or so. We cautiously returned towards the jetty only to spot the gun happy policeman and two of the potential muggers, for want of a politically correct description! I spotted one of my fellow passengers still approaching and asked him to quietly inform the ship that I would not be returning on board and would join the ship again after it had passed through the canal at Suez. The other lads managed to get similar messages back to their ship. We later decided that we were not that impressed with Port Said so organised a taxi to take us all the way to Cairo.

We had a great night in Cairo, visiting a nightclub for the mandatory

Visit to Egyptian Pyramids while 'on the run' Early 1950

belly dance, then a day out at the pyramids and the tourist traps. We got another taxi on down to Suez and I got a ride out with the pilot boat and rejoined the ship. The other two, I assumed would manage the same thing the following day They were great lads and I regret not being able to keep in touch. One was from Glasgow (the Gorballs, where else?) and the other from Nottingham. This was my first but not my last semi or unofficial/indirect encounter with Egyptian officialdom!

The ***Shillong's*** next call was Port Sudan on the west coast of the Red Sea. This turned out to be by far the hottest place I have ever experienced. The baking heat even made it impossible for the locals to work in their offices until dusk! It appeared that for at least three months of the year the senior management never came to work, only the clerks. So the efficiency of the place was not great and coupled with a strike meant that we were stuck in port for at least four days, just to unload five fridges! Even lying in our bunks we just dripped continually and even turning over soaked another pillow. I have never drunk so much fluid in my life. There was an up side though, which was that the underwater scenery was wonderful, great and colourful coral with an amazing variety of fish. While diving it suddenly went dark overhead and it turned out not to be a ship but a group of Giant

Manta Rays 'flying' slowly by - a great thrill. The sun was so hot that even with a shirt on bending down looking through a glass bottomed boat for a couple of minutes at the fish, the skin on our backs were so baked we could hardly straighten up again.

Then to the next port of call, Aden, another dump, hot-ish and stinking of fuel oil. Some of us went up into Crater City, so called because there was not a building that did not have dozens of bullet holes due to the differences in 1948 between the Jews and the Arabs! The residents were sour and generally anti-social. This was the place where the famous Col. Mad Mitch and the Argylls sorted the locals out in no uncertain manner, some years later. I was delighted.

Next call, after a very rolly crossing of the Indian Ocean, was Columbo in Ceylon. The ship's rolling gait was so pronounced that flying fish were landing on the deck and hatch covers! At Columbo a great school-days pal and close friend had arranged for an aunt, who was married to a local solicitor, to meet and entertain me. This they did in fine style, including a trip up into the mountains to Kandi. It was a nicer and cooler resort than those on the coast. Next stop, Penang, which over the years, has finished up my all round favourite place. It's as though all the best of Asia has been miniaturised and rolled into one place. Since my employer's had an office there the local manager, who's name I can't remember, collected me from the ship, gave me a tour of the office and to meet the staff that I would be in touch with on and off. I was then given the grand tour including a visit out along the coast past Palau Tikus (mouse island) and towards Batu Ferringhi,(the now internationally famous holiday resort) to the European Swimming Club situated below the road and right on the beach. I was royally entertained during my short stay by this manager and his wife so was able to experience the first samples of Malayan food, which I was to take to with great enthusiasm.

10. Singapore

After Penang it was straight down the Malacca Straits with the large island of Sumatra to our right and the Malayan coast on our left passing the island of Pankor, then the entrance to Port Swettenham and on past Malacca itself. As we entered Singapore harbour one could not help but be impressed by how busy and efficient it all appeared. I was met at the ship by the personnel manager whose name escapes me again. I was given a splendid lunch at the famous Box Club which is in fact the cricket club. It looks out over a large cricket field or Padang, then on out over the harbour and distant islands. I knew then that I was going to like it out east. After tiffin I was taken to the very nice residential area of Tanglin Hill, several miles north of the bustling city itself. I was delivered to a splendid house named Hazelwood and allocated room No.7 (lucky me!). This house was just two away from the managing director's abode (until recently June Toppy's home). Hazelwood was in effect the company's mess, housing up to half a dozen company bachelors and several more visiting firemen as required. The houseboy was most helpful and pleasant. My room was sunny and equipped with roll down cane blinds for the heavy monsoon rains. A wonderfully wizened Chinese woman was our 'cookie' and wanted to instantly feed me again. Everything was "can do", an oriental characteristic that I came to admire and appreciate more and more as time went on. The grounds were quite extensive, secluded and with a large tennis court on the only flat area at the back. The monkeys were known to steal some of the tennis balls!

My first evening meal in the mess was excellent and I met several of my future colleagues who worked in the main office in Singapore. The next morning I went into the office which was situated at 132/6 Robinson Road which was halfway between the city and the docks. The view from the upstairs general office was quite clear out to sea despite there being several parallel streets in between. The reason being that the war had left virtually no buildings on the south side of Robinson Road or on any of the other streets in between.

The exception being a Chinese school and some hastily erected 'Godowns' (warehouses). The scene was that of a huge, all but derelict cleared bomb site. I met the heads of all departments and their chief clerks (who really ran things!). I became aware quite quickly of a bit of an atmosphere, a sort of 'them and us' situation. It appeared that those that had got caught and spent the war 'in the bag' as prisoners in the infamous Changi camp seemed to resent those that had got out in time. Even though quite a few of them had came back to fight the Japs from the jungle, as part of Force 136. They in turn had little respect for the ex-prisoners. Not, I thought a very healthy situation generally. I trod very diplomatically! There was a distinct anti-attitude to me from one of the shipping office managers, which I could not pin down to anything I had said or done. It was hampering my ability to get essential information before I went up country, so I tactfully asked Mr. Lionel (John) Davis, my Tuan Besar, (big boss) what was eating the man. He laughed and said "did you not know that he was sweet on June Topsom before she went home and although they never dated he had accompanied her on the odd social do and was not amused when he heard that she was going out with someone in the London office." He was apparently a bit of a social climber and Mr. Davis said he was only made a Lt. Commander just after the war and had probably "never commanded anything bigger than a rowing boat. He may not remain with us much longer so get to know his senior Chinese clerks, they will be the more useful contacts, later on", was his advice.

To me, the cold *Coca Cola* drink machine in the office was quite a luxury. It may seem strange but I had never drunk a coke and do not remember the product having reached the UK at that time though it would go on to replace *Tizer* in due course as the drink of the masses. I quite liked it in its very cold distinctive glass bottle. My main complaint was that one was never quite enough and thirst always seemed to require another! Initially another mystery to me in those first few days was the regular shout of "Thamby" from different parts of the large, almost open plan, office. It turned out that a Thamby was an office cum errand and messenger boy. Boy was a bit misleading as one of them (there were three) was about seventy years old! Apart from being a bit of a dogs body or go-for, they were responsible for rushing round the city with very valuable documents to banks and shipping offices often potentially worth tens of thousands of dollars and in situations where minutes could mean a lot of money.

Once familiar with the various office departments it was then visits to several ships, cargo warehouses, (known locally as Godowns) and to meet all the representatives of shipping companies, stevedore companies and people like Customs and Port Control. The chief storekeeper at our port office and Godown where rubber was selected and packed, was a very cheery and friendly Chinese, whose name was Wee Wee Poh. Initially I did not believe it but it really was true. He had a motorbike and gave me a pillion tour including stopping under the sign for Henderson Road, which was an area also undergoing post war resurrection. All the bunkering or refuelling was and still is carried out on an island well off shore called Pualu Bukam. A lot of the loading and unloading was into lighters or barges as well as onto the docks themselves. Singapore is an entrepot port and very much the hub of the orient.

Wee Wee Poh, apart from familiarising me with the practical and physical rubber selection and packing procedures, also introduced me to the equivalent of today's so called modern technology. He was having a problem with their Jaga, a local night watchman and usually a tall Sikh armed with a big stick! They tend to put their charpoy against the front door or entrance to the establishment they are responsible for and usually sleep on it all night. The charpoy bed is a simple wooden bed frame with woven sisal strings for support and no mattress. This particular Jaga was required to get off his bed a specific number of times a night and tour several buildings, opening and closing the odd gate in the process. The suspicion was that he was not doing so despite his exaggerated claims to the contrary. Wee Wee Poh got hold of a gadget that we would call a Tachograph today. It is wound up like a clock with a rotating paper disc inside that has a stylus which draws a steady line until it moves and the a sort of pendulum moved the pen or stylus and this shows up as a blip on the paper disc and records the time any movement happens. When the Sikh was confronted with the facts of his every move or not as the case may be. He was very upset and demanded to know why the gods had betrayed him. He never did come to realise that the gadgets bolted to the gates were these gods but his superstitious fright did encourage him to do his job more conscientiously after that.

One of the first things that immediately struck me about Singapore was its contrast to the rather drab and somewhat resigned shopping situation back in the UK. At that time next to nothing could be imported and everything had to be made at home and then even the majority of that had to be exported. A visit to Raffles Place was a revelation. Robinsons Department Store, which was the local answer to Harrods and seemed to have everything plus many things I had not seen since before the war and many I had never seen at all! Being a bargain hunter I found my way down Change Alley which was along a narrow lane running from Raffles Place to Collyer Quay on the sea front. The large number of tiny shops/stalls on both sides had almost everything you could imagine at what seemed like unrealistic prices to me at the time. I threw caution to the wind and bought a few things I needed to go up country with, plus an Olympus 120 camera (Japanese of course) a simple range finder, a German light meter and a good Swiss watch which I still have to this day and when I wind it up and use it, it still keeps good time but has lost most of its original gold plating over the hard years. A few novel gifts and the odd souvenirs were also added. All my snaps of Singapore, Malaya and later Indonesia (plus Egypt and Lossiemouth in the Mosquito days) were taken with this camera and it certainly stood the test of time.

The mention of Collyer Quay reminds me of a trip down to Singapore from K. L. a year or so later and soon after I had my XK120. I had parked it on the quay and taken a launch out to the famous floating Chinese Junk Restaurant a mile or so off shore where a huge variety of sumptuous Chinese food was served. During the long lunch one of the Sumatra monsoon storms had arrived and passed. By the time I got back ashore everything had dried out and looked as if it had not rained for days! Unfortunately when I parked the Jag I had not fastened the tonneau cover properly so that when I opened the door literally gallons of water cascaded out over me. On that same trip I visited the famous Aw Boon Haw or Tiger Balm gardens. Why gardens I'm not too sure as it is largely a sort of Madame Tussaud's outdoor display of medieval Chinese torture and some pretty revolting exhibits of various forms of disembowelment! One display on a grassy slope was a war between good and evil depicted by white and black rats at each other's throats and tearing each other to bits! In retrospect its maybe not so far from the truth after all. If I remember rightly Aw Boon Haw was the founder of the world-renowned Tiger Balm, an all round curative ointment or balm and I think Tiger Beer and Cathay Pacific Airways as well. These gardens were just one of many examples of him putting something back into the community.

I was taken to several embassy parties, business get-togethers and met too many people to remember, which is, I fear where my bad habit of not remembering names, but always faces, started. They, as already settled residents only had to remember one new face and name at a time, whereas I was trying to remember literally dozens every day. Separately I had several quiet briefings with various military intelligence groups and with Special Branch. At this time I little realised what a huge part they played in the overall security situation. I was to learn! The thing that was bothering me more and more was the apparent lack of understanding or concern about what was actually happening up country by the Administration at large. I imagine that this must have been the same sort of attitude that led to the disgraceful fall and surrender of Singapore to the Japanese during February 1942.

In part, this was aggravated by the total ignorance and lack of experience on the part of the immediate postwar Labour Government in colonial matters. The High Commissioner for South East Asia was one Malcolm MacDonald, a descendent of Labour's icon, Ramsey MacDonald from Lossiemouth. He was a very nice and charming man but seemed not to really understand what was going on under his nose. All very presumptuous of me I know but I would liken him to a parent who is more concerned with being popular than a being good one. And we all now know what that has done to the western family unit and society as well!

I managed to get some flying in as well. The Singapore Flying Club was a remarkably active one. The civil airport at that time was Kallang on the eastern edge of the city and when you drove out there the road was often closed with a simple swing barrier and flashing lights, rather like a rail crossing. A plane would come in then go past and the barrier would be raised. We could then simply drive across the runway and on out along the East Coast Road that eventually leads to Changi probably stopping off at the Chicken Inn, Sea View Hotel or the Swimming Club, all on the beach and very popular. For a mile or two the coast road in this area became a gastronomic paradise at night with dozens if not hundreds of eating stalls, nowadays know as hawker stands. The choice was enormous and a splendid place to stop, relax and eat in the middle of the night enjoying the gentle sea breeze and all the aromas. Often sitting on stools half way across the road. It was at this same swimming club that my father witnessed a leg being removed by a shark about thirty years before.

Thanks to some new friends at the Singapore Flying Club I managed about twenty hours in a variety of planes including the one I started in, an Auster. I also wangled my first flights in twin-engined planes. First was in an Avro Anson, then into a DC 3 Dakota. Kallang airfield was on the verge of Kallang basin, which in effect is the wide mouth of the Kallang river and the aquatic commercial area for many Chinese import and export businesses. My first aeronautical clanger was to run off the end of the runway and park the borrowed Auster axle deep in water and mud in the basin as a result of my miscalculation of distance while landing over and ahead of a just landed Malayan Airways DC 3 on a flight from Penang. There was no reported incident, just a rude comment from the owner who still let me fly it again a week later. You don't get much better or more generous friends than that! The Kallang basin no longer exists today. It has all been filled in, reclaimed from the sea and is now just part of the Singapore skyline. Changed days, as today you will have to look quite hard to find the Cathay Building among the literally dozens of now even taller buildings. Many of them around the Raffles Place area and several in what was the Kallang Basin!

While I am talking about skylines, in those days the only reasonably tall building was the Cathay Building a mile or so inland and off to the east of Orchard Road if my memory serves me right (this building was locally referred to fondly as, Singapore's little skyscraper). It was build into a small hillside. On the lower side at normal road level was the entrance to a cinema with a restaurant and nightclub above. If you drove round and up the hill to the back of the building the ground floor there was above the cinema and in turn led up into a block of luxury flats.

One of the young managers at work and his wife invited me along to this Cathay nightclub for a dinner/dance as there was a visiting artiste from Australia, her name was June Hamilton. She turned out to be a lap dancer but not in the modern sense. She drifted around the dining tables singing romantic songs to all and sundry and occasionally sitting on the odd male knee while continuing to sing intimately, eyeball to eyeball. I became one of her victims(?), was very embarrassed and blushed a lot to the great amusement of everyone else. The next day, of all the victims to have suffered her attentions, it was my picture that appeared in the local press with June's ample cleavage right under my nose. The whole thing was totally innocent and just part of her show. We never even exchanged a single word in conversation. I was of course teased no end at the office and in the mess. Unfortunately one of June Toppy's Singapore friends sent her the picture and indicated that there was more to it all. I often wondered if it was the jealous creep of a Lt. Commander from the office who was responsible. I shortly received a scathing letter from June back in London to the effect that she was shocked at my behaviour, was very hurt and embarrassed by it all and could not understand why I had been so unfaithful and untrustworthy. I was not amused to be falsely accused and that she chose to jump to so many erroneous conclusions and think so ill of me. She had made no effort to check the truth of the situation with my chaperones and alibi from the night in question who, just happened to be friends of hers as well. Coupled with this was the fact that I had only just gone to visit June's Alsatian pup that she had had to leave behind in Singapore rather than subject it to a long sea journey and then six months quarantine when it finally followed her back to the UK. I had taken several snaps of it, now a very large and healthy pup, which I had sent to her with assurances that the animal was in good hands and happy and that she should stop feeling any twinge of guilt about leaving it behind. So I felt justifiably aggrieved.

My rather impulsive answer was one of great indignation, suggesting that with such little trust and confidence in me, she would not want to consider herself bound by any understanding would she? In addition, I quite understood that she would be happier not to continue any association with anyone so thoughtless and selfish as me. Of course my sarcasm was lost on her but she did sort of apologise but despite that and some months later when her father visited K. L., there was a distinct coolness from him and he made the comment that had it not been for his long friendship with my father he would not even be speaking to me. I have no idea what angle or misinformation he had swallowed or whether he thought I had jilted his daughter, so upsetting some long-term plan our families might have had in mind. On the other hand he had probably heard about my association with Connie, a Eurasian (frowned on and generally disapproved off socially) by then and took it as adding an insult to the original imagined injury! I was glad that, by then, I was making so much money for the firm and that my job was not at risk! I did however consider myself free of any vague constraints that the understanding would have inhibited me girlfriend wise.

Apart from singer/dancer June Hamilton I met quite a few famous and interesting characters at social events in Singapore including King Kong the Far Eastern wrestling champion who I had watched one night at the New or Happy World. He was a fantastic actor. In the ring he was totally convincing as a mad and wild monster. Socially he was a mild quiet and well-spoken man, a perfect gentleman although his goatee beard still looked fiercesome. On, I think a subsequent trip down to Singapore I also met Han Sulyin the writer of the book that later became the famous film with Jennifer Jones and William Holden namely *Love is a Many-Splendored Thing* (American spelling, of course!). She was a very elegant Chinese Eurasian and clearly not yet over losing her British reporter boyfriend in Korea. That being the story which was the basis of the book, with the film appearing about five years later. I should have got her autograph. She did, however give me a better understanding of the Eurasian social problems that they often had to contend with.

11. Up country

Within a month or so I was off up country. First stop Malacca. On the way I again slightly blotted my copybook by putting the firms Willeys jeep estate wagon gently into the ditch (one plane and now a car ditched). The Willey's steering was so indirect and suspension so soggy - well that's my story anyway. The manager at Malacca was one Alan Acton, a late middle-aged man with great charm and enthusiasm. Another Force 136 member, I was led to believe. I was billeted in the Government rest house on the sea front looking over a football pitch that had just been reclaimed from the sea. After breakfast on the first morning and with time to spare before being collected for the office I decided to take a swim, out several hundred yards to some small islands and back. Alan, when he arrived, suggested it was not a wise action as there were sharks in the vicinity! I enjoyed my few days in such an old town with its traces of both Dutch and Portuguese historic influences. One night we did a tour of the old town and dock area on the river in a police Land Rover. Armed with a floodlight and rifles to shoot any stray pariah dogs (pronounced, purrier, locally). This was a regular activity since there was rabies in the area. Some may disapprove but when you have seen a young child going through long, deep needle injections into its stomach, in an effort to save it from such a horrific death, they would be wasting their breath.

Next stop was Kuala Lumpur. To me an attractive city set in a sort of volcanic looking hilly depression. The city itself had a ring or boundary road that nearly circled it. Radiating out from the centre and passing through the ring to the North was Batu Road leading, via Batu Caves on up to Ipoh and then to Penang. The Southerly route, leading up over the surrounding hills towards Seremban, Malacca and all points south on to Singapore. The radial road east was Ampang Road that in those days petered out beyond Ampang village and tin-mine, today it is a shopping complex! Then, lastly there was the westerly route through the only low gap in the hills. This was by far the busiest road, leading via Klang to Port Swettenham, the main and only real port in central Malaya. I was put up for the first few nights in K. L., at a splendid hotel, which could have come straight out of a Somerset Maugham novel. Very old colonial and multi floored, set into a hillside close to the very famous Station Hotel. I was on the third floor where the window opened out onto the rock face with monkeys just strolling in and out. Sadly on Fay's and my last visit to K. L. I noticed that the whole rock face had gone along with the hotel to make room for one of K.L.'s versions of Spaghetti Junction.

My next temporary home was the Griffin Inn on Ampang Road. A nicely located night club, almost on the edge of town and further out than our K. L. office on the same road. At night I would fall asleep to the sounds of George Shearing on the piano, unless I was downstairs in the club itself. To me, he had that sort of haunting refrain to his playing in the same way that Nat King Cole had with his singing. In reality it was a brilliant Chinese pianist who led the club's dance band and who could have got a job anywhere in the world as a George Shearing play alike.

12. Finally to work

The K. L. office was the first air-conditioned office I had been into since leaving Singapore. I was to be assistant area manager (Tuan Ketchil (pronounced kitchy) or small boss), there in K. L and branch manager (Tuan Besar or big boss) of Klang and Port Swettenham.

K.L. was mostly a regional head office, which coordinated all the areas activities and the general pipeline back to Singapore. Klang was where a lot of the rubber trading and physical work was done, purchasing, taking delivery, selecting and grading the rubber and then packing it to our standards and responsibility. Port Swettenham is where it all would be shipped out from, along with several other exporters. The office there had its own Chinese chief clerk by the name of Yap Cheng Eng, separate staff were responsible for the shipping agency work for four different shipping lines, Blue Funnel (North America); Klavness, a Danish line; Charges Reiuney,(?) French and finally there was, Pacific Far East an American West Coast company. Everything they loaded and unloaded had to be arranged and booked, be it dock space, barges, stevedores, water, fuel, pilot-age both in, and out and sometimes medical help too. Ships are not always good timekeepers and often turned up in the middle of the night.

 The Klang office and Godown was beside the river and on Harper Street, which was on the inland or K.L. side of the river with of course Port Swettenham and most of the town on the other. The main road bridge was a tangled mess of steel from the Nippon period as it was often called locally and euphemistically. There was a local jocular phrase used at the time, "Nippon Go, British Come". The British forces when they returned had built a couple of pontoon bridges about a couple of hundred yards apart allowing constant two way traffic from the capital K. L. via Klang to the main sea port, Port Swettenham. Unfortunately the odd pontoon would spring a leak on a regular basis, which then almost sunk, leaving the other bridge to become an alternative one-way system until repairs could be effected, often days later! Queues would build up on both sides causing half hour delays. One of these bridges was exactly opposite the driveway into our office so if I timed it right I could park my car out front and jump the queue, almost legitimately. The other break down problem with these bridges was the fact that they could break up in the middle when the river was in full flood during the monsoon season. On one such occasion a couple of heavily laden old lorries and their frightened drivers floated off down river on a broken off section of four pontoons! Not terribly funny since, although the river was not infested with crocodiles, they were about! On occasion the odd hunt would be undertaken after a rogue croc. became a bit too sociable at night and entered a village to steal and kill chickens, pigs and goats. After, one such hunt, when the crocodile was opened up, a considerable amount of gold, jewellery, tin cans as well as only partly digested limbs were found inside. The locals had superstitiously thought he could be appeased or bought off!?

In addition to general goods and cargo being brought in/imported for all sorts of other businesses, we as a company also had agencies ourselves, from Beck's Beer (known locally as 'Key Brand'), tinned goods, tin plate, Ultra radios, a real variety of things that the K.L. office wholesaled out to many retailers. Right down to tea dust that was in fact the sweepings off the floor. This was turned into a cake and sold to the poorest customers. If we scoot forward thirty odd years what do we now drink that is embedded into water absorbent paper sachets? Why,the same tea dust in tea bags of course! So who are the tea 'mugs' now then? The paper work at the Port Swettenham office was frightening to me but as always the Chinese clerks coped remarkably well at any time of day or night. Unfortunately, as manager I still had the responsibility of individually signing all the many copies of Bills of Lading and Insurance Certificates (yes, we were insurance agents too!) The Bills of Lading, being the banks negotiable documents, had to be signed individually, not just in duplicate but up to seven times. Fair enough, I thought for a shipment of a hundred tons or more but not for a few tons only. Sometimes several thousand tons of different goods were involved, in total.

I was shortly to meet my saviour in the form of a Special Branch man who had an employee that specialised in forging documents and who kindly produced several variations of my signature in rubber stamp form which I used to save writer's cramp, often at 3 am with still a jungle drive home. Totally illegal of course but then, I was still almost three years too young to be signing such legal documents in the first place!

13. Action man!

Now, I come to probably the most dramatic, adventurous, exciting, sad and dangerous period in my life (well the first, anyway). It is impossible to get it all in any sort of order let alone chronologically as well. For nearly two years life was almost a blur of action and experiences. Some will seem almost impossible if not unbelievable in today's climate of political correctness and health and safety regulations. Despite all this I can assure readers that the gist is, if anything, understated! I can relate some incidents only to other occasions. Such as when I first got my M.G. Model T.C., or later when I collected my beloved Jaguar XK 120, or even when the two closest of my friends, out of nearly a dozen, were killed and then buried in Cheras Road Cemetery up on the hill, just south of K. L., or, again when The High Commissioner for Malaya, Sir Henry Lovell Goldsworthy Gurney K.C.M.G. was assassinated on his way up to Fraser's Hill and his subsequent burial in the same Military Cemetery.

Perhaps then I should start entirely out of order with Sir Henry. He was a regular at The Selangor Club in K.L., known by some as the Spotted Dog, (no, not Sir Henry!) which even today has not changed in appearance. A sort of Tudor style long pavilion that still looks out over what was and often still is, a multi cricket pitch known as a Padang (which is Malay for field or pasture) and on to the main road with, on the opposite side, the picturesque Moorish Govt. buildings, courts and the famous Little Ben clock tower. The only visible changes to the Padang today is an almost discrete section at the eastern end which now has a quite small area set aside as a paved garden and known as Merdeka (freedom) Square. At the other or western end is mounted what is reputed to be the tallest flagpole in the world (the Americans and Chinese will not like that!) The totally discretely invisible but massive change is that under the acres of cricket turf is a large underground car park! If you were not told you would never know it was there.

Sir Henry Gurney was keen on his tennis and would play with

any club member. On one occasion, knowing that a group of us were going up to Fraser's Hill for the weekend and staying in the bungalow next to his, he very kindly suggested that we use his personal tennis court, while up there. This we did and he was duly thanked later in the week on our return. In fact two days before he was killed on his way up there himself, as he was approaching the so called gap, which is where the road gets quite steep and becomes single track for the last few miles. Traffic goes up and down on alternate hour and half hours, even today. Fraser's Hill is a nice, relatively cool hill station, about 6,000 ft up.

It used to get quite cold at night, large log fires and thick woolly pullovers were the order of the nights. Amazingly, even the Chinese staff had rosy cheeks! Because of the low night temperatures it was regarded as a bandit free area as it would not be possible to get up there, taking several days, without large fires at night which would easily be spotted. On this occasion a group of C.T.s (Communist Terrorists) had pushed up as high as they could with extra clothing and set up an almost perfect ambush site and waited for a suitable convoy from which they could capture the maximum number of arms with the least risk to themselves. According to later captured documents, it appeared they waited some days before they attacked Sir Henry's escorted convoy. Sheer chance that it happened to be him but at the time it was thought that there had been a serious breach of security. Not so. From our, or rather my point of view, it was a sobering thought, that the previous weekend we had possibly driven quite nonchalantly under a dozen guns, through this prepared and described these days as a killing field. In those days it was less dramatically described as a field of fire. Sir Henry was killed on the 6th October 1951, just sixteen days before my teenage local friend James Bardell was killed on the 22nd of October while serving with the West Kents (like Donald Latter, later on) and finished up buried in Cheras Road Military Cemetery in grave no.1056, just a few yards from Sir Henry's .

Rather than the Spotted Dog club, I tended to use the K.L Selangor Golf Club that was located just on the countryside of the Boundary or Circular ring road that ran round the edge of K.L. This road is now renamed Jalan Tun Razak. I did not play golf but its swimming pool was the real attraction. They also served excellent meals at any time and I enjoyed the country surroundings and the view. Looking out over some Ulu, past the Ampang tin mines to the distant mountains whose appearance was constantly changing.

James Bardell's grave with 'stolen flowers'
Cheras Road Cemetery Early 1952

Typical Hashie funeral

14. Theft?

Some time after Sir Henry's funeral at Cheras Road, I am afraid I committed the second theft (temporary this time) in my life. I stole some of the many flowers from Sir Henry's grave and placed them on my friends' graves and then took pictures to send home to their families. In, perhaps the vain hope that they might feel slightly better if they thought someone was visiting their sons' graves, in such a far off land. Bodies were not flown home in those days! Sir Henry was killed on Saturday the 6th of October 1951 and my two closest friends Donald Latter (grave, 1094) and James Bardell (grave, 1056) are buried close by. I cannot date Donald's death for the moment, as there is some confusion in my mind or possibly the wrong dates on his gravestone? With the aid of my old passport and some original snap shots of the graves I will try and resolve the matter later. *(later I can confirm 6th November 1952)*. Donald Latter in particular was a very close friend. When I was the Captain of Courtyard Dormitory, at boarding school, he was my No.2. When revisiting my old school many years later I was particularly pleased to see Donald's name commemorated on a plaque in the school chapel. I had visited and stayed at his home outside Marden in Kent. His family home was a marvellous, and very old, Tudor timber framed house where the floors were far from level. In the bedroom the slope was so bad that one end of the bed was blocked up higher and when you stepped out of it onto the floor you could slide down the room on a mat! James, on the other hand was a neighbour for many years. He was one of two brothers (James and John) who lived just round the corner and two houses down in Vernon Walk, off Shelvers Way, Tadworth, Surrey where I had lived for most of my life and throughout the war years. A few months before I left for Singapore James had taken over one of my local dancing partners/dates who was just one of the several girls named June (Walder) that I have known over the years. It is a further sobering thought in retrospect that out of about a dozen of us friends, acquaintances and school chums that went out to Malaya, Singapore and Korea at that time only two of us came back!

Granny Frazer, who I think never left Singapore to go up country at all and myself who suffered no more than two bullet wounds and a bit of grenade shrapnel in my knee. This name, June has slighted haunted me throughout life, particularly since my mother had intended to name me Stella–June, had I been a girl! James Bardell's mother was a great character and insisted on teaching me to dance before I went off abroad in my dinner jacket! Her efforts with the Fox Trot, Waltz and Quick Step are to this day my full repertoire.

Since writing this many months ago I have been in touch with the Commonwealth War Graves Commission and the Royal West Kent Regimental Association (now amalgamated with several others) and their museum in Dover. I have unearthed more information that I was not aware of but which I think adds to the general story and reflects further on the general bravery and character of most participants. It is, in retrospect, perhaps to my chagrin that I did not know that either James Bardell or Donald Latter were in Malaya until they were dead! The West Kent's main base was at K.K.B. (Kuala Kubu Baharu) not many miles north of K.L. near the turn off up to Fraser's Hill and from where they operated in areas such as Tanjong Malim, Batang Berjunta and Rawang all very dangerous bandit hot spots. I had passed their base many times without knowing they were there and they in turn on weekend leaves in K.L would have passed within yards of my own haunts. I had been in and out of their K.L. establishment called Wardieburn Camp collecting and returning guns and equipment on several occasions! My fellow M.G. TC owner, friend and later landlord, Basil of A.K.C. (Army Kinema Corp.) I know had regularly delivered and collected his movie films from these same camps and since I have now discovered that Donald Latter was Company clerk, it is almost certain that their paths would have crossed. To this day I have retained some slightly haunting and reminiscing thoughts, that had I met them early on could I have given them any jungle tips that might have varied their ultimate history. We will never know!

James Bardell's story would appear to be that on that fateful day he and the rest of No.11 Platoon, "D" Company were returning to base after a three day jungle patrol and while driving through Ulu Caledonian Estate came under withering cross fire from 40 or more C.T.s in well prepared ambush positions. Some of the Kents would have died in the first hail of bullets as the rest de-trucked or baled out of their transport as they were repeatedly trained to do, in only seconds. Diving for whatever cover was available and then to return fire, which they did for about an hour against impossible odds. Even the badly wounded continued to bravely fight-on, to such an extent that they finally drove off the C.T.s, having wounded several and killed six of them. They even captured some of their arms and ammunition! Unfortunately this skirmish, although a victory in some respects for the Kents, left them with TEN immediately dead, ONE who died later of his wounds and a further TEN wounded who survived. The C.T.s captured not one gun or bullet, which had been the main object of their exercise, as in the case of Sir Henry Gurney's ambush a couple of weeks earlier.

James Bardell was a big tall lad and therefore possibly an easier target than some? Although I was aware of this terribly tragedy at the time I did not know it involved anyone I knew. The scale of this incident was such that it made the news back in the U.K. as well as locally and coupled with the very recent death of Sir Henry Gurney resulted in the lowest ebb of morale during the whole conflict. I am not literary enough to do this heroic battle descriptive justice but in the annals of war I would rate it along with the Glorious Gloucester's battle in Korea during the same period and the same enemy - the communists. It should also be born in mind that most of our lads were not professional soldiers but new short-term conscripts barely out of school! Korea was an 'official' war whereas Malaya was ONLY an 'emergency'. So I will rely on some of the messages, signals and congratulations send to the battalion afterwards. They will speak much better than I ever could:

From Major General R.C.O. Hedley, C.B., C.B.E., D.S.O.

"It is obvious that the men involved must have put up a magnificent show and I congratulate you on their conduct".

From Lt-Col. D'A. J.D. Mander, D.S.O., Comd. 1st Green Howards.

"I do want to say how tremendously we admire the magnificent scrap that your fellows put up on Ulu Caledonia. Not to lose any arms and ammunition and to kill six bandits into the bargain was an absolutely first class show. It was utter defeat for the bandits inflicted under the most difficult conditions".

From Chief of Staff, G.H.Q., F.A.R.E.L.F., Maj.-Gen. J.H.N. Poett, D.S.O.

"The reports stress what a splendid show the patrol, especially the wounded, put up. It was a really magnificent effort to have driven off the bandits in spite of the initial casualties and to have safeguarded all arms and equipment".

From Comd. 48 Bde. through 18 Bde.

"Please convey the admiration of all ranks, 48 Bde., on the splendid show put up by 1 R.W.K. in Ulu Caledonian Estate".

From Officiating Comd., South Malaya District.

"Am distressed to hear of your casualties. Your chaps must have fought well".

From O.S.P.C., North Selangor.

"We would like you to know of our admiration for the courage and tenacity shown by the survivors and victors of the battle".

There was a particularly poignant Remembrance Day Service held on the airstrip at K.K.B. on Sunday 11th November and attended by the men of all three companies based there (a mere five days later)!

~*~

Donald Latter's story is not so clear or well recorded as he appears to have been the only member of his patrol to be killed on that fateful day. Donald had been appointed Company clerk only a couple of months before his death but even clerks have to do their share of guard duty and patrolling even if they have less experience than the others. Donald was not a military type and was truly one of nature's gentlemen and certainly not cut out for jungle warfare but he would have tried his hardest and never complained or lost his friendly sense of humour. He was apparently on a routine patrol in an area where there had been no serious bandit contacts for a while due to patrols, such as his, finding and destroying the C.T.'s food allotments/gardens and driving them further into the jungle. It can be assumed that he was just unlucky on that occasion to be the one victim of a sniper that particular day. All very sad. Later in the letter to his parents and after the official announcement that he had been "killed while on operations in aid of the civil power on 6th November 1952, in Malaya while serving with the 1st Bn.". Donald was described as "a good soldier and popular with his fellow men". In another report as "a popular and respected member of his platoon".

In my searching I now have a copy of a picture of Donald in a group photograph of his "D" Coy., 1st Bn., taken in Penang just a few short months before his death which will now join the one and only picture of him I have from our school days taken on the beach below our school on the I.O.W., the last summer we were all together there.

Donald Latter on the beach below Bembridge School, my last summer there.

I am not too sure that any comments from me would be regarded as in good taste but they may be appropriate in the circumstances. One of the problems with the military mind is that they insist on sticking to rules and routines and it takes them a long while to adapt and change to meet different circumstances or even learn from their mistakes! As the reader will gather later on we 'Hashies' (any reader will discover what the Hash House Harriers were all about further on in this screed) did not conduct ourselves in this way and learned very quickly to adapt. We did not just go out onpatrol as a sort of show the flag way as the Army often did. We were systematic but irregular hunters not just regular members of a patrol. If we were going into the jungle for a hunt then we were secretive and traveled incognito as far as possible. Then, when we came out again it was never to the same spot where we had initially entered which would have been inviting an ambush welcoming party of CT.s. We would always go at least a few miles cross-country and come out at a different road, estate or village so thwarting any such communist plans. The other fallacy that did not seem to penetrate army behavioural patterns was the fact that they did not seem to understand that on leaving the jungle and say, crossing a plantation, particularly and when naturally starting to relax a bit on the way home was often a more dangerous time than actually in the jungle itself! Why? Simple. In the jungle you are only a few feet away from hidden cover unless it's a well-trodden path so that being shot is almost a 50/50 equal chance between them and you! And the best man should win, ambushes aside. In such circumstances a shotgun was often the favoured weapon. But once leaving the cover of the jungle and crossing between the plantation trees with their cleared ground cover, one is exposed to sniper fire about 70% of the time over the relatively open ground and with only the odd tree for cover. Then before a counter attack can be organized the sniper would just step back a few feet into the jungle and disappear again.

It should have been blindingly obvious to anyone that if a patrol goes out on regular three day patrols and are dropped off and then collected again at the same place the temptation for the bandits to plan and execute an ambush was bound to be seized. The Min Yuen, the communist civilian 5th column of spies and suppliers would soon get word to their pals in the jungle of any troop movements, numbers and general locations. They, in fact got so good and efficient that for example they would report what the brightly coloured identification/ security hat flashes the troops were wearing that week. Giving the bandits time to attach similar colours to their jungle hats so causing, often a momentary hesitation, by our troops to shoot, thinking for a possibly fatal second that it might be one of their own. We Hashies never wore any kind of identification until we were in the jungle and only Special Branch would know, on the outside, our code colour (often assigned by them). The army, after many moons woke up and finally did something about it. The order went out that all jungle hats should be worn inside-out until the start of the actual patrol, so giving no advanced colour warning to the commies. There were so many, often little detail things like that that ensured that our Hash House Harrier casualties (despite us going out and looking for trouble) were so much lighter than the regulars. As this saga goes on many of these jungle fighting techniques will become obvious without me stopping to list them here.

Final point and personal thing at this stage is that in all those days and circumstances, never ever did I hear the term stress used as an excuse or even at all! Nor was there any wishy-washy patronizing counselling indulged in. A hand on the shoulder and a kind word was all that was wanted or required in that era of rather more backbone-orientated characters. There were no psychological gibbering apes as a result of it either, as anyone will have observed, in the numerous wartime reunions and anniversary get-togethers witnessed throughout the media recently.

Malayan Postscript No.1
Over a year after I had finished writing the Malayan section of this C.V. My wife Fay found a book in the local charity shop about the jungle war in Malaya by an ex-reporter from the Straits Times. The Straits Times was and still is the leading English language newspaper in Singapore/Malaysia and was always a respected, restrained, conservative and fair newspaper. Their only rival was the Singapore Standard. I was very pleased to have the opportunity to read this book and thought that it might be very useful as a cross reference for names, dates and details that I had long forgotten and not bothered to research. Overall it gives an excellent blanket coverage of the period (1948 to 1960) but naturally I disagree with some of the author's political, policy and operational conclusions. But, he had at least appeared to have left Singapore island and worked in Kuala Lumpur itself, unlike so many others. I was also very impressed by his collection of running statistics whereas mine were all from a fallible memory and impressions, which appear to have been remarkably accurate in spite of this! I was almost prepared to withdraw some of my scathing and critical comments about the press coverage of the 'emergency' both locally and back in the U.K. at the time. Unfortunately however when this author came to cover the terrible West Kent ambush in which

my pal James Bardell was killed, my inherent lack of respect and cynicism about the news media returned with a bang! The following paragraph is an erroneous account of what actually happened on that fateful day This then followed by my true account supplied by first hand reports of the wounded and other survivors as recorded in the regimental records made at the time when all was only too fresh in the victims minds. So from this reporter's book I will now quote with some anger. *(WITHOUT PERMISSION AND ILLEGALLY NO DOUBT!?);*

" In October 1951 the Royal West Kent Regiment lost sixteen men and seventeen others wounded in a battle in an estate in north Selangor. Thirty terrorists had blazed away at twenty-five soldiers as they had traveled in two open unarmoured trucks on their way back to base after a three-day patrol. And in relieving the dead men of their arms and ammunition, some terrorists took other 'souvenirs'- they sliced teeth out of mouths.... "

The first flagrant error is how, out of twenty-five soldiers does he get sixteen dead and seventeen wounded? When I went to school that made thirty-three not twenty-five! Even ignoring the one wounded who died later the error on both counts is in excess of 50% on top of the basic inaccuracy of 30 or so %. In truth, ten soldiers died (including James Bardell) another one later died of wounds and another ten wounded survived. A total of twenty-one not thirty three. Perhaps historically more important is the complete reversal of the truth about the capture/non-capture of arms and ammunition. The mostly wounded Kents had fought and held off the ambushing C.T.s for about an hour and managed to kill six of them as well before the C.T.s finally withdrew with NO captured arms or the chance to mutilate any bodies (that is not to say they would or did not; when and if they got the chance to steal gold teeth and fillings!).

It is absolutely disgraceful to deprive brave young lads of the credit of their success in preserving their arms under such overwhelming conditions. Their battle was a success and a sort of victory in as much as capturing arms was the main purpose of the C.T. ambush in the first place. Perhaps an even greater disgrace was to state that the dead soldiers bodies had been mutilated at all when in fact the C.T.s never got anywhere near enough on this occasion to do so. They were driven off with six of their own killed and therefore they never got any nearer to the Kents than when the ambush started. What would the victim's families have felt on top of their loss to have been given such terrible news? Where did this reporter get the false information? Gossip in a nice safe pub from 3rd or 4th hand rumours? Surely not from the Straits Times reports at the time? The true story and facts of the matter any reader will have already read earlier in Chapter 14, THEFT?

If any reader thinks in the course of this C.V. that I am prejudiced against the world's press then they would be right and justifiably so, as indeed I am also in forming such an opinion and judgements. We are all continually fed mostly bad news, exaggerated, sensationalized, full of errors and often the exact reversal of the real truth to say nothing of total inventions as well! In this particular case even allowing for the odd printing error it remains a huge distortion and reversal of the true facts and an insult to the dead, the living brave survivors and the families and friends concerned.

The book in question certainly from my point of view suffers from other inconstancies too; 1. There is no mention of Nicholls the Commissioner of Police at the time.

2. Evan Davies is not given the credit for re-organizing the Special Branch at Winston Churchill's behest. It gives the impression that Ewan Davies was just an odd S.B. officer who operated out of Kluang. That was however the base from which he later launched his famous personal and successful 'hands on' operations.

3. John and/or Lionel Davis are mentioned as having the initials of J., L., and H. which still leaves me unclear as to whether my ex. Force 136 boss and Managing Director in Singapore was the John of almost legend or was it his brother?

4. I have also now found the forgotten name of the C.T. leader of the murder squad that killed Sir Henry Gurney on his way up to Fraser's Hill a couple of weeks before the West Kent ambush. This C.T. leader's name was Siu Mah who continued to cause serious trouble for some time. He was regularly hunted down but seemed to lead a charmed life often escaping in the nick of time while more and more of his gang were slowly eliminated. We Hashies went after him several times with accurate intelligence from Special Branch and while we wiped out several of his gang we never got him. For a while our quest was a bit personal since after all we liked Sir Henry and we

had used his private tennis court. We sort of thought we owed him something. Some years later Siu Mah who was continually on the run was sold out by his few remaining gang members and then shot like a mad dog in a lime stone cave just outside Ipoh. An overdue and fitting end to an exceptionally evil man.

The Bentong area (just outside Selangor and into Pahang State), which is where I was going that fateful day in my XK120 to collect Basil of AKC, my friendly landlord and which was where the car and I became wounded: This was an area of very dense jungle and the home and headquarters of Chin Peng the overall boss of the C.T.s, He being the Secretary General of the M.C.P. (Malayan communist party). A few years later the area got too hot for him and he retreated up north and over into southern Thailand leaving his minions to fight on in the loosing battle with the security forces. A really brave and fanatical hero!? (pardon my sarcasm). Of course all these years later when discovering this, I allow myself the very small but satisfactory thought that my XK120 wounding incident may have contributed at least a tiny nail in the communist H.Q coffin. I was not demoralized nor were the Malay army lads, I was just very angry. The C. Ts though would be at least slightly demoralized as their ambush had failed, they had killed no one nor had they captured any arms or equipment. They had been forced to retreat having lost at least one member who was shot while shamefully running away from me, a mad running dog (a British one at that!).

In my early weeks, mostly at Klang and Port Swettenham, I had transferred down to the Govt. Rest House at Klang for convenience and to save some time as I was still driving the company's Morris Minor. This was one of the original models, still with the possibly pre-war little 850cc side valve engine, split or two-piece windscreen and with the rather ineffective headlights set low in the grill. I think it would only do 65 mph and then only downhill. It was not long before I acquired my own M.G.-T.C. model (reg. No. BA5412) which was much faster and alot more fun to drive. I wore the tyres out in under 5,000 miles though. This was my first introduction to relatively fast cars and driving. I went everywhere flat out. The only accident I had with the M.G. was when returning to K.L. after work one late afternoon and driving through the 'S' bends that came after the Petaling straight. Halfway through the bends I spotted a goat and several kids. She was on one side of the road and they were on the other. In both cases they had turned away from the road clearly aware of my approach. Unfortunately at the very last moment one of the kids, missing its mother, reversed and dashed back across the road right under my wheels. There was quite a thump but since what I took to be the herdsman and several others were close by I decided not to stop (coward!). I looked back in the mirror but could not see the animal but still felt quite bad about it, particularly if it had been injured. The car seemed ok but as I drove through the next village some of the locals were looking at the front of the car and pointing. I assumed there must be considerable damage to the front of the car but waited until I was on a deserted bit of road (coward again) before getting out to inspect the damage. Walking to the front there was not a mark or sign to be seen. However something prompted me to get down and look under the car only then to see the kid hanging by its neck on the front axle of the car. I had a problem removing it as it had clearly died instantly as the axle had half severed its head, passing through the bone which then closed over again looking as though the axle grew out of both sides of its neck. I finally got it free and was just about to dump the corpse in the ditch and drive off before anyone came along when a voice made me jump (clearly a guilty conscience). This belonged to a Tamil who just appeared from the undergrowth and asked if he could have the kid for his family's dinner, I readily agreed and hastily drove off.

For reasons that I cannot remember now the M.G. was never involved in any ambush or other emergency situations so never had the scratch and small dent problems that the Jaguar suffered on several occasions when driving into a ditch to avoid mortality problems! The Jag, apart from these sort of incidents never had a normal road accident either but did nearly come unstuck on a very wet road quite close to where the M.G./goat incident had occurred. This I will cover later on and more in context.

On the social side there was not a lot going on apart from the nightly chat round the Klang Rest House bar among the rubber and palm oil planters who would come into town to break the monotony and sometimes loneliness of plantation life. Not being a drinker this had limited appeal to me. It did however enable me to learn a lot of what was going on in the remoter areas of the district, re. bandit activity! Gun battles and intimidation of estate workers was a daily problem. In the short time I stayed in the Rest House there were several occasions when it would be asked, "by the way, where is so & so tonight?" Often the simple answer was "did you not hear? He bought a Burton near the 'X' milestone on the Banding (or some other) Road last Wednesday. The reaction was always much the same. A round of drinks to toast his memory and that was it.

One of the regulars was a Bobbie Bapty, who managed a Palm Oil Estate. He came in one night absolutely furious having had, I think, at least two of his fingers shot off earlier that day and still bleeding a bit through his bandages. His anger was not so much about his injuries, since his trigger finger was still ok, but because his firm insisted on sending him home on leave, before he was due! Needless to say he was back out to Malaya, to his old job within two months. I mention all this to enable the reader to have some idea of the conditions and the spirit of the people involved in the so-called 'emergency'. Britannia still really meant something.

Klang Group Xmas 1950
Malcolm Norfor, Jean Allison, Dolly with one son plus
myself and selection of local Asian friends.

15. Port Swettenham

In my work around the docks of Port Swettenham I met a lot of very nice and helpful people of all types, races and positions. Among these was a charming man from the borders of Scotland by the name of Allison who was the railway superintendent in the port area. He kindly invited me home to meet his wife and daughter whose name was Jean and who was about a year or so younger than me. We got on fine but her mother (a small plump lump) was continually asking me if I had thought about getting married yet and did I not think Jean would make a good wife?! Both Jean and her father were very embarrassed and I tried to be as humorously diplomatic as I could in the circumstances. The mother would repeatedly find some excuse to rush out and leave us alone, even inviting me to a family dinner and then to do the same thing.

The Malayan railways had a beach bungalow called *Headlands*, some miles down the coast at Port Dickson, which could be used by senior employees. I was invited down there one weekend to join them, only to find that Jean had a younger cousin named Norma staying as well. I can only describe her as a budding example of future jail bait in her efforts to steal her cousin's boyfriend! The best part of the weekend was the beach and swimming in the sea. The facilities included a Pagar, which is a bit like a well fenced tennis court on the beach with a board walkway round the inside about six feet up. When the tide came in we could swim inside it without having to watch out for sharks. I had not forgotten my recent, possibly lucky escape while in Malacca, just a few miles further down the coast. The other claim to fame for Port Dickson was that it was the headquarters of the Malay Regiment with all its splendidly attired soldiers. Their uniform included immaculate white trousers and bright blue sarongs on top. After this particular weekend I extracted myself very diplomatically from the Allison family and occasionally ran into Jean in very public places and it had no effect on my business relationship with her father, I am glad to say. In fact I think he was relieved and grateful.

Malcolm is the name of the next influential character in my early days in Malaya. He worked as a dockside foreman for a very wealthy Chinese owner of the leading stevedore company in Port Swettenham. This Chinese stevedore boss quickly became a very good friend, his full name was Eu Eng Hock, Eddie to his friends, Mr. U. or Eddie U in general. A while later he also bought a silver Jaguar XK120 like mine except that it had red upholstery. As coincidence would have it, his ignition key had the same number as mine so we often played pranks by taking each other's car. He also had two wives, one of about his own age who was the mother of his children and the other who was the 'show' wife for social occasions and of course a bit younger. I got on very well with both of them and they, it appeared, with each other, but in separate homes. On one occasion when he had taken my car his No.2 wife became very confused, as she was certain that he had changed the colour of the upholstery! It was at about this time that I was to meet a friend and business associate of Eddie, by the name of Kim Ling Lee, or Lee Kim Ling, it seemed to alternate. He would reappear in my life a few years later with almost lethal results.

Back then to the milestone person, Malcolm whose family name I think was Norfor but I'm not entirely certain after all this time and it being such an unusual name. He was a very friendly and fairly handsome Anglo-Indian who was married to a local Chinese girl with the unlikely name of Dolly. They had two wonderful children named Johnny and Andrew. They in turn had a pet monkey named Jacko who has to be the most long-suffering pet monkey ever. Malcolm talked me into leaving the Rest House and moving in with them on the strength of his wife's cooking. The address was 78b Telok Gadong Road, which was on the north side of the Klang to Port Swettenham main road about a mile or so out of Klang itself. He was right about Dolly's cooking as she introduced me to just about every option of Oriental vegetarian dish you could think of. Socially Malcolm introduced me to a very wide circle of friends, including many of his fellow Eurasians, Chinese and several Indian groups.

16. Enter Connie

Malcolm also took me to many places in K.L., at night where very few Europeans normally went. Nothing wrong with them, it was just the social/cultural/race thing and mostly cultivated by the European wives! On one such night out he introduced me to an exceptionally personable and vivacious girl who I was to call Connie McGregor. She had just returned from Singapore having won the South East Asia Jive Championship. I was most impressed and spent most of the evening testing out the dance steps that Mrs. Bardell had taught me. Bless her! The fancier dances Connie danced with her more experienced partners, which brought the house down with the applause. She certainly was a champion dancer and as I would find out in due course an extraordinary girl in other respects as well.

About the same time, I got up one morning at the Norfor's home as usual, had breakfast, drove my little M.G. down the short track past some workers who were spraying kerosene into the ditches to destroy the mosquito larvae and then up onto the main Klang to Port Swettenham road, only to find the smouldering remains of a burnt out bus right in front of the Towkay's house (in the back of whose garden Malcolm's house was built). In other words less than fifty yards from where I had been sleeping. A very sobering thought, as I had heard nothing. This was luckily, not one of the C.T.s murdering attacks, this one was purely political and an almost ritual burning of the passenger's identity cards. These, of course, the commies hated as they caused them a lot of inconvenience. It restricted their movements considerably.

For a night or two I slept with my gun under the pillow instead of hanging over a chair with my other clothes. If the local Min Yuen or C.T.s got wind of my gun, as they were bound to and if it was decided to add it to their collection, I would not stand a chance. Even more important it would bring serious danger to Malcolm and his family. He was very reluctant to let me leave but I had to insist, in all our interests. I kept in touch with them and continued to see Malcolm at work at the docks regularly. I still visited them often for a good meal and took their whole family up to K.L. on the odd occasion. Borrowing on such occasions a car from a certain Kim Ling, the boss of Soon Joo, (not to be confused with Kim Ling Lee, who will be introduced shortly) who owned a large American Ford car, for the outing. In those days it was regarded as almost limo size compared to British cars.

Connie McGregor's father, I discovered, came originally from Angus in Scotland and worked as a manager on several rubber estates pre-war. He met and married a local woman who was part Burmese Princess, part Siamese and whose father had been a titled Danish diplomat in Bangkok and other capitals, including K. L. pre war. When the Japanese occupation started, Connie's father went into the jungle to continue to fight them as part of Force 136, having exceptional knowledge of the jungle, in the vicinity of the rubber estates he had been responsible for. He fought in and around the Batu Caves area, which is just a few miles north of K.L. and on the way up to Ipoh, the tin mining capital of the country. He left his wife and two daughters in their house in K.L. during the Japanese occupation. It would appear that the occupying Japanese Governor, who loved children, took them all under his protection, partly due to their semi-diplomatic status and to my mind more probably that, in return, Force 136 would not harm him personally! Father McGregor managed to secretly visit them quite often and ironically was able to take some of the food and medicines back to the jungle with him, that the benevolent Japanese official had kindly supplied to old Mac's wife and daughters.

I tried to chat Connie up with a view to a date and was politely rejected but was told that she would be happy to dance with my two left feet any time. Needless to say, whenever Malcolm let me know that she was dancing again I made sure I went up to K.L to see and dance with her. Her mother always sent a trusted taxi with chaperone to collect her from her nights out. So the usual offer to "drive you home" did not work either. After some weeks, she surprised me by inviting me to drive her home and buy her dinner on the way. I was delighted but to this day I don't know if it was my charm or my M. G. car that she was more interested in? I then met her mother who was very polite but I thought a bit disapproving. She did however invite me to return to their home at 152, Ampang Road, for curry tiffin the next day, which I hoped was a good sign. After that, as they say, is history.

Connie's older sister, whose name I do not remember, had previously married a Staff Sergeant in the British Army and was back in England at that time along with their first child. Again I do not recall his family name but he was always referred to a Ebok, instead of Stanley (some months after writing this I came across a photo/negative

Self, Connie & MG
Port Dickson Beach New Year 1950/1

wallet with the name and address of; Mrs. S. G. Harper (Connie's sister), 2, Bukit Aruzah, 3-1/4 Mile Klang Road, K. L. So of course Ebok was Sgt. Stanley Harper). This nickname I thought meant goat, but I have yet to find it in any Malay dictionary. However, as it turned out a long time later, that some of the other expressions that Connie came out with were in fact Gaelic, not Malay at all, picked up from her father in an unguarded moment, one imagines. It transpired that Connie, unlike her elder sister, had never shown the slightest interest in boys and regarded them as just something to compete with. Being a vain young male I was flattered but more importantly often grateful for her tomboy side. She was a better shot with my long barrel Hart revolver than I was and could lob a fair grenade as well. This coupled with her apparent fearlessness under attack made her a wonderful companion up country in sticky situations, of which we shared several.

The next person and possibly one of the most important and influential in my life was Thor Hor Chooi.. He was chief clerk at our Klang office and very well educated in the real sense. A total gentleman and had the best balance between Chinese and British culture and manners I ever encountered. To this day I treasure the memory of his loyal, helpful friendship. The Chinese, like many others write from right to left, so when they Romanise their names it is back to front to us. Therefore, since his first name is his family name, he would be a Mr.Thor. His birth or given name of Chooi is pronounced by us, as "chewy". If for religious, business or social reasons the Chinese take on a "Christian", name such as David then they would reverse it to David Thor. Chooi, in effect ran the Klang office and Godown as chief clerk. I had another chief clerk Yap Cheng Eng and half a dozen staff at our Port Swettenham office, which was entirely separate. As branch manager for both I was the only common link.

*Thor Hor Chooi (Klang Chief Clerk) and family,
Kapar Road, Klang 1950*

*Yap Cheng Eng (Pt. Swett. Chief Clerk)
Klavness Captain and me 1950/51*

The commercial operations at Klang were based largely on the local Chinese rubber dealers and some estates who, against an agreed base price would deliver tons of rubber on consignment and almost on spec. We then took responsibility to select, grade and weigh the smoked rubber sheets into, usually five grades. Grade one called for an almost totally clear sheet. Grade two allowed just the smallest flecks of bark and impurities. Grade three, a few more and slightly bigger particles and so on down to Grade five which allowed several bits of not too large items! Firms like ours employed dozens of local girls who would hold up the transparent sheets to the light and snip out what ever they could which automatically raised the grade accordingly. Some sheets looked like sheets of Swiss Gruyere cheese. This was a very responsible job and the company's reputation could be affected, not only locally but thousands of miles away. To say nothing of the loss of profit, since there was often a considerable difference in price between the grades. The basic market price was based on Grade one with varying differences or differentials between the others. It was even possible to sell at a slightly lower basic price if the differentials were small and the lower grade could fetch a better price than, say the week before, when the base price was higher but the differentials were bigger! The dealers would be advanced payment on an agreed percentage and based on their average final grade breakdown. Then, when that batch had been sorted and graded they would be paid in full based on the original agreed market price and differentials.

Our reputation at ultimate destination was at stake, so we had to be discerning. Whereas the Chinese dealers, for obvious financial reasons did not like we exporters to be too fussy and would often vote with their consignments and deliver them elsewhere if they thought someone else would be less stringent but always, of course, coupled with the basic agreed buying price. It was all a bit of a financial and diplomatic juggle on occasions. If we shipped a slightly inferior batch and this showed up on sampling. An arbitration hearing might down grade the whole shipment and we would be responsible financially for the difference and costs! This coupled with the inconvenience, loss of reputation on world markets made the selection more important than generally realised. I was glad, in this instance that I had gone to college! I was quite happy to take on this responsibility until I found that there was a hidden "(you know what) in the proverbial wood pile".

After reading and studying the files and accounts for the previous several months I noticed a distinct change in the branch's profile. Soon Joo, (the one with the big car) had been historically the firm's largest Chinese dealer/client but had lately drastically reduced their consignments and those they did make were largely of lower grades. Initially I had to overcome some reluctance from Chooi to be taken to meet the Towkay of this concern whose name as I've already mentioned was Kim Ling. When I finally met him he turned out to be large, as Chinese men go, a bit po-faced and possibly did not speak a word of English and of course my Cantonese amounted to about four words. Everything had to be translated by Chooi both ways. Finally, like pulling teeth I discovered the problem. It appeared that the man Edlin, who I had met in London had in fact, for a while been my predecessor before being transferred. He had been over advancing payments to Soon Joo for what I can only describe as financial and social advantages. This in turn led to Soon Joo over extending their business position (just the usual and typical Chinese business gambling).

When it had all come to light it was decided to let Soon Joo work and trade their way out of the situation. Our head office in Singapore had agreed with Soon Joo, to allow a small percentage of their advance payments on all future deliveries to be withheld to slowly regularise the debt. Soon Joo naturally reduced their deliveries in both quality and quantity so reducing the rate of their repayments to us. Not a very smart arrangement I thought on the part of my company. We had allowed ourselves to be outwitted and lost a lot of business as well. I also discovered that Chooi, as a result of all this had lost his right and authority to co-sign the large company cheques involved. So loosing face and the respect of the local dealers. I was shocked and annoyed that no one had told or warned me of the situation.

At the first chance I climbed onto the phone and very arrogantly demanded to know if I was the Manager or not? If so then I wanted authority to resolve the matter in my own way and was, perhaps unwise enough, to guarantee an increase in business in the process. Within a few days I was summoned to head office in Singapore to face the big boss or Tuan Besar, the aforementioned Mr. Lionel (John?) Davis. As I had just that week lost a fair sum on a futures deal I was a bit apprehensive. My copy book was blotted, I thought. In Singapore I was still very indignant about not being briefed properly and stated that I considered the scapegoat treatment of Chooi very unfair and then, letting the real culprit Edlin off, in effect

While admitting the scenario, as I presented it, I was told that my over concern about the treatment of Chooi, while it did me credit, showed me as being naively honest, not a formula for future business success! It was clearly meant as a criticism but to this day I take it as a compliment. I went on to admit my recent financial losses. Mr. Davis got out the trading log for the period concerned and said, "you have made over five times what you lost, congratulations", and then went on to say, "Remember as long as you win at least three transactions out of every five, we all make money and can move ahead. Unlike politicians who are afraid to do anything in case it goes wrong. Which then means nothing gets done in a reasonable time and it costs us all a fortune subsidising their incompetence long term. In our case we still have to pay overheads regardless of any inaction". AND FURTHER, "we have decided to give you a free hand and to allow you to take a market position of up to five hundred tons. We will also be authorising Chooi to resume his co-signing status with you. BUT it will be entirely on your head though, young man!"
Game Set and Match, maybe.

Then later, in a private chat with Lionel &/or John Davis we discussed the security situation up country and he suggested that I did not worry his nephew Arthur (my immediate boss in K. L.) with the details of any of my now planned nefarious activities and that he had already warned Arthur that I may appear from time to time to have erratic movements and schedules but not to enquire into them!

It was about this time that I was told that "John" Davis (some seemed to believe that Lionel was the John concerned but others claimed it was a brother?) along with a Richard Broome had been the main instigators in setting up guerilla bases behind the Japanese lines, even before the fall of Singapore. They were then working with the further travelled, more publicised and higher profile Spencer Chapman who seems to have got a disproportionate amount of credit in recorded history when compared to many of the other unknowns. Probably in part due to his quite famous book, *The Jungle is Neutral*. Davis and Broome set up the foundation jungle bases and camps from Johore, up through the peninsular to around K.L. and even on up into Perak (Ipoh area). They were responsible for filling these bases with, initially a skeleton force of Chinese recruits passing through the 101

Special (Jungle) Training School in Singapore. They had no problem in obtaining willing recruits since the Chinese in general hated the Japanese for what they had been doing in and to China for many years already! The serious problem was managing to get any sort of co-operation between the two Chinese factions of the Kuomintang (KMT) who were loyal supporters of the nationalist leader Chiang Kai-shek and the growing Malayan Communist Party (MCP). It was of course well nigh impossible and squabbles kept breaking out about the distribution of arms and other equipment. These groups had to be largely segregated which was not the most efficient way to run a war! The communist Chinese finished up being by far the bigger and more influential group within Force 136. This of course laid the groundwork for the post Japanese occupation and the Communist actions from the jungle against the returning legitimate government, administered by the British during most of the so called emergency. This was not really an anti colonial war as the communists liked to make out but an out and out civil war for a complete communist take over.

The next day I returned by train to K.L. which got shot up as usual while passing through Johore, the most southerly state in the Malay Federation. On my return to Klang and when I informed Chooi that he was to be a reinstated signatory the tears came to his eyes. He would now regain face and respect locally and I found it also vastly improved my own reception among the local Chinese dealers and trading circles. Next, I went about winning back Soon Joo's regular business with my 'free hand', via Chooi, of course. He, I noticed was now treated with greater attention and respect, particularly after I told Mr. Soon Joo (for that is what I had re-christened Kim Ling, to his apparent amusement and acceptance) that in future Chooi had my authority to close deals and bargains with him (an unheard of situation). I also told him we were tightening our grading policy further but I would increase our advances to him only by 5% but only on the higher grades. This would help his working capital, pay us off sooner and ensure we got better quality deliveries from him. I also offered him the chance to sell us futures. He was obviously excited by the idea (the Chinese are inveterate gamblers).

In addition I asked him to keep either Chooi or me advised of up to date Singapore market prices as soon as he knew them (thanks to his bribing of the phone operators). I told him if he did this we would be able to come back to him quicker with offers and bids and would always give him first chance or refusal. Up in K.L., Arthur Davis never did figure exactly how we down in Klang had such accurate Singapore market information ahead of them, while they were often still waiting for their booked calls or telex to come through. He accepted it though and often had the chance for his main branch to make extra money as well. In return for Mr. Soon Joo's new cooperation I would reciprocate by giving him exclusively the latest thinking about futures from both the London and New York markets. (the information being from my father, of course and nothing to do with my company). This sort of information was just, not even remotely available locally. Now and for the first time the usually totally inscrutable Mr. Soon Joo smiled and promptly invited me to attend a large Chinese dinner the following weekend. I was the only European out of about fifty Chinese and other local businessmen and officials present.

Within a month Soon Joo's volume of business had trebled and despite our lack of direct verbal communication, I think we finally struck up a sort of rapport. Whenever I visited him at his 'shop' he hastily brushed everything off his desk, offering me the best seat and ordered tea and fortune cookies. My next ploy was to persuade him that I should go up country into the non-European areas to meet his Chinese estate and small holding suppliers. Reluctantly he agreed and even came with us initially. My front was ostensibly to inspect production and advise on quality control (in the modern parlance), which would make it more profitable for them and us. The Chinese are happy enthusiasts for that sort of proposition. After a couple of these visits I arranged to take a different interpreter with me, claiming that I had to leave Chooi to hold the fort at the office.

My new interpreter was in fact a lad from Special Branch who had been trying to get into this area of Selangor surreptitiously for some time. He now obtained a lot of very useful information from the estate workers, as to the numbers of bandits operating in the area, the extent of the food and money they obtained by intimidation. He also discovered that there was a very active cell of the Min Yuen. They were the local, usually non-fighting Communist support group who helped the operational members with food, money, intelligence and often recruited new, ideal-a-logical youngsters to be trained and then fight with the C.T.s. The Min Yuen did sometimes operate in the towns and cities, throwing the odd grenade into a restaurant or dance hall.

The next personality to be introduced is Basil, who also had an MG TC that was green and bore the registration number SC 5101.. He was the central area and K.L. manager of A. K. C. (Army Kinema Corporation). He and his part Chinese and petite wife Barbara lived and worked from a large house on a big plot of land, rather like an orchard. This was located just beyond the northern outskirts of K. L. on Gombak Road, one of the roads out to Batu Caves and eventually on up to Ipoh. Basil was responsible for supplying movie films to entertain the forces dotted about the country, often in quite remote areas. His garden/yard was used to service and maintain his fleet of delivery vans. So I had access to any tool ever required. Basil could be away for several days at a time also acting as one of his own drivers while doing his round of drop-offs. Basil maintained that he should morally not send drivers into areas that he was not prepared to go himself - his wife Barbara needless to say disagreed!

As a general policy, even in the many dangerous areas he visited, he always went unarmed as he reckoned that this fact would become well-known and since at that particular time most ambushes were for obtaining arms and not just killing, he might actually be safer. That logic was an individual one and not shared by all. A single killing could bring down a disproportionate amount of heat and interest for no constructive gain to the bandits, from an area that might have large numbers of military personnel and who, until that point, may not even been aware of the C.T s presence in the area. Trips with Basil were always interesting and the information I gathered direct from the active troops, planters and miners who actually faced and experienced being shot at most days, all added up to a better and general understanding of conditions and the day to day situation and security problems.

Barbara, Basil's wife, was a sort of adopted aunt of Connie's and as a result I was offered a nice self-contained flat adaptation in their big house. Plus, the ability to use and congregate in a shared communal dining/sitting area on any and every suitable occasions Such as when, as frequently happened, anyone of us might invite up to twenty friends back for Curry Tiffin. Basil and Barbara's staff only seemed to need about an hour to produce at least three kinds of rice, up to eight different types of curry and about twenty side dishes (sambols), plus afters, including slightly scented steaming small towels. There was an occasion when one of the cookies opened up a Durian fruit too close to the house and stank the place out for days. I can only liken the result as being a bit like a skunk in a confined place! It was almost a sacking offence. Although no one likes the smell and unlike most other foods, is not related to its taste. Which although an acquired one, is one I too share with the majority of Malaya's residents.

The four of us got on very well and were the best of friends and shared many happy times together. One day a pet monkey came into the garden and we discovered that he had a fence-wire collar on that had eaten into his flesh. Eventually we built up enough confidence for him to let us cut it off and gently dress his wounds. He became great fun and continually tormented the servants. On one occasion he got drunk and hid on the top of my wardrobe and when anyone came close he would throw shoes at us and anything else that came to hand.

17. Politics and incompetent policies

I have already alluded to the inept post-war Labour Government in colonial matters. Some of them were, in retrospect, so left wing that they were in fact communists, but without the courage of their convictions! One has to wonder if they really wanted to defeat communism or were they kidding themselves they could live side by side with them. Which simply means that they were either incompetent fools or knaves, there is no other option. They were indirectly responsible for many hundreds of lives lost in Malaya alone. I think it was they that disbanded the S.A.S. after the war because they were too successful! They also discouraged undercover operations because they seemed to think they were using unfair methods. How can you reason intelligently with such logic? It was largely thanks to the return of Winston Churchill after the awful labour years that finally, almost too late, put a proper and positive policy into operation. I don't think that it is generally realised that it was largely thanks to Churchill that Malaya and possibly even Singapore were saved from the Bamboo Curtain in the same way he was the saviour of Greece at the end of the war, from finishing up behind the Iron Curtain as well. Most of the older Greeks are still well aware of it and remember to be grateful. I have, perhaps naughtily, often wondered if Churchill via Sir Walter and others was not already doing something about it, even before he was returned to official power at Westminster! No record for posterity, of course. I was taught that once anything was in a file, even labelled Top Secret it was already too late as it had by definition ceased to be one. We will never know since these things are never divulged and may only come to light via people like me who can only speculate at situations that might have been observed from only the fringe. In my own case over fifty years on and a sort of mixed kaleidoscope seen only through a smoky glass situation. We should all be grateful as a nation that there are still some very patriotic people about prepared to devote their lives to real public service without any recompense or recognition, unlike regular Civil Servants.

However this sort of thing would most certainly be disapproved of by our present day criminally and so called politically correct and over liberal democracy. (I wonder if they would allow me visitors in the cells at the Tower of London?).

The following experiences and stories are mostly from the period before Churchill appointed General Gerald Templer to take over after the death of Sir Henry Gurney. The planters, estate managers, miners and many other civilians who were bearing the brunt of communist murders and appalling atrocities were all getting very fed up by the lack of action, help, protection, arms or even a clear policy. In the early days of this war, euphemistically called an emergency, an ex-Chindit from Burma days by the name of Mike Calvert was appointed. A former Brigadier I think, clearly he thought that the war should be taken to the enemy, as in Burma. He organised a sort of new Ferret Force, which was initially, and for only a very short time, quite successful but unfortunately not entirely approved of by the extreme left wing or the liberals at home. Despite being on the right lines, the wisdom from Whitehall was that he and his men would be better employed in the Korean war which was raging at the time. They would have had minimal impact in Korea compared with the undoubted and later proven success of their actions and methods in Malaya. Meddling politicians!

One of the first things Winston Churchill did, presumably officially, was to appoint one of his war time body guards, who was an ex-commando I believe. This man's task was to report back direct to Winston on the state of the Special Branch and carry out whatever changes they agreed on. This is what I believe led to the Special Branch being separated from the C.I.D. branch of the police so that they became a sort of M.I.5 and largely a secret law unto themselves! This man's name was Evan Davies and he was the brother of Rupert Davies the star or the award winning *Maigret* TV series. He even wore a French type beret like his brother. They appeared to be so visually alike that I thought they might even be twins? Evan certainly made many worthwhile changes and the double agent and rewards policy certainly more than paid off. But he was not happy sticking to the administration side of things so took off every chance he could to be hands on or more correctly, guns on. He built up a fearsome personal reputation with the C.T.s in any area where he often led the operations against them himself. On the civilian front he seldom travelled escorted and was more often than not to be seen driving his own M.G. TC about K.L. and even on country roads with no more armament than the rest of we casual travellers! Latterly I believe that he tended to base himself down in Kluang, central Johore and was personally responsible for coordinating some very important "clean ups". Coincidentally or just ironically was the fact that the Kluang jungle area was also one of the first Force 136 development centres against the Japanese. Old Mac would appear to have been correct when he suggested that a lot of the C.T.'s camps and routes were similar to the ones that Force 136 had used against the Japanese.

Our own plan, that is, that of a large number of dissatisfied and very impatient and aggressive minded civilians was simple and obvious, if the Government would not react in the right way, then this very angry and sometimes frightened group would try to take some unilateral action for themselves to put the bandits under pressure in their own backyard rather than always awaiting their pleasure and then being constantly being caught out. Their 'we' would include planters, miners and other civilians, who would also be entitled to rewards rated on the rank of the C.T.'s importance and whether dead or alive. A live bandit could be worth double as he could be turned into a double agent and always had a piece of the enemy jigsaw to contribute. Initially about seventeen of us from K. L. and its environs met and made our first plans, which had to be basic, simple and realistic. Tailored to our abilities, experience and resources. By this time most up country civilians in the front line had some experience of shooting, both giving it and receiving it. This had been limited to ambushes, running gunfights from vehicles and from fixed, sand bag protected positions. Some jungle hunting experience was now required. This was obtained by hunting each other in the local fringes of palm oil, rubber estates and at the back of the botanical gardens in Penang. All this with air guns and protecting ourselves with some old fencing masks often made out of meat safe mesh covers. We had never bothered with such sissy protection at school! (I just KNEW that our strictly illegal air gun fights on the cliffs would come in handy!). Soon, most became quite good at picking out any incongruous shape in the undergrowth. Any sort of movement was always the first possible give away.

18. Conspirators

One of the favourite gathering places for us in K.L. was the Coliseum steak restaurant on Batu Road, now Jalan Tunku Abdul Rahman, renamed after Malaysia's first Prime Minister.(I have since been corrected and that it was named after some minor royalty of the same name?) The other half of this edifice was a cinema and the whole place got its name from the several columns included in its architecture. The steak restaurant was often like a scene from a wild western film with a vast selection of guns, belts and boxes of grenades having been checked into the cloakroom. Many plots were hatched there. Being a vegetarian and for other good reasons (most Special Branch chaps that I dealt with were Asians who would stand out too obviously inside the Coliseum). I usually had my meals in one of the many cafes and more cosmopolitan restaurants on the same street. I would join the others for any final plotting after having consulted a member of S.B. who might or might not approve and give clearance. They always had to be consulted as they had so many irons in the fire themselves and it was essential that we did not muddy their water, so to speak. Plus the fact that, their intelligence was vital to our own enterprises and they would often accompany us as both competent fighters, observers and to identify any C.T. victims of any skirmish!

The S.B. or Special Branch were largely a law unto themselves once they had been separated from the normal C.I.D branch of the police force. This in turn tended to throw up some very distinct characters. The classic to my memory was a man called (Big) Bill Stafford, a police superintendent who, when out on a raid, (to escape paperwork) would wear what I can only describe as a pair of black Chinese pyjamas and a black trilby hat! He would lead from the front and on kicking the door in would enter with both guns blazing! The both guns were reportedly often shotguns which he wielded like a couple of ordinary revolvers. The results, as can be imagined were spectacularly effective. Bill became know and feared as Two Gun Stafford and by the the Chinese as the Iron Broom.

19. First Sortie

Our first project was to help a member of our own group who had a rubber plantation about twenty-three miles outside K.L. He, like many others, was shot at night after night. Usually this would occur about one a.m. and again about four a.m. The bandit's policy at that time and area seemed to be to intimidate, wear down the resolve, through lack of sleep and nervous exhaustion. All this was done with a view to stopping production and causing financial hardship, even to the estate workers themselves. The usual and typically selfish, traitorous and treasonable left-wing tactics that, we have all seen in many parts of the world, including our own country.

Most estate manager's houses had similar layouts. The ground floor being concrete walled and floored containing the ablutions, kitchen, scullery and staff quarters. Above, usually constructed of wood would be the manager's bedrooms, dining and sitting room, which was usually over the entrance porch, a sort of carport below. This sitting room was therefore open on three sides and very airy, ideal for the sticky weather. With the advent of the troubles, another ridiculous euphemism, the downstairs would be sandbagged at doors and windows with a special sort of sentry box in the porch for the Malay policemen to stand watch in relays night and day. Upstairs most rooms would be bagged up to about window sill height with gun slots at strategic points and with an array of guns just lying there for instant use, often with the trusty Bren gun facing the direction thought to be the most vulnerable to attack. Frequently this Bren gun would be manned by the woman of the house! Plus the odd box of grenades and a flare pistol to back up the radio to summons for assistance if the phone lines were cut, which they often were.

Outside a typical layout would be a tall perimeter barbed wire fence about 50 to 100 ft away from the house, floodlit from the house on all sides, not only to see what might be going on but to partly blind the approaching bandits and impede their choice of targets. Beyond the fence the ground would be kept as clear as possible. There would be a double gate manned by another relay of Malay constables, in twos with a full height defence post. Finally there would be patrolling dogs within the fence. Tin cans, bells, old saucepans and anything that would rattle and set the dogs off would be draped here and there along the fence. This, our first enterprise was based on the planter having found the flattened laylang (sort of local grass) from where the bandits now regularly fired at the house. Having become so confident, they had even left a clear track back to the ulu where they came from. Their shooting visits usually lasted up to an hour and then they would go away again. The return defensive fire was totally ineffective other than it stopped the C.T.s from coming up to the fence to cut it. The clear path that they had left, to and fro was an invitation to us. We would sneak out after dark and wait for them in ambush. We would set up two firing positions, one on each side of the path several yards back into the bush. The bush had grown up very quickly round the old rubber trees that were no longer being tapped for their white milky fluid. These would be well behind the C.T.'s usual and regular firing position. An ideal cross firing situation and with them also silhouetted against the floodlights, with us in the dark, behind them.

One side position would have a Bren gun, a Sten and a rifle, on the other side two Stens and a shot gun and a flare pistol, which would be the signal to open fire. We also made sure that the poor Malay constables were clear of our fire path too. We arranged for another Sten to guard our rear in case any additional bandits rushed in an odd reinforcement. For the first time locally, we were picking the field of fire (nowadays called the killing ground), not them. Two of us had gone back with our host the weekend before our scheme was due. Quietly we very nonchalantly walked round the designated area. He was right it was a clear and trodden path from the jungle. We carefully paced it all out and took a couple of directional bearings and left a indistinct peg or marker at each of our chosen ambush lay-ups.

There were nine extra mouths to feed on the estate that weekend. We extras had been almost smuggled into the house, just after dark, from the usual array of armoured family cars and Land Rovers. The staff had been given the weekend off so the woman of the house and their two young children did the catering for us. Consisting of a splendid curry and a very sweet sago pudding plus a lot of tea and coffee.

At about eleven o'clock we turned the perimeter lights off for just ten minutes only. This was to enable us all to move into positions without being spotted by a stray estate worker or anyone else. There was just enough light from the rubber tappers quarters a few hundred yards away. We filed out of the gate and made our way along the fence to a marker we had left last week. Took a bearing and walked exactly 180 paces, past the commies firing platform and on to a rock at the side of the path that we had left as a marker. We then split up into the two prearranged groups and at right angles on opposite sides to the path then proceeded into the deeper undergrowth to our two pegs. We lay down on our ground-sheets, put on our mossie net head gear and waited in total silence, lying dog-o, showing that long patient training does work, with the one exception of a grateful burp, that was the sign and aftermath of a good meal.

The floodlight came on again a few minutes later. We waited a full two hours, eventually to see five C.T. s showing up well against the lights, from our positions now behind them. They were so confident that they just stood around smoking for several minutes, which seemed like ages to me. The temptation to open fire was almost overwhelming but the plan was to wait for the signal flare from the English Ghurkha Officer who had brought two of his lads along for the fun(?), as they had the weekend off duty! This waiting may also be part of we Brits being mugs for the chivalrous attributes of fair play and giving the benefit of the doubt, even to our deadly enemies! These days of course our wishy-washy liberal supporters of unrealistic rights would argue that until they (the C.T.s) actually opened fire they might have been innocent estate workers, just taking a stroll for a smoke! At one o'clock in the morning for a quiet smoke in a no-go zone and carrying illegal weapons for walking sticks, I suppose? It would appear that our modern rights champions ignore any and all overwhelming circumstantial evidence to the level of criminal negligence to go with their overwhelming incompetence.

Eventually the C.T.s started firing at the house as usual, which occupied their attention and would drown any slight noise we might inadvertently make. The flare went up and all hell broke loose for about twenty seconds. Then followed a total silence, apart from the dogs barking back at the house. The two Gurkhas went forward and signalled O.K. Three were dead, one almost cut in half by the Bren and two very badly wounded. We called for one of the Land Rovers, then patched up the wounded temporarily and loaded them all on board. We gathered up their weapons that also included an antiquated Japanese long rifle that should have been in a museum but no doubt captured by Force 136 during the occupation.

The Gurkha trio and the S.B. representative loaded up a Land Rover and the Standard Vanguard (yes, you can get three bodies in its boot) and then wanted to head back to K.L. The patched up wounded prisoners were secured with those nasty, spirally wound brass small animal snares. Any movement and they cut into the flesh. These days, of course, plastic ties are used. The S.B. boys were anxious to get the load back to one of their non-existent facilities to possibly identify the dead and persuade the living to turn and become double agents, for a suitable payment, of course. This worked on many occasions. Even the uncooperative ones all helped to put the communist jigsaw puzzle together. The rest of us were left with the task of gorging on one of the children's birthday cakes, along with gallons of tea, hot chocolate and coffee, some of which was laced with the almost ubiquitous brandy, 5 Star Hennessey, I think.

Well, the idea and plan had worked flawlessly and it boosted morale no end. This was not exactly beginner's luck but we had proved that we were on the right track. However, that is not to say that we would always be so successful. We were not. It did confirm our belief that getting behind them or taking the war to them, was potentially a winning ploy. Not only from a practical military point of view but as time went on I noticed that there was an increase in the panic level and considerable psychological confusion among the C.T.s. It was not just a war of bullets and ideology but more of hearts and minds. Morale on both sides was vital to success. From that night onwards, some of us thought we were finally doing something useful and constructive. It would help the country grow, one day, into the most diverse but ethnically integrated and civilised nation on earth. Needless to say the usual 4 a.m. delivery of bullets from the C.T.s did not arrive, or ever again as far as I know. To the locals and estate workers, it was all a bit of a frightening mystery and they never knew what had actually happened. If they and the commies wanted to believe in mysterious avenging angels in the night let them. Superstition can also be a good weapon and fear of the unknown certainly is. I have gone into broader details about this incident, first because it was the first of quite a few and so that any reader might better understand the general ambiance of the place and times. Any following examples will be more concise and less specific.

20. The Melshams

Next, a visit to a rubber estate on a somewhat lighter note. I met the honeymoon couple from the P. & O. ship *Shillong* again - the Melshams. They were in Klang shopping one day. The blushing bride claimed to be settling in quite well but was glad they had brought out the Great Dane dog. It appeared that their own guards were petrified of it and the word had got out that they had a supernatural monster guarding them. Whatever the truth was, the C.T.s. had not attacked the house since its arrival. They were however shot at on a regular basis on the long road into the estate and on the driveway up to the fenced and guarded house. There was about a mile of older rubber trees on the approach to their estate, on either side of the road with the ulu starting immediately behind the trees and from where the shots were fired at them from cover. Not with any great accuracy it appeared and they merely said that they were regularly pinged at. Not shot at, please note! The noise being bullets bouncing off their armour plated car or Land Rover. I was invited to the usual Sunday lunch with the casual comment "we'll send the armoured car for you at 11 o'clock". Just like that. Obviously a perfectly normal and obviously a generally accepted situation. I was collected as promised and we were indeed shot at just after leaving the main road at Batu Tiga (three rocks) very close to where the present day Proton Car factory is situated. We drove through the guarded chicane into the garden at the front of the house. Not quite a typical English Rose garden but the bride had done wonders with the aid of her Gabon (sort of gardener). As I then walked towards the stairs leading up to the living quarters and later the sumptuous lunch we were nearly knocked down by one of their Alsatian guard dogs, in a great hurry, with its tail between its legs and letting out a strange howl. On reaching the top of the stairs in the gloom all I could see was a kitten. A well built little fellow with broad feet and short ears and with very attractive markings. Its sort of growling purr did not seem natural until it was explained that it was in fact a very young Tiger cub.

A few days earlier when the security forces had done a sweep in the area they had shot its mother by mistake. The result of movement in the undergrowth and a nervous trigger-finger. Quite understandable, but rather unfortunate all the same. The Melshams had adopted the only cub and were still hand feeding it, even through the night. Unfortunately I was never able to get back to their estate to see if they managed to train it to assist the guard dogs and Great Dane on their patrolling to discourage the C. T.s from hanging around their estate. The apparently cowardly Alsatian, I presumed had reacted instinctively to the tiger's smell and growl. The dog concerned was certainly no coward and in reality had chased the odd C.T. into the ulu and was thought to have managed to bite at least one!

I have particularly mentioned the Melshams because they typified the staunch young and brave Ex-Pats who stuck it out through thick and thin. And often, in some very dangerous and lonely places too. Sometimes not seeing another European face for weeks at a time. They were salt of the earth types and a very important element in saving the country from the evils of communism.

Some several months later, soon after I got my XK120, I was approaching the same Batu Tiga cross roads, where there was a small humpbacked bridge on its approach from Klang. Not for the first time I was taking it too fast and on this occasion the yump dislodged the driver's side rear wheel spat or cover. Then as I slowed, it passed me skimming along the road like a flying saucer, rose up and just missed the Malay constable's head that was on guard in his sandbagged guard post. The, quite heavily fortified Police Station was located on the South East corner of the crossroads. I finally stopped and reversed back to the entrance gate and felt a bit like a small boy asking for his ball back (please mister!).

My Malay was not very good and his English almost non-existent. He was clearly shaken and I gathered that he could not leave his post and certainly not allow anyone unauthorised in through the locked and heavily barbed wire covered gate. After about ten minutes of browbeating and erroneously using some senior police officers names in K.L. he reluctantly backed out of his haven, keeping me covered with his rifle, retrieved my wheel cover and poked it out through the fence to me. As I took it and backed away, the relief on his face was clear and I finally got a sheepish smile out him. He then scurried back to his post and tried to retain or regain his dignity and look as if he had never moved!

Whenever I passed by after that I would slow right down hoot the horn and wave at whoever happened to be on guard at the time. This was soon reciprocated by all the guards and with very UN professional and cheery waving of their rifles. Racial relations restored, I hoped. Now after over 50 years I have finally had the scratches on that wheel cover (from the skidding along the road) repaired and replaced the broken off flap, over the carriage lock, that retains it all on the car.

21. Petaling

Petaling was a quite notorious area which in reality was mostly an opencast tin mine. The village or even small town was on the main road between K.L. and Port Swettenham, bounded on the north side by the main road and railway, which were easily patrolled and guarded. To the south it was all several square miles of tin mine tailings and pools with the giant dredger operating somewhere about the middle. This was the area of approach the C.T.s used, to creep into town and extort food and other supplies. There was a well-known Min Yuen group helping them. One of the engineers on the dredger who had sat in on our early meetings asked if we could discourage them and their constant efforts to sabotage his machinery. Apart from the cost, tin was a vital strategic material during a war (Korea, remember?). The idea this time was to secretly redirect some of the dredger's floodlights into the open area at the back of the village, so forming a potential illuminated ring, where the C.T.s were thought to pass through. Plus a couple of old vegetable carrying lorries that could have their headlights turned on, manned by Chinese coolies sleeping in them overnight, who in reality were S.B.s. For three nights we waited in vain but on the fourth night the usual signal went up and on went the lights and a few shots were fired. One lone figure was all there was to be seen. He was lying down on the ground, not because he had been shot but because he had fallen over with fright or tripped when suddenly blinded. By rights, I should perhaps add that there was a curfew in operation and it was known that anyone breaking it could be shot on sight. So, only desperate Communists were likely to risk it.

The prone C.T. was shaking with fear and had been carrying the usual coolie yoke across his shoulders with the big shallow baskets on either side, which roughly balanced out. He was carrying rice, dried fish, dried ribs, vegetables, hard boiled eggs, salt, kerosene, some medical gear, clothing, several pairs of boots and flip-flops. At a guess it weighted all of 100 lbs. Potentially we had reduced the support route from the local Min Yuen to their pals in the jungle. Unfortunately Petaling remained a problem and hot bed of trouble. Finally, some months later, it was decided to destroy the place and resettle the whole community into one of the fenced and guarded new villages.

Toward the end of 1951 I was driving back up to K.L. one morning at dawn to find the whole place surrounded by a large security force of army and police. Each Petaling household was given a dedicated lorry and less than an hour to load all their worldly goods and themselves on to it. The young British troops were so kind and helpful it was almost touching to see them assisting the old folks and children, knowing that anyone of them might well have a grenade. The lorries then drove off in an escorted and guarded convoy to their new homes. New houses, more land and running water but all fenced in and they would be screened and given passes, to go in and out as they pleased in daylight. They were not prisoners but new members of what were called resettlement villages. As they left Petaling the whole place was burnt down. In the process there were several explosions from hidden ammunition and grenades going off in the heat. Need I say more to justify the action of the authorities? The operation had lasted well under two hours from beginning to end. The next day when I passed again there was absolutely nothing but a sea of black ash and burnt beams. The C.T.'s were never again going to get any supplies from Petaling. However the dedicated Min Yuen still attempted to beat the embargo by trying to smuggle rice out of the new fenced and guarded villages in the saddle tubes of their bicycles and even grenades inside fruit. All this in spite of the possible death penalty. This will give some idea of the level of almost mad fanaticism that communism can generate.

These new secure resettlement villages were fenced, lit up at night and well guarded to cut off supplies to the C.T.s in the jungle. To reduce the communist intimidation and blackmail of estate workers and villagers in general and to isolate the communists as far as possible with the addition of Identity/Pass cards now required. This plan was referred to as the Briggs Plan. Named after Lt. General Sir Harold Briggs, the recently appointed Director of Operations. He had been dragged out of retirement, rather reluctantly by Sir Henry Gurney. General Briggs had served in Burma during the war so was well-qualified to understand the needs and methods of jungle warfare.

As in the case of the Burmese Chindits very efficient and successful action against the Japanese.

Another Petaling story was that on several occasions C.T.s had been spotted in the far distance at the old dredgings close to the edge of the ulu, busy doing something but what, remained a mystery for some time. On very discrete investigation there was nothing to be seen except very barren mud and gravel pools. Discarded tailings from the dredging after the tin had been extracted. This process leaves a selection of lombongs (puddles, ponds and almost small lakes). Hence some lake gardens in several ex-tin mining areas around the country today. Eventually it was discovered that the C.T.s were fish farming in these ponds to supplement their smuggled diet. Very ingenious and a good example of the often bold and creative enemy we were facing and had to deal with.

The other Petaling story that involved me most was soon after I got my XK120. I would regularly open her up to about 110 mph as I left the village and headed up the Petaling straight towards K.L. The strait was somewhat undulating as well and ran parallel with the already mentioned railway line. At the start of this bit of road there was one of the entrance tracks to the tin mine. Often waiting for me was a young chap on his Vincent (Black, Knight, Prince or Shadow, I'm not sure which) 1,000 cc motor bike which was the Rolls Royce of bikes in its day and very fast. We would have a flat out blind up the straight. He would always get ahead of me up to about 90 mph and I'd then catch him again. He would then slow down, turn round and go back home with a cheery wave. All he wore was a pair of white shorts, a singlet, a pair of flip-flops and no crash helmet. He would just turn his head to one side to reduce the wind in his eyes and insects too I imagine, judging by the sort I collected on my windscreen. I never actually met him or knew his name. We were just two lads with our toys enjoying the odd chance to try them out in company. So, sadly, in retrospect, we only exchanged a wave and the odd salute in mutual respect.

And last, but only closely related to the Petaling stories, was when a now close S.B. contact and friend invited me out one Saturday evening. Connie was away visiting her Danish relatives in Penang at the time. He took me to a large concert cum dance hall opposite the B.B. (Bukit Bintang (Star Hill)) Fun Park, where the Miss Malaya contest was being held. He did not tell me initially that he was on duty and that we were not there just to enjoy the spectacle. He was involved in investigating a Eurasian estate clerk whose daughter was one of the contestants. He was thought to have some unsavoury connections and contacts. It later turned out that he did, but that they were of a criminal nature not terrorist connected. So the matter would then be turned over to the C.I.D.

This man was at the contest with his daughter and a motley selection of supporters. Cutting the story short, the daughter won and my S.B. pal urged me to introduce myself and chat her up as a possible 'in' to the father's extra curricular activities. Not only did I chat her up successfully, but I got to take her on to the celebrations and later home. She lived in a small Kampong (native village) just on the K.L. side of Petaling. I was able to include my friend along too, so the S.B. got his 'in'. The girl's father was a pretty revolting slob and the mother, sadly was a fatter version of the same and not a very attractive type either. One did wonder where the daughter got her looks from and how long they would last? Plus what was between her ears did not match her outward appearance!

The girl's father was a scrounger and repeatedly invited me to date his daughter, as long as I brought at least 200 cigarettes for him. I'm not sure if this was some early form of commercialised sex or not. At my colleague's behest I visited the girl with him about three times and we had a foursome dinner once. Luckily it became clear, quite soon that it was not a terrorist matter after all and I could get off the hook gracefully and before my stock of Kools cigarettes ran out (more about these later). Plus, of course before Connie returned even though she knew what was going on. It turned out that she knew the girl from school days and shared our general opinion of the whole family. I can't remember the family name, but if any reader wants to look up the records on Miss Malaya 1951 they will certainly find it there.

Now to a more informative and in some ways personal series of snippets from a series of estate or plantation visits. The first case was a visit to Connie's father, who seemed to manage several estates and own the odd one as well. On our first weekend visit to him he had instructed us to come armed. We did, with Connie carrying a shotgun and an old Webley service revolver and I had a Sten and my favourite long barrel Hart .38 plus a box of grenades between us. The 50 odd mile journey was without incident this time! Old Mac as he was usually referred to, still had his old pre war family cook, who had also joined him in the jungle and caves as part of Force 136 during the Japanese occupation. Although, it appeared that he often braved the journey himself but was away in the farthest reaches of his domain much of the time, which made it usually impractical, not to say downright dangerous and foolhardy.

The slight apprehension I had at meeting him for the first time, he quickly allayed. Much to my relief, for despite the very worldly experiences for my age, meeting a possibly disapproving father of a girl was not one of them! He was almost charming, which was not his reputation, which was normally being a bit old fashioned and on the prudish side where his daughters were concerned. He was clearly proud of his girls and almost immediately organised a shooting contest. He had taught his daughters to shoot in their early teens. I was a bit shaken to see that Connie with a rather heavy Webley could knock cotton reels (not bottles or tin cans, please note) off the garden wall more often than I could with my long barrelled and theoretically more accurate Hart. My respect for her went up no end. Some team I thought and I never ever again hesitated to take her up country to dangerous places, when she wanted to go with me, or in some cases, us. This included social and reconnoitring trips, not actual jungle patrols though. Old Mac also showed me the best technique for using a Sten gun. He pointed out that the barrels were never straight and one should regard them more as a garden hose. Never aim at the target, as you will seldom hit it. Spray the area with a circular or oval burst. He also told me to stop taping the spare magazines together, as in emergency it took too many extra seconds to separate them and re-load. Use cut down inner tubes like rubber bands, as they separate almost instantly and you can carry more of them in any block. Never use full magazines, always leave out at least one bullet, as these guns are prone to jam otherwise.

I think I and the few other civilian weekend guests learned much more jungle craft from Old Mac than months of bitter and sometimes lethal experience could have taught us. He explained that in the jungle the C.T.s priorities often change depending on whatever shortages may be prevalent at the time. Plus any short term changes that might be politically expedient at the time. i.e. don't draw too much attention, if the area is heavily covered with security forces. Wait until they go or are reduced. Don't always murder for the sake of murdering but tend to use it to intimidate and frighten the populace into supporting them with food and money. They clearly found that by murdering say, a rubber tapper, in cold blood in front of other estate workers, that the rest of them, in that area would be more forthcoming with illicit support. One particularly nasty incident happened when a tapper had refused to pay his subs. He was tied to a rubber tree in front of the other workers and his pregnant wife was brought out and beaten in front of him. He begged them to stop, making some comment about wanting to see his child born safely. They promptly cut her open with a Parang (machete) to expose the foetus and then jeered and killed them both anyway. In such circumstances it is very understandable that the non-communist populace would give in and pay up. It should not be forgotten that, contrary to the communist propaganda this was not a colonial war, but just the communists against everyone else including, Muslims, Hindus, Buddhists and Christians. Many, many more locally born people were killed than all the Ex-Pats and combined British forces put together. All loved the country so much that it was probably THE country that people least resented dying for. It should be also born in mind that most of the Ex-Pats were happily working and fighting to put themselves out of work in due course as the country was being given (often against the local and particularly the Sultan's wishes) entire Governmental independence. Not freedom, they already had that! And national freedom was actually what the communists feared and resisted most.

At this point perhaps a small bit of potted Malayan colonial history might be enlightening. Since it is contrary to the colonial rubbish that the sickeningly ignorant and totally un-pragmatic liberals bleat on about. In the case of Malaya it was never even remotely like the wicked image they deceitfully put forward to justify their irresponsible and selfish political aims. A little of what follows is slightly plagiarised, to save hours of research to aid my memory.

So, whereas both the Portuguese and Dutch had originally come to the Malayan area as Viceroys, regents, missionaries and conquerors, the British came as merchants. Their object was largely to trade, their economic principles laissez-faire, with no more interference with local culture and custom than was entirely consistent with the maintenance of law and order. The ports were made free, in almost brave defiance of the traditional jealously guarded trade monopolies. Tuan Raffles drew from Edmund Burke the idea that colonies were held in trust, and that the welfare of the inhabitants was to be a major concern of the governing power. While therefore seeking and encouraging trade to his utmost abilities, he did cultivate the closest relations with the people of the country while becoming an authority on the language, customs, flora and fauna of Malaya and encouraged education by establishing many schools. Although his stay was relatively short, his influence remained and remains an inspiration to this day!

Penang, Malacca and Singapore all thrived. Up country in the Peninsula there was constant strife among the different states, and, within each state there were often ruinous dynastic (Sultanic) struggles. The discovery of large deposits of tin in Perak and Selangor not only brought wealth but the usual lawlessness of robbery and violence. The tin was near the surface so could be worked by opencast methods. Rival gangs of miners and their labourers disputed claims (a bit like the American Gold Rush?) while the local administration was only interested in levying the maximum tax they could. With communications totally inadequate, supervision necessarily devolved to local headmen whose abilities only seemed to stretch to setting up customs posts on all the exit routes. Like America, again, mining camps became a lawless or at least a law unto themselves with hardly any policemen to enforce anything! Finally the Sultans of both Perak and Selangor requested the then Governor of Singapore to send them a resident to teach them the art of government.

Peace and prosperity marked the next fifty years. This was all helped and strengthened by the advances made in agriculture but which in turn also had its own setbacks. The spice trade declined, sugar and coffee failed and even rubber was subject to the disastrous slumps in the 1920's and 30's. Malaya in capturing a disproportion of this world trade was then of course exposed to trade cycles and felt forced to embark on the potentially dangerous course of restrictive methods for both tin and rubber. This rather arbitrary act did work and achieved for Malaya the highest and sustained standard of living in Asia. Such action was again carried out on the financial markets some 70 odd years later and worked again, much to the greedy international speculators annoyance if not fury! But I digress again.

The residential system was successfully introduced and by the end of the nineteenth century Perak, Selangor, Negri Sembilan and Pahang had formed themselves into a Federation. The large state of

Johore remained aloof for a while but finally accepted a British Adviser in 1914. Kedah, Kelantan, Trengganu, and Perlis came under the British umbrella in 1909. The Peninsula was, of course occupied by the Japanese from 1942 to 1945. Cut off from the rest of the world Malaya saw just how hard the austerities of autocracy were although lessened by the large stockpiles that had piled up in anticipation of war shortages. Never the less suffering and hardship were wantonly acute. After the war and on the welcome return of the British the Malayan Union which had been planned 'in vacuo' lasted only from 1946 to 1948 when it was succeeded by the Federation of Malaya which was what was in operation during my time out there. Singapore became a Crown Colony with its own administration.

The full history of Malaya has yet to be written and until the erudition of a George Stubbs and with the imagination of Arnold Toynbee, the history will remain a bewildering chronicle of petty states and even pettier chieftains. Their pre-history is still very obscure and even approximate dates of their stone-age are conjectural. It's a country that needs to be personally experienced rather than read about. A country of so many greens, the pellucid shade of young rice through to the deep dull olive of rubber trees, or the trace yellows of coconut palms, to the infinite variety of tints in the forest. The land is permanently green, and about three quarters of it is jungle/ rain forest so thick and dense inside that the maximum visibility is never more than thirty yards and frequently barely even ten feet! This almost impenetrable jungle defied human occupation until tin and rubber attracted enough labour and finance. Before the advent of the automobile, which led to the planting of literately hundreds of thousands of acres of rubber plantations, all transport was by river alone. (rather like most of Borneo today). In 1870 the records indicate that there was not one mile of paved road in the Malay states! Here and there a small group of Malays would clear a small bit of ulu (sub jungle) and plant rice and build small residential kampongs(villages). Then they would have to wage a continuous war against the jungle's return, just as modern day plantation have to do. Some of the more enterprising went fishing or went on jungle trips to bring back rotans (Malay for rattans), ivory or various gums. It was not until the latter part of the nineteenth century that tin was mined on a large scale and that estates of coffee and coconuts were superseded by rubber and now more recently palm oil. The labour for these new enterprises was imported from India (mostly Tamils from the south) and China. Then foreign capital was attracted and roads were built, railways laid and land instead of only water communications between all states became possible at last.

Such introduction of large amounts of foreign labour have, as always, and still do, produce profound social and moral changes and risks. Taking the two territories together (Singapore and Malaya) the Malays now found themselves in the minority to the Chinese. The Malays accustomed to centuries of easygoing kampong life, then almost suddenly found themselves thrust into the complexities of international trade with its unintelligible cycle of boom and bust. Often thrust aside by the more industrious and harder working immigrants they finally saw that they would lose out in the survival of the fittest (or greediest) stakes and belatedly woke up to the beginnings of a political consciousness. The Malays in particular still had (in my day) a malaise that had to be cured without fail. All, but a tiny fraction of the population are Asians who for centuries have based their lives on a unit of society that was very small. Their own family, their clan, the village. There was never a particular loyalty to the state as an abstract idea, and now the state had become very large and internationally complex. The territory had become unified but the hearts and minds had not. They were being expected to cherish and show an undivided loyalty to an entity that in their experience was almost incomprehensible. Malaya had acquired great wealth but had not developed a soul, or a common national patriotism, or common standard and values. The most pressing problem was to find a way to make them all feel good and become fellow citizens and even brothers under their various gods. The Muslim religion/cultural mentality had not yet reared its head! The communist situation was hardly helping matters though and I feel almost proud to have had even the tiniest part in enabling the country to succeed, which it has. How?

Simply by retaining and improving all the British colonial administration systems and values that we left behind for them. Unlike all those disgustingly corrupt African former colonies that have not only thrown out a perfectly good baby along with clean bath water but have then filled the bath with foul, perverted and evil systems that starve and kill their own people by the thousands as a regular matter of course. The mealy-mouthed liberals will not honestly face the truth in these matters and should be considered and held guilty of multiple murder by association and by, in effect, and association both before and after the act! In this country not so long ago people were hanged for even one similar example and on a lot less circumstantial evidence. All the African countries and to a much lesser extent in India have changed names of almost everywhere. Malaya on the other hand has with few exceptions, retained most of the old British (majority Scottish!?) street names and have even added more since full, so called medeka, independence. The main seafront road in Penang is now Gurney Drive (after Sir Henry, the murdered High Commissioner) and just north of K.L. not far from the Batu Caves is the large Templer Park and Golf Course (named after General Sir Gerald Templer, the appointed Supremo, after Sir Henry's demise). The only major exception is that, what was Port Swettenham is now Port Klang, which being their main and largest port is understandable and I am sure not done with ill will or malice towards the former British Resident Frank Swettenham. However still related to sea port work is the Jetty Swettenham as a main quayside in Georgetown Penang even today. The three main hill stations and resorts are still called Cameron Highlands, Frasers Hill and Maxwell Hill. The Malay Regiment's original home is still called Port Dickson. The ferry port and town on the mainland opposite Georgetown Penang is still called Butterworth and was a main R.A.F. air base in my day. Just from memory and after Fay and my trip to Malaya 45 years later I can still remember nearly 30 of the original British street names still in use on Penang Island. Mostly Scots of course, from Argyll, Campbell, Carnarvon down through Farquar, Leith, MacAlister to Stewart. There is still a Love Lane plus King, Queen, Duke and of course a Victoria as well. Even back in Klang where I once worked and although my old office is long gone Harper Street is still there on the riverside.

If, in the course of this history, anyone gets the idea that my seething hatred of communism goes too far, then just remember the incident I've recently mentioned plus the following and many other similar incidents. Communism, along with drugs and other forms of murder, should not be given the dignity of even being regarded worthy of discussion or debate, it's a total No, No. If it had not been for me, acting out of respect for the S.B., I would happily at the time have been responsible, both directly and indirectly, for as many communist deaths as possible. However, captives, wounded or not were worth a lot more money. Apart from the fact that each one converted or turned was reckoned to be worth ten or more lives saved. Be it civilian, services or even the rank and file terrorists themselves, who were often only in the jungle due to some coercion and having been subjected to brain washing. When this was added to the millions of dollars it was costing to wage this war and the loss of national income from all sources it was more than a convincing argument. I have also, since learned in life that we should never hate the person, only their behaviour. We humans do have ability to see the light or reason and unless already deserving the death penalty, as in the instance mentioned above, should always be given a chance, even if only for the pragmatic and cost reasons. But once only though!

That's enough of my personal attitudes, back to Old Mac and his jungle skills. He advised us never to pursue terrorists directly after an attack unless they were in sight. Because if it was a genuine and planned attack or ambush they would have good routes for escape, often with several false trails, some of which could be booby trapped. They often adopted the wild boar tactics, making them even more dangerous. The wild boar appears to run away and then turns and circles back and attacks from the side and low down, which can give it both the tactical and psychological advantage. If it was an attack on an estate they could be expected to leave the area as quickly as possible. Because if there was a chance of any of the guard dogs coming after them they would be sniffed out of any possible ambush that may have been laid. Another change of tactics might be because of a shortage of arms and ammo, in which case they would try and attack a small convoy with overwhelming odds, just to capture the arms. As was the intention of the ambush that led to Sir Henry's death, which was in fact entirely and tragically incidental. If the C.T.s were short of food or medicine that would lead to a series of concentrated raids to obtain new stocks of such items.

Old Mac was quite sure that the C.T.s general command and control system would still be much the same as in the Force 136 days. Often still using the same camps and jungle paths, connecting up the three basic type of camp. Apart from the flimsy front line operational Bashas. These being the post office, relay and operational transit points at path junctions or jungle cross roads. Next and further into the interior would be the small strategic camps which would house a full operational group for a particular area with possibly half a dozen semi permanent buildings, a vegetable patch but not big enough to be spotted from the air. Plus of course, mistresses for the more senior ranks, which was known to cause some resentment among the lesser grades. This sort of camp was guarded by lookouts posted several hundred yards from the camp with a variety of warning methods from runners to a long string attached to tin cans and bells.

Then there were the very remote regional camps that may have several dozen permanent buildings. Including classrooms for lectures and the essential indoctrinations. Full kitchens and even a parade ground complete with flagpole! Also a printing division, tailoring facilities and a sort of field hospital. A much larger, small-holding of crops, pigs and hens. Again some women for the officers with the most red stars on their caps. These camps were usually so remote that little caution was required which only changed later when the Lincoln and later the Canberra bombers found them! In both cases these last two types of camps required to be close to a good and regular water supply and this common denominator was, on occasion to be their downfall. If the rough area of the camp become known, then by studying the watercourses it was possible to narrow the search considerably. This sort of information was frequently obtained and after months of patient work by, often a woman S.B. plant or latterly by a turned C. T. for money. They, in turn would come out again with more information and even a few more surrendering bandits to further enhance their financial standing.

In addition to these camps there were numerous caches dotted all over the country, usually in the form of oil drums and old ammo boxes taped up. These would contain spare arms, ammunition, grenades, tinned foodstuffs and a wide variety of items down to cotton and thread. Mostly the same items that had been used during the occupation and against the Japs. On one of our weekend field trips and after about five hours on the go, Old Mac showed us two of these, well hidden caches. Mac had, a couple of years earlier, at the beginning of the emergency, broken the seals and poured water into them to render them useless.

It appeared that Mac's 136 lot had covered a large area, both north of K.L., and then sweeping west and to the coast in the area of Pankor Island and to the east into the central mountain spine that runs down the centre of Malaya for most of its 500 mile length, from the Siamese border down through Perak, Kelantan and on into Pahang towards Johore. This included the lime stone Batu Caves, just north of K. L., which was an area that the Japs had all but given up on, as in fact had our own forces, to a large extent. These caves are vast and complex and have been washed out of limestone cliffs, over a great deal of time. In several places the roof has collapsed in and then been grown over by the jungle above. There are a limited number of easy ways to climb the cliffs from the outside, again through heavy undergrowth. During the occupation Mac and his merry men would hit and run back into the caves where, if they chose to, they could hold off an army. They would often retreat up rope ladders through the holes in the roof to the complete mystification of the Japs. Who then might have the odd grenade dropped on them, for good measure! In the gloom they never knew where they had come from and became convinced that there were secret inner cave passages that they were too frightened to spend time looking for. On the odd occasion that the Japs had climbed the cliffs to investigate, they, not knowing or seeing the carefully marked routes, several of them had fallen to their deaths through the grown over holes in the roof. The Batu Caves themselves are a sort of Holy shrine for the Hindus and are reached by climbing about 275 steep steps up to the first entrance, as the caves themselves are well above ground level in the first place.

22. Mc.G. tech

On these arduous weekend jungle treks we were always armed to the teeth, Old Mac would have a Sten chained to his belt with the forward part slung through a very stretchy rubber strap enabling the gun to be ready almost into firing position without tying up his hands. He would have a slightly sawn off shotgun slung over his shoulders but with barrel down so as not to catch in undergrowth. He too would carry an old Webley and several pouches on shoulder webbing and belt containing ammunition for all three guns plus a few grenades for good measure. We learned how to creep slowly and more importantly, quietly. Listening out for the tell-tale changes of animal and bird calls from usual chatter to alarm calls. Which of course meant that either we, or an enemy, close by had caused it. At which point a silent hour or so was essential. We learnt that sometimes we were only able to cover three miles or so in whole day without getting frustrated or despondent!.

He advised us to always work with a patrol of six or seven, because the nervous strain of both the lead scout and also the vanguard man was considerable and they should be changed ever hour or so. Secondly because on average we should expect at least one of our patrol to be either injured or wounded and if that person was receiving attention from another it disproportionately reduced our fire power potential in such an emergency. In the case of only four it would be halved! Lastly the radios fifty years ago, were heavy and cumbersome and the load should be shared, in turn. He also advised that we always take a Sakai with us (the seventh man) as these aborigines of the forest were totally at home and could sense things we would never even know about. Although they would not fight, they also hated the C.T.s, who were continually raiding their villages, deep in the jungle to steal the hard worked for food and even taking their dogs and killing them for food. (in those days all aborigines were referred to as Sakais, but these days, the politically correct name is Asli People, of which the Sakai are but a main tribe).

Finally, some surprising weapons, a catapult and some soft lead shot to be used as a method of causing a diversion to distract the attention of the enemy sentry or to attract the attention, silently of a team member. If we were going to be away for a while. We should then consider carrying at least one crossbow, which was handy to dispose of a C.T. lookout or sentry, silently or to kill some food without waking up the neighbourhood with gunfire! This would certainly be the case if we shot any game for the pot. Old Mac kindly gave us the name of his craftsman supplier who worked at the back of Wearne Bros. This garage was the Nuffield agent at that time (before they became B. M. C.), and who sold Morris and M. G. cars. This was off Pudu Road, going up the hill towards Bukit Bintang and which then led onto Pudu Road Jail, where most hangings were carried out, of the murdering terrorists. There was also a lethal selection of Rambo bolts to go with these crossbows.

Another very useful tip was to pin the sides of our floppy camouflaged hats up so as not to impede our hearing in any way. In addition we stuck small rubber wedges behind our ears and taped into position to make them stick out almost bat-like. This reduced the need to turn our heads as far when cocking an ear for faint sounds. The eyes have a wide sweep range compared to the ears so the head does not need to be constantly swivelled as much or as far. So many of these things may seem small but could literally be the difference between life and death. Another good piece of advice was not to use grenades in the jungle unless you are sure there is no obstruction. It is only too easy to lob a grenade that hits a branch, drops and goes off, nearer you than the enemy! So ends lesson ninety-nine. The next lesson concerned rivers, their crossing and negotiation. Under normal peaceful conditions rivers and steams are the easiest and most used routes. Unfortunately, they also offer ideal places for ambush with little cover for the victims. The noise of running water also drowns out any tell tale or warning sounds as well. So in any possibly active area do not use rivers as paths, only for crossing and then with great care.

All water ways of course run downhill and if one were lost by following them on down, eventually they open out into a plantation or paddy field with the almost certainty of a local kampong in the vicinity. With only sketchy maps the rivers remain the only way to double check one's position. Because, in most jungle situations you never see the sky for hours, if not days and cannot even see the next hill, in most instances. Not even if you could climb the odd 100ft tree.

If it is necessary to follow a river then this should be done away from the bank, often up a slope above the water, where the water can be kept in sight or at least within hearing. Since sound tends to rise, the patrol moving above cannot only hear the water but also things, like voices. Whereas anyone down on the river can hear next to nothing, apart from the water. Although moving along through undergrowth above the water is slower it does have real advantages in a sudden shoot out, because those above have height and cover whereas those on the river have little initial cover.

Although Mac and his visitors had to be armed while travelling to and fro along the approach roads to his estate, that bordered jungle and were notorious at that time for quite serious ambushes. To such an extent that most of the immediate road side trees had been felled to stop them being used in the usual manner, of dropping them just in front of the ambush victim and just after they had come round a corner. Mac and his estates had little direct problems with the C.T.s, simply because he knew some of the older and more senior members and they in turn knew him from 136 days. There was a element of mutual respect and I think some superstitious fear on the Commies part. This had all turned to a mutual hatred of each other's ideologies. The joint wish to defeat the Japanese is what had brought them together in the past, but for entirely different reasons. Mac, of course for patriotic reasons but for the communist party it was more to do with long-term political opportunities. Expecting to be in a very strong political position after the Japanese were finally defeated, they thought that they should have and deserved disproportionate political treatment. However when the returning British made it quite clear that it would be one man one vote, in due course, the communist party just went back into the jungle and continued to fight for what they wanted and against all their general political enemies.

As in France during the Second World War it had often only been the communist party that was well organised enough to work and fight alongside the Allies against the Germans in one case and the Japs in the other. Wars can at least temporarily, make strange bed-fellows.

The C.T.s also left Mac alone because he had made it perfectly clear that he would personally go after them and kill them all if they dared to attack or try to intimidate his workers or even come onto his estates. They knew he meant it and was still capable of doing it! He was always well-armed because, if the word got back to the bandits that he was vulnerable, then they would murder him at the first chance they got. He knew that they had put a price on his head but only outside his domain. Not only was this a possibility for local kudos, but they wanted access to his estate area for intimidation, for food, money and so on. However, they knew that if an assassination attempt failed they would have good reason to be fearful of the unknown repercussions from him. In this case the Chinese instinct to take a gamble, they clearly thought better of.

Although it did not publicly appear that Mac was actively fighting them. But as I have already mentioned he had spiked their caches and he was also actively working with the Special Branch, who had managed to plant members into the local branch of the Min Yuen, among estate workers and even two into the nearest jungle group themselves. All this was unknown by the local police whose security could not be guaranteed, as office staff or typists could be Min Yuen spies. As a result of which a local, recently arrived and over zealous Welsh Ex Palestine policeman with a bee in his bonnet was regularly insinuating that Mac, due to his previous associations was co-operating with the C.T.s, for old time's sake and in effect buying his immunity from attack and intimidation. Mac of course resented this very much but could not clear himself without seriously jeopardising the local S.B.'s security. So he just ignored it as best he could. A different type of bravery and a thankless one at that. Sad to say Mac was not the only Ex Pat and former 136 member to be misjudged in this way. To me this was further reflection of the sort of inability that the immediate post-war Labour Govt. had to make knowledgeable appointments in a serious Colonial situation. Be it either at the top or the bottom of local administration.

23. Innovative jungle clothing

Starting from the head down; Basic jungle floppy hat with camouflaged pattern that is so important to help break up the lines of a face which is the easiest part of the body to spot in undergrowth. Hence a painted or oily looking face make-up as well. Lamp black or even Cherry Blossom boot polish could be used. In addition to this we fabricated four quarters of heavy felt and sort of hinged together which could be folded and stowed easily or unfolded and put on top of the bush hat giving the appearance of a Boy Scout or Canadian Mountie. This for the very wet conditions and which would throw off the rain from our faces and helped to prevent the rain running down inside our clothing. It was quite handy for use when sleeping or on guard and used with a poncho at night when sleeping vertically crouched with one's back against a tree, again to disperse the constant rain. On the poncho front we favoured the very light cycle cape of oiled silk, again dyed darker and streaked for camouflaged effect in preference to the hot and heavy rubberised ground sheet material usually used. Next a head net used mostly for sleeping when we would not immediately be conscious of landing and biting insects. Facial bites are much more serious than the odd body ones. These net coverings were made up out of dark dyed mosquito netting and looked a bit like beekeepers equipment. They worked though! We used simple Terry towelling for sweatbands for head and wrists, elasticated and with the ubiquitous local sweat towels round our necks. Two of these were strung together so that while one was getting soaked the other could dangle and dry off. These small towels are used universally as face cloths, then wrung out and used as a drying towel as well. Ours were dyed dark of course but the originals are white and emblazoned with 'Good Morning' and the equivalent in Chinese characters meaning Chu San in Cantonese, literally translated as Morning Freshness.

Next, a good quality cotton bush shirt (I tended to favour long sleeved versions to avoid some scratches, cuts and to reduce the exposed flesh area for the ambitious leeches) with additional pockets on body and sleeves plus a spare one, a couple of singlets and very non-restrictive underpants. Prickly heat or any form of heat rash is not funny, particularly in the nether regions! Next, very good quality and strong lightweight trousers and with the obligatory extra pockets. A selection of both cotton and woollen socks and the standard issue jungle-boots. I managed to get hold of a pair of Japanese jungle boots and found them very good as they had even smaller lace holes and therefore helped to keep out the leeches which worm their initially very thin way in through the smallest of holes or openings to become thicker than a finger, having gorged on your blood, before they are discovered at the end of the day! In some very strange places! These Japanese boots had distinct cross bars on the soles that gave better grip, particularly on muddy slopes. Since they have smaller and broader feet than most of us in the west I (size 8) was one of the few that could use them. Unfortunately some of the C.T.s also had them so on one occasion we were not sure whether the tracks we found were ours or theirs! Simple answer. I just cut an additional and distinct groove on the bar of my boots and any others that we might use in the future. The additional footwear carried were the traditional plimsolls with the toes cut out (to let the moisture both in and out quickly) plus heavy woollen or string socks to wear over them for exceptionally slippery surfaced or even climbing. On a jump sortie we would use reinforced industrial gloves to reduce the risk of rope burns as we slid down very long ropes. On non jump outings I always wore a pair of thin chrome leather cycling fingerless mitts to reduce the risk of cuts, scratches and things like thorn wounds which could flare up very quickly and render one single handed which could be both fatal from an infection point of view and by slowing down ones deftness in an ambush situation.

24. Jungle equipment

Apart from the obvious arms and ammunition, which could vary depending on terrain and target and even if being jumped or just foot slogged with. Side arms and grenades were always the basics. The question of rifles or machine guns of various types or shotguns would vary and often there would be a mix. This would call for slight variations in the sort of webbing and pouches that would be carried. The basic haversack or rucksack would be much the same (the modern term Bergen, in my day referred to a specific type of Norwegian rucksack that had an inbuilt support and padded frame). We would often take two very luminous watches, at least one compass and a couple of pencil torches.

The heat rash and prickly heat problem in the nether regions in particular were the next biggest worry after foot rot of any sort. So, some favoured braces to keep their trousers up and so reduce the loads on a belt-only configuration. The obvious water bottle with a funnel attachment which containing fine sand and charcoal to filter debatable water supplies and some purification tablets as well. Either one or two Billy cans or mess tins for cooking, eating and drinking use. Numberless tobacco tins for matches, solid fuel tablets, salt tablets (not for me), needle and thread, gun oil and flannelette for a pull-through, for cleaning, as wet and muddy conditions can render guns almost useless and very dangerous. A couple of lighters and fuel, a basic first aid kit including some morphine, iodine, a few plasters and a wide crepe bandage. Anything smelly was out, so no chewing gum, soap, toothpaste, coffee or cigarettes. The lack of cigarettes proved a bit of a nuisance, as they are the most effective way of removing leeches. When this was not safe we had to be patient and use salt, iodine, a lighter flame and even hot curry powder instead! Salt was also carried for drying up wounds and for the others to add some taste to their basic food. A small powerful telescope in a case with plenty of desiccant to stop the lenses from steaming up.

On the tool side the standard army knife on a lanyard, a parang (local machete), commando dagger, good sheath knife and usually a small pad saw with coarse teeth, which enabled us to quietly saw small branches off (slashing with a parang tends to be a bit noisy!) to use as cover and camouflage or to even widen our field of fire in an ambush plan. Some of the lads ground extra saw teeth into the backs of their sheath knives making them vicious weapons as well. An entrenching tool which could be used as a sort of ice axe, but in our case for mud climbing. The entrenching tool was essential to dig deep enough to bury our excreta, urine and anything we had to leave behind. First because we did not want to leave any obvious trace and secondly that if we did not, then within minutes a mass of beautiful coloured but evil flies would appear making so much noise that it could be heard hundreds of yards away. On more than one occasion our first warning of a C.T. sentry or even a commie camp was the noise of flies! While on the subject or urine and at a time when the term dehydration was never used in relation to the human condition, only when referring to preserved food! We could simply monitor our condition by noting whether the smell of our urine was growing stronger and if the colour was getting darker. In other words the less smell and the weaker the colour the better! Not just relying on our natural thirst.

A short fine rope that was stowed in an oiled-cloth or silk roll to prevent it catching when not deployed. Several of these oiled bags were kept for various purposes from sticking in the occasional bandit head and fingers for later identification or to carry wet clothing separately from the dry. On our swamp trips we would fold up our specially made hammocks very carefully into bags as well to stop them tangling up. These hammocks we had made up out of the silk cords from damaged parachutes. An ill wind and all that! Then the net covered inner tubes to float our equipment along when ever possible, which also saved a lot of drying out later despite the liberal use of the semi waterproof oil-cloth bags. No such thing as a bungee rubber ties in those days so we used the typical school boy's elasticated belts with the 'S' buckles along with several cut up inner tubes for strong elastic bands used singly as in the case of ammunition magazines or knotted together to support one end of a gun or to strap down various items securely but with some give in an emergency. Always, of course several reels of strong fishing line that we used for tripwires and booby traps and remote signal wires for guard or sentry use or even to co-ordinate the springing of an ambush when out of sight of each other. The catapult idea was used if within sight. On some trips a Verey pistol, flares and the crossbow would be taken if appropriate or required. The flare pistol would be used to signal an air-drop or the start of an attack and very good at starting a fire in a C.T. camp we wished to destroy.

On the food front all sorts of dried or dehydrated meat, fish, vegetables and fruit plus a few tins. Tea, sugar, dried milk, egg powder, OXO and a variety of stock cubes. High-energy honey, nut or seed bars, high melting point chocolate bars and glucose sweets. Rice and curry powder to mix with almost anything. (hence the salt for some!) Even the odd bit of lime would help transform drinks and food.

On the jumps there would be the additional long rope, leg bag, goggles and a tight fitting pair of overalls (called a jump suit today!).

25. Salt, the fallacy of?

When I became a vegetarian in my early teens I also gave up taking any additional salt either in cooking or as a condiment. There was, and to a large extent still is, a fallacious belief that we need additional salt for bodily health and to prevent cramps and other problems. I dispute that as any added salt is almost always IN-organic unlike the natural organic salts we derive from green leaves (preferably raw) which are ORGANIC and can be absorbed, utilised and essential to the human body. Plants and often weeds with their long tap roots pull up the trace mineral elements we require and convert them into a form that can be properly assimilated and so that they can be truly beneficial. Whereas IN-organic mineral salt just passes through us and emerges just as it entered, diluted in the form of sweat etc. Totally unchanged but having caused potential chaos in the process. Only in recent times has medical opinion finally realised that salt is a major cause of many heart and circulatory problems as it dries and thickens the blood to say nothing of hardening the arteries. Salt is also a stimulant and in nature you will always get a reaction after any action. There is always a price to pay when you either go against or try to short circuit nature. So when people, particularly in the tropics, take salt tablets they may get a temporary boost but will always pay for it later, often without realising it. In Malaya and later in Indonesia I was frequently the only one that never, ever took inorganic salt in any form. My sweat level is well above the average so as well as loosing more moisture I would also be loosing more salt making me more likely than the average to suffer the supposed consequences. All total nonsense. I was one of only a very few that never ever suffered from either heat stroke, exhaustion or collapse. My strength and stamina was well above average without any salt or other stimulant!

My childhood calf muscle cramps (before my non salt taking days) were clearly a hereditary condition from, at least my father and on down to my own children in their youth. Things like salt licks for cattle are to encourage them to drink more, to produce more milk, even if thinner and of poorer quality.!? It has nothing to do with their health. Cattle and other natural grazers should always get all the salts they require if grazed on suitable natural pasture. Domestic salt is used to bring out the taste but unfortunately the palate gets conditioned and tends to want even more, as is the way with sugar. The more we get the more we think we need which leads to habits being formed if not on to addictions! Potatoes and cabbage if properly cooked (not over cooked) have adequate taste of their own once the palate is clean and clear of salt dependence.

The body is a miraculous design and creation and can cope with reasonable amounts of poisons, toxins and other alien substances for a while at least. Some can be discharged on a continuous basis with not too much harm being done but others like heavy metals such as mercury just keep building up, fatally. So as with food in general it is often not what you eat so much as how much the body is abused in the process. If we over eat then we would tend to be over poisoning ourselves as well. Obesity is not just a question of excess fat and weight but also a build up of poisons and toxins to attack an already weakened system. A final family thought; Grandfather Walter (my mother's father) seemed to survive all the Central and South American diseases and fevers when building railways in remote areas. He reputedly would never eat cheese until it had grown hairs, shave it then he would eat it with gusto. This was about forty years before penicillin was discovered. Often modern science is now discovering that what was thought of as old wife's tales have a real basis after all. Grandfather Walter was also apparently a firm anti vivisectionist as well so his health was not safeguarded by vaccinations or inoculations. He was probably thought of as mad at the time but he survived (as all of us can vouch for) as did his wife and all his children in the same climate when many others around him did not!

26. Jumping

Having gained all this knowledge and experience it was time to put it into action, although I can't claim that we were the very first to jump into the canopies of trees, we were not far behind. Our first practice jump was into the jungle fringe at the edge of a tin mine just outside Ipoh where one of our members worked. We all learned a lot more than we bargained for. One broken leg and all with countless bruises, scratches, cuts and sprains. It appeared that we needed more weight to break through the upper branches because out of the fourteen that jumped that day eleven of us finished up swinging well off the ground. Three hours later, three were still dangling. The useful lesson learnt was that we needed to carry a good quality rope of at least 100 ft in length and that we could do with a much heavier load.

So the idea of the leg bag was used which meant that we could carry a lot more combat equipment in with us and be less dependent on debatable air-drops later. The bag was attached to our right legs with a quick release device which at first meant that we could descend, faster, which should help to break through the branches (and theoretically bruising ourselves even more!). Release the bag that was attached to the long rope and which was still attached to our harness at the other end. If we were stuck up in the branches we could unhook the rope and attach it to one of the offending branches and then lower ourselves down it to the ground and the bag. We had heavy chrome leather industrial gloves to reduce the risk of friction burns to our hands. It rapidly became clear that the less we carried, in the way of arms and anything that stuck out or could get caught up in the branches, the better and so these item should all be stowed in the leg bag, out of the way.

Everything that could be put into the bag, was. This enabled us to ball ourselves up, in much the same way as when doing a honey-pot at the swimming pool or a sort of defensive foetal position. It also enabled us to put our elbows in front of us with arms up to protect our faces as we crashed through the tree canopy. So the idea of the leg bag finished up serving two purposes instead of one. It also occurred to us that on operations in open countryside or desert could take advantage of the bag idea, too. In their case, with the additional advantage that descending quicker than usual, until the last 100 ft or so. Then the bag could be released and able to fall away, which would reduce the weight as it hit the ground and slow the descent at the last minute to make a normal landing. This faster drop would make it more difficult for snipers to shoot a helpless descending Paratrooper, as had been a favourite sport among the Germans during the previous war!

27. Enter Geoff 'B'

The biggest problem was a more practical one. Namely the shortage of parachutes. On each occasion we would tear and damage several and even lose the odd one stuck up in a tree. We did get some back by offering rewards to the Sakais to rescue them for us later and then hand them into the nearest remote Police Post. Unfortunately they were almost always beyond repair. So again, the quartermaster concerned was not amused. Our whole plan and methodology was at risk. However, as is often the case, luck, (which I do not believe in), fate, providence, call it what you will, turned up unexpectedly. On one of the American Pacific Far East ships, (that had the big Kodiak bear on their funnels), the *SS Luckenbach*, I think, that came into Port Swettenham was a very nice and very friendly Executive Officer and Purser by the name of Geoff. "B". Called this because his father was a Geoff "A" and "B" did not want to be called either Junior or Geoff the Second. His father was either a director or large shareholder in the shipping company. During the war, a very young Geoff "B"

Self with Geoff 'B' our American gun runner on SS Luckenbach

had been part of the American Airborne invasion on D-Day into France. His group had been dropped too far inland by mistake and finished up well behind the German defence lines. They had had to fight their way back through the Germans to rejoin their comrades. He found the otherwise efficient Germans very confused by this and as a result they suffered many less casualties than those confronting the Germans head on. He therefore thought, as a result of his own experience that our, 'get behind them' policy was a good one. He was still active in his local National Guard group outside Seattle and offered to find us some equipment, including some chutes.

He and I got on very well. Frequently, after his ship docked or moored out in the roads and when all the paper work was finished, often at three to four in the morning, he would grab some kit and return to K. L. with me. There we would usually finish up at the Golf Club and turn on the flood lights over the swimming pool for a good swim at five o'clock in the morning. After which, as the staff came on again at six we would get a hearty breakfast, sitting at the poolside looking out across the golf course towards the jungle and mountains to the east, as the sun came up, wonderful. His swimming trunks were a very bright florescent yellow and when swimming underwater it was possible to see his trunks moving in the gloom but not him. I think, he thought I admired them because the next time he arrived he had brought me a pink pair. I got used to them and had them for many years, long after the florescence had faded and until the sort of elastic construction, gave up as well.

Like most Americans around the world, he was hospitable and generous to a fault. Even though I did not smoke, he always included among his gifts, hundreds of cigarettes, mostly Kools, the menthol cigarette with the Penguin on the packet. His comment was usually "well give them to your buddies then". That is how I came to have stocks of cigarettes to bribe Miss Malaya's father. The only time I ever used them personally, was when working with the odd dead body, when the smoke was far preferable to the stink of putrefying flesh up one's nose. On one trip, he came on one of our weekend excursions to a rubber estate to indulge in a bit of commie hunting. He was a very good shot but was not exactly enamoured by the jungle itself! The terrain was hardly like the D Day Normandy landings.

Well, Geoff "B" was not only as good as his word but unbelievably better. He later arrived at Port Swettenham with about a hundred parachutes, bundled up in numerous bales. Inside these he had arranged to secrete some American carbines, two mortars, two Chicago type Tommy guns, some powerful shot guns, assortment of grenades and some booby trap mines for covering an escape route to delay pursuit plus, literally thousands of rounds of ammunition and detonators. A few American Walkie-Talkies were to come in handy as well. The British radios were so heavy to lug about the jungle. About the only thing he had not brought was loose explosive material. Loading at

Seattle had not been a problem, partly I think because of his father's influence and partly because of the growing American paranoia and fear of 'Reds under the bed'. This coupled with their losses in Korea at the time, meant that no American was going to inhibit any action that would hit back at the worldwide Communist threat.

One Seattle customs official had said "anything we can do to help our Limey friends in Malaya to kill the ……commies, the better". So the un-inspected gifts for his Limey friends left America with no problems. Customs at Port Swettenham was another matter though. Smuggling arms was a very touchy matter anyway and from our point of view operating outside officialdom, even with the unofficial blessing of Special Branch we would not want any Min Yuen plants in the docks to get wind of it. We enlisted one of our S.B. contacts at the port, who kindly had a quiet word with the customs duty officer and suggested to him that unless he wished to be taken away for possible interrogation as a suspected Min Yuen sympathiser he could demonstrate his loyalty and patriotism by ignoring the bales of personal effects and gifts. This he duly did. He was still to received his usual tea money (bribe?), as was the local custom.

I should explain that this was, at that time, not necessarily either a bribe or even a tip. Even today, Malaysia, as it now is, discourages the habit of tipping and on most restaurant bills, printed with a different colour ink, is a note to that effect. A very pleasant and refreshing attitude in this modern world of constant scrounging. Tea Money was more often a token gift, given out of respect for the position that the official may hold. It may be just a coin or a very small sachet of tea, itself. Really only symbolic and rather like an exchange of gifts between our western heads of state. If it was intimated or suggested that it was any sort of tip or bribe, great offence would be taken and regarded as an insult.

28. Hash House Harriers

Another background or back up situation that had to be solved was the problem of the meeting(s), of we, the like minded civvies and the involved military members. The old colonial snobbery, cultural and financial reasons generally precluded these groups meeting socially very often. We had to be able do so regularly but without attracting any attention. The only possible common denominator was something sporting. It was proposed that a running or sports club would 'cover' the situation. So, it appears that was how the original post-war Hash House Harriers came into being. We, sort of hijacked this pre-war colonial fitness and exercise club and formed our own chapter. It had no H.Q. or regular clubhouse, so meetings would be held at alternative clubs, with the non-members or guests being duly signed in. Meeting at alternate military and civilian messes also worked well and allowed the catering to be better organised. It would be accepted that after a long period of exercise, a slap up meal would be appropriate. The fact that it was sometimes two weeks later that some of us returned from a hash, never seemed to be noticed by the catering staff, who could be Min Yuen spies as well. Just why the Americanism of hash slinging was adopted I have no idea. We did do quite a lot of obvious P.T. and running round the neighbourhood including on the roads of estates on the outskirts of K.L. Even today, having developed into quite a widespread international organisation, a hash would still appear to be combination of a paper chase, a treasure hunt, a cross country steeple chase or a Hare and Hounds event.

I now stop to dwell on the two most frightening experiences I ever had. They have nothing in common, either in time, place or even circumstances. One could be regarded as real life and death stuff and the other a huge joke but only in retrospect. On one of these jogging or running hash occasions and just before dusk a group of us were jogging along the laterite (red clay) track on an estate just on the town side of the hill where Cheras Road cemetery is located. The lead runner, a young detective inspector suddenly shouted over his shoulder, to the rest of us, "Don't look right. Don't look right.

Whatever you do! Needless to say I for one did, carefully and without obviously moving my head. There, slightly above us, against a rock face, sitting round a small fire were at least five C.T.s. Two even had the usual caps with red stars on them. They were that close, probably within 50 ft. We being entirely unarmed and to them looking quite mad had no option but to bluff it out, keep going and pray. The next thirty seconds or so were the longest in my life, just waiting to feel the slam of a bullet in my back. It did not come, to the surprise of us all. The C.T. s motive for not killing us all was probably manifold.

Needless to say the location was officially reported and a security sweep was organised for dawn the next morning by the official forces. The bandits had already left but their ashes were still warm. This was the only occasion that I, almost felt pleased that they, on this one occasion had got away. The old British instinctive sense of fair play, I presume. However, I never again allowed my focus to waiver or weaken, in such communistic matters.

Three typical nonchalant 'Hashies'
armed and ready

29. Frank's mobile

The only other sickening grip of fear that I experienced was when driving with an older chap who was some sort of Civil Servant.(we tended not to nose into each others work details). We had originally met when he introduced himself to me with a couched message that, he was not aware, was from a S. B. contact. We met several times but apart from cars we did not have much in common although he clearly envied me my friendship with Connie! His casual attitude to women appalled me and to what is often euphemistically called a 'social disease' which he claimed was "nowadays no more serious than a bad head cold, which the new antibiotics take care of easily". I did not share his opinion and nearly sixty years on still don't. Anyway, back to the point of the story, we were driving down to Singapore for some reason or other. On this particular occasion, it was in his Jowett Jupiter sports car. It was very fast for a 1.1/2 litre, flat four engine in an E.R.A. (English Racing A.) designed chassis. The usual route south to Singapore, particularly at night was to stick to the coast road via Muar and Batu Pahat, after leaving Malacca and on down through Johore. Unfortunately it also meant waiting for two river ferries and if after queueing up for an hour or so a military convoy turned up then they would get priority. Causing further delays.

So unwisely, of course, we set off on the dangerous inland route via Gemas, Segamat, Labis, Yong Peng, Ayer Hitam and Kulai (all terrorist hot spots) on a longer but faster inland route (which was, under normal circumstances the real main north/south road anyway) and where the two rivers were much narrower and were crossed by bridges. It also meant that we had a chance to make Singapore in time for a good breakfast!? This was a notoriously dangerous area and I think we reasoned that because it was so, the C.T.s would not expect a lone vehicle to risk it. Only a large armoured convoy and even then, not often at night, when the headlights could be seen from a considerable distance in the open plantation districts. As we were driving across a large moonlit pineapple plantation there was a tremendous bang and the car almost jumped in the air, it felt so violent and then started shaking like a mad thing. Frank rather panicked (not surprising for an office worker) and was trying to slow down. I thought it was a grenade or a mine and almost screamed at him to keep going to get clear of any ambush. After a frightening few hundred yards when it was clear that it was not an ambush, we stopped, turned off the engine and I got out with a torch to looked for a flat tyre but they were all ok.

We rolled the car back and forth and all seemed fine. I lifted the bonnet and told Frank to start the engine and the mad shaking started all over again. He switched off hurriedly but I could not, immediately see anything wrong. Frank then asked what the dark mark on the bonnet was. It turned out to be quite a big jagged hole! Still a bit of a mystery until it became obvious that one of the four metal fan blades had broken off and gone up through the bonnet with great force leaving the whole engine miles out of balance. Being a practical chap, I just bent the opposite fan blade back and forth until it broke off, too. Started the engine, perfect balance restored, no more problems. Frank's car ran like that for a couple of months until a new fan arrived and the body was repaired. It was all very funny in retrospect but very, very frightening at the time.

30. No go area?

To understand the next incident it is necessary to know that one of the communist's original stated aims was to capture parts of Malaya and claim them as Free Malaya. This to disguise their true aims of subjugating all races and classes. They wanted to give the impression that they were the liberators of the Asians from the British yoke and all that sort of rubbish. All about as accurate as the communist's usual meaning and definition of democracy! The examples of the former East Germany and of North Korea now, tell you all you need to know, about that fatuous claim. Their planned Free Areas would then be joined up progressively. It was essential that the C.T.s should not be allowed to make such a claim over even a small town or village and be prevented from claiming, even the smallest political coup, of this sort.

As a result, in one particularly remote area of the state of Pahang and which was probably over 95% jungle anyway. This area had been chosen by the C.T.s as their first target. They thought that as they already controlled the jungle cover that the very small remote population could be taken over easily. In modern parlance they wanted to establish a no-go area or a total exclusion zone. But first, of course they had to kill or get rid of the relatively few planter/managers, plus a few admin. types and the odd police posts. The communists had vastly superior numbers and were sure that they could win the ideal-logical war in this area easily. To contain this required a disproportionate security presence with even greater defence systems and guards on the plantations and other vulnerable places. As always the wives stayed on which was one of the best counter propaganda points made. The locals, seeing the Mems (the Tuan's wives) staying on, made an obvious lie out of the C.T.s claim, of overwhelming control.

To support this enclave, everything in and out of the area had to be transported by an armoured convoy, along the one and only access road. Almost every convoy was attacked but with no great success. The commies seemed to think that if they caused enough trouble it would demoralise everyone and then they would then give up and move out. They never succeeded, so this key communist aim was defeated resoundly. So to help support the families concerned it was policy for volunteers to travel up with the convoys to visit and give moral support and jovial company. The news of these parties was known to infuriate and frustrate the C.T.s, no end and must have been demoralising for them to see an increase in social life and normality despite their almost frantic terror efforts.

Connie, who was a very humourous, vivacious and ebullient girl, was always a welcome visitor to these isolated wives. They in turn, unlike their city counterparts, were not snobbish over class, race or position. She was always very popular and not only with the women! On one of these trips she, I and a couple of Malay policemen plus the Cyce (driver) were travelling in convoy, at about fifth position in a late forties American Ford, a sort of fast-back shaped car. It had been armour plated all round with gun slits, (about the size of the average letter box opening but slightly wider) in the window panels, which had hinged lowering covers in case of attack and while not in use. These cars were like ovens inside. However, more worrying was the fact that a very serious weakness had only just come to light. This Achilles heel was the fact that the underside of these cars was still the original, only very thin steel panels. No one had thought to reinforce them as well! If the car ran over a mine or a grenade was rolled underneath the consequences to those inside was catastrophic and horrendous to say the least. The explosive power was trapped under and inside the car, building up a fantastic pressure, enough to lift the car well of the road. Any unlikely survivor would wish they had been shot instead. One rather graphic description I remember was "they looked as though their brains had burst out of their eyes and ears". All very nasty!

Now to the actual incident itself. We came under, the almost half expected hail of bullets and for some reason the lead vehicle stopped, blocking the narrow road. It appeared that the firing was only coming from one side, which is always, almost a blessing in itself. We fired back somewhat blindly through the slots but suddenly one of the Malays yelled something that I did not understand. Connie shouted, "we've to get out quick". It appeared that one of the C.T.s had got close to the car in the roadside ditch and was below our field of fire. The thought of him rolling a grenade under us was not one we liked!

We all bailed out rapidly and with little dignity on the leeside. Semi panic! Taking cover, over the road edge. Then the Malay policemen took up positions over the bonnet of the car and returned the C.T.'s fire. Connie was firing under the car to discourage the lone C.T. from getting too close, again blindly I think. I rolled round the back of the car under the boot with my Sten at the ready and told Connie to lob a grenade over the top of the car.

This she did and the moment after it went off, I leapt out into a sort of crouch and opened fire at what was already only, in effect, a tatty rag doll and who now, thanks to me, lost most of his scalp as well. The Malays continued shooting up the slope. Shortly, after a couple of mortars were fired up towards the C.T.s everything fell strangely silent again. Cautiously the police went forward to the ambush point, to find four dead C.T.s, presumably from the mortars. Plus of course our very own dead grenadier, literally at our feet. Making the score five in all, with only two on our side slightly wounded. Connie seemed not the slightest bit fazed by the few short minutes of hell fire. She merely complained that it took too long to reload her Webley in such an emergency and would consider carrying two of them in future. Oh, and she was not happy about breaking a fingernail when pulling the pin out of the fatal grenade. Women!

The rest of the weekend went very well and I think that, the almost captive residents really appreciated our company. As a sort of bonus for our efforts, there was no attack on our way back or on our hosts for the next full week or so. It appeared that we were making at least, a little difference.

Connie, lightly armed Penang 1951

31. XK120, wounded!

Next comes a very personal incident. I was driving up to an area near Bentong to pick up Basil, who's A.K.C. van had broken down and could not be fixed for several days. Bentong was quite a notorious area for C.T. activity and ambushes. It is located about fifty miles out of K. L. to the North East, a bit over the border from Selangor and just into Pahang. Most of the route was on dodgy roads at that time. Basil's wife Barbara had asked me if I would go up and collect him. As my Jaguar XK120 was only a two seater I could not take her with me to collect him, so I was on my own, and as it happened, just as well. After several miles of very winding roads I was finally able to get past a small convoy of Malay Regiment troops in four Land Rovers. On the very next decent straight I was doing up to about 100 mph when the car was hit with no warning and I felt a numbing pain in my right elbow. I was absolutely furious and promptly broke all the rules. Instead of keeping going to get out of range quickly. I ground to a halt and started reversing back to the impact point. The car was barely in control, at nearly 30 mph in reverse. In the meantime the convoy had arrived, stopped and deployed in a matter of seconds and were already firing into the ambush point.

To, I think, everyone's surprise a C.T. broke cover on my side of the oil palm plantation edge and started running off into the trees but away from the cover of the ulu. I leapt out of the car, unhooked my Sten, so as not to impede me while chasing after him, with only my .38 and the odd grenade. As I ran after him I heard a Malay voice shout, "Tuan, Tuan, nanti sikit jam—Saya........(Mr. or Boss, wait a moment. I.......) but I heard no more either due to the shooting or my own blood pounding with adrenalin. I don't know, but I was gaining on the C.T. and having missed with an earlier shot I was not going to miss the next time. He turned and took a shot at me, missed and ran on. I got to within about 20 ft. of him, all ready for the coup de grace, when two bullets whistled past my head, from my right and I thought that I was being shot at by another C.T. But no, because the one I was chasing then dropped like stone and as I reached him, I could see that he had one bullet in the head and another in the shoulder. I simply put two more into him for luck and felt a lot better for it. How dare they even think of shooting my beloved first wife, my precious XK.!

The Malay soldiers came up, including the one that had shouted to me. He had been trying to tell me that he had already got my C.T., in his sights. I, of course had nearly got in his way! He looked down at our joint handy work, spat and said "Gila Barbi" (Mad Pig, the lowest form of animal life as far as a Muslim is concerned). He then politely pointed at me with his thumb, grinned and said "Ini Tuan Gila, Gila Bunya (this Mr. or boss is even madder, very). They were all very nice and solicitous and concerned about the jelly-fied blood I was oozing. I had been shot once along the right forearm and had a groove about 6 inches long, running back to my elbow. The second bullet had nicked my gun belt and taken about, a two-inch bit of skin off my right hip. In both cases, missing my bones, by barely an inch. They kindly dressed and bandaged me up and made me promise to get to a hospital as soon as possible. So after half a flask of hot-minted tea I left them to clear up and I resumed my journey to collect Basil. More importantly from my point of view, the two bullets had gone through the car's aluminium door skin before hitting me. I was not amused at all, in fact quite upset about it! My pride and joy.

The hospital, in due course and several hours later cleaned up my wounds and cauterised them both. I did not become a fan of the smell of my own burning flesh. It appeared that I was not going to be able to wear a gun belt on that hip for a while, either. A sort of final thought on the matter; I have never ever again, been so angry or so stupid in the rest of my life. Yet! That look of startled unbelief on the face of the C.T. when he saw me chasing him and tried to shoot me (again?) was almost funny in retrospect. I have often wondered since, if in his last moments it, finally dawned on him that people like me, (that his communist masters, had the cheek to label Running Dogs) were fully prepared to run at or after them, not away from them as their propaganda liked to infer?

Thought for the day; Fast driving is dangerous? Rubbish, if I had been doing, say only 99 mph instead of 100 the bullets would have hit me in the body area. Dead. No one has since yet convinced me that speed or fast driving, in itself ever killed anyone. I'm the living proof. Officer! I never found out if the dead C.T. was the one that shot me or not or how many had escaped back into the ulu or why they so unwisely(?) shot at me in the first place. Perhaps a very fast moving lone car was a tempting, almost sporting, target. Just for fun!? We will also never know why the dead one broke cover in the plantation, whereas the others just melted back in to the jungle as usual and disappeared. Initially he may have thought that he was still screened from the troops and may not have considered me, a mere civilian, as a potential menace. I take some personal satisfaction in knowing that he never got the chance to learn the lesson and ever put it into practice.

Ah Hoi, Self & Ah Kwan rebuilding XK120 after bullet holes repair & repaint

Back home in K.L., later, some skilled lads and friends of my two pet mechanics, Ah Hoi and Ah Kwan who worked at the back of the local Jaguar dealer on Batu Road re-skinned the door in alli for me. I then had the whole car repainted a nice shiny dark blue, as the original silver paint did not hold a good polish in the tropical sunshine. The X.K. was involved in quite a few ambushes and associated incidents. The usual procedure under fire if the road was not blocked was to just run the gauntlet but if the way was blocked then to drive off the road into the rough or ditch on the side away from the firing which meant that the car, even if it was on its side (some finished on their roofs!) gave some cover from the flying bullets and gave a barricade to return fire from safely(?). The Jaguar was so strong that in all these episodes no real damage was done to the car apart from just small body dents and scratches. Later the ubiquitous Land Rover or army lorry would hitch a rope round the Jag's rear bumper-ette mounting irons and pull the car out in reverse. These same irons are the ones that later towed 7 ton Mosquito aircraft in and out of hangers at Lossiemouth and even later were used to pull the Jag out of a frozen lake in Canada during the Winter Rally there. They are the same ones still on the car today!

While making comment on the usual method of driving/diving into a ditch to avoid gunfire if practicable, reminded me of a story which I heard, many years later and have every reason to believe. A young rubber planter was involved in a very serious ambush which led to his car being involved in some sort of crash/road accident a few miles from Ipoh, Perak, which very seriously injured him. He was repatriated to U.K. rapidly and lived to tell the tale (or not as the case may be!). Later and still on sick leave he was to meet the young woman he intended to marry and while obviously having to mention his serious car accident omitted to tell her that the car had been riddled with bullet holes as well! Being a bit naughty here and knowing the spirit of the old Malayan hands I wondered if it was because, had he told her the full story she might have declined to marry him if he was set on returning to Malaya. She may well have been put off the idea, not liking the perceived risks involved? We will never know but it remains an intriguing thought, does it not?

I have already made the odd disparaging comments about the British automobile industry's poor backup in parts and service. I suffered from this badly in the case of new tyres for my XK120. I had gone through the first set in six thousand miles (slightly better than with the M.G.) and was horrified to find that there were no replacements to be had either in Singapore or in Malaya, anywhere. They were Dunlop Super Sports (so called!) and very poor in my opinion. Some years later I switched to Michelin "X" and promptly got FOUR times the mileage even when driving harder and faster. So there I was with four bald tyres in the most powerful car on the road and at the start of the monsoon rainy season. I drove as though I was on ice all the time. I learnt a lot which I attribute to my exceptional results later on, both in ice racing and in the Canadian Winter Rally. Then later still gaining most of my successes in Saloon Car Racing in very wet conditions and to say nothing of being a very useful skill to have in every day wet and icy road conditions.

The nearest I ever came to an accident in the XK120 was with the bald tyres during that same rainy season. Again, one day on my return to K.L. and not much further on from the goat incident in the M.G. I entered a left handed bend only to find that the area had been newly tarred which the heavy rain had set before the road men could get the gravel spread on top of it all. The surface was like a skating rink and I drifted/slid over onto the wrong side of the road halfway round the bend with no chance of getting back onto my own side before a lorry coming in the opposite direction reached me! So, with great presence of mind (or so I kidded myself) I continued across and off the road and onto the far verge finishing up on top of the heap of gravel that was waiting to be spread on the slippery tar surface. I was stranded like a whale and felt very foolish all the while pretending I had intended to park there all along! The lorry passed me safely on the wrong side. Then with the aid of the sheltering road men and wielding a shovel myself we dug enough gravel away from the car so that with a bit of a push I got free and continued home to K.L. as if nothing had happened. Just dirty and very wet.

I should at this point state the Jaguars themselves back in Coventry were the exception and were always very helpful and prompt with any parts that I ever required. Always by return Air Mail (not cheap in those days) and the parts never charged for! The situation being that because my car had not gone through the local dealership they, the local dealers, were very unhelpful so I wrote direct to Jaguar themselves who presumably could supply parts free without breaking any dealership contract locally or maybe because I was a competitor and this was their way of supporting a private entry. These were the days when Jaguars ruled supreme at places like the Le Mans 24 hour race and they were very conscious of their reliability and stamina reputation.

32. Airborne

In between all my other activities I would always try to go along for the ride on as many air-drops as possible. Usually, in an ubiquitous D.C.3. Dakota. Needless to say, that if I got the chance of a drive as well, so much the better. I think, I managed to log up nearly 40 hours on the Dak during this period. Apart from just wanting more time and experience on twin engined aircraft, I was almost, always more interested in studying the jungle from above. The contours and rivers look entirely different from that perspective. I later found this sense of topography helped in difficult navigational situations in otherwise featureless areas when on the ground itself.

I do not have anything like a photographic memory but my hours of practice playing 'Kim's Game' in my scouting days stood me in good stead. Helping to remember odd clearances, swamp patches and so on. This also helped in the planning of, not so much the actual area of jumping but how to get out again afterwards. The Sakai villages were particularly worthy of note, as were the odd paddy field, small native plantations and of course the rivers or small streams which I have already mentioned. All these can be crucial when you consider that possibly over 99% of an area could still be untouched, almost primeval jungle.

Most of these reconnoitring (reckies) and drop flights would emanate from K.L.'s old airfield (which is all it was) unless they were coming up from Singapore, as were the bombing raids and photo runs. This airfield was used mainly for commercial flights such as Malayan Airways and their Dakotas. As I remember it, one just carried on up Pudu Road, heading south and past the jail turn-off for about a mile or so and onto the main Seremban road. This area was a sort of shoulder of land well up from the Klang river and town centre but still a bit below the hills that surround K.L. itself. The flying clubs and the odd Canberra bomber could operate from it as well. I don't remember a club house, only a bar below the control tower (for want of a better description!) and alongside a long tin shed with an almost equally long polished wood table for folding and packing parachutes.

An amusing and typically incongruous angle on all this was not only that officialdom refused to call the emergency or the troubles a war, despite over a hundred of us being killed a month at the time. To add insult to injury, the insurance companies would not insure us for any form of motor sport -too risky, they claimed! Yet they would pay out, day after day, large sums to the dead and wounded and literally by the thousand, over these worst years. Even a driving skill test or a treasure hunt was too big a risk. And as to flying, they absolutely panicked at the thought!

Our various companies therefore had a general policy of forbidding participation in motor competitions. So, just like being back at school again, we did it anyway and used assumed and invented names. Flying was less of a problem, because, unlike motor sport, there would be no press coverage at all. In this ridiculous situation, a planter or miner who had bullets bouncing off his house and car on a daily basis was not allowed to further risk his life (or maybe his earning capacity for his firm!) by driving round a car park at less than 30mph, if a few others might be doing the same. Absolutely ridiculous. Perhaps the birth of today's dangerously stupid, even criminal political correctness and erroneously called Health and Safety may be traceable back to just such a farce?

33. Damp squibs

The ongoing death toll on our side would have been often worse but for the happy situation that the C.T.'s munitions tended to be old having suffered from the damp and humid climate of the ever present jungle. The atmosphere and damp, over time tends to spoil the explosive powder or cordite. Leading to a damp squib effect or nothing at all. Even in our case, with fairly fresh munitions we always laid everything out in the sun to bake after any period of jungle work. Once, my own Hart failed to fire properly and just went crack instead of the usual firing noise. I luckily, stuck it away again as I had the Sten gun with me.

Later I found that the lead bullet had stuck halfway down the barrel and in effect, only the detonator had gone off properly. Had I fired again with that blockage, it could have exploded back in my face. I chucked out all the other bullets in my belt as well and opened up a fresh box of .38 cartridges. Another and typically lucky such incident was in the Great Easter Hotel (just off Ampang Road, over the Klang River and behind our K. L. office) one night with the dance floor packed with both civvies and military personnel. A grenade was thrown into the middle of the floor which very fortunately did not go off but everyone had already dived for the floor. A bunch of, as usual, badly behaved Malayan scouts, sobered up very quickly and one of them, to give him his due promptly found a shovel from somewhere and with one of his mates then grabbed a small metal topped table to give them some protection as they approached the hopefully dud grenade. The table had the usual umbrella hole in the middle but hardly affording either of them good visibility or protection. The first scout scooped the grenade up and with now, some very sober mates directing them in a sort of blind man's bluff, then went through the most dangerous egg and spoon race I have ever seen. They were verbally guided up the stairs and out through the main door where the offending grenade was dumped into a rain water tank.

We all resumed the dancing as if nothing had happened. The only, barely noticeable, difference was that the Red Caps (military police) at the door, (who we thought had arrived to calm down the over ebullient scouts), now had their side arms out and ready. Half an hour later and right on schedule, the so called exotic Javanese dancing took place, a great night, however you want to look at it. These occasional attacks at crowded venues were probably carried out by the odd and over ambitious Min Yuen member, trying to prove himself. Rather than by, say an active C.T. coming into town from the cover of the jungle. Their attacks could and did cause multiple injuries and the odd death but totally failed to stop people from socialising, almost normally.

I should explain that the Malayan Scouts were best described as a rather motley and not entirely satisfactory international group. Hurriedly brought together to try to bridge the gap after the original S.A.S. had been disbanded and until at least something like the 'originals' could be selected and trained up again. There were some Brits, some Kiwis, some Rhodesians and reportedly the odd Foreign Legion renegade as well. I was involved with them only on a few occasions but thought that they rather lacked discipline and certain of the essential graces required in a war of hearts and minds. They were too inclined to behave like selfish mercenaries, throwing their weight about as though they were doing all the rest of us a big favour.

34. Hills

The majority of jumps or foot slogging jungle sorties were largely uneventful from the actual contact with C.T.s and the fighting point of view. But it must be remembered that both our hunting and other patrolling groups would reduce the terrorists total freedom of movement and certainly reduce their ability to hit and run and terrorise in general. There were several methods of attacking their remote base camps, which were usually located in potentially easily defended areas. The actual camp complex would be almost a small village as I have already described. Usually, where possible, protected on two sides by hills or rock faces so reducing the actual area of their perimeter needing to be guarded or defended.

If we could drop in, higher up and behind them this would work well and dislodge and drive them out of their camp and down the valley to be met in the relative open by another force waiting in ambush. At other similar locations where it was not feasible to get behind them, then our preferred method or due to the logistical problems of not getting enough force to pincer them. Then, a simple frontal attack was favoured with mortars and grenades driving them back up into their well-prepared defensive positions. In holes, caves and even sand bagged machine gun posts, producing the sort of winkling out situation the Americans had to deal with, island after island, to clear the Japanese out of the pacific during World War 2, with corresponding huge loss of life. We were not gung ho Americans! We would just keep the C.T.s penned in from a relatively safe distance and call in a Lincoln bomber by radio and indicate and mark the area to bomb with a flare, when the bomber arrived, often hours later. We would then burn the camp and destroy all of their infrastructure, like the long bamboo piped water supply, food, clothing, medicine and any arms and munitions. Sometimes it was policy not to bomb them to total destruction but more to demoralise the survivors to such an extent that surrender would seem, not such a bad idea after all. Leaflets were left and dropped, making financial offers to those who wanted to come in out of the cold, so to speak. On principal I have always been against rewarding criminals of all types but in this set of circumstances where the money paid to each individual seemed unfairly large it always, in practice turned out to be a good buy. For the reasons I've already explained, earlier.

But it still sticks in my throat despite the large savings in time, money and, more importantly, lives. Perhaps that's why I would never be a happy and often hypercritical party politician. However leaving some of them alive and in some cases wounded without any, even primitive basic facilities could not help but demoralise them further. They would start wondering where next as more of their secret lairs were targeted. Terrorism ceases to function effectively when they have to be more defensive and it completely upsets their established psychological framework. If one such incident does not work then, such terrorists will be even more emotionally vulnerable the next time.

There were occasions when we were running out of operational time and had to give up, sometimes after days and nights of patient waiting. Then we would cut our losses, so to speak and lay booby traps on discovered C.T. tracks and paths. Favourite was using simple fine but strong fishing line used as a trip wire attached to the ring-pull pin on a grenade attached to a suitable tree. My favourite was to attach the fishing line to a branch that had to be brushed aside at, say chest height and then on up above eye level with the grenade just jammed into a small branch fork so that when the pin was pulled the grenade dropped onto the passing patrol, with much more devastating effect. It was known to kill up to three, as against the average of seriously wounding one, at leg and mid-riff level. War is dirty but is never won with one hand tied behind your back in the way politicians tend to do. With the result then, that it all goes on longer and kills more people in the end. The only slight concern about leaving booby traps was that innocent Sakais might stumble into them. I was assured that, one, they would spot them, the proverbial mile away. Secondly the Sakais stayed as far away from the C.T.s as possible and used their own, almost invisible trails rather than the commie tracks, anyway.

35. Swamps

The other form of 'getting behind them' related to some of the lowland camps, often backing onto impenetrable mangrove swamps. This protected their backs in the same way a hill or rock face did in the highlands. These camps were almost impossible to find without very localised knowledge but could be spotted from the air on occasion as there was no primeval jungle cover only short mangrove woods and brush. They were usually approachable, only by easily defended narrow soggy paths. This would give too much warning, back at camp and any possible element of surprise would be lost. Casualties would be bound to rise in any gun battle that ensued. The obvious answer was to creep in from the blind or in effect the seaside, through miles of maze and tangle of apparently impenetrable mangroves. There was an exceptionally successful example of this method, carried out by the Green Howards a largely Yorkshire regiment, who sent a patrol in by that method. They took several days to wade, often chest deep through the swamp to finally arrive and attack the camp in southern Selangor by surprise early one morning. The leader of this group of C.T.s was a particularly nasty piece of work and unusually for the Chinese, had a very distinctive black beard and whose local reign of terror was one of the worst examples. The locals thought him invincible, were petrified of him and firmly believed that he could only be killed by a silver bullet! That's how far and bad the local superstitious fear had got. There was therefore, understandably great reluctance locally to cooperate with the authorities. The whole area was deadlocked. The Green Howards finally crept ashore and caught the bandits totally off guard. As I remember they killed or seriously wounded the whole group. The black bearded horror was shot right between the eyes by a young National Service conscript. Dead centre.

Unfortunately the locals would not believe it at first so the only way to convince them was for his head to be stuck on a stake and exhibited in the kampongs. (officialdom, of course denied the whole thing, as usual). It turned out to be the turning point and cure for the apathetic morale of the area. The local population were amazed and so impressed that such a young Tuan soldier could be so accurate in his shooting. This awe and respect almost immediately swung round to the troops who were now greeted with smiles that had not been seen for a long time in that locality. The whole area was psychologically transformed over night and the C.T.s never dominated that section of Selangor again.

My own swamp experience was nowhere near as successful but was still worthwhile. Our team of waders decided that we did not want to spend days, often chest high with all our gear on our backs as usual. So we made up some fishing net covered inner tubes that we could float along with our equipment and supplies on the top. This would at least take most of the load off the straps and belts that tend to dig into water softened flesh. We would collect enough leech, insect and scratch sores without adding further sores to them, at least on this occasion. On the very few dryish parts of our route in, we found that the floats weighed next to nothing but were inclined to catch every snag or branch. Next time we decided that we would take a pump! In addition to the floats we made up rather rudimentary hammocks so we could at least sleep or rest above water and dry out to some extent overnight. This considerably assisted in slowing the softening of flesh and helped prevent that fell asleep in the bath look, particularly important where our feet were concerned.

The C.T. base was almost deserted apart from five fairly junior rank commies, rapidly disposed of, an old cook and a couple of leathery middle-aged women. These belonged to absent officers including the local committee member who was responsible for doctrinal lectures almost every day. It appeared that the missing force were not due back for at least a week. After interrogation we released the two women and the cook who were so surprised that they offered to guide us out of the base along a sort of isthmus that had led onto their island in the swamp from the inland side. We burnt everything including the dead C.T.s who would otherwise soon pollute the neighbourhood with their smell, almost within hours. It was decided that the identification of these lesser mortals was not important. So no heads or fingers were taken with us that time!

The journey took about seven miles of several ziz-zag diversions until we reached the first kampong and then on to a straightforward jungle and plantation path to a secondary paved road in the neighbourhood of Bandar. We had radioed ahead and were then met by two Land Rovers, an old Bedford army lorry and one armoured car. All belonging to a nearby rubber plantation where we were treated to a splendid feed, after washing off the almost dried on swamp slime initially with our clothes still on. By the time we had finished the feed our team transport had arrived from K. L. and we were all very pleased to get a hot shower at the club and apply an excess of talc to our feet in particular and iodine to our cuts, scratches and open sores. We all sat up late discussing the enterprise but slept late the next morning. I think we could fairly claim another very small success and hopefully continued a sort of link from the very short lived Ferret Force onto the later properly coordinated efforts under General Templer.

Some retrospective musings; There were so many variations in the sort of actions taken against the C.T. s and these varied from time to time and place to place. Some, locally to meet specific circumstances, like our plantation and mining weekends. The more general, wide spread and longer duration actions that we took were sadly thought essential due to the often, inactive, rather inept and badly coordinated security reactions. The majority of up country planters, miners and other business ex-pats continually complained and sought help and action. This was, for a long while, totally ignored at least as far as constructive assistance and official defence was concerned. The defences round plantation homes and the armouring of private cars was arranged locally. This with panels cut off abandoned Japanese vehicles left over from the occupation. There was a considerable shortage of new steel imports. All this and many other potential problems appeared to be the sad result of 'too many cooks........' and petty rivalry and jealousies between the civil and military commands.

The emergency was often regarded as a simple civil war, which it was not. There were outsiders and backing coming over the Thai (Siamese) border from the Red Chinese. Mao regarded Malaya as just part of his vision for world communism just like Korea at the time. Luckily for us the back door route was not very easy or efficient. Although the C.T.s could cross back and forth easily to hide or rest, there were no large reinforcements of either men or supplies. They made a few attempts to land supplies down the South China Sea coast but almost all were thwarted. They soon gave up on that idea to concentrate on their Korean war-effort against the United Nations.

Being therefore a civil war, the police, regardless of their inabilities on occasions to deal with a situation, would often be reluctant to call in the army to assist them. Such was, too often the attitude of some of the local senior police officers. This then coupled with the resentment and frustration from the military having to follow what they often considered militarily inept and possibly disastrous actions by the police. Although fortuitous it was still very sad that it took the combination of the C.T.s ambush and killing of Sir Henry Gurney and the happy return of Winston Churchill to Westminster to break out of this possibly no win situation. Churchill did this by appointing General Gerald Templer as an overall Supremo, to run both the civilian Government, and the military system as a whole and as an integrated and coordinated manner.

However, and always threading through both the bad and the good systems were the Special Branch who were the most consistent and only form of reliable continuity throughout the troubles. They were above (or possibly below?) it all and that enabled them to coordinate and liaise with us and other sorts of unofficial defence actions. These in other circumstances would have been classed as vigilante and with a faint trace of a mercenary motive. I would claim with absolute certainty that all the people I was involved with absolutely hated communism and its methods and had a real affection and faith in Malaya as a country, then and in its future. Looking back now, I am more than a little proud, along with my dead friends and colleagues, to have had even a tiny part in saving the country from the evils of communism. In my correspondence with the recent Prime Minister of Malaysia, I made the point that, of all the Commonwealth countries today, Malaysia had turned out to be the only member to prove to have been worth fighting and loosing good friends for! I can pay no greater compliment than that.

Having already touched on the political ineffectiveness of both London and locally the 'them and us' added to by the situation between those that had been in the bag as prisoners of the Nips., mostly in the Changi prisoner of war camp at the eastern end of Singapore island and those that had got away to either fight from the Malayan jungle as Force 136 or elsewhere in other theatres of war. This was only one of the reasons for lack of 100% cooperation between the military and the civil authorities often worsened by petty civil service incidents. The ex prisoners appeared to sometimes be almost resentful (maybe almost jealous?) of those that had escaped their fate. With even the suggestion that those that had not been bagged had in effect deserted their posts to make their escape. There may well have been the odd example of this. However the prejudice flowing the other way was more serious. There had been an almost total and pointless loss of troops due to the too early, partly unnecessary and certainly premature political surrender of Singapore to the Japs. When they could, with advantage, have fought on longer and allowed many more troops and civilians to get out first. So preventing the large loss of personnel, troops, civilians and members of the civil and emergency authorities including the police who by remaining loyally at their posts and by, as far as possible, retaining and controlling the developing civic shambles and general breakdown. This enabled almost all women and children to be evacuated in time. Probably saving many hundreds of lives at the time and possibly thousands had so many vulnerable people not got out in time but finished up in Changi for three years or more! The Brits and others concerned did their duty without question. They served with loyalty, bravery and often knowingly sacrificing their own freedom in the process. Such duty is to be commended not criticised. I would equate it with a captain staying with his ship, at least and until all others are off safely, even at the risk of going down with the ship! Although being neither a writer or a historian it has occurred to me since I started these ramblings about my life, that I may be one of only a very few still here today who can give a neutral view on the happenings at the time since I was never part of the military or civil establishment and have no vested interest in covering my tail.

36. A fine Policeman

To now follow on from that and in the same vein I would mention and introduce the next character and for the same reasons that I may have laboured on about the Melshams. They all, in their own ways exemplified the staunch British spirit that got us all through the war and that was now going to get us through the so called emergency. The Melshams who would continue to work away at the country's very important basic produce and help to pay the cost of freedom from insidious communism. Now to the leading policeman who had the massive responsibility to oversee and organise the civilian protection from the communist terrorists. The man's name was Nicholls, the Commissioner of police in Malaya. I am not sure if I ever knew his first name and it is too long winded to keep referring to the Commissioner of Police so with no lack of respect he will be just Nicholls. I never actually met him but had passed him in the corridors of power from time to time. I did however deal on a regular basis some of his managers of his various departments, C.I.D., Special Branch and Jungle Force. They without exception had the greatest respect for him and he clearly inspired them in return. This was essential in such critical national circumstances. Nicholls had been one of the loyal and brave police officers that had stayed on at his post doing his duty in Singapore before being captured and imprisoned by the Nips in the infamous Changi jail for at least three years. Many did not survive but he did, which in itself speaks of exceptional willpower, a positive and constructive outlook. As with all survivors his health was compromised and he probably returned to the Far East sooner than perhaps he should have done. Few people who have suffered so much in a country would ever want to return to it, whatever the change of circumstances. But there has always been something different about Singapore and Malaya! It certainly never stopped Nicholls from tirelessly pursuing the highest standards of the force. He had been largely responsible for the Chinese members of his C.I.D. division to dissuade the Tongs (Chinese Mafia) from moving into Singapore from Hong Kong. The Chinese business fraternity were forever grateful to him. His rapport with his Chinese officers was crucial to the success of both the C.I.D. and Special Branch during the emergency. He instilled into them a sense of belonging to Malaya and not just being, almost temporary residents who worked only for mercenary reasons.

This flair for inspiring his officers also worked to great advantage with the Malay officers as well. The Malays until then were very parochial in their loyalties to their Sultan and state. Nicholls seemed to get them to feel part of the greater, whole country with a growing national pride and responsibility. He certainly seemed to find the way of overcoming their natural inertia! He also got the Malays and the Chinese officers to work together as a team so paving the way for a properly integrated police force essential not only for the emergency at the time but also for the coming independence where it would be vitally important. It may be possible to have different racial regiments in an army but not in a national police force. Perhaps, and without fully realising it, Nicholls had paved the way for them all to become Malaysians first. This was long before the fourth? Prime Minister, Mathir pursued and promoted the idea years later. Perhaps this is yet another example of a prophet not being credited in his own time?

The practical side of this policy is best demonstrated by Nicholls, as the emergency grew, in forming the Police Jungle Force consisting mainly of Malays. If my recollection from that time is right, it consisted of about two dozen well armed and trained groups that could be split into several patrols and located in relatively remote areas where the C.T.'s had thought they were safe from interference by the authorities. By their regular sorties and patrols the Jungle Force ensured that the C.T.s had to hide deeper and further into the jungle and less able to accomplish their usual intimidation and collection of food and money from the kampongs. Being mostly Malays the patrols were always welcomed without hesitation by the local population whereas they would always be a bit apprehensive of the other nationalities making up the security forces. This Police Jungle Force was very effective, largely underrated and not particularly secret as of course the Special Branch have to be. This being so I have always found it strange never to come across any mention of them anywhere. Very strange! These jungle force patrols operated out of some very remote and dangerous police stations in Johore, up through Selangor and into Perak that

I knew of. There may have been more. Nicholls was a frequent visitor to his far and remotely flung Jungle Force bases, which was very risky and brave of him and beyond the call of duty. He would always have an armed escort of course but it should be remembered that it did not save Sir Henry Gurney or many others! Nicholls was reputedly on occasion to be a bit aggressive and UN-diplomatic. So what? That was his job, not to be wasting time playing silly politics. I would use the analogy of it being much more important to be a good father rather than just a popular one! Lets face it, all the destructive liberal do-gooders opinions finish up wrong, costly and should have been avoided like the plague in the first place. We should always remember the fact that Winston Churchill was the most unpopular politician in the 1930's reaching the point of almost hatred! No one wanted to hear, believe or face the truth about Hitler. The war came anyway and largely because people would not listen to Churchill's warnings and believed that appeasement would work. It never has and never will. Bullies have to be stopped. As always, the sooner the better.

To my knowledge Nicholls did a remarkable job in almost impossible circumstances and that, after a terrible prison period under the Japs., when he must have seen many close friend and colleagues die. Yet despite all that and in far from perfect health he returned to duty and acquitted himself exceptionally well. The odd misinformed comments about him in supposedly responsible historical, part-novels just goes to prove that historians can only build up their parasitical opinions from dead information that might have been recorded by someone with a biased opinion, or with a political axe to grind or was not even there! To say nothing of being out of context in the first place as I am quite sure the quoted comments by General Templer were. I am certain that they were not made in a directly critical way but merely stating the dirty political realities of Nicholl's 'non compliance' and personal decision. In other words a plain honest political fact of life and not a personal criticism of his ability in any way. Whatever Nicholls's real personal reasons for finally going were, I would suggest that he made the right one as he was too honest a man to be stuck with a changing and largely political situation.

My own judgement overall would be that the world and particularly history should be repeatedly reminded that it was ONLY in Malaya that the communists were ever defeated in battle. The Americans in particular should have learnt from our lessons in Malaya and then the outcome of the Vietnam war could have been very different for them and the world today! We should not forget Korea either, it's still not resolved fifty years on and potentially more dangerous than ever. All because an American President allowed misguided politics to stop General Douglas MacArthur from finishing the job when he was certain of victory. Again the Americans did not learn and made the same obvious mistake, again and again with Iraq. Plus now Afghanistan.

Back in Malaya, once Churchill had appointed Gen. Templer as a Suprimo, with the authority to bang a few heads together and force full co-operation between all services and departments, people like Nicholls could fully and finally do their jobs no longer frequently being frustrated as before. It had needed a man like Churchill who understood history and the biblical declaration that "a house divided cannot stand (for long)" and certainly not when built on sand or a poor foundation as well. Nicholls certainly implemented the revised policy and like so many others, deserves credit and recognition for their historical part in making Malaya a unique success story in today's shambolic world.

Finally, the sequel to this story was that entirely coincidentally and many, many years later I was to meet Nicholls' two youngest daughters who were born in Malaya during the emergency and while I was there. I found this a slightly eerie experience or coincidence at the time but am very grateful to them for helping me to make up my mind to return to Malaya some 45 years on. Whether my reluctance was born of past jungle experiences or my fear that the country might have gone to the dogs as is the case of almost all other ex colonial countries, particularly those in Africa, I don't know. How wrong I was. In all salient ways it had not changed at all except for the city skylines. The people were just the same - friendly, polite and helpful. There was no anti-social behaviour, litter or graffiti. The school children were in neat uniforms with a wish to learn. No pornography and some censorship of the totally unnecessary violent and crude scenes that we are subjected to all too often. None of the liberal modern clap-trap we suffer daily about homosexuality and drugs. They have literally kept the laws and standards that we left them with nearly fifty years ago and they (politely) do not understand why we have not done so too?! As well they may ask.

37. Islands

Now the tales of two islands; many miles apart but very much related in historical use and activities. They are both off the west coast peninsular of Malaya. The first one, Pankor is, perhaps about 120 miles north of Port Swettenham and just off the coast of Perak and the small town of Lumut. It is the larger of several islands at this point on the Straits of Malacca and looks out over towards Sumatra which is the very much larger island forming the whole other side of the Straits. Old Mac had told us, that during the Japanese occupation his area of Force 136 had used Pankor, first to take delivery of arms and equipment from allied submarines who found it easy in those waters to play cat and mouse with the Jap. patrol boats. They then stored everything in several caches around the island for distribution inland later in small batches. The island is quite small but has very dense jungle right down to the beaches except for the main town and several very small kampongs (villages) that just span the narrow coast road and no more. The island has numerous beautiful sandy bays and a small number of look outs can cover all the sheltered bays easily. The sound of a motorboat can be heard long before it would come into view round the headlands.

The jungle is so dense that it could hide hundreds of people only yards from the shoreline. The other use for this island was for rest and recuperation with the salt water and sunshine resuscitating the sallow and rotting skin and reduce the irritation of prickly heat. Old Mac, having told us all this, suggested that it was possible that the C.T.s may well be using it still for holidays, particularly the multi red star officers. He suggested we might like to investigate and he even drew us a map, roughly from memory, showing the beaches and the camp areas they had used in the past. "If you can't find the paths in, just cut through, because nowhere is ever a mile from the shore and you will break out easily within a couple of hours", were his instructions and he was right. So, one weekend, sixteen of us drove up to Sitiawan a small port just short of Pankor and out of its line of sight. We had arranged to hire a fishing boat that had been organised by a local dormant S.B. agent. They were certainly not expecting the majority of the fishermen to be Europeans! Carrying large kit bags and strange strapped rolls. We turned the boat north after we had got clear of the river mouth.

We arrived north of and near Pankor Island itself rather late and anchored off one of the smaller islands, out of sight of the town of Lumut and of Pankor itself. Just before dawn we landed on the north broad and raised part of the promontory, which is connected to the rest of the island by a fairly narrow neck of land. This landing point was picked because we had no idea whatsoever what we might encounter and we might need to evacuate very quickly! Plus the fact that it is a lot easier to defend or repel attackers on a very narrow front and with no chance of them getting behind us! However, we found nothing and advanced over the narrow neck, then turned south along the coastal track on the seaward side of the island and then just before the Kampong Nipah, at the start of the first small bay we headed inland along a track. Whether it was an animal or a village footpath we did not know. We climbed up to the central island ridge, near the base of Bukit Pankor and where the path divided, we then split up.

The northern fork finished up in a possibly abandoned camp. It had only one decent hut and about ten simple bashas. It did not appear to have been used very recently but we burnt everything anyway. The other forked path, finally led down again to the sheltered beach, now on the east side of the island. There were signs of a boat having been pulled up and down fairly recently but no boat. Having joined up again we all headed carefully down the coast for about a mile in the general direction of Pankor town itself. We discovered more boat marks on the sand but even with the rather indistinct footprints it took several minutes to find the start of the jungle path. So we went back inland again and up the hill. Instinctively we were very cautious this time having smelled smoke but the jungle was so dense we could not see where it came from. We followed the path even more carefully now and came out into a manmade clearing. As we spread out in a semicircle to approach a group of huts, a solitary C.T. sprang out to open fire at us. Unfortunately for him he was dead before he had even fully raised his rifle. The camp indicated the fact that there could be nearly thirty in residence, all the rest, presumable in town doing their shopping or having been out for a night and might return very soon!

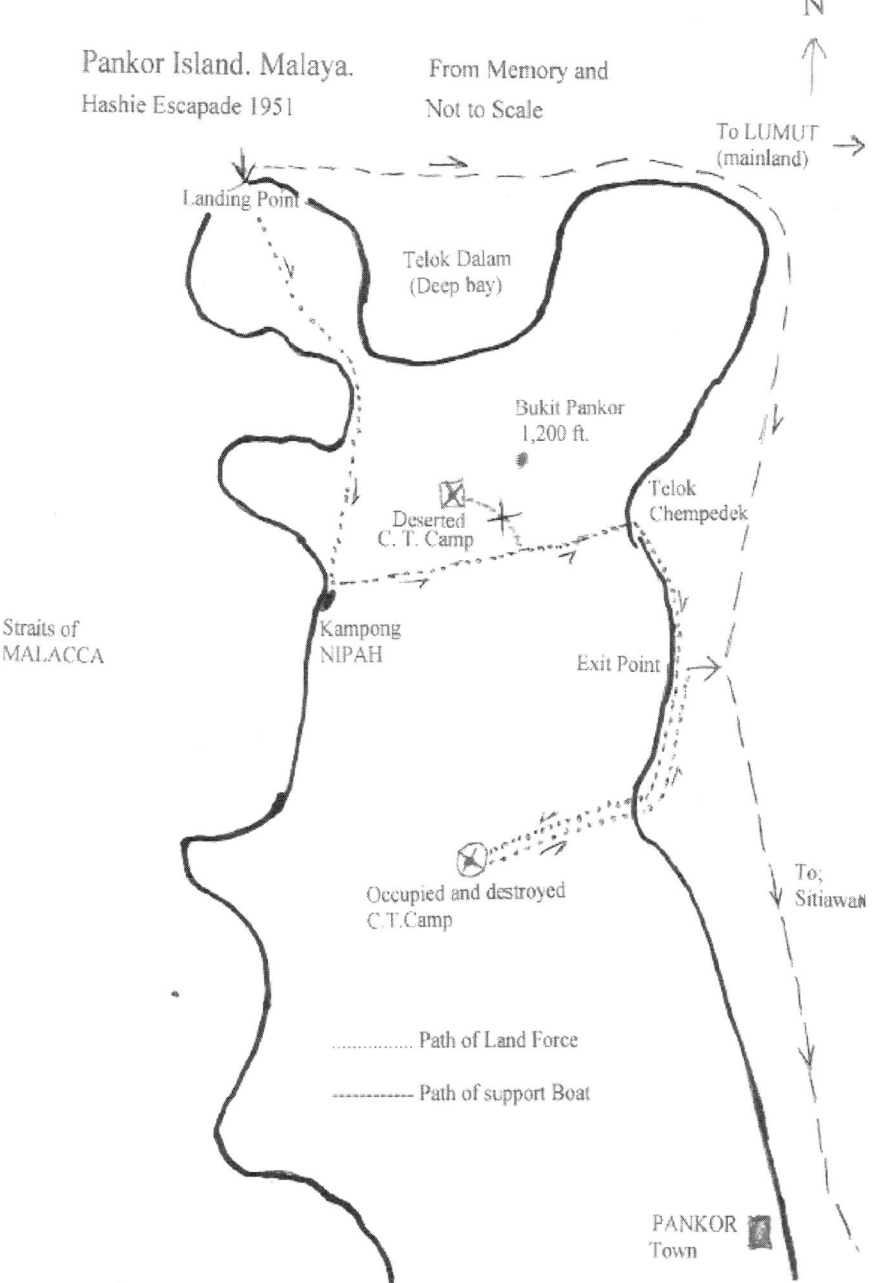

We hastily piled up all their gear, which included a lot of bedding, clothing, a few arms and ammunition, a radio, several batteries, medical gear and a lot of books and writing paper. We poured some of their kerosene over it all and set the lot on fire, along with the other huts. The body was added to his own funeral pyre.

Well knowing, that even in dense jungle our shots would have been heard we decided that rather than face the unknown size of the enemy on their own territory, particularly when there was every indication that we were badly outnumbered that discretion was certainly the better part of valour. Since we were out on a limb as it were, with no possible assistance for hours, if at all, we hastily retreated along the way we had come, back down to the eastern beach. We radioed to our boat, which immediately set out round the top or northern end of the island, past Telok Dalam (deep bay) to pick us up, close to where we had found the first set of boat marks in Chempedak Bay. Within, about half an hour we were on board and heading back south and up the river to Sitiawan, busily congratulating ourselves. For what? I later wondered. For killing just one C.T. and burning their holiday homes or because we had stuck out our necks into the unknown and undeservedly got away with it? We did however legitimately enjoy the irony of launching our escapade from Sitiawan, reputedly the original home of the top communist Chin Peng and where his family had had a cycle repair shop pre-war. He had had the audacity to go to London to take part in the Victory Parade and represented the Chinese element of Force 136. And this when he already knew he would be returning to the jungle to fight on but against the British and all the vast majority of non communist Malayans this time. He was no ordinary bandit, was well educated, highly intelligent and had evaded capture by the Japs for several years and managed the same for even longer from our security forces during the emergency. I believe he finished up his days in retirement just over the border in Thailand. There was some talk that the first Malaysian Prime Minister, Tunku Abdul Raman, as part of the final sort of amnesty made some financial deal with the Thai Government to keep him out of circulation. Chin Peng, I imagine was one of the thousands round the world during the 30's, of over educated and very naïve intellectuals who seem to live on another planet at times and thought that communism was the best way of defeating fascism. How stupid they proved to be since communism is far more dangerous and insidious. Fascists are usually more easily got rid of and in a shorter time frame than communism. The world should remember that Stalin was responsible for far more Russian deaths than Hitler and they were his own people so imagine what he would have been like to and in other countries had he not been held back by the Iron Curtain and the cold war?

Looking back about half an hour later we could still see the smoke rising from our handiwork even though the island of Pankor itself was well out of sight by then. We got back to port in time for a late lunch at a Chinese eating shop, paid the fisherman, who had no idea what his boat had been used for. We certainly had no fish on board! That evening we were all back in K.L. and some wag at the company mess suggested that it must have been a boring weekend as we were back sooner than usual. Little did he know. We naturally notified the S.B. of the Pankor situation, they thanked us and bought us all a round of drinks but they did not know when and if they would consider doing anything about it. They felt we may have already given them such a big shock that they would be very unsettled and unsure as to what and when to expect anything next. Let them stew in their own psychological juice for a bit, was, I think the final decision, for the moment at least.

Much further north is Penang, a much bigger island than little Pankor and is densely populated in George Town itself. Penang is the name of the island not the main city. The only other islands even further north are the Lankawi group, which are almost up to the Thai border and in the Andaman Sea. Quite apart from my business contacts on the island Connie and I went up there quite often and stayed at her Danish relation's holiday bungalow which was always staffed just in case of spontaneous visitors. This was a few miles out of the city along the northern main road, which leads to the beach and holiday centres of Batu Ferringhi. The bungalow was set up the hill a bit above the coast road and looking over it onto the local beach and to the North. It was located within a three minute walk of both the European and the Chinese swimming Clubs. They in turn were literally on the beach themselves. Many other ex-pats, liked the area and to this day I think of Penang as being my favourite, all round and concentrated bit of Asia. However, ironically and slightly funny was the fact that the C.T.s also used the jungle and hilly hidden centre of the island for their R. & R.. There seemed to be an unwritten truce on the island. Neither side seemed to bother the other and in truth there were hardly ever any incidents of consequence. I cannot vouch for this but that was, in effect what seemed to happen. One day however the relative peace of Penang was shattered by a big bang in a car park one very hot afternoon. This time it had nothing directly to do with the terrorists. A young tin miner from north of Ipoh had driven up through some dangerous countryside armed to the teeth and with a box of grenades on the passenger seat of his little open Singer Roadster.

In the gung-ho atmosphere prevailing at the time, a common practice when in a dodgy area, was for the safety pins to be taken out of the grenades. This was only a temporary measure and then being replaced with rubber bands to hold the sprung detonator arms down, instead of the ring pins. This enabled the grenades to be flung out and around without the time consuming and awkward, when driving with one hand, pin removal. When the grenades hit the ground the jerk would overcome the rubber band and fire the detonator. In these sort of drive-through ambushes the grenades flung out were merely and hopefully to put the C.T.s off their aim, at you. On this particular occasion the lad had gone off shopping and forgotten to replace the pins. Needless to say the direct hot sunlight perished one of the rubber bands and the grenade went off, along with the other dozen or so. His car was wrecked and about ten others badly damaged! Miraculously no one was hurt or killed. He did finish up in court, though, probably because the insurance companies would have been furious. Innocent lives had certainly been at risk and it had happened in normally peaceful Penang after all! I think, due to the appreciation of the strain of up country living and his previously good record he was only admonished and ordered to stop and put the pins back into his grenades in future BEFORE he next crossed over on the ferry from the mainland!

At about this time I was getting a bit upset and probably more annoyed at the number of funerals I went to. I suppose that we had all become a bit blasé at the time. And I have to say that it was very much more emotionally upsetting visiting my friend's graves, nearly fifty years later. When perhaps the significance of their loss finally crept out of my subconscious. It had all been 'on hold' I imagine for all that time. We all play psychological games with ourselves during such trying times.

People sometimes ask what was it like to kill people. Wrong

question because in such circumstances the enemy are not people and don't warrant the same concern that may be given, even to a mad rabid dog that has to be shot. No dog, however mad, would have thought to do the terrible things that the C.T.s did to so many innocent people. We were not killing human people but killing an idea (communism), bit by bit. The exception comes when someone is killed at short range. That does stick in your mind, on and off for a long time. Not necessarily with any guilt but just hovering around in your mind and one has to remember to balance the overall good that finally came out it all. Plus, of course the number of innocent lives it will certainly have saved as well.

Only two of the many funerals were for members of our Harriers who did not die on any Hassie escapade but in the normal way of things. Which even so, when worked out on numbers, in relation to C.T. contacts and their losses would statistically indicate that we were vastly more efficient by attacking them on their home ground than just waiting for them to surprise our side, almost unawares, with superior numbers. Attack really had proved to be by far the best form of defence. Add to that the demoralising effect we had and the number of their efforts that we were able to thwart. It proved again that the Chindits in Burma were on the right lines against the Japanese. I think, but for the ignorance and incompetence in Whitehall, from the postwar Labour Government, in stopping the Ferret Force early on in the conflict, probably hundreds of unnecessary deaths could have been avoided and the emergency shortened by several years. We will never know for sure.

38. The influence of cars

Perhaps I should return to my growing love of sports cars and flying, before I start getting a bit morbid. The advent of my first sports car, the M.G.- T.C was very exciting. It had belonged to one of the Selangor Princes, who are known as Tunkus. I drove it flat out all day and every day and wore the first set of tyres out in just over three months. The car had been painted in a two-tone blue. Light blue body and dark blue wings and running boards. Plus a lot of extra chrome plating. It's still the best looking M.G. I have ever seen, even to this day. It spent its life at, never under 65mph and as close to 80mph as often as I could manage. I was convinced that I was King of the Road. Particularly with a girl like Connie sitting in the passenger seat. I was definitely invincible. Then one fateful evening when we were both on our way back up to K.L., after a reception on board one of the ships in Port Swettenham, the worst happened. In the area of Petaling (yes, that place again) and while driving flat out I was amazed to notice some headlights coming up behind me fast. I could not believe it. I checked the speedo and which gear I was in and still did not believe it. The lights and the car they were attached to swept past, doing at least 30 mph more than us. Impossible! They were not racing us and in fact hardy even aware of our existence. The driver was driving one handed with a fag in the other and the female passenger had her scarf covered head right back, presumably admiring the stars.

That image was so burnt into my brain at the time that it remains vivid, even today. I was really cut down to size but could still hardly believe it all. At the end of the Petaling straight the other car eased off a bit and I was able to stay within sight of his tail lights but only by driving like a man possessed (of what?). Then as we reached the last fast stretch into K.L., known as the Lornie Mile he simply disappeared off like a rocket. I just managed to catch sight of his lights again, from about half a mile behind as he turned left onto the bridge over the river Klang and then right down into the city centre past the Padang. I too entered the city and broke all the speed limits to try and catch up and find out what this car was that had so comprehensively destroyed my ego. We did not catch it up or find it. Sleep was not easy that night. A terrible thing ego, particularly when in the company of a woman(girl).

A few days later, when next in Klang, I relayed the story to Chooi. He immediately suggested it was one of the amazing new Jaguars he had read about. I made enquiries only to find out that I might have to wait over a year to get one. Then by sheer coincidence Chooi was reading the *Straits Times* of Singapore newspaper and noticed an advert for an XK120 already on its way to Singapore and surplus to requirements! It appeared that the wealthy Chinese businessman concerned had thought that as they were in such short supply (most going to America for the dollars to help the export drive and reportedly there were only a dozen British owned XKs in the whole of the U.K. at the time) he decided that he had better order two and then he might get one. He had now discovered that he was getting both of them, much to his surprise and embarrassment. He was more than happy to sell me one of them.

'Hashie' Alan Pitt posing in my Jaguar XK120. KL Lake Gardens. May 1951

I chose the silver with blue trim, so in May 1951 Ah Hoi, Ah Kwan and I all squeezed into my M.G. and headed down to Singapore to collect the car from the docks. It never went through the local dealer, Cycle and Carriage (1926) Ltd. in Orchard Road, much to their annoyance as they were adding over 20% to the price. I got mine for the basic, tax-free U.K. price plus freight and insurance. A well worthwhile saving. The charming Chinese seller (as a result of a phone call (February 28th 2008) from an Australian who is writing a book on XKs in the Far East and Australia and still doing further research into the records I am now able to remember the name of this Chinese seller, it was/is Chan Lye Choon) had already arranged for it to be registered and taxed in my name at Ipoh in the state of Perak. The reason was that the Chinese, it would appear, like numbers with straight lines (perhaps like the modern day Feng Sui?) so he had got AA1771 as a number for me and for good luck. In addition he had fitted a quite expensive silverplated, St. Christopher badge to the dashboard as well. I am not superstitious or believe in these sort of things but I have kept it more as a reminder of the nice man and the remarkable and almost unbelievable set of circumstances that enabled me to fulfil an obsessive dream so quickly.

I drove the Jaguar back to K. L. while the other two lads took turns in driving the M.G. It was very interesting journey as the Jaguar came with a stop on the throttle pedal which was wired and sealed until its first 500 mile service, if it was broken, then the guarantee was null and void. This restricted the cars speed to 58 mph which meant that the boys would leave me behind on the straights but the Jag's handling and ride was so good I could not only catch them up round the corners, I could pass them as well! By the time we got back to K.L. I had been pressing so hard on the pedal it had made such a dent in the carpet and underfelt that I was able to do nearly 63mph instead of the restricted 58mph. I do not remember too much of the next few days but they passed in a blur of happiness. A honeymoon period? This was certainly my first wife!

I had already been doing the odd motoring events in the M.G, and the Jag. now encouraged me to do more. There were, in a short space of time, several XK120s in Selangor. Derek White, whose passing of my M.G. on that fateful evening, was personally to blame for my ownership. Eddie, the wealthy Port Swettenham stevedore company owner that I've already mentioned, the one that shared my ignition key no. Another up country estate manager by the name of Ferguson and who was also a close friend of the White family. Another wealthy Chinese owner, of a tug and barge company in the port, had an unusual green XK. with tan upholstery. His name I do remember was Saw Kim Tiat. I remember because of a story against myself. Chooi, who by now considered he knew me well enough (you might say he had become my personal Jeeves on all matters local) to give me tactful advice to the effect that it was impolite (not rude, please note) to point or wave a forefinger at anyone. I thanked him for his advice but was sure it would not apply to me anyway?! However only a few days later at a motoring event at the Port Swettenham airfield he photographed me, obviously sounding off at poor Saw Kim Tiat and waving my finger almost under his nose. Even worse Chooi had taken the snap with my camera and left me to discover it when the film was developed later. Oriental tact. My face should have been red but I did learn the lesson. The aforementioned Ferguson car was later sold to a British Colonel type. He mounted a machine gun on each wing so that he and any passenger could fire back at C.T.s single-handed while still driving along. Fergie's car, being an early one, was an all aluminium body type and it took a lot of restoration by David McLeod, a Glasgow businessman many years later.

I suppose, looking back, that I was always mechanically minded. From the early days of Meccano and then on into building my own bicycles in my teens. Of the practical subjects at school I tended to enjoy geometry the most and possibly physics next. The writing was on the wall, so to speak. With Ah Hoi and Ah Kwan having my M.G.'s engine apart, almost on a monthly basis, I learnt a lot. They were always thorough and meticulous in their work. When I got the XK120 they were so enthused and felt almost honoured to be able to work on such an (then) exotic vehicle. A typical example of this was one Sunday morning when they had come out to the Harper Gilfillan Mess to service the Jag. I just happened to mention that the steering box was leaking just a spot of oil and might need a new gasket. A couple of hours later, returning from a good tiffin at the Golf Club we spotted Ah Kwan cycling back into town with my steering column on his shoulder.

It appeared that they had the whole steering system stripped down and decided that one of the machined faces was not quite true. So, instead of just fitting a thicker gasket they were off into town to a little back street machine shop to face off the column properly using (to us), a primitive treadle and string type lathe. No messing about with any sort of bodge or "if a job's worth doing---" and all that.

In addition to my very wide range of jobs, the company had decided to get involved in tendering for generator systems for the rapidly growing number of resettlement villages. I should mention that we had a branch in Hong Kong by the hardly British name of Yu Tung Tai. I have no idea how it originally came about but that was what they were called. We also had a branch in Saigon as well, but that was named Alcan et Cie being the French influence of its parent company in Paris whose boss was an Alan Alcan. In Hong Kong there was a company by the name of South China Iron Works that occupied several acres of corrugated tin roofed building and works. They were completely self contained, having their own foundry and furnaces for forgings etc. It transpired that they were licensed by Mercedes to build one of their diesel engines and that they had a great business going. These engines seemed to power almost every Junk boat in Hong Kong harbour and had converted many of the very uneconomical Bedford army lorries left over from the war. My firm were interested in these engines as the motive power to drive the generators that they were going to import from Italy.

British companies were not very interested, had poor delivery dates and were already building up their very poor reputation for not backing up sales, in general, which, unfortunately also applied to British cars. For example, I had to wait for over four months for a new radiator cap for my MG. The quality of these Hong Kong made engines impressed me a lot and dare I say it, better than anything I've seen come out of Germany since. Their two boffins, who came down to see us and who in turn I visited several times were named, believe it or not, a Dr. Su. and a Dr. Wu. Both were graduates of Shanghai University and quite brilliant in all aspects of Mechanical Engineering. I learnt so much from them, way above and beyond the task in hand. They seemed to take a liking to me and were exceptionally hospitable and not just because of the possible contract involved. They saw my genuine interest and decided to educate me. They brought pages and pages of mechanical study material for me on each trip and then gave me a gruelling examination on their next visit. It was very tough but I got a real sense of accomplishment out of it. After about nine months of this, they announced one day that I had completed, with distinction the full three years course and for all intents and purposes I had graduated from Shanghai as a Mechanical Engineer, having not only covered the, over three years normal work but had demonstrated and put a lot of it into practice as well. It was better than any formal graduation ceremony and was accompanied by a ten course Chinese dinner as well.

These amazing men were really impressed with my Jaguar, particularly (so was the rest of the world) the engine. And offered to design and produce some high performance camshafts for it. It would have been very churlish of me to have refused! They taught me almost all I know to this day on the subject. They understood the relationship of lift and valve timing to different bore to stroke ratios and then to different rotational speeds. This, to me, almost sacred knowledge I have never seen in any publication or informative literature from either cam designers or producers, anywhere in the world.

It has continually proved its worth to me in almost fifty years in the engine tuning business.

The good Doctors and I hit it off, I think, because I was the first European that would laugh, joke and socialise with them like friendly equals. Even though I was certainly not equal to them, in ability or knowledge. In due course they were as good as their word and produced a pair of camshafts that they had machined and ground out of solid steel billets. It must have taken hundreds of hours. They fitted and set them up along with Ah Hoi and Ah Kwan. What a team, two of the most brilliant engineers (in the world?) and the two best mechanics in the country and I was really only just learning to drive fast. The cams changed the note of the XK's engine and with little noticeable loss of flexibility, produced a clear improvement in the mid ranges and it revved all too easily into the red zone on the tachometer.

All this helped my amateurish competition results locally and impressed the other Jag. owners who were not aware of my secret weapon(s). I also developed other small techniques that all helped shave the odd fraction of a second off my times but the real advantage was those cams. My car was fitted with the low compression pistons for export to poor fuel countries. In Malaya at that time we only had rather low octane petrol from the Caltex oil wells in Sumatra. With the lower C/R my engine could be advanced a bit more than the others. Although this theoretically produced a little less power it did give a smoother and more responsive engine. This more than made up for it and generated less heat in the first place. As I was to learn more about the subject in the ensuing years it became clear that it is not always how much power you have but how well it is delivered. It was on such a competitive occasion that I had been wagging my rude finger under Saw Kim Tiat's nose.

The 'impolite' author sounding off at poor Saw Kim Tiat. Port Swettenham Airfield 1951

When we had rigged up one of these Hong Kong made Mercedes "junk" test engines to one of the generators we had to make work and prove it had the overall capacity and more importantly, the reliability. All our competitors had works backing and test documentation. Our combination, being never tried before, had to be subjected to stringent testing. But how? There were no test facilities in the country. Stalemate and great frustration! I asked what was needed to prove the set-up and was sarcastically told "the equivalent of several hundred electric fires but we don't have very many in the tropics, do we?"

Silly man. My brain went, tick, tick, inspirational thoughts. Enter one electrical ignoramus. Me. I consulted the good Doctors who thought I was almost mad but might get away with it. My brainwave was to get hundreds of yards of a sort of fence wire and coil it up like a long spring. Then lay the coils out on wooden trays filled with ash and gravel as insulation, rather like giant electric fires. These wooden trays, in turn were insulated with sheets of rubber (no shortage, there). However when the generated current was applied initially the 'fires' promptly melted and disintegrated into lots of very hot bits of wire. All about the colour of my embarrassed face.

Fortunately one of the invited witnesses was a City Works Department Divisional Manager. He quite rightly suggested that as we were not sure of output current and had no idea at all about the resistance or load involved with our makeshift fires, it would make better sense to incorporate some type of rheostat and he knew where he could get one that might do the job. This, it turned out to be part of the electrical equipment taken out of a Japanese warship for scrap. He was quite right. A week or so later we tried again and fed in the power very gently until the first block of 'fires' just glowed dull red and melted off some of the coating. We then made up more and more fires and included them into the circuit until we had a large workshop, open at each end (rather like a small hangar), glowing happily and with so much heat that we could have baked bread without an oven.

After a few more teething problems the system settled down and ran for many hours. The Govt. specification called for minimum of 'X' amount of K.V. A. to be generated for so many hours and then reduced to a lower level for so many more hours. Then repeated daily for twenty-one days. This, of course to simulate the demands of the villages for floodlights at night and everything else during the day.

A visiting assessor from the Crown Commissioners Office came out to inspect and report on our tender (concerned, no doubt about the taxpayers money). He arrived with his instruments and was finally able to tell us just how much current we were generating. It was more than enough. His initial reaction was one of horror at what we were doing. But when he saw that it was all working quite well he grudgingly congratulated us on our remarkably efficient, simple, economical but a very dangerous method of load testing (health and safety, what's that?). Apparently, even in those days, an approved test facility would be expected to cost tens of thousands of dollars and would always be within the factory facilities. Not out in the field like ours.

The mess belonging to Harper Gilfillan was where I lived for a while after meeting Connie and moving out of Malcolm's house near Klang after the burnt bus episode. Harper's mess was off Ampang Road but beyond the ring or boundary road and verging on the ulu countryside. Of the average number of residents living in the mess, about ten people would have been well armed, so it was unlikely that the C.T.s would bother us, particularly as their escape route could be easily cut off. Because of this, they seldom roamed much nearer town than the tin mines at Ampang village itself, a few miles further down the road from us. The other advantage of Mess-ing there was that Connie too lived on Ampang Road, but just on the town side of the ring road, barely a mile away. The mess was therefore, at that time outside the city boundary, but today, within about a quarter of a mile is where the new K.L. city centre is, along with the famous Petronas TwinTowers. That will give some

Family group: Self, Connie, her sister & baby, her husband Sgt Stanley Harper with Basil's Chinese/ Eurasian wife, Barbara, sitting in front

idea of how far the expansion and development of K.L. has progressed in fifty years. In the same vein, Connie had an aunt (I never entirely understood the numerous aunt relationships, some were related, others had been historical baby sitters. Others appeared to have lived with the family for a period of time and others, just adopted) that had a large house and fruit orchard, producing Rambutans and Mangosteens on the south side of Ampang Road, almost alongside a convent and up on a slope known locally as Bukit Nanas (Pineapple Hill).

This is where now the K.L. Tower is located, which although not the tallest in the world, as are the Petronas Twin Towers, is still in the top half dozen or so. I have often wondered if this particular aunt had retired a millionaire or not, from the sale of her house and orchard?

This aunt's property was secluded and had a summer or guest bungalow at the bottom end of the orchard that we were able to use quite often. With no one noticing the numerous cars and strange and motley gathering of Harriers. It was like a remote and hidden oasis, close to the city centre. Ideal on occasions for our purposes and coupled with the fact that the aunt seemed to really enjoy catering for us with a variety of snack foods that we had never even tasted before!

It may seem strange that while I was living this comprehensive life of, often instant life and death decisions, there was one decision that I found by far the most difficult of all. In fact it took about six months to reach and then only because Connie was used by one of my best planter friends to nag at me or at least regularly reason with me. The problem was, should I keep my wonderful little MG. T. C. car as well as the Jag or not? This demanding friend John, already had the more up to date MG. T. D. model that had smaller wheels, rack and pinion steering and independent front suspension but he regarded it as being too civilised and was desperate for me to sell him my T.C. model M.G., so that he could get his kidneys further pulverised on his bumpy estate roads. I considered him daft in this respect. He was such a good, loyal and trusted friend that I did finally but accidentally put him out of his misery. One night while we were all out after a particularly successful C.T. episode and when the drinkers amongst us were toasting the number of red stars (on the C T.s caps) that would never shine again. I was asked just how much I would sell the T.C. for and I unwisely stated a price well above, even a new one. Stupid of me of course because John immediately said done. I was a bit embarrassed and hoped that he, being one of the drinkers, may have forgotten by the next morning. But no, he had not and was round at the mess the next morning for breakfast with his cheque book in his hand. I could not back out of the deal but did insist that he paid me a thousand dollars less than the ridiculous price he had agreed to.

Since that was the end of my MG days I must add the final story that connects, the MG car, Connie, the emergency situation and Batu Caves. Some time after we had heard all the stories about the wartime Force 136 activities in and out of these caves from Connie's father, Old Mac, and after a very good curry one Sunday afternoon, Connie and I decided to visit the caves, as she had not been out there herself for several years. It was known as a dangerous area but we were well armed and thought that in broad daylight it should be ok. As we got within sight of the caves the roads were empty and there was not even a bicycle in the large car park. So we parked the MG at the foot of all those 272 steps and climbed up among the cheeky monkeys who were on the scrounge as usual.

View from Batu caves during 24hr 'snoot to kill' curfew

We went into the caves and wandered about for an hour or so looking into gloomy corners and up through the collapsed holes in the roof that Mac had told us about. They were still there and are, even today! The smell of bat dropping was pretty awful and the signs of very old Hindu celebrations gave the place a far from hospitable atmosphere. We left the caves and took the typical tourist snap shots which included one looking down the steps at Connie, complete with tartan skirt, her gun belt on one hip, plus the lonely MG below in the empty car park. We drove off back to K.L. for some tea and again did not see a single person or vehicle until we got back onto the main North-South road again. We casually mentioned this later back in the mess and we were greeted with blank stares, a load of derision, total disbelief and then some very rude remarks. We finally convinced them that we were not kidding, only then to be told that the whole area was totally out of bounds and under a 'shoot to kill, 24 hour curfew'!

Nearly fifty years later when I took Fay there, the car park had hundreds of cars and other traffic. The place was cleaned up and had several tourist buildings, shops and cafes. The caves themselves have been cleaned and floors concreted over with new Hindu shrines, images and statues dotted about the various cave branches. The partly overgrown holes in the roof are still just the same. The place is now a major pilgrimage point for the Hindus who now come from abroad as well. For one of their festivals, the year before Fay and I visited, over 800,000 had flocked there in one day alone. I could not help but look down those same steps, remembering so many different things! No MG this time at the foot of them, just buildings that had never existed before and the usual, mere hundreds of weekday visitors and tourists. The monkeys were still the same timeless pesky characters though.

Perhaps one final friend and character to be mentioned because he somehow typified the enterprising, crafty and some times devious mentality required to adapt and survive during those years. He was a fellow mess mate of mine at Harper Gillfillans and one of the tennis partners at the Spotted Dog club of Sir Henry Gurney. Plus one of our group that had been up to Fraser's Hill the weekend before Sir Henry's ambush and murder. His name was Allan Pitt and apart from his regular job with Harpers and his nefarious activities with the Harriers he had a part time job as a Disc Jockey at the local Redifusion studio. It may seem strange but in those days of shortages and relative impecuniousness, most locals could not afford a modern radio. So the more economical alternative was for the wider population to have a speaker only, set in what looked like a small radio set and connected by land lines back to a broadcasting station. These lines often shared the telephone poles but in the remoter kampongs and plantations, they were draped through the trees for miles. Quite often, at night when Allan's duty at the studio clashed with some social or other activity he would record his general spiel, good night and closing down message, well in advance. Then, later a trusted engineer would play these messages at the appropriate times for him. There were times when he would already be in bed at night listening to himself saying good night to his wider audience. On other occasions he could be with other Harriers fifty miles away up country laying up an ambush and waiting for a dawn raid on some C.T.s.

Malay, in its many variations, is spoken by all national groups with their own words often mixed up into the general conversation. A bit like the Gaelic in Scotland where you will often hear "--------------- spare wheel-------" or "---------Carburettor-----" because the language does not have the equivalent modern word or the speaker does not yet have sufficient command of it. We would often literally translate anything from swear words, exclamations to funny descriptions into a pidgin Malay which would totally confuse local listeners. As an example, if one missed hitting the ball at billiards and instead of saying "hard cheese, old boy", the locals would be totally mystified as to what a bit of old "Kedju Kras" had to do with the game we were playing at the time. And even more remote for them to follow was something like "On the whole, I think", this or that. This became "On the hole" and the nearest we could get was "atas lombong" or, above a ditch or hole. Sounds awfully silly in retrospect but in those tense times, humour often took on a strange guise.

39. Air recces

I now come to what was one of those few epic occasions in my life that are for ever etched on my mind with great clarity. The one before this was of course, being passed by Derek White and his wife in their Jaguar XK120 as though I was almost standing still! First though I need to explain that we were lucky enough, on occasion to scrounge a flight over the area we wanted to operate in. This enabled us to get a better idea and feel of the general lay-out. Hills, rivers, clearings, paddy fields, kampongs and even on occasion the bandit camp we wanted to attack. This was often, to find the best way out again not just how to get into a dodgy area in the first place. The mapping of Malaya was very poor, once out of town or off the main roads. It is well nigh impossible to judge contours from ground level, in dense jungle and swamp areas, so, low recce flights were the best way to overcome this problem. Mostly these would be in a Dak., which was fine but it was thought that at some bandit locations too many low level passes might alarm and warn them of impending interest and attention, causing them to move before we got there. Higher altitude photos worked quite well but could not give us the important changes in terrain that were only clearly discerned at very low level. The other problem with the Dak., was that being relatively slow it could be heard coming, so giving the C.T.s time to take cover or hide and even pull into the side of a river if in a boat at the time.

On the odd occasion we were very lucky and were able to do these runs in a Mosquito. The only disadvantage of them was that they could only take one observer, which put a great responsibility on the person concerned. A mistake could always later be fatal to us rather than to the bandits, which was not really the object of the exercise! The Mosquito being so fast might catch the C.T.s napping so to speak, but made it more difficult to make adequate notes or sketches. So we used a simple domestic 8 mm movie camera, which we could replay at a slower speed. We also used thin celluloid sheets over a map to wax crayon on additional details while lying in the Perspex nose of the plane and looking forward through the optically perfect oval bomb site window.

At that time Changi (the notorious prison camp under the Japs. and today the International Airport) was one of Singapore's two operational military airfields. The other being Seletar, which was off the beaten track on the northern part of the island, close to the Straits of Johore. Johore Bahru or New City is the capital of the most southerly state of Malaya. At that time famous for its troublesome C.T.s in its interior and for having the only full road racing circuit in the country. The Johore Grand Prix became quite famous in its own way. Of course none of us raced there did we?! The usual fictitious names were often used but on the odd occasion someone else's genuine name would be used. This caused great confusion when the company or employer concerned was about to take serious disciplinary action found that, what they thought was the guilty person was either away on leave or had a cast iron alibi. They and the daft insurance companies did not find it at all amusing but we all did! From all this the reader will realise that the historic and published results were therefore not very accurate. Singapore is joined to Peninsular Malaya by a road and rail causeway that also carries huge water supply pipes to the island. Johore was quite well known for its Sultan, who seemed to spend most of his life sampling the bar maids in the Chelsea area of London. To keep up his prowess in this department he had claimed to have had some monkey glands implanted! It has to be nonsense, as we all know now that the rejection factors of such transplants would not have allowed it. The story was a good one at the time and did typify the man's perceived lusty character.

40. Epic flight

It was on one of these flights in a Mosquito and while being piloted by a war time Pathfinder that the memorable episode occurred, quite unexpectedly. After taking off from Seletar, Singapore and flying west over the Johore Straits and the causeway, then out into the Straits of Malacca before turning north up the coast passing Malacca and Port Dickson on our right until we reached the general area of Port Swettenham (now Port Klang) and all the islands and mangrove swamp areas that characterize the Selangor coast at this point. We took several series of pictures in and around the various waterways and river routes before 'beating up' the Port itself. We came inland swinging and skimming above the water at less than twenty feet above the sea and below the deck line of several ships moored out in the roads. Then a tight climb up and over the docks and buildings, all at close to 300 mph. I felt glued to the seat with a very heavy weight on my lap. The observer's seat being on the main spar or leading part of the wing construction with only an excuse of a cushion between us. The pilot sits on his parachute, which makes a good cushion and the navigator or whatever has a backpack chute, which is often only put on when and if required! After this thrilling experience we climbed and turned out to sea, levelling out at about 10,000 ft. within sight of Sumatra across the Straits and ready to head for home. But no, my friendly pilot asked if I had ever flown a Mossie. I replied no and that my only real experience of twin engined aircraft had been on D.C. 3s. He said, "now is your chance lad". I thought he was kidding, but no, we exchanged seats which is a bit of a tight squeeze and not easy to do without moving the controls. We managed and only lost about a thousand feet in the process. It took a further several minutes to readjust straps and chutes etc. I then spent about half an hour going through all the simple manoeuvres and getting the feel of the plane. It was great fun, exhilarating and exciting beyond my expectations. In addition the plane was much more chuck-able than I imagined for an aircraft of its size and weight (about 7 tons). I felt at home with it very quickly. My mentor obviously thought I was almost a natural because he then suggested that I should try a landing. I was certain that he was joking this time as there were no airfields nearby except Port Swettenham and I knew from my motoring events there that it was not suitable. He was not joking and told me to head south down the coast for a few miles where at the end of the mangroves swamps was a very long, wide and flat beach and the tide was way out. This was a small place called Morib and was where the allies made their landings to oust the Japs. The only beach anywhere in the country with these characteristics and apparently with very firm sand as well. Unique.

I was to try a few circuits and bumps, the traditional landing and take off training method. If the runway is big and long enough you have the option of changing your mind if you make a bit of a mistake! The man was clearly mad but I was not going to turn down such an opportunity was I? I flew over the site once and noticed from the nearest kampong smoke and the state of the sea that there was next to no cross wind to worry about. I turned a bit too sharply to starboard and lost more height from side slipping than I wanted but still had enough in hand at about 1,300 ft., as I lined up for the final approach. I was told that he would take care of all the trim adjustments and all I had to do was to get the speed down enough to about 160 knots A.S.I. (air speed indicated) or 180mph (but not too slow), switch superchargers to MOD then to lower the undercarriage, (checking that both lights turned to green). This in itself causes a lot of drag or wind resistance and slows the aircraft quite dramatically to about 140 knots (or 160mph) at the same time the brakes must be released and their operational pressure checked (landing with locked brakes is not recommended!). Then at about 5 to 600ft and about a quarter of a mile out, the propeller pitch is set to fully fine to enable the engine to reach maximum power, which, except in combat, is only normally used for landing and take-offs. The radiator flaps opened to allow maximum cooling at full power and the reduced airflow through them at the lower speeds. The throttles are eased back to reduce speed and height on the approach then the fuel is switched from main tanks to the outer and higher gravity tanks which ensures that the fuel will still be available if a engine fuel pump fails on the final approach. Some pilots prefer to do this at an earlier stage of the landing routine! Then lower flaps to perhaps 15 to 20' which in turn causes further drag but with extra lift to enable a more gentle and slower touch down at about

110 knots. At this point it is a bit of sight and feel, as altimeters can be a few feet out due to barometric changes in the weather and if landing at an airfield with no such advice available one has to visually judge the last 200 ft or so as the plane comes over the airfield edge but still short of the runway itself. The next few seconds I found a worry as I was not too sure how hard I was down on the sand or if I was still almost skimming over the puddles. Well there was plenty of room if I wanted to throttle back and stop anyway. Then, if needs be we could swop seats while parked on the beach and he could take it off again. But no, we were loosing speed and were well below stall speed (about 90 knots) so I knew I was safely down. But I kept the tail wheel up in anticipation of going round again routine, with careful positioning of the joystick.

Then it was wake up quick, engage brain, as it was take off time. Remembering the Mossie's reputation for a quite unpleasant swing to port on take off, I opened the throttles very gently and progressively, while easing slightly back on the stick (I was worried that I might tip it onto its nose apart from the swing tendency) and with the port engine leading the starboard by a noticeable amount until I reached full power on both and was still pointing in the right direction! Great relief. At about 125 knots I eased the stick further back and the plane seemed to lift off the beach, almost by itself. Wonderful. Then back through the reverse routine. Up undercarriage, wait for both unlocked red lights to go out, indicating locked up, having already applied the brakes to stop the gyroscopic effect of heavy spinning wheels as they are being retracted while still climbing. Then switch back to main fuel tanks without the trace of a splutter. Up flaps and reduce throttle but only as far as required to enable the rate of climb (at about 135 knots or 150mph) to be maintained, from about 3,000 rpm and about 12lbs boost at take off down to about 2,650rpm and about 6 lbs boost. Watch the coolant temperature and if finally dropping back below the ideal of 90-95c., then close rad. flaps. I was quite surprised that these rad. flaps had a distinct effect on the lift of the craft but obviously much less than the main flaps. It still has to be adjusted for, by using the elevator trims. The change from nose up to nose down, and vice versa, while not dramatic is noticeable. Then level out at about 3,000 ft., look round, check all gauges and controls, if ok, start all over again. My next landing was not quite as good or as level and I was glad of the very wide beach. In an airfield situation, I might have finished up off on the grass, halfway down the runway, a bit of a crab-like bomber rather than a plane fast enough to be a fighter. The Mosquito is, of course both and exceptionally versatile and thankfully quite forgiving too. My next two efforts were quite good and I felt very confident, comfortable and all tension was gone. I became quite nonchalant but still very much aware of the incredible trust and confidence that had been put in me. To say I was flattered would be the understatement of a lifetime. My tutor, mentor and lunatic friend decided it was time to go home as we were getting low on the outer gravity fuel tanks and we still had the final landing back at R.A.F. Seletar to do with them.

I was getting all ready to swop back seats while still in empty airspace over the Straits of Malacca, rather than when closer to the busier skies near Singapore itself. But no I was to drive back and told to open her up, while at about 10,000 feet and put her into a very shallow dive down to about 3 to 5,000.ft and then level off. A full 350 knots A.S.I. came up very quickly and that is very fast even in the air. Small clouds went by at unbelievable speeds (for me) and I felt that it was all getting a bit out of hand for my very limited experience so I pulled out of the shallow dive and into a slight climb as I eased the throttle back and put the C.S.U. lever (constant speed unit, which controls the propeller pitch required and can feather the prop in emergencies if an engine fails, to reduce drag) into a coarser pitch and backed off the boost to only about 3-4 psi for cruising speed again. We headed straight down the Straits and only turned to port as we almost entered Indonesian air space above their smaller islands that are like stepping stones up to Singapore from Djakarta (Batavia in my father's time). Then to port again heading up towards the South China Sea, then to port once again just off the Changi end of Singapore island itself. Now, having throttled back to about 180 knots at 1,000 ft. My navigator having already got clearance from Seletar control to land plus a small change in the millibars to correct the altimeter. Plus having to allow about 20ft or more for the false reading caused when the flaps are down that upsets the airflow and pressure at the pitot head, high up on the tail plane. I was then waved on in with a cry of "Tally Ho" and a big, "thumbs up". All I presumed to encourage me over any possible growing sense of apprehension as I turned in and got into line with the operational runway.

Here we go again, this time with a very taunt stomach. The difference between playing about in the wilds with only our lives and a plane at stake is very, very different from landing illegally at an official and regulated military airfield, with possibly hundreds of critical eyes on you. I think my conscience almost got the better of me. Silly really because no one out there would be any the wiser unless I made a hash of it. It was to all appearances, just another routine flight returning. Not to me, it wasn't! Now lower undercarriage, both red light on as they lowered turning to green as they finally locked down, check freedom of brakes and plenty of pressure available (I was going to need it this time!) rad. flaps open, prop. pitch to full fine for maximum power, fuel cocks turned to gravity outboard tanks. I selected full flaps to enable me to land at a slower speed, in case my judgement of the landing point at the start of the runway was wrong. This would give me the option of slowing down sooner and before I ran out of runway or alternatively if the worst came to the worst I could apply full power and take off and come round again. I had visions of making a real mess of it all and having to fly off over the South China Sea. Then swapping our seats again in relative safety and letting the real pilot bring it back in himself. I need not have worried the wooden wonder behaved perfectly and dropped onto the tarmac in an almost perfect landing.

Unfortunately, I then nearly wrecked it all by not throttling back quickly enough and continuing at, albeit reduced speed, for too long down the runway before I eased far enough back and dropped the tail wheel back on the deck. The feel of the brakes was unexpected so I was very cautious and only used them to any real effect when the runway end appeared to be coming towards us a bit sooner than I expected! It was ok, I need not have worried but we had gone past the perimeter track turn off we should have used for taxiing in, so I was told to just go to the furthest dispersal point and park there. This I did, all the way feeling the relationship between throttle control and rudder pedals, which have the brake differential control linked to them. As you touch the brakes at full rudder (or even partly will give some progressive differential effect) one way, that side brake works allowing the other to stay free so the plane will turn the way you and the rudder wants it to (on the ground and at low speeds the rudder has no effect in itself). Some additional steering can be done by opening one engine further than the other, always taking care to keep the control column back so as not to tip forward and touch the prop tips on the ground!

Having parked at the remote dispersal point we had only just managed to both get out before the ground crew drove up, somewhat mystified at our choice of parking spot but too late to see who got out of which seat! My guardian angel just said, (tongue in cheek) "I think the compass is out a degree or two, do a swing and see that a fresh correction card is fitted before I take it up again. Thank you". Off we went, being driven back to control in a nasty little Hillman Estate car. The relative silence was finally broken after my mentor's obstinate pipe was finally lit up and I was then patted on the back and told "consider yourself checked out on Mossies, lad" and "always remember the pilot's mnemonic adage of BUMPFF. B., being brakes, off and pressure up. U, being undercarriage, locked up or down. M., being for Mmmm, I wonder what I might have forgotten. In our case, just praise the wonderful Rolls Royce MERLIN engines, whose temperature must be watched and controlled by the radiator flaps. P., being for the propeller(s), which must be at fully fine pitch for maximum power. F., being flaps and the final F. being fuel cocks". I had heard it before, of course but on this occasion it finally got burned into my flying soul permanently, like a good mnemonic should.

It will need little imagination as to who bought more than his fair share of drinks that night in the Officers' Mess. The pictures when developed from the authorised part of our flight were very good and served their purpose for several months to come. Our own Harrier escapade in the swamps had been made much easier by a similar recce, beforehand. The very successful swamp effort by the Green Howards (Regiment) that I have already relayed was assisted greatly by the sort of Mossie flight we had made that day. I managed to wangle five more Mossie flights but only one more with me driving. Little did I know that all this would put me in a very strong position, some years later, when working on Mosquitoes, to become junior test pilot as well as a Chief Engineer with Short Aviation, back in Scotland and later still with Spartan Air Services, in Canada.

It may appear to any reader that all the risks we faced were of a rather exotic type and on occasion could have resulted in us being killed, even two or three times, during the same episode. The exception to this came late one evening, just after a very heavy Sumatra monsoon deluge had finally eased off. Several of us were sitting on the veranda of Connie's mother's house which was set back off Ampang road. We all heard a skidding slither and a resounding thump. We rushed up the drive to the road only to see one of those Forties fast back American cars upside down on its roof, which itself was a couple of feet under water. The radiator was issuing steam having hit and broken a pole and the local power cables it was carrying, some of which were now snaking about on the car and wet road, sparking in an alarming manner. To cap it all, the upturned car was leaking petrol onto the road and into the ditch full of rainwater. We grabbed anything we could, from the odd fence post and broken tree branch from the storm. This was in an effort to fend off the lively, dancing and sparking cables so that we could get to the car itself to try to extract the two occupants who appeared not to be moving much. Luckily they had already opened their windows after the steamy rainstorm. We finally managed to drag them out through the openings, as both doors were stuck. Regardless of any injuries that they may have had, because we were all expecting the leaking and floating petrol to go up at any moment, ignited from the sparks. One of the occupants turned out to be a local Reuters correspondent and the other, a visiting fireman.

We all thought it a bit ironic that here were two international correspondents that had come to report on the dangers of living and working in Malaya. They themselves, with no help from the C.T.s, had turned their car over which could have killed them (once). They had hit a pole and almost stopped dead, which could also have killed them (twice). Then, as their heads were partly underwater in the upside down car, they could have drowned (thrice). If they had been wearing modern seat belts they would certainly have drowned in their very dazed condition. Then, the wriggling, live electric cables should have electrocuted them, particularly with all the water about (four times). Finally, if the floating petrol had ignited they could have been burnt to death while still trapped in the car (fifth death). So what is dangerous or risky, what is the relationship between life, perceived risk and death?

Apart from the short term fright in the Frank-mobile incident by far my worst worrying time was during one of the regular slap up meals on board one of the ships we were agents for (perks of the job and all that). On this occasion it was one of the French Charges Reuney(?) ships. As I have often indicated I did not drink alcohol. On this particular occasion I was offered an interesting and very refreshing drink, which was harmless. This I took for meaning it was not alcoholic. It was called *Pernod* and I had not come across it before even on my nefarious Scout trips to France at the end of the war. I was told to water it down, one to seven. They gave me seven parts *Pernod* to one of water, to make it cloudy! It was a long drink and I downed it in one and started on another, it being a hot thirsty day! Within a few minutes I was feeling a bit strange and it dawned on me I was perhaps a bit tiddly? I was not amused and spent the whole meal slowly and carefully feeding myself so as not to demonstrate any symptoms. Every move was methodical and deliberate. No one else seemed to notice but I was one step short of being petrified at the possibility that I might be getting drunk. Bearing in mind that I had to drive back to K.L. in my recently acquired XK120, after I had signed all the usual mountain of paper work. I was very, very worried about the situation. After the long and very relaxed meal we finally went ashore, with me gingerly plodding very carefully down the long steep gangway, step by careful step while hanging on to the hand ropes very tightly, to the motor launch waiting to take us ashore. Once on the launch I stood up, hanging onto a rail grimly with my head out into the breeze. Within about five minutes my head had cleared and by the time we landed I was able to run up the steps feeling normal and as if it had all never happened. It was none the less a very alarming experience in the circumstances, for me and caused worry for a longer period that I would normally have allowed myself to indulge in.

41. Impending sadness

I now come to, for me and from an entirely selfish point of view, the biggest and entirely unexpected blow. I have perhaps written more than I originally intended, to perhaps postpone the telling of the evil day when I had to leave a country that I had come to love and feel so much at home in. So many wonderful people, some of whom died for certainly, at least to me, the almost only worthwhile cause that has arisen since the Second World War. So many experiences, adventures, personal tests, both mental and physical that would be impossible in today's world, or even in several life times now. The harmonious blend of several cultures and almost total tolerance and acceptance of each other's differences. The variety of food and feeling of freedom to do anything that you wanted or aspired to. The only proviso being that you always conducted yourself in a civilised and considerate manner. The country never seems to show any negative attitudes about anything. Never an excuse, always a "can do" reaction to any request and with only a simple basic payment required. Never tipping as their pleasure is in the "giving". Fifty year on, K.L. remains my spiritual home. Here I go again. I'm stalling and postponing the inevitable.

In my many up country adventures, I, like many others had picked up (developed) a non-specific jungle fever that laid me low for several days and nights at a time. This coupled with my obvious over working led to the powers-that-be sending me on leave early, in an effort to save me from myself. I was not at all pleased and since I was assured that it was not malaria, I thought I should be allowed to work it through. In retrospect, they were right and I was wrong and blinded by an immature sense of mission. Mr. Lionel Davis, my overall boss, made the comment that I had "run out of candles to burn at both ends" apart from needing to be "saved from myself".

For the last month or so before my departure, life became one long social whirl. Chooi, Soon Joo and some of the other Chinese dealers organised a fantastic 10 course Chinese Dinner at a local Buddhist temple. Instead of the usual suckling pig. strange fish and the usual wide variety of debatable dishes, this one was all strictly Buddhist/vegetarian. Everything still looked like meat etc. but only when it entered your mouth did you finally believe that it was all based on mushrooms and soya beans in their many forms. Again I was the only European there. For once it was the Chinese that risked the hangovers not the Europeans! A lot of 5 star Hennessy brandy was consumed and a lot of faces became less inscrutable than usual! I still did not drink and had not lost the respect of local traders, as my ex-pat colleagues had originally predicted.

Arthur Davis and his wife invited Connie and me, for the first time as a couple, to their house for dinner. Arthur, although officially a bit disapproving, had always been very polite and friendly to her. His wife, as is the custom for European wives, was always a bit aloof. Despite all this Connie and I had spent quite a lot of social time with the Davis family on days out to the beach at Port Dickson and such like. Their children absolutely adored Connie as they played endlessly on the sandy beach. On this occasion, perhaps because I was no longer going to be a possible social embarrassment to her, Mrs Davis (yes I've forgotten her first name) was charming and her usual self, to us both. On another occasion the Harriers, some close contacts with S.B. and several regimental operational partners put on a 'do' for me at the Golf Club. Also invited was "Old Mac" who was, in today's parlance, our Guru. When I got there I was slightly disappointed at the few members in attendance. However that soon changed, as a few minutes later there was a deafening roar as a Dak. skimmed over the club house and pool at Mossie height and climbed rapidly (for a D.C.3) towards the mountains beyond Ampang. It turned and headed back at about a thousand feet altitude. Then as it crossed the edge of the golf course a dozen or so parachutes were disgorged. Some were to land within a hundred yards of the pool where we stood watching. We were then attacked at a rush with lots of noise and hopefully, only blanks being fired. The rest of the gang had arrived in style but certain golf players out on the course and some other club members were not amused and must have thought the emergency had finally caught up with them personally. The lunch that ensued lasted on into dinner in the evening and only finally wound up at about 2am. Memorable stuff and I was emotionally touched and flattered by it all. The price of madness?

The K.L. office started getting phone calls from several unlikely places, some military, some police and one from Government House. I walked in one morning to a very confused Arthur Davis and was greeted with something to the effect of, "what's your connection with all these people and what the hell have you been up to for the last two years?" One of the messages was from Alan Acton in Malacca, who invited, no, almost ordered me down to visit him before I went and to bring M.M. with me without fail! I now need to explain that Connie was known to most people and to her family as Mabel. I had an aversion to that as a girl's name, possibly as a result of a thieving maid that my parents had to fire for jewellery theft pre war. So M.M. was of course Mabel McGregor or Connie to me. We went down to Malacca the next weekend and were treated royally by Alan. He and Connie rabbited away in Malay to such an extent that I could not follow most of it. I should have known that via the Force 136 days Alan had met Connie's father, Old Mac but had not seen Connie for about seven years. She had grown up a bit, he informed me! I then got a repeated lecture about how lucky I was to have her as a girlfriend and all that. He thoroughly approved (unlike all the other European staff) and was pleased that she was following me home to the U.K. on my hopefully short leave. Alan was also obviously another one of Sir Walter Fletcher's appointees.

Alan was not yet supposed to tell me but they had almost agreed that when I returned to Malaya I was to join him in Malacca just long enough to learn the ropes with a view to taking over the whole area as the Area Manger (instead of only an Assistant Area Manager and a double Branch Manager) on his impending retirement. Alan insisted that in unstuffy Malacca, where all sorts of strange marriages were the norm, due partly to the Portuguese and Dutch historical influences, there would be no social or other impediment to us! No amount of persuasion from us both that marriage was not on the cards or had ever even crossed our minds, would dilute his enthusiasm for the idea. He thought he had it all worked out for us. My future nefarious activities would be mainly with the local Special Branch (as were his) Operational Groups and would not require long stints in jungle or swamps only in the local secondary ulu or bush, plus a bit of coastal marine patrolling with of course much less risk of recurring fever. Commercially there was much less shipping work than at Port Swettenham, very few imports by comparison and the local rubber market was less competitive and communications with the Head Office in Singapore were much better. Alan was almost entirely his own boss and had a completely freehand as would I, having apparently more than proved my worth. It was nice to know and sounded good. Alan had laid on the usual but more multi-racial dinner for over thirty local business contacts and officials that I would be dealing with in due course. They included an up and coming local Malay Councillor who was later to become the Governor of Melacca district or province (the spelling was changed from Malacca in due course, if not the pronunciation, in the same way Penang is today written as Pinang). He was apparently to become a close associate of the fourth Prime Minister, Dr. Mahathir Mohamad. We left Alan reluctantly and headed back to K.L. for another busy few days, which, would you believe, included a couple of talks or lectures on jungle craft and warfare to quite a number of recently arrived National Service lads who had no idea of what they were in for. I really did hope that my comments and advice would save at least some of them from finishing up in Cheras Road cemetery. The more experienced soldiers present thanked me and said that they wished that they had heard my comments before they were "thrown into the deep end", so to speak and that it might have saved some of their mates!

42. Templer, the General and the man

A few nights before I departed for Singapore, for the last time and to catch my ship home, several of us were invited to a special dinner at Kings (Govt) House. I had been there before in Sir Henry's days, but only for the odd drink and nibbles, this time I was to meet Gen. Gerald Templer, who I liked and admired (Churchill was right again). I gathered that he had been briefed by Sir Walter Fletcher as well as several meetings with Winston Churchill. During the meal one of our three Johns presented the General with a pirate type eye patch that he had painted gold. This was of course to signify the famous Nelson blind eye which we thought very appropriate in all the circumstances, (the real meaning would only be clear to he and we). The General's response was, roughly to the effect, "to the non-existent and long may they continue". Later during the evening the General made it clear that he was not only referring to the likes of us, but to the various other activities that are often required in a dirty conflict. Those, that if reported out of context, would raise an entirely unreasonable furore in the liberal and left wing press and elsewhere. The question of bandit heads occasionally being used for identification or in the instance I've already mentioned to counter communist propaganda and set many hundreds if not thousands of good people free of fear. A very good example of a biased press at that time was the fact that even when over a hundred people were being killed by the communists per month it took the death of at least 3 to 5 in one incident to even warrant an odd column inch back in the British press!

It was nice to have been recognised, if only in private. I reluctantly decided that the new General was more than capable of taking good care of my adopted country during my, hopefully not too long absence! Perhaps, here, a final story that also reflected the new general's down to earth, pragmatic and caring character. At one of the resettlement villages, the former squatters but now proud smallholding owners (and Home Guards) had been supplied with some shotguns to help defend their new independence. Unfortunately, the first time that the C.T.s turned up with their usual demands and threats these hapless new villagers meekly handed over their guns to the bandits. Templer was furious and considered it a very poor show, if not downright treachery. He flew down to them the next morning in a helicopter, lined them all up for a really good dressing down.

Reportedly, and through a Cantonese interpreter, he cursed them up and down and called them all sorts of bastards amongst other things. He then went on to tell them that he could and would prove to be a much bigger bastard than any they had met before. There was considerable confusion and not at all the reaction he expected. In the Cantonese translation it had come over rather like, "I know that most of you do not know who your parents are" but "I have to tell you that I have many more parents that I do not know, than all you lot have put together". After some merriment it was all sorted out and the ice was broken. Almost immediately a new hearts and minds situation developed and the General responded by ordering that they should be given a second chance and re-issued with shotguns. His faith in them turned out to be well placed and the C.T.s were driven off afterwards with repeated success.

I made a final visit to the office of another Eurasian friend, one Henry Grenier Junior who worked for his father and whose accountancy firm ran the Automobile Association of Malaya. They promoted and organised many of the car events that I had competed in including the famous Lornie Mile just outside K.L. On this occasion I was there to pick up my International Driving Licence with my almost criminal looking picture in it.

And so, sadly I flew by Malayan Airways down to Singapore having sent the Jaguar on ahead by train. I do not recall the reasoning behind this, as I would always rather drive anywhere, any time I got the chance. Having already handed in all my arms and equipment with the exception of my Hart .38 which I was going to leave in the Singapore company safe on Robinson Road, so that on my return, I would at least have it, on my imagined return drive up to K.L. or Malacca in due course. Ha, the best laid plans of mice and men... and all that. The many, not too sad farewells would have been very different had I known that I would not be able to return as planned. Within about six months or so as I expected, this being the usual contract leave period. I had managed to book a passage on another ship for Connie to follow and join me back in the U.K. later. She had already been shopping to get equipped with temperate climate clothing, which would be essential for her at any time of year!? Particularly when I was planning to take her up to Scotland to visit her father's roots. Her sister had been there twice but Connie had not yet done so.

43. Singapore, some thoughts

Singapore, being more formal and socially staid, was not as much fun from the goodbye and social point of view. It was enjoyable but not the same atmosphere at all. I was going to miss the informality of up country living (and dying!). The people on the island had no real idea of what was going on over the Johore causeway. It was another world to them so I should not have been surprised at the almost total ignorance in the U.K. 7,000 miles away and which largely pertains to this day. Who knows, perhaps this epistle will one day slightly change that? I feel the urge once again to demonstrate the incompetence and the ignorance of some of the Civil Servants that the Labour Government had sent out to Singapore to run things.

Some, recently arrived, new health chap was horrified to find that the vast amount of the Chinese staple, bean sprouts, were being grown in what he decided was far from ideal conditions. In a press interview he stated that these conditions were tantamount to sewers and would be banned. All future bean sprouts would have to be grown in approved conditions. Within a few weeks 'sewer' grown bean sprouts were fetching a financial premium! A black market in bean sprouts, can you imagine anything dafter? The next do-gooder change of policy was to ban suckling pigs, a long established Chinese food which featured at any special Chinese dinner. It was usually served up early in the meal when the crackling would be eaten then taken away and then later served up again as sliced meat with sauces. It was often the dinner centre piece in the way a boar's head was in medieval England.

On the other hand and rather more constructively, the Singapore Police employed a certain Colonel Young, recently retired from Scotland Yard to try and resolve some driving and traffic problems. He introduced double white lines to stop drivers cutting a particular long corner on a hill and which had caused several fatal head-on crashes. He then posted several constables along the double lines with batons to enforce it. At the same time a by-law was passed to stop people from driving one handed and with the other arm outside the car holding their roofs on. The same constables were instructed to strike the offending arms. It worked almost miraculously and overnight the habits of a lifetime were changed. I'm pleased to say that this no nonsense approach has carried on down through the years, making Singapore today, probably the cleanest and safest city or state in the world.

44. Racial prejudice?

Some personal thoughts on this subject; I've lived in it, experienced it, met and had good friends on both sides, in their own respective, natural or original domains. I think that to always labour on about the racial angle is very misleading and very counter productive. In truth, very similar prejudices abound over colour, race, religion, class and the status between military and civilian aspects of an administration, to say nothing of inter club football violent rivalry, all over the world. I maintain that it is all largely nonsense. It has more to do with habits, cultural values and behavioural patterns and rarely develops into anything very serious between individuals alone. It tends to be a group thing. Often, just a gang of troublemakers looking for an excuse to create mayhem. The sort of thing we see all too often from supposedly football fans and dangerous elements of the National Front. All looking to make political hay out of, often genuine, local concerns about unfair distribution of resources being used too favourably, to subsidise immigrants and asylum seekers, legal and otherwise.

The fact that a certain character trait, that we don't like seems to occur in a particular group or nationality, should only be regarded as incidental. It is often said that the individual American is very hospitable, generous to a fault etc. but that as a group they can be a pain in the neck, on occasion. That's with a nation that we have so many things in common with, from language, colour and religion in general. If we are travelling in some form of public transport and one of the occupants coughs, sneezes and spits in an anti-social way we get up and move away. That's nothing to do with his colour or religion but his, to us, unacceptable and selfish anti-social behaviour. You would not invite him to your house or be very pleased if your daughter wanted to marry such a person, even if he had the same coloured skin. Further, if your daughter brings home someone that you find, tends to urinate in the kitchen sink or over your door step you would not happily give them your blessing, be he a black, blue, pink or white man from either darkest African or the bogs of Ireland!

In some countries people pick their noses and teeth with vigour, in others they burp as loudly as they can to show their appreciation of a good meal. These are not habits we would welcome into our family circles. Even when ignoring all these points one has to conclude that mixed marriages are still not to be recommended as with the divorce rate running at about 50% and with a large proportion of the rest being only a form of armed neutrality, far from happy or content. It is surely very unwise to add another major potential stumbling block for a newly married couple to cope with? And is it fair on their children even in our growing ethnically integrated communities?

Whilst I was in Malaya and Singapore the gutter press at home would frequently try to make an issue over the supposedly exclusive British/European clubs. I see no provocative harm in people who are ex-pats., choosing to spend some of their social time with like minded people who also share their values. Particularly after a long day or week in a slightly alien environment. The Press never make an issue out of the fact that the golfers don't encourage tennis players to join their club and vice versa. People have always tended to be at variance and rather cliquey. It is normal and natural and certainly not always racially motivated, for like-minded people to want to socialise. I've already made the point about the fact that the military and civil administration did not share social activities and clubs, despite them mostly sharing skin colour, nationality, religion, cultural pursuits, sports and a common life and death cause and struggle. This often making it a bit difficult for our Harrier planning meetings to be held. Most European clubs did have their Asian nights, several times a year and they always went off very well. There being absolutely no them and us situations arising. Conversely there were Asian clubs that were so exclusive that no European had ever set foot over the front steps in a hundred years! The same Press did not make an issue over that. Usually I found that the average Asian had no interest or wish to visit a European club anyway, except on a business occasion and exceptionally, the odd misguided social climber.

In Malaya and Singapore I was criticised for being too friendly with the locals, sometimes by the men but mostly by their wives. With exactly the same attitude once back home in U.K., I was criticised for being a bit of a racist. On such occasions one tends to remember Churchill's answer when he left the Liberal party and joined the Conservatives. He pointed out that he had not changed his ideals and policies but the whole political spectrum had moved to the left. He remained where he had always been, consistent and rock like. So the question and definition of racial or any other prejudice is largely a nonsense and anyway, it always depends on where you view it from in the first place. We now live in a world where the majority of the Press and other media criminally abuse the subject for the sake of making and maintaining sales of their so called news which has, over time, conditioned the masses into accepting that only bad news on such matters is newsworthy. Very sad and certainly portrays the end of the sort of civilisation that many of us grew up respecting and unwisely taking too much for granted. We now have a situation where the Liberal/Left wing attitudes always choose to be blindly ignorant of the honest realities of life. The ongoing American, hasty and almost fanatical zeal to foist their idea of Democracy on, often tribal cultures and societies, has a lot to answer for. This has been clearly the biggest single cause of the criminal shambles in most post colonial countries. Now in Africa, after 10 to 40 years, I think it can be clearly seen and without exception that corruption and murderous mayhem rules, on and off in every single country. Economies in disarray, millions dead and the vast majority of those that have escaped death at their brothers hands are much worse off now than under the Colonial system. Any honest African that does not have a corrupt vested interest political or business will admit this point. The original status quo and a slower transition would have saved many millions of lives. That is not to say that colonial rule was always particularly good, fair or ideal but it was at least more equitable, practical and humane from the local population's point of view. The relatively few that were killed by colonial forces probably amount to less then 1% of those killed by their own brothers after home rule or had the Colonial Governments not managed to keep the inter tribal warring to a minimum beforehand.

The lying Press continue to cover up the real truth in South Africa, which amongst its many awful statistics now has a murder rate, realistically and reportedly approaching a HUNDRED times greater than before gaining their idea of freedom! They have a President who will not publicly denounce the rape of little girls as a cure for Aids and will not admit that H.I.V. is even related to Aids! Then there is Rhodesia, where the interfering outside world forced the acceptance of a murdering communist as a supposedly democratic Prime Minister.

Result? What was the wealthiest and largest exporter of food in Africa, on a per-capita basis is now starving, bankrupt and killing off any political opponents. Yes, it has featured in the news but not for long. Perhaps it is because only hundreds are being murdered each month not thousands. Will they wait until it runs into millions like Rawanda? People tend to forget that both the ruling A.N.C. in South Africa and Mugabe's lot in Rhodesia were always Communistic! The world should not be celebrating the growing success of these groups (on paper) as it will only lead to greater entrenchment and democratically impossible to shift or change them. Exactly the situation we now see in so called Zimbabwe. The other, over hasty transfer of power, was to India when the separation or partition of India and Pakistan led to more millions of dead, this time Hindus and Muslims and all that could have been avoided. But at least that area has settled down and progressed far better than anywhere in Africa, apart from their high risk of atomic warfare! And the ongoing Kashmir problem that was not solved at the original breakup surely proving that undue haste is very unwise. India being a relatively success was because it already had the infrastructure and a very large and efficient Civil Service, of mostly Anglo Indians, already in place.

The biggest and ongoing mistake almost all developed countries make is to allow ghettos and the mentality that then goes with them. Many years ago when I emigrated to Canada we were told on arrival and in no uncertain terms that we were to be New Canadians and if we did not like that life then we could "go back where you came from" We were free to practice any religion, have any interests or hobbies but to also respect and tolerate any other legal and acceptable conduct from others. We were to muck in and expected to integrate socially and particularly at work. We could live almost anywhere we wished with the emphasis on mixing and integrating and that colonies and ghettos were frowned on. The exception seemed to be the Chinese (again). Unemployment benefit was available but only after contributions had been made and amounted to only just enough to cover a basic roof over your head and one square meal a day. For anything else, you had to go out and find whatever menial task you could to pay for it. Incentive based and with no subsidising of lethargy. Unfortunately it would appear that Canada has now gone even further than some other liberal countries, by pandering to the idle, their screaming minorities and perverts.

These often being the parasites of society some totally ignorant and others, over subsidised students that still have so much to learn and often being cynically used as fronts by quite sinister elements of our society. This coupled with their lack of experience of life, to even start towards an intelligent conclusion. Nothing, in fact, based on any wisdom at all, to temper their erroneous judgements. Then there are, the great 'unwashed' and the criminal abusers of the system. While I fully accept the old slogan of, "no taxation without representation" I would maintain that anyone of a working age who receives the taxpayers money in benefit of any sort should not have a vote as to how other people's money is spent on themselves. After all, in business meetings and even in our highly inefficient council meetings, it is accepted practice for any parties with a vested interest have to leave the meeting and have no say or vote on the subject, contract or money that may be concerned.

The other major provocative action that often leads to resentments and a backlash is positive discrimination. This has been more prevalent in recent times and has led to women being promoted ahead of better qualified and experienced men and the appointment of an obligatory minimum of Asians, Africans, Arabs (more correctly, probably Muslims) and any other agitating minority, from homosexuals, feminists and abortionists onwards. This will inexorably lead to, not only a lowering of standards but be counter productive in that it will cause further resentment and racial and other prejudices. So society will loose out again, on at least two counts that could have been avoided. Particularly by the minority vote seeking hypocritical politicians. The almost silent and hard working majority will once again be largely ignored and taken for granted, making the practice of democracy very close to a farce.

Positive discrimination, as a social tool should only be used very sparingly, in special circumstances and for as short a period as possible. I will return to my favoured society, Malaya. After the close ties with Singapore were broken, mainly as a result of the lack of common ground on the same thorny subject of positive discrimination. In Malaya's diverse population, the Chinese were the ones with a work ethic, entrepreneurial drive, enthusiasm for a gamble and therefore had most of the money, businesses and local banks. Rather like the Jews in other parts of the world. The Malays, on the other hand were a quiet, gentle and mostly rural people. Most of the land was owned by the Sultans of the different states. To outsiders the Malays appeared lazy and apathetic and only prepared to work, just enough to make a basic living, even most of this was done by their women! The smallest group, mostly Tamils (southern Indians) were largely a labouring class only, although there were amongst other Indian minorities, many Indian shops and quite a few professional people, from doctors to lawyers, amongst them.

So, when the fourth and the only just retired Prime Minister, Dr. Mahathir came into power he had the almost impossible task of motivating his own race to seriously compete with the Chinese in particular, if the whole country was to progress into a modern integrated international nation. He insisted that they were not to be individual competing groups but all were now MALAYSIANS together. He insisted that every business, office, department, banks and all institutions had to have an obligatory number of Malays on board. The Govt. spent millions on sending the Malays, in particular, overseas, for advanced education and training so that when they returned they would be more than qualified to retain their new jobs, in every field. This then largely reduced the short-term need of positive discrimination and any short-term resentment hopefully just faded when it was seen clearly that the Malays now, had earned and more than deserved (hopefully) their positions in all aspects of society. Nothing is ever perfect and there are still cases of the odd Malay being given promotion over the head of an equal and sometimes better Chinese candidate. It did, however need a very strong, steady and highly respected leadership. The Prime Minister was to be seen day after day visiting and taking a real interest in every conceivable undertaking. Always approachable and prepared to cut any red tape required (Remember the formula of getting it right three time out of five being essential for progress?).

He did not suffer fools gladly he just did not suffer them at all! He was always prepared to stand up to be counted and was totally fearless in dealing with the biggest international businesses and even other governments in the outside world. Often making himself unpopular with them in the process. At the general election before last, which was held just after one of his leading ministers was being jailed for homosexual and possibly treasonable activities.

The outside world's media who clearly took the felons side in the whole matter made great efforts to paint the legal government as tyrannical and likely to loose the election and claimed right up to the polling day that it was neck and neck, and spent a disproportionate amount of time putting the minority opposition's case. The result was not anything like they had hoped and the Prime Minister and his government were returned with an even bigger majority! The outside media hardly even mentioned the result, as it clearly did not suit their liberal agenda. So what had occupied very heavy media coverage right up to the election was suddenly dropped as not now newsworthy. The news hypocrites, having failed to get their own way by influencing things politically just dropped the subject as it was not the news they either wanted or were interested in covering anymore.

The Muslim Malaysians still do not drink alcohol but you will find them in a hotel bar with Chinese or European friends or business contacts showing no concern about everyone else drinking round about them. At swimming pools you will see the Muslim women wearing T shirts and leggings while all the other groups will be wearing bikinis and anything else suitable. Again, no them and us problem. At restaurants you will see Muslims sitting at the same table with other Malaysians who may be eating pork and other unclean foods. There is a religious police force but they seem to be entirely for Muslims only and have no connection or even authority over anyone else? I'm sure my possible readers may think I am prejudiced but can you imagine all this in any other country in the world? No, of course not and further, they run their schools, legal system, all Government departments and businesses in exactly the same way and with the same discipline that they took over from the British, forty plus years ago. They politely ask why we, back in the U.K. have not retained the same high standards. Good question.

In all my years of hearing the archetypal Scotsman, Englishman and Irishman jokes I do not remember even one being of a malicious or unduly prejudicial manner. They and all the others including the Jews have always joked about themselves and it seems unfortunate that so many people spend too much time looking for trouble that may not even exist instead of worrying about the many more important problems of this world. Surely and very often the most important thing is to be laughing at ourselves, on occasion, first? There is less and less these days to laugh about so I'm all for more good humour and for once I will expose my own racial prejudice by actually agreeing with the French and their historic cry of "Viva La

Difference". Be it sex, race, colour, hobbies or any other non antisocial activity. The world is meant to be full of entirely different individuals not moronic stereotypes.

When I arrived back in the U.K. I claimed or prophesied that the Chinese with their numbers, abilities and business flair could one day take over the world. I was laughed at of course. However here we are today, only fifty years on and they are more than half way there, already!? Another piece of my prophesy was that the world will need to watch out for the Mad Muslims (meaning the fanatics and fundamentalists) in due course as they came into, mostly, oil wealth. My other prophesy was that the mad or fanatical Muslim fundamentalists would replace the communists as the world's greatest threat in the twenty-first century. Again the idea was pooh-poohed. They are however totally impossible to reason with if they can in anyway include their religion into any situation or dispute. More worrying is the fact that the Palestinians in particular, choose to teach and preach absolute hatred of the Jews to their children. Ignoring the fact that their plight was brought on themselves by starting the war that left the situation they now hate so much. It is and will always be a total waste of time to try and meet them halfway because from their religion's point of view they are always 101% right! Today it is only the Israelis that get anywhere near understanding this and knowing how to deal with them and they are of course being steadily undermined by our western ignorant liberal appeasers and do-gooders. That is not to say the Israelis are always right but it should always be remembered and allowed for, that the Israelis have absolutely no option but to fight to the death for their survival whereas even the most unfortunate Arabs have several, although not necessarily comfortable options open to them. Their fellow Arabs, seldom do anything to assist or relieve each other except provide arms and encourage terrorism. In some ways the Israeli's best allies are the Arabs themselves that can never seem to agree with one another!

45. Underway (finally)

On arrival in Singapore I left my Hart revolver and ammunition in the company safe and my Jaguar car with a friend by the name of Freddie Pope who ran a very good sports car garage, located between our office in Robinson Road and the docks. He also had the local dealership for Peugeot and owned an XK120 himself. His name will also figure in the winners list of the Johore Grand Prix. My company had done me proud and booked me a first class cabin on the *Willam Ruys* which was one of the flagships of the Rotterdam Lloyd shipping line. The other being the *Oranje* which is Dutch for orange their National colour and William of......, I presume? It was a large mail and passenger ship and should get me home again in about half the time that the P. & O. *Shillong* took to get out to Singapore in the first instance. The first class accommodation was up front and on the upper decks with its own swimming pool. Most of the passengers were unfortunately a little old for me and a bit stuck up and set in their ways. One of the few exceptions to this was the daughter of the British Ambassador to Saigon who was travelling home on her own. She was a very nice girl and joined some of we, relatively juveniles who sought younger company towards the rear of the ship with the Tourist Class passengers who had their own separate swimming pool. We all had a lot of fun and made many friends there. Little was I to know that later on I would meet several of them again in a different place and entirely different circumstances. Someone discovered that the Ambassadorial daughter was due, within a few days, to be 21 years old. So we got together and arranged a wonderful 'do' for her and later received a Cable and Wireless telegram from her father thanking us for our efforts. He by the way, or at least, so his daughter told us, had found a way to attend several diplomatic parties in one evening and stay sober. He lined his stomach with up to half a pound of butter first!

46. Cultural shocks?

The first cultural shock on board with regards the Dutch was that most of the males were indeed boors and treated the women in a very offhand way verging on the rude and disrespectful. We few young Brits., who chatted to the Dutch girls/women with normal, to us, common courtesy were inundated with female companions around the pool and at games. The Dutch males seemed to spend most of their time at the bar getting even more boorish and glowering at us for pinching their potential girl friends/companions. The girls were truly grateful and certainly appreciated being treated as fellow human beings! My conclusion was that the Dutch men and women come from different planets! By the time we got to Columbo in Ceylon (Sri Lanka) friendships were well established and since I was the only one who had been ashore there before I was elected to organise a suitable day trip for a couple of dozen passengers. Mail ships like this one only stay in port a few hours unlike the cargo ships, which might stay several days. Hence the reason that the mail ships could do the journey up to three weeks quicker. I tried to contact my hosts from my trip out on the *Shillong* but they were away at the time. I therefore organised a small fleet of taxis to take us out to Mount Lavinia. This is not up in the mountains like Kandi but a few miles along the coast from Columbo. The hotel sits up on a small promontory, which catches the sea breezes and has a nice beach. I still have some of the fun snaps of that trip showing a Dutch girl, whose name I've naturally forgotten, sitting on a vintage road roller with the makers name being Huber so of course it was labelled "Hubber Hubber", the popular American expression at the time meaning a bit of all-right!
A wonderful day out that was enjoyed by all. Back to the ship and the relative long leg across the Indian Ocean then north into the Red Sea having passed that dump (fuel) Aden.

47. Egypt again!

On arrival at the southern entrance to the Suez Canal there is always a wait to form a convoy queue before going through. Roughly halfway along are the Bitter Lakes where the convoy may have to stop several hours moored to one side to let the convoy travelling in the opposite direction pass before being able to proceed on, up north to Port Said and the Mediterranean Sea beyond. Unlike my trip out I stayed on board and actually saw all of the canal this time although not without incident! This was the period in history where Arab nationalism started to get even nastier than usual and the Egyptian authorities were getting even more difficult and Egyptian than usual! Col. Gamal Abdel Nasser while initially hiding behind Gen. Neguib's coup to get rid of the monarchy and depose King Farouk was encouraging all Arabs to throw their weight about. One sign of this was the announcement to all ships that cameras were forbidden while traversing the canal. They clearly had something to hide?! The new military junta was trying to convince the world that the coup was an entirely peaceful one with no nasty incidents occurring (an unlikely story I thought) no fighting or acts of sabotage involved.

Very early the following morning just after we had passed Ismailia where the road from Cairo then runs alongside the canal, the so called Sweet Water canal and the railway for the rest of the way North to Port Said, I spotted several burnt out and derailed trains that had not been cleaned up or cleared away. Problems were obviously still occurring and this was the sort of news that the so-called authorities were desperate not to get out. Hence the banning of the foreign press, censorship and the ban on cameras being used while passing through the canal. I was up on the top boat deck at barely dawn taking the odd snap shots of the evidence when one of the military guards must have spotted me because before I knew it I was under fire from the clown. At least five bullets passed quite close to me and two made holes in one of the lifeboats. Something told me that this was going to lead to possible further problems. So I hid my camera under one of the lifeboat coverings and having a well-developed criminal mind I found myself wiping off my fingerprints, first! Ridiculous.

The rest of the journey towards Port Said was uneventful but full of strange mirages. These were apparent lakes of water that of course did not exist and the impossibility to judge distances of the very few objects in the desert and its odd haze. I was therefore rather surprised to spot several ships apparently floating across the desert about a mile or so away. This turned out not to be a mirage and explained by the fact that recently the Farouk canal had been opened which appeared to be a short bypass canal presumably to assist and partly relieve the Bitter Lakes and reduce the normal delays. I had not even heard of it before nor had any of the other passengers. We must have all had other things on our minds in our Oriental backwaters!

On arrival and docking in Port Said the ship was invaded by literally dozens of thoroughly ill-humoured uniformed Egyptians. They rushed to the upper deck (as if the culprit would have still been there!) then demanded that everyone with a camera should assemble in one of the dining rooms with their cameras and all films. A few did turn up but most clearly ignored the order. They then confiscated a few films and threatened to keep all our passports unless the culprit owned up. At which point the ships officers told them in no uncertain terms that they were far exceeding their authority and if there was any further delay the shipping line would no longer bunker (refuel) at an Egyptian port ever again. "Try and explain that (loss of a large amount of hard foreign currency) to your superiors back in Cairo!". We left Port Said with only a short delay in the end and I rescued my camera from the lifeboat, unharmed. Two of my pictures were later bought by a London newspaper on my return to the U.K.

This incident was only the beginning of what was to become, the ongoing Egyptian interference and official obstructive-ness right up to Col. Nasser nationalising the canal some three or so years later when of course the British, French and Israelis invaded and took control of the canal for the original and rightful owners. This did not suit the Americans at that time so we poorer countries who were still greatly in debt to them from the war had to give in to the American blackmail. One wonders all these years later that if the Americans had not interfered then, would Nasser and then later, so many other murderous Arab nationalists that followed him have been allowed to get the Middle East into such a particular and insoluble situation. To say nothing of the terrorist activities all round the world now.

An amusing (though not at the time) part of my cultural education was to discover that the Dutch did not supply toilet paper in the tourist class loos. Nor could I find how to flush them on my first visit! While trying to find 'what did what' I finally came across a tap which I unwisely turned on and promptly soaked the front of my trousers with a very strong jet of water. It appeared that their loos were only equipped with a sort of bidet arrangement and I had found it when facing the wrong way! I sheepishly and a bit embarrassed then hurried back to my cabin to change the fly soaked trousers.

Then a pleasant passage through the Mediterranean, past the Rock of Gibraltar and into the Atlantic. Even the Bay of Biscay was uncharacteristically smooth. Southampton finally loomed up after passing Spithead and getting a good view of my old school on the Isle of Wight. I had very mixed feelings and although I was looking forward to seeing my family and all my friends it was not with any great enthusiasm generally. I felt something was missing, slightly apprehensive and a bit aloof about it all. Some of my new-found Dutch friends I was to meet again unexpectedly in due course.

48. Eulogy for a dog

On arrival home I found my family now living in a much smaller house but in a beautiful wooded estate well off the beaten track. Pat (the Kennel Club pedigree name being "Eugrawn" Welsh for Red Nymph I think?) the Pedigree Corgi pet dog that my parents had laughingly suggested originally, that breeding from her would help pay my school fees, went absolutely daft and leapt up into my arms at chest height and nearly knocked me over with her enthusiasm before I even reached the house that my father had named Court Echo. It appeared that every day without fail Pat had been sent out to look for me so that she would not forget me (my name). A nice touch and it certainly worked! I've since learned that a dogs sense of time is meaningless on our scale of things. They will be just as pleased to see you again after an hour, a week, a month or a year. It seems to make no difference to them.

Pat was meant to be my mother's dog but we had her a week or so too soon so that I might see her before I was due to go back to school. As a result she was crying all the first night missing her mother and fellow pups. I was the one that heard and went downstairs to stroke, comfort and keep her company. My parents came down in the morning to find me asleep in a chair and with my hand still stroking the back of Pat's head. So that was why the Corgi became imprinted on me. I was never a fan of what I considered toy dogs particularly after a big dog like Stengah. Corgis however, are not toys and have the heart of lions.

They were Welsh cattle dogs originally and have a great propensity to climb rather like mountain goats. As a puppy we were forever lifting Pat down from windowsills and the top of furniture to prevent her from later jumping down and becoming bow legged before her bones matured and set enough to properly support her stocky body against the constant impact on her feet. We were also instructed to never lift a dog under the stomach but to use two hands one to grab the scruff of her neck and the other the scruff just ahead of her hind legs. This supported her bulk and spread the load evenly right round and over the length of her underside. People thought it was cruel but it was not and she was perfectly happy and certainly in no pain at all. I have proved this with many other dogs since and if the ignorant do-gooders stopped to think about it they would realise that it is akin to the way a mother would carry her pups in nature as well. The other popular objection to Corgis is that they are constant yappers. They can be but this is picked up from their owners when and if they insist on rushing to answer a ringing phone or the doorbell etc. These highly intelligent and reactive dogs pick up on their owners responses, reactions, moods and are only rushing to please and be part of or join in their apparent mood.

Many years later Pat proved to be a remarkable dog. Even when she was well past the normal life span of Corgis, with kidneys riddled with cancer that barely functioned properly and when the vet thought she only had weeks or at best a month or two to live she would keep my mother going by insisting on being taken for a walk regardless of barely being able to do so herself. Pat kept this almost impossible effort and routine going for several years and was certainly responsible for my mother getting over the immediate and worst shock (wrong word) of my father's death. My mother was totally devoted to my father and had no other interests or hobbies to help distract her. She was almost lost without him. Hopefully my brother and I plus by then the grandchildren Laird and Laura helped a bit but on a daily basis it was Pat.

As usual I have somewhat digressed having leapt forward and now back about eight to ten years. The first week or two back from Malaya I spent rushing round seeing most of my cycling, swimming and childhood pals both male and female. Some were now working and no longer living at their original homes, which meant that I would only see them in the evenings and at weekends. The days were often unproductive and even when able to socialise I rapidly realised that we had all grown apart and had very little in common anymore. I had after all been living in what must have seemed to them another world. Our values and philosophy had changed. I am afraid I found it very difficult to get excited and enthusiastic about going to the cinema once or twice a week as a sort of ritualistic centre of ones life. We had, of course an interest in cars and driving in common but they found it almost impossible to believe that I had a post war M.G. let alone a Jaguar XK120! They had never seen one on the road only at the Motor Show! At this time over 90% of car production was for export only and you needed to be a Doctor or some essential worker to even get on the waiting list for any sort of car. Even the children's sweetie ration was lower than it had been during the war! Although the total shambles of the post war Labour Govt. was starting to improve now that Winston Churchill was back at No.10. Not much but just discernible.

A business friend of my fathers by the name of Skinner was anxious to sell off his splendid 1934 Lagonda 4.1/2 litre Pillar-Less saloon car, which was costing him too much to run during those austere days. He had married a French wife at the end of the war and had a very young daughter who at our very first meeting wanted to marry me! I only mention this because many years later she phoned me up one day and asked me again. That's another story, which I will get to in the appropriate time slot and in due course. The Lagonda car's registration no. BGW100 was very appropriate as it truly was a "B.......Good Wagon" and would certainly way exceed 100MPH. It combined real quality with high speed performance and was of course designed by W.O. Bentley after he left the Rolls Royce organisation but was not able to use his own name as this was still owned by Rolls Royce as indeed it was until very recently when it all got split up among the Germans. The Lagonda had a very strong chassis and a quite light aluminium 4/5-seater pillar-less saloon body mounted on it. The engine was a 4.1/2 litre Meadows straight 6 engine with both coil and magneto dual ignition.(aircraft practice). Twin large S.U. carburettors stove enamelled in black and with a Ki-Gas starting/priming hand operated pump (again aircraft practice) mounted on the dashboard. Which when starting the engine with the cranking handle up front made it a bit of a race to get back past the very long bonnet to the pump again to keep it going before it stalled, again. It was really a two-man operation and if only to share the hard work of turning over the large engine fast enough to start it in the first place. The front radiator grill had thermostatically controlled vertical slats which opened up as the water got hotter. The headlights were German Zeiss and had glass mirror reflectors and the glasses were actual focusing lens. The resulting headlights were better than anything I have ever seen since, even among modern rally spotlights. When they were dipped there was a clonk and they literally hinged down actuated by electrical solenoids. The suspension was controlled by Andre adjustable friction shock absorbers or dampers but in addition there were Tele-controls to the front and rear with their own pressure gauges so one could adjust the addition pressure differential to suit the load, speed or surface and while driving along. The car was trimmed in good leather and the seats were inflatable, again to suit the weight or comfort of the individual. There was even a rear window roll up blind for additional privacy or to cut out glare from a car behind. Controlled by the driver/chauffeur who had to get in and out with care to avoid the gear and hand brake levers from getting stuck up their trouser leg as they were both located on the outside of the driver's seat and leg space! (quite traditional, at the time). The car would do about 115 mph on any reasonable straight and cornered quite well for a saloon. My friends and I had many miles of fun with this high-speed limo and upset quite a few sporty types. It was clearly a car well ahead of its time and a credit to W. O. Bentley and much better than the cars still carrying his name in the late Thirties.

I accompanied my vegetarian conversion friend, Grant Tyler to both Pinewood and Elstree film studios and met Diana Dors and some of the old Sugar Bowl swimming crowd again. Diana had some total clown in tow by the name of J. Hamilton Gittings. She however impressed me then as not just another dumb blonde after all but a girl who could actually act given half a chance. My friend Grant seemed to only be getting bit or walk on parts and as far as I know never got a star billing again after his original *Danny Boy* part. I became very bored and my parents suggested that I should go off to Majorca for a holiday and relax. I never did and then Connie arrived and came to stay with us which gave me something to do, like taking her up to Scotland as we had arranged and for her to meet several of my friends who without exception were captivated by her. My parents however were not so enamoured and while liking her as a person obviously considered her to be too 'suntanned' which coupled with the usual mother thing about no girl being good enough for their son etc., did not help much! After a few weeks Connie went off to stay with some of her relations and her brother-in-law's family, then enrolled as a student nurse at Paddington Hospital in London.

To help negate my mid-week boredom and to rekindle a sense of doing something worthwhile, it was suggested that I have a chat with my father's older brother, Dr. James (Dr. of maths I think?!) who was either then or shortly afterwards appointed Academic Registrar at London University. With his help and advice I cooked myself up a suitable mechanical engineering course, which today would be a sort of Open University, work experience and correspondence course programme all rolled into one. I was not really aware that I was starting a dramatic change in future career. My father in his wisdom, looking back I think realised long before I did! In some ways he would have been very sad about it as it had always been understood that I would follow in his footsteps, which of course I was already doing by working out in Singapore and later in Batavia and Surabaya. With my comprehensive training and experience in rubber dealing I would hopefully and eventually have made as good a rubber broker as him? Thanks to my Shanghai remote university experience and qualification, I found most of the London course and practical work very easy but struggled with some of the complex (and to me often pointless) maths. It was good experience and discipline for me because a year or two later out in Java the lowest maths mark I got was 98%! At school I doubt if I ever did better than 60-70%. A clear indication that, an enthusiastic amateur will always do better than a bored, (so called) professional. To be the best in one's own field, work or job it has to be a vocation as well. This was proved to be so, more and more often as I progressed in life.

A month or so after returning I received a message to contact Sir Walter's parliamentary secretary who arranged for me to meet a certain Major Smyth at the Pall Mall Club for lunch. He was clearly a Guards Officer in both posture and manner although not in any uniform. I did not believe his name was Smyth and it was only a sort of keep in touch meeting when I was informed that they (whoever 'they' were was always a bit of a mystery) would be in touch again in due course to see how I was feeling (I was already feeling bored, frustrated and not very productive). It was indicated that it might not now be Malaya I would return to. To sum up; a very depressing and unproductive meeting from my point of view. However there was something I was finding much more disturbing, at about this time.

My mother had suggested that I should meet the new vicar of the local church as she was sure that I would find it of interest particularly with my now more worldly ideas plus having lived at first hand with so many other religions and that we would have a lot in common. How wrong she was! The man, if he deserved the title was a disgusting pervert by the name of Ten Bruken Cate or something very similar. I regarded it as an unlikely name at the time and still do today. All the women parishioners thought he was marvellous and doing such good work with the youngsters. I was horrified when I met him and promptly warned my parents not to let my brother ever be alone with this man and to, preferably, stop or discourage him from being involved in any way with his church activities for the youth which seemed to be largely boys. I witnessed his vile reaction to a choir practice when his leering was clearly demonstrating his greater interest in the boys than their singing! Yes, he seemed charming, was a good actor and very plausible at least to the unworldly and naïve. I was a bit naughty when he was trying to talk me into Christianity and he was horrified when I told him that almost all the best Christians that I knew were Buddhists! He, of course missed the point I was obliquely making. One, the Buddhists were not two faced hypocrites like most church going and professing Christians I had met at that time. Two, they actually practised, in their every day life, meekness and genuine outward concern for their fellow man, in fact all the supposed fruits of the spirit Christian attributes but without the benefit, knowledge or understanding of God and the ins and outs of his sacrificial Son.

My parents could not believe that he was a raving homosexual and suggested that the church would never appoint such a person and I must be wrong in my assumptions. Needless to say I was adamant and strange (?) to relate several months after I had gone off abroad again I received a letter to confirm my opinion and that there had been a huge scandal concerning several little boys and the vicar had been transferred. Even worse and to help avoid criminal prosecution he had hastily married one of the young girls to try and give the impression that it was all a misunderstanding and that he was really normal after all! The girl's life was of course ruined, having been pushed into such a marriage by her own parents who were church wardens and more concerned about the church's reputation than their own daughter happiness. Even more disgraceful was that other church wardens, our neighbours in fact during the war, by the name of Griffiths, even admitted that they knew what sort of animal he was when they appointed him in the first place! He already had a track record from a previous parish.

This was also about the same time that the disgusting Lord Montague had been charged with sexually molesting Boy Scouts camping on his land at Beaulieu. He got away with it the first and

I think even a second time but he went to jail for it finally. Today I presume he is regarded as some sort of pioneering martyr amongst his associates when here we are fifty years on with the same church appointing these abominable criminal perverts to senior positions including that of Bishop. Is it therefore at all surprising that the churches are emptying today? The clear anti-biblical teaching and the total hypocrisy are there for all to see. I am afraid I will never accept the modern euphemism for such perversions as being just an "alternate life style" anymore than rape or murder is acceptable as an alternate life style in any decent society. History also shows that homosexuality always leads to further perversions like be(a)stiality, paedophilia and total moral breakdown of civilised society. Finally I see the at the misuse of the English language when the word 'Gay' is used to describe such an abomination when it clearly should continue to mean the traditional and exact opposite such as something nice, happy, friendly, jolly, full of fun and humorous. A suitable non-perverted girl's name.

49. Setback? (or just a delay?)

Another business friend of my father's was a man by the name of van Beugen Bik who had a son, Tony. Our fathers thought we boys would get on as Tony had obtained an export XK120 (Dutch Quota?) and was anxious for us to meet so that he could pick my brains and share experiences about the car. This we did and arranged to drive up to Scotland overnight to visit Charterhall race track, near Berwick, on the borders which was another of those post war converted air fields where the racing was usually done on the perri (perimeter) track. So we set off late one cold and bleak autumn night with the hood down but well wrapped up in old leather coats, woolly hats and scarves. We headed off up the Great North Road, the old A1 and had agreed to share the driving, doing about an hours stint each. We would then stop and have a quick cup of soup or tea out of a flask and then set off again..

A few miles south of Catterick and after I had been driving for my hour or so Tony took over and seemed a bit disgruntled that I was averaging between ten and twelve miles more than him in each hour without any apparent effort or drama. He started driving beyond his skill and ability as if to show me he was a equally good driver. It started to drizzle on the straight bit of road past the well known military camp and as he turned into the village far too fast on the wet road, he lost it in a big way, mounted the sort of double stepped pavement and hit a stone cottage well above ground level damaging the top part of its front door. Seeing the inevitable impact looming I turned my head to the right just before I was thrown out catching the left side of my face and in effect pivoting on the top of the windscreen as the rest of my body spun over the top and landed on the pavement outside the cottage door. The car continued spinning backwards for a considerable distance and finished in the local pub forecourt.

I got up rather stunned only to find my mouth full of blood and teeth, one of which I remember picking up a throwing away in disgust. I think it was at that moment that I suffered the only serious vanity and depressing thoughts in my life coupled with the erroneous conclusion that neither I, my life nor my looks would ever be the same again! Then I quickly realised that had I not had all that woolen padding round my neck and face I could easily have been decapitated by the top of the XK's windscreen! That immediately switched my negative thoughts to realising that I should be counting my blessings, in all circumstances. The owners of the cottage were very nice about it all but I did hear later that the poor woman who had almost been knocked out of bed, had a miscarriage and I always hoped that it was not directly due to Tony's stupidity. They kindly produced the usual hot tea and I then realised, as it promptly ran out again from the side of my face under my left ear and down my neck that I was a bit of a mess!

I really do not remember how quickly the ambulance came but I do remember that it seemed to take a long while to reach Darlington to deliver me to the Memorial Hospital. Again it seemed to take ages to get any attention when finally the doctor stitched my gaping face together again. I was dumped into a ward with no other attention until morning when it was a kindly char lady who went and found a sort of pot with a spout that I could just use to pour tea into the uninjured side of my very swollen mouth. Tea administered in this fashion and the odd grape, again forced into the good side of my mouth was all the attention or sustenance I received for three days. It seemed that if I could not manage the food supplied it was just my hard luck!

Tony, it appeared, had told my parents that I had a bit of a cut face and there was nothing to worry about. They in turn could get no satisfactory information from the hospital so decided to come up and visit me. When they arrived I could see that they were horrified at what they saw. I was insistent on leaving hospital at once and returning south with them. The hospital refused to release me and my parents naturally thought that they knew best. Remember that I was still under the age of 21 and my parents had to sign the release documents for me. A bit daft when you consider the life I had been living and the magnitude of the decisions I had had to make on an almost day-to-day basis. However I was very insistent as I felt that I was going downhill rapidly but I even had to walk outside the hospital front door in my pyjamas on a very cold and wet day before they relented and after signing release and responsibility documents I finally got my clothes back. The train journey back south was grim and I felt like the proverbial death warmed up.

I did sleep better in my own bed that night but was on the verge of delirium the next morning. This I presume prompted my parents to phone our local doctor in Chipstead, a Dr. Steward who was on his day off. Probably because he knew the Henderson family propensity to only bother a doctor if it really was a matter of life or death, he, in fact came as soon as he arrived home and got the message. As he walked into my bedroom I can still remember his shocked expression and wrinkled nose. (it appears septicaemia was well under way and I stank of it). He rushed off only to return quickly with massive doses of some new antibiotic. I was not to be moved until (if?) I recovered from the infection. Later Dr. Steward admitted that he had never seen anyone recover from such an advanced stage of septicaemia before and suggested himself that it was probably my otherwise exceptionally clean (vegetarian) blood that was responsible. Plus of course the latest antibiotic which unlike the original massive doses of early penicillin did work on me this time. Thank God.

Within a few days I was out of danger and Dr. Steward had arranged for me to go into Guys Hospital which is of course one of the finest in the world. He had arranged for his brother-in-law to do the initial operations on my face/jaw bones to remove one tooth from the roof of my mouth and the other from pressing under my left eye! This wonderful surgeon's name was Pip Reading, so called because of his diminutive size but even more importantly his tiny hands which were world renowned for the fine precision work that he was almost uniquely capable of. He even had to stand on a box to operate! My operation should have taken well under an hour but it was discovered that the impact on my upper jawbone was so great that the broken bit was dead and would not therefore repair itself and would have to be removed. This he duly did and spent a lot of time tidying up and doing some groundwork for the plastic surgeons later, taking a full four and a half hours in the process. When I came round I was a bit confused as it was dark outside and I had missed a mealtime! I was even more confused to find tubes, drains and dressings emanating from mouth and nose that I was not expecting. It appeared that in addition to the dead bone job one of the errant teeth had badly damaged my lower left sinus or antrum in its travels and I had undergone a 'cordrul luk' (I'll try and find the correct spelling later) operation as well.

During the following week I was progressing quite well with

chatting up a very attractive and socially acceptable nurse so that when the very painful time came to remove the stitches from the roof of my mouth I was prepared to sweat blood rather than this nurse see me react to the pain inflicted on me by a rather (in my opinion) ham-handed ward sister. That was bad enough but later much worse was to follow. With what I can only describe as a hollow metal or tubular coat hanger hook a bit like a question mark. This was worked up my nostril and hooked through the side into the sinus then some flushing fluid was pumped up it into the sinus which expanded a bit as old blood and bits were flushed out down my nostril and some up and into my throat as well. It was b......y agony but I dared not move even a fraction as the hook itself would hurt even more, if that was possible. Then the antrum was collapsed and left to seal itself off and I was told never ever to blow my nose again as any resultant sinusitis would require an operation in future. The final removal of the hook was even more painful. Of perhaps the three most nightmarish experiences that I have had in my life that was by far the most painful and when coupled with the total inability to move even a muscle or to even cough out the old blood and fluid which felt as if it was going to drown me as well at the same time.

Naturally I soon got over it all and took the said nurse out to a London theatre about a week later. We got on very well and really did have a lot in common, I was quite smitten with her and it appeared she with me. However being, what I thought was a considerate gentleman with a still badly disfigured face with even the edges of my lower lip not matching up and to say nothing of the ugly scar still swollen and discoloured. I was not therefore prepared to inflict myself with even a perfunctory goodnight kiss on someone I respected and was getting very fond of. Was I? We parted with what I thought was a slight atmosphere and I thought nothing more about it until I phoned her about a week later to confirm our next date only to be told that she was disappointed in me and had been badly hurt, insulted and that I had been leading her up the garden path so to speak! She was keen on me but as I had not thought enough of her to warrant even a good night kiss, that was it! I tried rather pathetically to explain my motives to which I was told that I obviously did not understand women. She was right of course and I still don't.

Next came a series of plastic operations, which were carried out at Guys annex on the edge of Orpington in Kent. The surgeon was one of the wartime pupils of Archibald MacIndoe (later to become, deservedly a Sir) the very famous burns and plastic surgeon who pioneered such valiant work at East Grinstead on so many Battle of Britain pilots during the war. I was very lucky. I became such a regular that I was moved into a little end ward with only a couple of other patients. This had an exterior door so that the inmates could go out to a pub after lights out if they wanted and without going through the main wards and the hospital in general. I used this facility rather differently. I would drive up, often late at night in my Lagonda having been out for the evening and just change and climb into bed. The change of staff in the morning were none the wiser and I would just go along to the operating theatre when they were ready. Having not eaten anything while out the previous evening of course. At the later operations I was allowed to stay awake and watch in a large mirror as I was regarded as not prone to operational shock. It was very interesting but a bit strange to see oneself cut open and dealt with in an almost mechanical manner, hearing crunching and other noises but feeling nothing.

One instance I remember well was when they decided to remove the worst of the badly cobbled up scar material from my lip back down to under my chin towards my left ear. They started by very carefully marking out either side of the scar with what seemed to be a mauve indelible pen as they were to bring my lip line back together and in line while removing the hardened scar material from across my lower cheek. The local anaesthetic was then injected in and my face blew up and distorted quite a lot and bore no resemblance to its original shape. Hence the careful marking out beforehand as one side of the scar was now much more swollen than the other. The cheek was then cut wide open again with a fine scalpel very close and down one side of the hard scar material. Then with what appeared to be a pair of kitchen 'Kumfi-Kut' scissors the hard scar line was cut off the other side of the gaping wound with a strange grating cutting noise from the partly serrated blades. My lip was then opened up from the inside, some slicing, layering and repacking was done to leave the lip about the same size or thickness on either side of the planned join. Finally it was time to pull all the indelible matching marked pairs together and stitch the rather swollen and distorted two halves together again with very fine stitches and some clips. I was quite surprised at how little blood was involved and just how mechanical it all seemed.

I drove home a few hours later and returned for the stitches and clips to be removed about a week later. The swelling had almost all gone and there was only a small pale line where the thick scar had been and my lip was almost perfectly level and normal, I had witnessed an almost miracle. My healing rate once again surprised the surgeons and on one occasion they operated on top of another operation only four days later! As long as I live I will always remember with gratitude the Health Service, at least in the form of Guys Hospital and its many departments. I think I was involved with five different departments. One - E. N. T. (ear, nose & throat). Two - Dental surgery. Three - Plastic surgery. Four - Orthopaedics. Fifth - I can't recall at the moment but it certainly was not Psychiatric and no one even thought of or suggested the other modern bane and claptrap of counselling.

Some time later I was invited by Guys to be a prize exhibit at one of their International Open Days. Not often did they have so many departments involved with one case over such a short period of time. I happily and gratefully spent a whole day being poked at, peered at, tested, inspected and questioned by so many students and doctors from many different countries. Guys had (from my point of view at least) rebuilt me in as many months as it should have taken years! The speed at which it was all processed was questioned by one Ward Sister who it appeared was told in no uncertain terms it was something to do with the national interest and none of her business anyway. I had certainly never thought of myself of being in the national interest and there were certainly many, many others who also were doing their best to keep our island afloat. That expression at the time was very apt as Britain was at risk of sinking and not just economically! We were largely saved, apart from our own relatively puny efforts (as was also the whole of Europe (the Germans and the French now have very conveniently short and ungrateful memories)) by America's good will and financial generosity in the form of the Marshall Plan. (The fact that we would all be an important future market for them was of course never even considered!?). Joking or not I was very happy and grateful to be the recipient of any strings that Sir Walter and 'they' cared to pull for me. For, apart from being rather bored I did genuinely want to be earning my (national?) keep again.

At about the end of my surgery sessions the clutch on the Lagonda started to slip a bit and I was not too keen to get involved with either the work or the time involved and although it had been great fun it was not really my sort of car anyway. So I traded it in for a splendid little Singer 9 "Le Mans" two seater sports car rather like my MG TC. It was reputedly the car that had come third in its class in 1934 at Le Mans behind the Rileys. It had the brass plate on the dash to prove it!? This car enabled me to scoot about the countryside in a much more flexible way. It was a blue car and my oldest childhood friend Barry had a red MG 6 cylinder Magnette from the thirties and our friend Brian had a white MG PB from about 1937. We could therefore drive about in a very patriotic manner. Barry, Brian and me; Red, White and Blue! When most of my medical appointments were behind me I started to travel about a bit more, particularly after I had been down to my old school on the Isle of Wight for Foundation and Old Boys weekend. I was particularly pleased to see the plaque erected in the school chapel in honour of Donald Latter. It was nice to see him remembered at his old school as well as in a military cemetery outside K.L., 7,000 miles from home.

Being back at Bembridge it was also nice to meet old friends in the locality as well as school chums. While still at school I was lucky that another of my father's business contacts, a man named Stanton happened to own a big house close to the school named Howgate he also had a very nice daughter by the name of Hazel who had married Geoff the son of the main local boat builder, Wades. They had their main sheds on the Brading side of the harbour. When Geoff and Hazel first got married they lived in a converted war time MTB moored in the harbour and always had open house for several of us growing and hungry lads at tea time. Geoff was a very brave young man who had survived a bad case of Polio but fought back and although he still had a limp he had even become the cox of the Bembridge lifeboat by the time I had now returned as an old boy. I had great admiration for him. The Bembridge lifeboat was at the end of a long lane past Howgate that also led to the lighthouse. Located there, was/is a nice pub called The Crab & Lobster, which was frequented on a regular basis by our House Master, Mr. Stedman, (known to us all as the Beak due to the size, shape and colour of his nose) and Niel Rocke, the school's Bursar. They were both naturally referred to by us all as the Crustaceans. On more than one occasion very late at night on our illegal and out of bounds trips to and from the village to buy goodies to sell at a profit back at school the next day, we had to dive for cover into a ditch or over the Howgate wall to avoid being spotted by the Crustaceans weaving their way back to school in the Bursar's three wheeled Morgan sports car. Long after I left school and after Mr.Stanton died, the school bought Howgate as an annex and for overflow accommodation it being only just outside the school's original extensive grounds.

On my first visit back on the island I was introduced to the local yachting fraternity and went down again on several weekends to enjoy their company and a lot of boating as well. One of Hazel's friends, a big strong girl and local schoolteacher by the name of Margaret became my regular sailing mate. As can be imagined the social life apres-sail was much better at the Bembridge Yacht Club than with the toffee-nosed Spithead lot. To such an extent that a certain spirited Princess would come and slum with us, dancing with several of the members, complete with her chaperone and bodyguard in tow! On one occasion she talked us into helping her escape through the toilet window at the back of the clubhouse to join some of us at another party. She left a note explaining that she was absconding and not to worry, that she would be back to the hotel for breakfast! Her minders were obviously not amused because a couple of hours later when going from one party to another they spotted her travelling in the opposite directing, turned round belatedly to give chase. So we had great fun and with the Princess's encouragement rushing round the country lanes giving them the slip. It was a bit like a cops and robbers farce. The Princess thoroughly enjoyed herself and joined in all the good fun, we got the impression that she did not often get the chance? We returned her as had been promised in time for breakfast at the Spithead Hotel but we never heard what sort of music she had to face afterwards although I did hear later that it was not her last trip to the Isle of Wight!

At this time I finally thought my life was getting back into gear again and at the weekends that I did not go down to the Isle of Wight I would drive down to Torquay, sometimes in just my own car with the odd friend. The one that joined me most often was a lad from the village named Ken Foster who enjoyed dancing so we usually went to the Marine Spa Ballroom in Torquay. There, we had met two very nice local girls who were sisters and ran their own hairdressing business in Paignton (the twin town round the bay from Torquay) when we had first met we were unwise enough to offer to walk them home instead of driving them in relays (the car, the Singer, was strictly only a two seater). They claimed they lived just along the road but it turned out to be 4 to 5 miles each way, or so it seemed. It was certainly a long walk and nearly dawn before we got back to my car in Torquay.

We then drove along the coast the other way, towards Babbacombe for a bit and fell asleep in our sleeping bags on a grassy slope on the cliffs and it was late morning before we woke to blazing sunshine and noisy seagulls. A quick swim in the sea and then back into town for breakfast. On the several trips to Torquay we were able to sleep out on almost every occasion because the weather was so good and settled that year. Needless to say and very unflattering to the girls I cannot recall their names despite the fact that they came up on the train many months later to my belated 21st and farewell party at Court Echo, the night before I was due to sail from Southampton back to the Far East in the form of Djakarta this time. On other trips to Torquay the trio of red, white and blue cars would go down for the weekend as it really was a nice place, nice times and with nice people. My, almost, life long friends after a lot of encouragement finally seemed to break out of the dull staid British post war rut and allow themselves to enjoy some fun and semi adventure. I got the impression that they thought I must have caught something abroad and gone quietly mad. By the time I left them again they had decided that I was not totally daft, after all!

50. Gainfully employed again

During the period of these weekends to Torquay and the Isle of Wight I had been assigned to a new company (for me) with a view to going out to Djakarta (as it was still spelt in those days and called Batavia in my father's day) ostensibly to trade in rubber, tea and sisal mostly. There was also estate management, some shipping and to sometimes stand-in as my new firm's cartel rep., for cinchona-bark. This was very much a closed shop and a tight cartel on this vital substance from which quinine is extracted and used for the control of Malaria. Each year there would be a conference with interested parties deciding on how much would be released out into the market and what percentage each member would get out of it that year. I thought it was a disgrace that such a vital substance in saving many thousands of lives should be restricted since there was no actual shortage of the trees themselves. It was just another immoral world financial ploy like diamonds and more recently life saving drugs often costing little to produce but then charged at such astronomic prices that the world's poor and sick cannot afford them. These companies would rather see thousands die than, say halve their profits!

I was more than familiar with the rubber market of course and soon gained all the basic knowledge where Sisal was concerned. Tea was however something entirely new and I spent many hours tea tasting at the regular sessions on the top floor at our Eastcheap, London office which was only about a block and a half away from the office where I had received my original commercial training in one of the few remaining (after the German bombing) office buildings down St. Dunstan's Hill just above Billingsgate Fish Market. Being inherently a coward I managed to avoid meeting June Topsom at our former luncheon places. I was however particularly pleased with my tea tasting but not because I had ambitions to be an expert in that field (although useful in my new job) but because the practice had helped to retrain my taste buds and palate after it was thought that the extensive damage to various parts of the inside of my mouth might have left me with little if any tasting ability. Where tea was concerned I would not claim to have become an expert but I could regularly get most of the basic brews right and well over half the blends. My new firm was in fact a subsidiary of *Brooke Bond* the world famous tea company who used to use the famous chimpanzee tea parties so often in their TV and other adverts. At this time the odd briefing/meetings I had with Sir Walter or his organisations were usually held in Plantation House which also hosts the Rubber market/Produce market, off Mincing Lane.

During this time an exceptionally good looking and pleasant young man came into the Eastcheap office, he was perhaps about five years older than me. I cannot remember, for the moment either his first or second name which is quite ridiculous bearing in mind the amount of time and experiences we would share together later! I think it was David so David it will be for the sake of this narrative unless, as has already happened, things have later jogged my memory. He was on his way back to Indonesia after his several months leave and like me could not wait. He was returning to our Surabaya office which he managed. I think we took an instant liking to each other and seemed to have a lot in common. He too had been briefed by Sir Walter's minions and it appeared that we would be working together on the Borneo project. He had already made some exploratory trips over there but had no jungle experience, which is where I was to come in, obviously! Our conversation was slightly guarded in the office but I remember his parting comment to the effect that "I look forward to your visits to Surabaya to join me in some pig shooting". I was left slightly mystified as we were not on this occasion being allowed to shoot the communists 'pigs' (unfortunately)!

51. The nefarious element!

This other job or Borneo mission would be to reconnoitre as thoroughly as possible the Indonesian side of the border on the very large island of Borneo. Accurate and reliable information on their military presence, strength and infrastructure would give some clear indications as to Indonesia's possible future greedy intentions. The other side of this northern border being British territory in the form of British North Borneo with its capital of Jessleton which was still being rebuilt after the town's almost complete annihilation to thwart the Japs. Then the small Sultanate of Brunei where there were vague rumours of greater potential oil finds that Indonesia was thought to have ambitions to annex and add to their almost sole supply run by Caltex in the central southern part of Sumatra in the general area of Palembang and Jambi.

The oil rumours were enhanced by the discovery of potential oil deposits on the east (Indonesian) side of the Borneo border in the region of Balikpapan, which is on the south coast and sort of diagonally across the island from Brunei and thought to be part of the same deposits. Some of the military elements of the Indonesian establishment were making aggressive innuendos about it all being theirs (by right or might?). This they saw as cornering the market in South East Asia at the time and in the foreseeable future. Wealth and power being of course the usual greed factors. Then, lastly on the British side was Sarawak with its capital Kuching (Malay for cat) the southern and largest British area which in total, taken with the others takes up about two thirds of the smaller northern segment of the island. The remaining much larger (about 2/3rds) southern and at that time almost totally undeveloped portion of Borneo was all Indonesian territory, as were almost all the other hundreds if not thousands of islands in the area, having all been part of the former Dutch East Indies.

52. The journey back East

That of course was all for the future so back to my remaining time in UK. It was decided by the family that I should have a slightly belated 21st and farewell party before I went off again to uncertain places and for an uncertain period of time. Court Echo was bulging at the seams and since several guests had come long distances they were farmed out with some kind neighbours and friends who helped with overnight accommodation. There were a considerable number of both male and female friends (all very civilised) including two old girlfriends who had asked me to marry them (on separate occasions!) as they really fancied the life (not me) out East that I must have described to them. Then, as now I must have been a good advocate of and for Malay(si)a? When the party finally wound down at about 3am, I decided to start packing, much to my mother's consternation as she thought I should have started weeks before! I had no intention of sleeping anyway since there would be plenty of time for that at sea over the following three weeks or so. We hired a big car to take me and my big tin trunk and cases up to Waterloo station to catch the boat train to Southampton. We dropped the Torquay girls off at Paddington station for their journey home. It will seem terrible but I do not remember whether either or both my parents saw me off at the station or whether our farewells had been already been conducted at Court Echo.

I do not recall any details of the train journey to Southampton but was quite pleased to be once again sailing on the *Willem Ruys* despite the déjà vu aspect of it. Some of the crew were the same as on my previous sailing and the first class accommodation and food were still of the best. The difference seemed to be the ages and type of passengers. It was always risky for a wife or fiancee to travel alone as often the usual shipboard romance developed into them wanting to marry someone else by the time they arrived at their destination! It is generally claimed that the Sixties were the permissive years but looking back the signs of a universal *Peyton Place* were already with us in the fifties! I was hardly settled on board and on my way to the first evening's dinner when I was latched onto by a very good looking older (than me) Dutch woman travelling alone by the name of Miriam. She was certainly in her late twenties if not as old as thirty! We got on very well over dinner and we danced afterwards. I escorted her to her cabin later and was invited in for a cup of coffee. She promptly got partly undressed and climbed into bed while requesting that I should stay and read some poems to help her sleep!? She showed little sign of going to sleep that easily. After a couple of poems and like a coward I excused myself politely and almost ran away. We met again for breakfast and lunch but later in the day she asked if I would be offended if we stopped 'keeping company' as she had met someone else she wanted to spend her time with, I agreed and tried not to appear too relieved. The man she spent the rest of the voyage with was much older than her and looked like the BBC T.V. Brains Trust personality, Professor Joad, complete with goatee beard. He was clearly much more worldly and sophisticated than me. Little did I realise that I was to meet Miriam again, some months later in her own home and with her husband!

This was but the first example of strange or non-conventional marriage arrangements that I was to encounter. None of which, either had I imagined or been initially equipped to deal with and did not conform to my idea of sanctity. We were obviously moving into a new moral age and it was happening at a great pace. The loose moral ideas were spreading almost like a plague! The next example and almost immediately after the Miriam episode was when I met and dined with a very nice and friendly American couple. He was an accountant for Mobil Oil and on his way out to Bangkok and was getting off at Singapore to transfer on. He, I think would have been in his forties and his very personable wife barely into her thirties. She had been a child bride from the deep south of the USA and had a very ebullient daughter who was already as attractive as her mother. It turned out that the father was not a social animal and turned in for bed early every night leaving his girls to party and dance as late as they liked. He asked me to accompany them on such occasions, which initially I was quite happy to do. The four of us spent a lot of time round the pool and in each other's company generally plus usually dining together as well. The two girls were continually flirting with me and competing for my attentions. Each would try to sit beside me before the other got the chance. All very flattering and the father/husband, if anything seemed to encourage it! However after about a week or so when the situation was leading to the girls squabbling like a pair of children over who sat next to me the last time or who had danced with me more times than the other. When they started arguing over whether it was fair for one to dance closer to me than the other I thought enough is enough. Again, being a coward I baled out of the situation diplomatically. It must have been diplomatic because at the end of their journey at Singapore they all kept on about me being more than welcome to stay with them in Bangkok and how many months would it be before I could visit them?

For the rest of the journey I spread myself about a bit thinking that there was safety in numbers, spending some days at the first class pool and others at the tourist deck and pool as I had done on my previous journey on the ship. The sports or entertainment master obviously relished the general laxity of so many women and was nick-named the "bed master" which did not sound too unlike his official Dutch job title of (it sounded like) Baad Master. Whether Baad is Dutch for sports I never found out. The food on board the *Willem* was very good as usual and I have to say that the Dutch ships were much better on the catering side than the British ones, in general. I should add that this time I managed to pass through Egypt without an international incident. I bought a nice camel skin holdall bag but with poor stitching while in Port Said. Third time lucky? I did not even go ashore this time so as not to tempt fate! I do not even recall whether we called in to Columbo or Penang on this trip. I must have been getting a bit blase and a seasoned traveller by then? I did get to know quite a few other people, mostly Dutch or mixed that I would meet again later in different parts of Indonesia.

Arriving in Singapore was almost like being home again but I did feel a bit nostalgic about not going off up country to K.L. in particular. Malacca would certainly have done as an alternative but it was not to be. I had little time to dwell on such matters as the ship was only in port for a few hours before leaving for the final destination of Djakarta. In that time I had to arrange to off load some hand luggage, being the new hard top for my XK120 that I was getting Freddie Pope to fit before he arranged to ship the car over to Java, to Tanjong Priok being Djakarta's port at that time. I managed to talk a local taxi driver into putting the ungainly loaded pallet on his roof rack for a very precarious journey from the docks into town. Customs had no idea as to how to classify the hardtop and just waved me on, to avoid the paperwork? In addition to all this I had to visit my old firm's office in Robinson Road to collect my trusty Hart .38 revolver which I wrapped in some oilskin and wound it up in copper wire with a view to Freddie dropping the Jaguar's sump and securing the gun to the oil pick-up pipe plus a load of ammunition to be stowed inside the car's headlight nacelles. This so that I could smuggle it all into Indonesia. Since, with a touchy new native government they were not going to issue me (us) with a gun licence, were they? And "for what" they would want to know! I could hardly explain that I had come to find their possibly secret forward military bases in Borneo and whether they had any obvious intentions of invading British territory! Several small boxes of fresh bullets were stowed behind the headlights in the pods! Time being short I settled for having bowl of curry noodles with Freddie and his Chinese mechanics instead of the usual curry tiffin at the Cricket (Box) Club.

53. Djakarta

Next it was straight down to Tanjong Priok where I was met by my new flat/mess mate John Hardy who it seemed came from Carshalton Beeches in Surrey not far from my parents new home, Court Echo, and that we had some mutual friends there - small world. At that time the port and docks were out on a long promontory several miles from the Kota (Kota in Malay literally means a Fort but is still used to denote a walled town or city or latterly just a town, usually the old or original part). I would be working at the company office in the Kota area of Djakarta but in the meantime I was taken straight through the crowded and bustling city inland where the land rises slightly towards the outskirts. There we picked up a brand new dual carriageway, which took us out to a pleasant area called Kebayoran Bahru, which loosely translated means New Garden City, a very apt name. We turned off left at the first big roundabout and shortly came to HarriPeek Flats, a brand new "L" shaped block, one storey high. Company property I was told, and that I was to share, what until then had been John's ground floor flat at the back, away from the road and that had better water pressure than the upstairs flats!

I took a couple of days to unpack and acclimatise and met several of the other office staff and their families who lived in the other flats. They all seemed a nice bunch at the time, managers, accountants and legal staff. John was on the estate management side but was not experienced in trading any of the estate's produce. This was where I was expected to take over and set up whatever was required. It appeared that I had a reputation that had got there before me! Great things were expected of me it appeared. I was really looking forward to the buzz of playing the international markets again. The firm supplied me with a brand new Hillman Minx, which reputedly cost more than the London Chairman's Rolls Royce!

The reason being that the Indonesian currency, the rupiah was really only banana republic money worth not much more than Monopoly money, so much so that a slice of our salary was paid into a London bank account and the rest in rupiahs locally for the every day expenses. Since the currency was all but worthless we could not transfer any out of the country and back home. So where luxury items like cars were concerned the hard currency had to be bought on a sort of black market which upped the basic price considerably then there was an import duty of about 300% and then a sales tax of 200% (it may have been the other way round!). The Minx, unexpectedly turned out to be quite a good car and I used it on a day to day basis to and from the office even after my XK arrived from Singapore. The local Hillman agents and garage were quite good and was run by some local Dutch chaps and I had sufficient confidence in them to let them service the XK as well. There was only one other Jaguar XK120 in the whole of the vast country of Indonesia and that belonged to an Indian millionaire businessman. With the tax levels I've just indicated he would have to have been one! Although I did hear that he kept re-exporting the car to Singapore and re-importing it again every six months to avoid the excessive taxes. The shipping costs each time, I imagine he paid in local, almost worthless rupes.

Driving in Djakarta was wilder and a lot more congested than K.L or Singapore but it all seemed to sort itself out in the usual frantic Asian way! I adjusted very quickly and turned native in that respect quite happily. The Indonesians drive on the same side as us despite all the Dutch colonialists best efforts to convert them to their (the Dutch or Continental) custom of driving on the right. The story goes that despite all the bullying efforts of the Dutch to instil their culture and habits on the locals but where the rule of the road was concerned they finally gave up. Reputedly the locals stated that Tuan Raffles told us to drive on the left and that is what we will continue to do. This must have got up the noses of the Dutch authorities since they had lost out to British interests in so many other parts of colonial Asia. This, despite the Dutch (being much meaner financially than the Scots?) having encouraged their ex-pats to marry locally and become colonists. Whereas we Brits were usually on 3 or at most 5 year contracts the Dutch were on 10 to 12 years. The motive being that in that time the chances were that they would marry a local girl (without the British sort of stigma) and set up a family home with little need to return to Holland, so saving their Company or organisation the cost of even the 3rd class or tourist fare home!

The other indication of this was of course the point I made earlier when travelling by sea on the *Willem Ruys* (a Dutch ship). The youngest of the Brits were always 1st class passengers whereas the younger Dutch passengers were all tourist class until they became very senior in their positions. All this was clearly related to a story my father had told me about his time in Java, even back in the twenties. On his first visit to Surabaya he had met a man to whom he had said "oh you are Dutch are you?" to which the very indignant man replied "no I am not, I am one of only three genuinely pure blooded Hollanders in the whole of the Dutch East Indies!" Indicating that the integration policy was in operation long before my day and may even date back several hundred years when ships could be away from their European home ports for years at a time. Very pragmatic!

I actually quite enjoyed the competition of the drive to and from work through downtown Djakarta to the Kota area each day. So much so that my immediate upstairs neighbour and fellow employee, an accountant named Jim Thompson, would often ask to drive in with me as well as my flat mate John who was also more than pleased to let me do the driving even once remarking "heaven help the poor London taxi drivers the next time you get home!" The last couple of miles down into Kota were alongside a sort of running canal on our right where literally the world and his wife gathered on and off all day to attend to their personal ablutions and laundry on the water's edge. Literally thousands were always there at what was a social institution as well and it certainly brought home how highly populated that part of Djakarta was. This stretch of dual carriage way (with the canal in the middle) was joined by the odd bridge at each block. The name of this entertaining and interesting stretch of city was Jalan (street) Gajah Mada, named after an early Javanese General and Prime Minister hero dating back to the 1300's, I think!? Then at the end of a day's work we would return up the other side of the canal with the bathers on our right again, seemingly the same people doing exactly the same thing in exactly the same way and in exactly the same place as hours earlier. It never seemed to change but was yet always fascinating to observe.

After about a couple of weeks I finally got to meet the managing director who had been up country on leave when I originally arrived. His name was Ekins and I don't think we particularly warmed to each other. I think he was slightly resentful of the fact that London had taken a local decision where I was concerned without consulting or discussing it in full with him. It was bound to generate some resentment of course but he was not in the need to know loop other than the strictly commercial aspects of my job. To paraphrase; he said "I understand that you are here to change/improve the marketing aspects of our estate management department, to set up a new system and take responsibility for the market risks involved. I also understand that you may be away for possibly weeks on end on other business so I do not understand how this can be equated with the day to day marketing decisions that may be required of you? (as I had not figured this out for myself yet I could give him no answer). I am also instructed to introduce you as soon as possible to as many of the diplomatic, government and military contacts that I have social contacts with myself. Oh, and by the way, there is a Mr. Bruce of the British Embassy who wants me to bring you to the British Sports Club (another colonial 'box' club!) one evening to be introduced to him. He's a strange chap, no one here seems to know what exactly he does. He calls himself a Commercial Liaison Attache!?" That's about as close a summing up as I can recall after all these years but it is an accurate gist of it.

Mr. Bruce of the Embassy of course turned out to be my contact and conduit back to Major Smyth (of the Pall Mall Club, remember?) in London. I was not to ever visit the Embassy or be seen to contact Bruce himself but rather to occasionally date one of the two English girls working at the Embassy who were also regular player/members of the Club. They were both tough and wicked hockey players, of which more later. The Club had a wide selection of members including a very nice English woman who was married to a far from handsome Dutch man. He was so attentive, caring and genuinely concerned for her, one of the few exceptions to all those Dutch boors I've mentioned. At dances or parties as a couple they would almost always leave early as they really preferred each others company to that of the rest of the world. Hugo, being this woman's husband was, sort of tolerated in the Club as an honorary Brit. I thought he was often treated unfairly so with my usual naïve sense of fair play I put myself out to be friendly to him, not that we had anything particularly in common. Looking back now perhaps I respected his loving loyalty which was the exception in that rather amoral climate.

54. Nonnie

As a result of which and as far as I know I was the only Club member to be invited to dine with this couple at their own home where I was to meet several of their Dutch friends including a stunning girl by the name of Nonnie. She was tall, very strong, wiry, slim, athletic and what I can only describe as a potential Amazonian. Yet so utterly polite and feminine but unfortunately already married! Despite my immediate disappointment I chatted away to her most of the evening and while paying her some sort of compliment made the usual silly comment to the effect that it was a pity she was already married, to which she laughed and said that it never seemed to stop other men, so why me? And further that she was not really married in the true sense and if I would take her out for dinner the next evening to an Italian Spaghetti House down in Kota she would explain further. Naturally I agreed!

Well the next evening the spaghetti, the sauce and some Chianti red wine were all exceptionally good. The candle lit dim booth added to perhaps my first intimate dinner ever. Nonnie turned out to be an exceptionally appreciative first date and I became quite smitten with her. Her story was simple but very sad. She had been born in Java and lived there all her life as had her parents. They had all survived internment under the Japs but not without some harrowing privations. After the Indonesians got home rule, Merdeka (freedom) they hounded as many of the Dutch out of the country as they could, even those that had been born and brought up there, some families even going back several generations!(I do not remember any cry of ethnic cleansing then!). The locals had to be given almost every job whether they were capable or not and of course most were not. Hence the countries virtual bankruptcy and worthless currency. Nonnie's parents had been deprived of their legitimate jobs, had their home confiscated and were then deported. Nonnie should have gone off to Holland with them but she still loved the country too much and wanted to stay as most of her friends were in Java. The only Dutch being allowed to stay were those in essential jobs that the locals could not even pretend to do.

One of these was a male school friend who was a first class newsreel camera man needed by the Indonesian Government. for all the national propaganda being dished out. He worked for the local equivalent of Movitone News or Pathe and until they could find or train up an exceptional local replacement he was given a series of short term contracts and allowed to stay even though his family had already been deported. Simple solution, he and Nonnie got married and she was allowed to stay as his legal and apparent wife but she would still have to leave with him when he was made redundant! Nice people! He was rarely home as he had to work very hard all over the huge archipelago making a non stop series of propaganda documentary films. So in effect he and Nonnie were not married in the usual sense and just remained good family friends as they had been from childhood.

Nonnie & me with Jaguar XK120 and its new hard top. Djakarta 1954

Nonnie was also not allowed to work at her career of hotel receptionist and public relations because the authorities always forced one of their own into such jobs. However the manager (an old family friend from internment days) of one of the leading International

hotels employed her as a volunteer and paid her unofficially at some risk, out of the tips pool I think. I met Nonnie's non-husband on a couple of occasions. He was a very nice chap (not typical Dutch) and genuinely pleased that she had found
a friend to takeher out and about a bit. I was pleased too! Of course it will be obvious that people like me and the company I worked for were allowed to continue to exist because the country was desperate for hard currency and required people like us to earn it for them as they did not know how to work the international markets for their country's produce and they were not going to nationalise all the estates owned by foreigners in a hurry either as it would lead to an overseas boycott of the same produce.

Well there is my second strange marriage story. The first being the Americans onboard ship on their way to Bangkok. The third one will be coming up soon. Nonnie and I spent a lot of time together and I would often pick her up from her work on my way home where the two women servants would just lay an extra place for her when we arrived. Other evenings we would go to receptions and house parties, eat at one of the clubs or return to the spaghetti scene! Some weekends we would go off up to the cooler hills behind Djakarta to Bogor which is only about one thousand feet above sea level but the change in climate is very noticeable and the rain and thunder storms are quite dramatic. Today, fifty years on, I believe it is almost a commuting suburb of Djakarta! The road up was not very good but fun in a sports car! The road could not support the size of population so I presumed that most journeys and goods were by rail. Bogor has one of the best Botanical Gardens in the world and is a truly remarkable place. The Kew Gardens people had a lot to do with it in its early days and reputedly Stamford Raffles himself was fond of the place. We all know of his founding of Singapore but it appears he was a considerable influence and much wider travelled than I had realised. The Bogor gardens had huge lily pond leaves that the local kids could walk across with the aid of pair of a sort of snow shoe! It was the first place I ever saw both Scots pine trees and palm trees growing beside each other! There was a large rare and special palm tree with high scaffolding and a platform round it. This to enable it to be pollinated at the first chance as it was possibly the only example of this tree left.

Carrying on beyond Bogor further into the hills and still on the railway line through the entertaining (for some drivers!) Puncak Pass is the city of Bandung which is still only about 2,500 feet above sea level, it was even milder but received a lot less rain. The city itself is not that attractive but its setting is. It appears to be ringed by volcanoes, some of which smoke mildly! The rural area is very fertile as a result and is composed mostly of tea plantations. We would usually stay at one or other of them since as a company we were their agents so had regular social as well as business contacts with the managers and their families, a nice arrangement. It had been mooted to promote Bandung to become the capital of the country but I think that in unsettled times the cost and practicability of improving the roads and general infrastructure would have been totally impractical.

After Bandung the area seemed to pass into what might be called rebel territory because it was not fully controlled by the central government. The area was, at least from a local tax point of view run by the southern central city of Djogyakarta. As you entered the district you removed your Djakarta issued car tax disc and bought a local one which had to be displayed all the time you remained in their area and hastily removed again before returning to Government controlled areas. If you were caught with the rebel disc you were in deep trouble because no one was supposed to support or subsidise the rebels. It was not unknown for the odd car to be confiscated! The whole area was one that Europeans were advised not to visit. Needless to say and with a competent interpreter like Nonnie I did venture there a couple of times and found the ancient ruins of long ago kingdoms very impressive. The infamous volcano Merapi a few miles north of Djogakarta erupted very seriously while I was in Indonesia (not in the actual area at the time) it wiped out some villages and cost quite a few lives. Nonnie's husband was there and shot some fantastic footage which we were able to see privately but which was extensively censored by the authorities before it was shown to the general public!

The next regular weekend escape was to the west coast of Java, south of Merak which was unspoilt, never crowded (local superstition about it being a place of ill omen, presumably as a result of the multi deaths and devastation from Krakatau's eruption) and had some excellent beaches which looked out over the Sunda Straits towards Krakatau the volcano that woke the world up (1883) with the biggest explosive eruption and tidal wave ever! The volcano/island of Anak (child of) Krakatau is still growing and is about 2,500 feet high already! Of course contrary to the Hollywood film about the episode, called *East of Java* it is in reality, WEST of Java! We found it quite eerie to visit the multi brick foundation that is all that remains of the original lighthouse that was completely washed away by Krakatau's tsunami reputed 100 ft. plus wave! At this largely deserted beach area we would often be the only car parked in the area but sooner or later some local chap would turn up with his mobile food stall to sell us roasted sweet corn on the cob, buttered and spiced to perfection plus a wide selection of fruits. Another vendor would offer a wide selection of fruit juices, well iced. The ice coming from a wrapped block and planed finely on an upturned carpenters wood block plane. Being so fine it almost instantly melted and produced a cold drink with out the usual rattling ice cubes. A simple but clever idea, so why do our pubs etc. not do the same thing? The sweetening of the drinks was produced by fresh sugar cane being put through a simple mangle to crush the cane and squeeze out the juice.

55. Commerce again!

Perhaps that's enough about the nice leisure times, so back to work. Within a few weeks of working in the Kota office and after I had been selling the estates produce into the world markets it was clear that it could be done better and more profitably. The established procedure was for the estates to phone or advise us that they would have so many tons of this, that or the other ready for shipment to the docks at Tanjong Priok. We would then find a buyer and arrange the shipping and insurance etc. The estates were responsible for their own quality selection and packing, (unlike the Malayan arrangements) and sold only when they were ready with a crop so were stuck with whatever price happened to be current at the time. This quite often meant they were selling at less than ideal times since many other estates might be selling on the same sort of seasonal basis. Which, with so much available would inevitably lead to at least a small drop in price, even during the then still current Korean war.

Solution? Simple, either sit on the stock if the market was set to rise which might be only days but often weeks! The better alternative was to sell in advance (as we often did in Malaya and Singapore) for a given future delivery date and in some cases before the produce was fully grown, tapped or picked! This would often give several months of market time to try and anticipate the best time to sell. So having demonstrated this potential several times by delaying even a few days, three of the biggest estates asked that we take a view of the market and in effect gamble on prices improving in some interim period. Having sold enough to cover their essential production costs and general overheads and take a gamble on the rest. Needless to say I was now once again partly dependent on my father's view on the world market coupled with my own developing nose for such matters.

My own company as managing agents were paid a flat fee plus a very small commission and therefore had very little to loose but a lot to gain so I was given the all clear from London as well, enabling a new system (for Indonesia anyway) to be started. I think I can say that we won at least eight times out of ten! We were now in a position to buy and sell both spot (current) or futures which could mean that we might sell one day at a reasonable price and then the market might drop a bit a few days later when we could buy it back at less than we had originally sold it for so making a profit on paper at least temporarily. Then wait a while until the market went up again and then sell again making a second profit out of, in effect the same original shipment (in practice it would be someone else's similar shipment in quality and tonnage).

If it was felt that the market would fall in the months ahead then we would sell at the current high price, production that would not be ready for shipment for three or six months. If we were right then a much better return was earned than would have been the case if we had waited until it was ready and then sold it off as spot. If we were wrong and the market went up we had not really lost anything but just not made as much. Even this could be guarded against by buying for one period and selling for delivery at another and other permutations on the same theme. Some of these techniques were referred to as straddling and hedging (as in hedging your bets at a race course with the bookies!) and go along with other market descriptions of being bearish or bullish meaning to be careful and wary or optimistic and aggressive, respectively. Other expressions were words like going or selling long or short on something or a particular period of delivery or shipment. Long indicates buying or stocking up and awaiting a higher market price in the future. Short would indicate selling off at a good price and expecting to buy back at a lower price later, so making a profit both ways.

It was also possible to intermingle all this with an alternative settlement market which in effect is only paper and often with no hard produce to back it up! There would be a regular settlement day monthly or quarterly depending on the market and the produce involved. One might find that out of the thousands of tons involved back and forth one might finish up say ten tons short of parity and have to go out and buy physically the ten tons to cover the deficit and to balance the books as it were. So then if you could buy in again at a lower price than the original paper selling price one would have made a further profit. But like dealing in shares it can also go the other way and one could come a cropper. I hope that all this will be of interest to some readers in understanding my active and calculatingly trained mind. I revelled in it but can understand others having mental breakdowns over it all.

Now a historic story that is directly related. When my father returned home on leave to Windygates, Fife all those many years ago and he described roughly what be was involved in at work to his mother, (my granny, Janet McLaren) was absolutely horrified and convinced that it had to be against the law to sell anything that did not yet exist or had not even been grown yet!

On to slightly more serious matters, in fact the underlying reason for my being in Indonesia in the first place (apart from just earning my keep financially and making a lot of money for my employers). Now that I had set up a marketing procedure for some of the estates I could go off and leave the planet for even a month if needs be just leaving very simple instructions for each estate's situation which could be summed up basically as "if the market price goes up to "X" then sell but if it drops below "Y" buy back in and when it rises again even only to "Z" then sell both lots! Confused? Don't be. If "X" = 10 and "Y" = 5 and "Z"= say 8 then "X" will have lost 2 but "Y" will have made 3 so the combined transaction will still have made 1 which is still a profitable down side bearing in mind that if the original "X" sale had taken place it would have been profitable in itself since it was a high market price to start with. So the final profit is really 1 + original planned profit combined!

In my planned social life I was instructed to make and encourage an acquaintanceship with a particularly obnoxious young Indonesian Colonel Kepala by the name of Yos. The kepala bit just means head as in a headman of a village (kampong) and the Indos. seemed to have a lot of spare colonels rather like the Americans! This particular one, Yos claimed to be one of President Sukarno's many nephews and was in contact with our Embassy (and others too, I am sure) involved in arms procurement and in the usual corrupt way expected to be entertained on a grand and regular basis while any negotiations proceeded. I'm sure the British tax payer would be horrified to learn that their money was used to ply little runts like Yos with good food, booze and women in the national interest. All of course to assist millions of pounds of business (usually on credit as well).

Yos was always keen to go to European based parties because as a supposed Muslim he could then get away with being drunk in their company and in the interests of business he would be found somewhere discreetly to sober up, usually with some hired female companion that he could be photographed with to ensure the growing strength of the business relationship! All that side was the Commercial or Military Attache's business not mine. I was to inveigle as much information out of him as to what the wild boar shooting was like on Celebes and Kalimantan (Borneo) plus arrange friendly introductions to military contacts in those areas to arrange for hunting and gun licences in those same regions. Plus of course, who apart from him was to be bribed and by how much? Tolerating this obnoxious little hypocrite socially and having to be a hypocrite myself by smiling sweetly did not come easily particularly when I was temped to flatten him on more than one occasion! However when be was in his usual stupefied state late at night he talked about anything and everything and was very easily led to any subject of our choosing! He felt he had to prove that he knew everything about everything and knew everyone of importance. He gave away a lot of state and military information and was even a bit derogatory about his uncle. Bung Karno. At that time the President, Sukarno was trying to give himself a benevolent image and encouraged his people to think of him as Ah-bahng, pronounced Ahbung meaning elder or big brother (a bit communistic?). This then became shortened from Ah-bahng Sukarno to just Bung Karno.

The President was another loathsome character who had been a lover or at least an admirer of the Japanese during the war for his own political ambitions and ends. He had been quite prepared to sacrifice many of his own people's lives if it was expedient politically. And now he was being far too friendly and tolerant of the Communists as well, even for the liking of most of his more devout Muslim political friends and supporters. Above all he was dangerous and unpredictable and several parts of the nation were on the point of erupting. A bit like their own volcanoes and as there were so many different tribes, races, religions and languages it was perhaps not surprising that it was an all but impossible task anyway without resorting to fear and repression. When a leader such as Sukarno needs to try and unite oil and water for political ends, fear and the threat of a just war will sometimes help to unite, at least temporarily, the different factions involved.

56. A sad faux pas

My most difficult task to date was a social one. Nonnie and Yos clearly disliked each other intensely. He, because his drunken advances had been repeatedly rejected which he was not accustomed to as he seemed to think anyone's wife or girlfriend should be available to (the great) him. She because he resembled a particularly sadistic Japanese officer in circumstances that she understandably would not talk about! The last thing she wanted were those sort of memories. This coupled with his rudeness and disrespect presented me with the problem of trying to explain to her why I was not able to defend her honour better and positively and also why I still associated with him in all the circumstances. Of course I could not and I must have sounded a bit lame if not cowardly as well. The explanation that it was a question of business did not satisfy her. And when I suggested that she not accompany me to such occasions the immediate response was "oh so you prefer his company to mine?" I was beaten and deeply resentful that I could not do much about it.

It all came to a bit of a head one evening when Yos was drunk as usual and none of the women present would even speak to him. He then flounced about shouting that "you are all a bunch of whores anyway so why should you be so choosy?" I very nearly blew everything, as in anger and with rapidly loosing patience with the worm, I snapped back at him in not very accurate Malay "then why do you not bring your own whores to these parties?" There was a horrified silence as it had come over to the effect that I was agreeing with him that they were all whores in the first place but that he should bring his own instead of using other peoples! In the heat of the moment I had also used the more serious word, sundal which means an outright prostitute!

Of course most people soon realised my mistake and even laughed about it. I may have imagined it but I sensed that Nonnie appeared to remain a bit hurt. This coupled with several trips to Surabaya without a full explanation may have given her the wrong impression, that there was another girl there. These really were only genuine business trips but not entirely the company's. As David was busy organising our future boar hunting trips to Celebes and Borneo and already had several useful contacts among the commercial and civilian boat people (some he claimed were ex (hopefully) pirates) who were continually going in and out of restricted military zones with impunity. The local police and army acquaintances were quite happy to issue both gun and hunting licences but needed Djakarta's agreement which was of course why it was important for me to keep in with Yos and his like, back in the capital regardless of Nonnie's feelings on the matter.

57. Surabaya

Surabaya, although a big city is a much smaller one than Djakarta and occupies the same sort of position on the north coast of Java at the east end of the island as Djakarta does at the west end. It had a much larger natural port area then Tanjong Priok. The whole atmosphere is different, it's very relaxed and not almost frantic the way Djakarta is. The streets are much wider, almost suburban and the buildings set back and farther apart. Once out of town its immediately into countryside whereas Djakarta has ribbon development that seems to go on and on. Its so long ago now but that is my lasting impression of the place. I liked it and always enjoyed my trips down there. The people were also more relaxed and friendly, more like the Malayan Malays. From the road and flight point of view its the last stopping off place before legendary Bali. David meantime had been very busy since we first met in London. He had made several trips up to Makassa, the main city on the island of Celebes (now known as Sulawesi). From there he had managed to organise a couple of boar hunting trips into the interior of this strange shaped island. He even had the trophies on his office desk to prove it! Four evil looking tusks! He had been part of a group of European ex-pats along with a couple of Indonesian army officers and a Dutch/Indo friend by the name of Hugo, who had been able to stay on and join the new Indonesian army. This, in his case because he was part Javanese himself, was married to a local girl, had three children and the wife's father was a district or provincial mayor. This was of course another useful and important bridge into our planned activities!

The pace of business and the social life were so totally different. The best way of making this point is to describe an average working day. Up before 6am, breakfast and into the office by 7am, work solidly until between 1 and 2pm (6-7 hours) then finish work for the day. Stop off for a leisurely lunch and cool drinks with friends at a club, open air restaurant or sometimes at home or at someone else's home until about 4-5pm. Then into bed in a cool air conditioned and almost sound proof room. One of the servants would then wake us at about 9 to 9-30 pm when we would go out to a club, restaurant or a party at a friend's home. The most usual seemed to be a dinner dance until about 2 am and back to bed for another four hours before getting up again at 6am and start all over again! This way we were living two full days in one. I thought it a splendid way to organise both one's commercial and social life. I have often wondered why such a good idea had never caught on elsewhere. We got a very full days work done, slept for full 8 hours and managed a weekly night out every night!

However this did not stop me, while dancing one night, from falling asleep on the shoulders of a girl by the name of Anastasia or whatever the Dutch equivalent is? The tune at the time was the haunting melody, *Oh My Pa-Pa* and I had been dancing in my sleep and had kept going even when the music stopped. Slightly embarrassing. Anastasia was very nice about it and we continued to dance now and again when I was in town and happened to meet in the same social group. It turned out that she was either the granddaughter or great-granddaughter of one of the Sarkie brothers who were the founders of the larger international hotel group which included Raffles in Singapore, the Eastern & Oriental in Penang and many others which I had not until then realised. The only time I had even heard the name Sarkie's hotel before was in the post-war film based in Vienna called *The Third Man*, involving drug smuggling/dealing, which starred Orson Welles who played the part of Harry Lime. Anton Carras played the haunting theme music on the Zither.

Another thing I liked about Surabaya was that we could go on a car rally most weekends which enabled me to see a lot of eastern Java that I would not have seen otherwise. A lot of attractive coast line, coral and other beaches plus amazing volcanic mountains. All of which was capped by the almost magical first sight of Bali, off the far east coast of Java. The day was a hot sunny one where we were but Bali itself was almost hidden in a blue tinged mist across the water. A sort of mythical Brigadoon type of setting. I could hardly wait to visit the legendary island, when I finally did I was not disappointed. On these amateurish rallies David and I would use his company car which was a Ford Zephyr or Zodiac, after my Jaguar seemed to have tiny wheels which in turn seemed to wear out the front tyres at an alarming rate. So Surabaya was a very relaxing place but where we all worked and played very hard. An unusual combination and I have often wished that I could replicate it but I fear such days are long gone. However I appreciate how blessed I was to have lived at a time when such a life style could be practised and experienced.

58. Smallie

Meanwhile, as they say, back to Djakarta and perhaps a good point to introduce my third strange marriage story. The firm's recently arrived accountant who lived in the flat above John and me, Jim Thompson and as I have already mentioned he often accompanied me to work as my passenger to avoid driving in and through the mad house as he saw it. On the several occasions when John was off up country visiting estates Jim would confide in me that his marriage was not entirely ideal and that he and Smallie, (he being well over 6 feet tall and she barely 5 feet high) whose real name was Marion were not properly married! (what another one?). Eventually it came out that he had been fostered by Marion's family who had brought him up as one of their own and as a big brother to Marion. They had just been like brother and sister all their remembered lives. When Jim got the job to go to Djakarta the parents had sort of said to him something to the effect "you'll be marrying Marion and taking her with you won't you? Such a thought had never entered either of their heads but they thought, with someone else paying the bills for such an adventure, why not? Jim being a really nice and very grateful chap felt obliged and agreed, so they got married. Immediate disaster as the initial failed effort to convert a brother/sister relationship into a physical marriage went so wrong as to generate almost revulsion on the part of Marion. Their one failed effort was their last!

They both kept the matter to themselves, particularly from her (their) parents and sailed off for a new life together without anyone knowing that they were only brother and sister again and on which basis they now got along as well as they had always done before. Unfortunately they did not have too much in common from a social point of view. Jim was a bit of an opera fan and wanted to spend most of his spare time with the local amateur dramatic society but Smallie was more sporty and wanted to play tennis and hockey. This of course meant that their developed circle of friends and clubs were very different and did not have too much in common anyway! The problem of transport then arose having only one car between them as they would be often going to different destinations which were not always with one being on the way to the other of even sharing the same time span. The inevitable soon occurred of course; "would I be kind enough to drop or collect Smallie somewhere?" Because Jim would be elsewhere at the time etc.etc. I should have realised that in effect I was setting myself up for gossip. Since I would be seen taking her 'out' whereas in reality it was only to drop her off somewhere before I went on my own date with Nonnie. Then it might happen that Jim would ask me to pick her up first and then him slightly later. So we could all head home in the same car. I noticed that this also raised a few eyebrows too but I naively ignored them. On occasion Jim would invite me to have dinner upstairs in their flat before taking Marion with me to pick him up at some 'do' (when his car was in dock and he needed to share my company car for a day or so).

This of course did not go unnoticed by one particular senior employee's wife in one of the neighbouring flats. Then one night after John and I had taken our respective dates home and I had returned alone, Marion was waiting in our flat with some coffee ready because she could not sleep (maybe our hilarity downstairs earlier had kept her awake?) and wanted to talk. On such occasions if anyone was up in the night, within minutes one of the servants (with proven second sight) would appear to see if they could do anything or were wanted for any reason. Even to cooking a multi course meal for unexpected guests or if one of us had only just got back very late from up country. The servants all lived on the premises and never missed anything! You might even say we were permanently chaperoned! Needless to say the nosey neighbour's wife just happened to notice this occasion and assumed the worst of course, and started feeding the rumour mill further. A few days later I told Jim what appeared to be afoot and he agreed to go with me to see the nosey neighbour's husband who obviously thought he should take his wife's side in the judgemental stakes! Unfortunately, Jim in his efforts to clear me of any wrong doing was unwise enough to say "and even if they were having and affair I would not care anyway!" This of course made matters worse not better in the director's eyes, who obviously had the same sort of mind as his wife. In retrospect and being fair to the director he may not only have been trying to ensure that there was no dissention in the ranks that might impede the smooth running of the office he was responsible for. He could also have been genuinely, and quite rightly so, concerned about the moral reputation of the company in a rather conservative country. I give him the benefit of the doubt but not his wife!

The situation became quite a problem because with Jim and I working together and living, in effect next door, travelling together to and from work frequently and with his wife coming along and needing to be collected from time to time. There was no clear cut escape from it all except when I was away up country or at Surabaya or later over in Celebes or Borneo. It was a salient lesson though and one I have never forgotten!

Marion Thompson 'Smallie'
Bali 1954

59. Kim Ling Lee

Next, a saga or series of stories that almost deserve a book in their own right! I was down in the smaller part of the port area which deals with the myriad collection of coastal and inter island (Indonesia has well over 10,000 island in its archipelago) ships and boats moving all sorts of spices and products and taking supplies back again to some very remote places. On this particular occasion I heard a loud voice saying "Tabe(k) Tuan Jagooooah X.K. Bob" (Tabek is Malay for greetings, the K is silent and is pronounced as Tabay. Tuan is Mr. or Sir and, of course some Asians have a problem in pronouncing the word Jaguar and the letter "R" in general, hence flied lice instead of fried rice. I turned round to see a very scruffy looking Straits Chinese waving his topi at me. I was rather taken aback initially until he came over and introduced himself. I did know him but certainly did not immediately recognise him. His name was Kim Ling Lee and I had first met him through my XK120-driving wealthy Chinese stevedore friend from Port Swettenham, Eddie Eu Eng Hock. Eddie had introduced him to me as the best and wealthiest smuggler across the Straits of Malacca. I had not taken the comment entirely seriously at the time. I was now to learn, happily, that Eddie was right.

When I had first met Kim Ling Lee I had been delegated by Eddie to take him up from Port Swettenham in my Jag. to the Chinese Opera and restaurant in the Bukit Bintang amusement park in K.L. Eddie was throwing one of his lavish parties largely in Kim Lee's honour. Kim was dressed immaculately in white dinner jacket and a very fancy and colourful bow tie, which looked a bit incongruous. Kim was one of those Chinese that it was impossible to put an accurate age to. My vague guess was anything from forty to fifty-five years old. We got on well and had a lengthy conversation about our mutual hatred of communism. He, it appeared, had lost several fairly close relatives back in China to both murder and torture at the hands of Mao Tse-tung and his Red Brigade. Of course I knew all about the smuggling that went on, OUT of Sumatra to Malayan ports of all sorts of produce. This because the sellers could get immediate hard currency instead of 'banana money' through the official Indonesian system. I remember that the worst smelling cargo of the lot was unsmoked wet slab rubber. It was slimy and horrid but was cheap and could be ground up locally and used for low quality products, so leaving more of the good Malayan smoked sheet for export. The other rather nicer product to handle and worth a lot of money but very bulky was patchouli leaves which when boiled down were distilled into an oil. This is then usually the expensive basis of high quality perfumes as it is very slow to dissipate or evaporate away so making the quality perfumes stick and longer lasting. It was such items as these that I assumed Kim Lee transported and traded in, along with tea, copra and all sorts of spices.

Well now I had met Kim again and regardless of his present appearance I invited him back to my flat since John was away at the time so I thought there would be no social problem about it. My motives were of course very selfish as I was very keen to get up to date news of my friends and associates back in Selangor, from Eddie Eu Eng Hock onwards. Although not normally a snob I did not think Kim's appearance would make him very welcome at any of my usual dining haunts. Wrong again because when I collected him from his boat he was once again immaculate. A very deceptive smuggler this one! My two women servants had produced a better meal than they had ever done before and I borrowed some of John's brandy for my guest. The evening went well and after extracting most of the Malayan news from him and several brandies later he got a bit maudlin about his family back in China and our mutual hatred of communism.

He said, "you pink devils (the Chinese regard us as only pink and themselves as white which in the case of Kim was funny because of the fact that his ancestors had clearly married into the Malays at some stage and therefore was distinctly brown for a Chinese, (Straits Chinese or, I believe sometimes called Baba-Nonya Peranakan?)) may be beating the C.T.'s in Peninsular Malaya but the commies are getting ready to go in through your back door from Indonesian Borneo into Sarawak. I have seen shipments of arms and equipment from China being delivered and taken up river to bases that some elements of the Indonesian army are cooperating with. As you know Indonesia wants all of Borneo and as soon as the British leave in a few years they will be ready to pounce and take over. (as of course they did later in East Timor as soon as the Portuguese left). In the meantime they will encourage the communists groups to probe over the border and cause unrest while claiming that it is nothing to do with them officially. It is of course known in certain quarters that some of the Indonesian border area bases are quietly feeding and supplying these marauding groups of communists and that Sukarno himself is knowingly turning a blind eye to it all in the hopes that later he will reap the territorial benefit. However many of his more staunch Muslim army officers are very concerned that they themselves and even the whole country may be taken over by the communists if they are not carefully contained." That's about as close as I can recall the details now but it is an accurate gist.

He then told me that he had often helped Force 136 during the war with smuggled goods and supplies and had even run guns into the Island of Pankor (small world!) and regularly smuggled rubber and tin out again and then transferred it onto British ships at the northern end of the Malacca Straits off Banda Aceh (the most northerly city on Sumatra) or among the Andaman Islands which were outside the usual Japanese aircraft patrolling area, before they in turn returned to Ceylon with it. He claimed that he had personally killed many Nippongoes as he called the Japs., and communists too he added. I pressed him on this and he said that he had been blackmailed by the communists in Medan on Sumatra, which was his home port, to carry arms and equipment into Malaya for the C.T.'s. If he did not agree then more of his relatives back in China would suffer. So he agreed but the crafty smuggler that he was (is) told the commies that he was sure that the British/Malayan authorities were watching him and it would be very unwise and dangerous to risk it but he was willing to try but it would be on the clear understanding that it was their responsibility if it failed! Along with the arms and supplies he was to take in four important communist officials to accompany the shipment. All of which were to be put ashore south of Port Swettenham into the mangrove swamps of south Selangor (small world, again!) which are diagonally across from Medan. Kim told me that he simply killed the communists wrapped them all up along with (my guess would be that he may have kept a few guns etc. for himself) the guns and equipment plus some rocks, into an unmarked sail. Then bound it all up in baling wire so that it would be many years before there was any chance of it coming up to the surface again after being dumped over the side.

Later when he returned to Medan he told the communists that their comrades and equipment had gone ashore in the dark, that he had heard a lot of shooting and thought that a naval patrol boat had spotted them. The commies seemed to swallow the tale, stopped their threats and never asked him to do it again. It appeared that this had all happened a few weeks after we had originally met and dined out in K.L.!

Since I was in Indonesia to assess the activities and ambitions of the Indonesians as regards the British parts of Borneo, this news was a bit of an unexpected bombshell and would indicate that the Indonesians were more ambitious than had been thought. Because if they grabbed ALL of the British or ex British territory they would get any future oil automatically. Of course, even worse if the communists were not then contained by the Muslim and other elements of the government, Indonesia would run the risk of becoming a communist state which would spell an international catastrophe. Without waiting for clearance and acting completely off my own bat I immediately talked Kim into taking me over in one of his ships on his next trip from Djakarta to Pontianak which is the main port on the south western coast of the Indonesian part of Borneo.

The next morning I phoned Bruce at the embassy and he arranged for one of the girls to meet me for a date at the sports club that same evening for a long dinner, on this occasion it was Grace. She was the brighter of the two girls and knew what she was supposed to know but never got curious about anything else. She was well trained and picked for her 'need to know only' job. After dinner I took her back to my flat, first to give the impression that it was indeed a date and secondly there was some information to relay to her that could not be risked within the earshot of even other Brits. and particularly not the odd journalist. I finally took Grace home at about 1am only to find Marion Thomson waiting for my return with some hot chocolate, having left hubby Jim upstairs snoring I presumed. Luckily Eu-Bah, one of the servants hovered about until Marion returned upstairs to her own bed. The next morning I told Jim about his wife's nocturnal visit, to which he replied, "Smallie can be very thoughtless sometimes, can't she?" And apologised for her! So who's naïve then?

A couple of weeks later when John was back again, Grace and her cohort Eleanor from the embassy came to dinner to make up a foursome. While John was busy trying to make his mark with Eleanor, Grace quietly told me that against their better judgement I could use my initiative as the possibilities and repercussions of my news were of such huge potential consequence it must be confirmed if possible. If it became necessary some plausible cover story would be fed into the company to explain that I might be away for up to two months! I was to give Grace a list of any extra equipment that I might need from telephoto lens camera to exceptionally powerful binoculars etc. Plus any special documentation that I thought I might need to explain my presence in such a remote but sensitive area, a naturalist, an anthropologist or just an all round nosey tourist. The choice was mine.

I did not tell them that I had recently retrieved my .38 Hart revolver from the Jaguar's sump while giving the car a service, of course! I had over fifty rounds of ammunition, which had been smuggled inside the Jaguar's head light pods. These bullets I dried out in the kitchen oven one day when the servants were off. I nearly forgot them and wondered how I would have explained the situation if they had all exploded? In the meantime I had found that the best place to secrete the gun and ammo was in lightly padded bags along with some silica gel desiccant, on the driver's side in the Jag. Up in the almost secret compartment, high behind the driver's seat which normally would hold the car's side screens. I had practised several moves and had got the time down to six seconds from standing nonchalantly beside the car to firing the gun while it was still hidden inside the soft bag. The problem would be different in Borneo and the question was, where to keep it most of the time and how to wear it with light tropical clothing without it showing but still quickly retrievable when and if I thought it might be essential. Visions of hornets nests and no escape came to mind vividly all too often.

I also started thinking that the days in the Malayan jungle from distance point of view they were going to seem like child's play compared with the vastness of Borneo more so since I was going to be mostly on my own and also from the back up point of view. This question can perhaps best be understood if I say that the remote areas of Malayan jungle were already perceived as vast in one's mind and in practice. Very roughly the total length of Malaya from the Siamese border all the way down to Singapore was not even 500 miles yet it could take up to three months to get a message through all the jungle tracks from end to end! The length of Java is about 600 miles and the distance on Java from Djakarta to Surabaya is approaching 500.

Then going north from Surabaya to Makassar at the southern end of Celebes is a little more at about 550 miles plus a further 300 odd miles up the coast to Palu and then across another 350 miles of water to Tarakan on an island just off the coast of north eastern Indonesian Borneo. At the western end of Borneo where I was to go alone, to hopefully confirm or otherwise the Indonesian and or communist threat I would have to start again with the same sort of long sea journey of about 450 miles from Djakarta up to Pontianak the main port on the west coast of Indonesian Borneo and which, as far as I know is the only real town exactly on the equator?

Islands like Sumatra and Java at least have roads that run the whole length of them whereas Borneo at about 800 miles long and 500 miles wide has no proper road net work and access to the interior is almost always by water along its extensive river and tributary network. Borneo is split roughly from end to end (S.W. to N.E.) by a long mountain range, which roughly defines the British one third to the north and made up of Sarawak, Brunei and British North Borneo and on the southern side, Indonesian Borneo. Although Borneo is largely jungle and forest there are still very large areas of mangrove, swamp and boggy ground (very popular with a huge selection of insects mostly of the biting and stinging kind!)

Unofficially I was going to be out on a limb in an inhospitable country with only trust and reliance in pirates, smugglers and some still very primitive tribal people. (Borneo head-hunters and all that!). While I would not admit to being actually frightened I was getting a bit apprehensive. In Malaya I was used to having a very strong team about me and supported by plenty of fire-power on most occasions. Plus anyone and everyone with the exception of the C.T.'s themselves were friends, be it the police, the army, the villagers, the estate workers, the general public and the whole establishment. There we could turn to almost anyone, anywhere for help and even limited support. Now, where I was going was largely rebel countryside where even if the police and government officers were not corrupt they at best would be resentful and unhelpful. The army would be like-wise and possibly even be the enemy in effect if they were one of the communist supporting units.

The locals, which I will refer to as Dyaks as a general description are actually a very diverse and localised small groups often with their own dialects, distinct social and religious customs apart from being rebellious, do not even respect or obey their own central government back in Djakarta (in general the Dyaks were the river bank tribes and Ibans, the more inland jungle dwellers.) They often resented strangers and were still killing off the odd innocent missionary. In all these worrying circumstances I could easily just disappear and never be found or heard of again. This was not patriotism, it was crass stupidity but due to the very tight immigration rules there was not another single Brit. in the whole of Indonesia who had the experience, ability and a semblance of a cover story to even make an attempt at it. Back in Malaya there were hundreds who could have done it. I really had to give myself a good talking to to keep my nerve and be at least slightly optimistic. As I think I have made the point before, fear of the unknown is the best psychological weapon but I had never expected or imagined for one moment that I would be a victim of my own making in this respect. Just imagine what modern day analysts would make of that!

That's enough of my musings for one evening. This occasion was meant to be ostensibly a social occasion and we were partly entertained by John after dinner with his usual party-piece(s) in addition to playing cards. His first one was waiting until a mosquito landed on the back of his hand and was biting him, then he would clench his fist, tightening the skin, trapping the insect's proboscis and preventing it from escaping. Secondly he could lie back in his seat with one arm round the back of his head/neck and smoke a cigarette with his hand in effect on the wrong side of his face. putting the fag in and out of his mouth while puffing away at it. It looked most odd and quite unnatural. Later John took both the girls home while I got an early night as I was due to fly to Surabaya on the first flight in the morning. While John was away I took my ablutions in our large fully tiled bathroom. This consisted of only a WC and a huge open tiled (to match the floor and walls) water tank. In the Far East at that time and particularly in Djakarta the water pressure was not very reliable. The slightly higher area of Kebayoran where we lived did not help much either, so the usual procedure was to fill and store water in the large Shanghai jars or tanks when there was some flow. We then used a sort of saucepan as a scoop to douse and rinse ourselves as an alternative to a shower or bath and to flush the toilet. The other similar restriction in our nice modern, up-to-date flat was the frequent power cuts, which meant regular use of candles plus the odd hurricane lamp at dinner and in the evenings. As a result of which no one used electricity for cooking, so we had an oil burning cooker and even a charcoal one for backup.

Despite all the apparent socialising I had also worked very hard at my engineering course (often by candlelight). On the maths side the lowest mark I got was 98%! Not bad since I doubt if I ever even got 65% at school. I remember one late evening I took a break from my studies to write a first letter to girl by the name of Prudence who lived less than a mile from my parents. My mother had met a nearby woman resident by the name of Lapworth who appeared to be a bit of a social climber but had a couple of daughters, the younger one my mother thought I might like to meet in due course when I was next home and who in turn had expressed an interest in becoming a pen pal meantime. Little did I know that due to the assignment I had just set myself which then resulted in recurring health problems, that it was all destined to occur, years earlier than expected and that she would later become my first wife (after the Jag. of course!).

60. Borneo-One

When I got to Surabaya the next day David had made all the arrangements for a group of we 'wild boar' hunters to fly by Garuda (a mythical Indonesian bird-man, a bit like our Phoenix, I think) Indonesian Airways north east over the island of Madura and out over the Java sea the odd 500 miles to Makassa on our first stage to Borneo. It appeared that the hypocrisy of my friendship with the loathsome Yos back in Djakarta may have helped in the obtaining of gun and hunting licences from the Surabaya police who were not too sure whether they really had authority to issue them for Borneo as well as Celebes! They even suggested that we should bluff it out with the inferior officials when we got there, a clear indication of local racial prejudice. Makassa, the main city on Celebes was a much bigger port and place than I had imagined. There were few large ocean going ships but literally hundreds of inter island trading boats and ships crewed by a diversity of peoples from all over the Orient, making the city the most cosmopolitan port on these trading routes.

Two days later we managed to finally get the small chartered plane under way to fly us all a further 300 miles north to the smaller and much less important port of Palu from where the rest of the group had previously gone inland to hunt. On this occasion David had organised the charter of a fair sized sailing schooner owned by a part Indian and part Sumatran trader. The ship/boat had what looked like a historic cannon partly hidden below the deck in the bow. We were assured that it worked and could be used with all sorts of ammunition from rock salt to nuts, bolts and scrap metal bits! It had proved itself capable of blowing a hole in a metal ship at the water line and could completely destroy a large sail -very versatile. The trader skipper claimed that he had a good reputation in the local seas and never had any problems with pirates. I think his definition of good really meant fearsome.

The 350 odd mile journey north by north-west to Tarakan took about two and a half days. The weather was good on the whole but there was a heavy sea running as we cleared the north of Celebes and the schooner pitched and rolled a lot. The food was very spicy with some tastes that were not familiar to me. The cook appeared to be a Philippino Chinese. His rice seemed to change colour and texture from day to day and a sort of nan bread was made fresh each day as well. There was no shortage of beer, wine (rice and normal) and a variety of teas and coffees. I hated the green tea and some of the coffee seemed to have sand in it!? Most of us stuck to fresh fruit and local bottled soft drinks to quench our thirsts. We slept in hammocks out on deck and under an evil smelling tarpaulin that kept the baking sun off us during the day. The only entertainment was our own company, reading and watching thousands of flying fish, some of which flew onto the deck and finished up as part of the crew's menu.

Tarakan itself was a bit of a nondescript and not very big city/town on an island of the same name. It is one of the larger islands that are distributed at the mouth of a very wide river estuary. There was a fairly large army/police barracks, grounds and a considerable number of long abandoned landing craft from the war. There is a large war cemetery nearby full of far too many Australians that died in an unsung and bitter battle with the Japs. My interest in this area was because of its close proximity to British North Borneo (BNB) (Sabah today). Inland from there is the very mountainous border and in turn the closest point and not very far from Brunei. The point being did the Indonesians see this as a suitable stepping off point to BNB or Brunei, or both? The first point of interest was that there were quite a few WW2 allied landing craft about the area although they did not appear to be in very efficient or pristine condition or immediately suitable for a sea invasion. Tarakan was obviously a garrison city in itself but was it also a staging post for other more forward bases and a link in a supply chain? Only up river and well inland would we find the answer to that question.

We wangled an introduction to a Senior Captain (soon to be a Major we were led to believe) who was a duty officer at the army barracks and camp. He was very friendly, particularly when he realised that we were British not Dutch. I had been discovering that as a result of the Dutch having no forces to spare at the end of the war they had asked the British to act for them in Indonesia (the Aussies were already there, both dead and alive). The British agreed but for a very limited time span, having no vested interests in the Dutch East Indies themselves but more pressing demands on their resources in Malaya, Singapore and the British territories of northern Borneo.

They were not going to get bogged down in such a vast country and as a result tended to help speed up the independence of Indonesia much to the delight of the locals but to the chagrin of the Dutch who were powerless to do much about it!

So the British were seen as good friends whereas the Dutch had long been seen as resented visitors who had long overstayed their welcome! They were not actually hated as I have found that in general Asians do not nurse hatred in the way Europeans or particularly Arabs do. The exception to this was the general attitude to communism which I think may be because it is totally godless and therefore can have no possible excuse or justification for its terrible conduct and behaviour (this is my own pet theory but it does seem to add up). The more usual attitude of Asians tends to be resentment, irritation, a initial reluctance to accept something that chances with time to a tolerance and mostly passive philosophical and psychological acceptance of their lot. They have an ability to be reasonably content with their situation if it is not unduly oppressive and to have a greater respect for age and authority than we Europeans do!

Our friendly and chatty Senior Captain whose name was Syed was innocently the source of some very useful information. For instance he said it was naturally assumed that in due course the British would naturally leave their northern Borneo territories and Indonesia would naturally take over, so uniting the whole of the very large island of Borneo, which was to be called Kalimantan. Their sole worry at that time was that the Philippines were claiming BNB and its close islands when and if the British vacated the region. This was why later when the British, who were the real instigators of turning all their Borneo possessions over to what was to become Malaysia. (the one exception being Brunei).Then resulted in the Indonesians being caught off guard and becoming so furious that they started an unofficial war to try and get these areas for themselves as they had always naturally expected. Syed therefore would have no inkling of why we might show any interest in his military activities and what they may be planning or were doing in the area! He was quite happy for us to go Babi (bah-bee)(pig) hunting up the rivers and wished he could have gone with us! He even directed us to the odd military outposts with strict instruction to call on them all? It was almost difficult not to laugh as we could not believe our luck.

We arranged to go up the very wide estuary past the biggish island of Bandul as far as Melinau where the river had already narrowed down to a normal type of river width. This, in a large family run cargo and trading boat which was crewed by some very smelly and fierce looking Dyaks. At Malinau we hired three much smaller narrow boats and headed off up the northern tributary of the main river to a small stilted village/town called Tangung. There was only a very small army post there with about a dozen soldiers. It had no storage area or the possibility to be used as a staging post. Quite apart from the fact that the massive mountain range just beyond the border in the distance was never going to enable any worthwhile military access or invasion, the logistics alone would make it impossible. We dutifully asked about the local wild pig population and were told they were rare. So we thanked them for their temporary hospitality and headed back down river, part of the way back to Malinau but then we turned south at the junction of another tributary and went up it almost as far as it was navigable. Passing several nameless stilted kampongs on the way where the usual hordes of naked children were continually leaping in and out of the river. The timber constructed long houses and walkways looked very risky for either man or beast. They all seemed to have large amounts of fish spread out and drying off ready to be taken down river for trading in the towns.

The majority of us left the boats at this point to yump south round the base of a 5,000ft mountain named Bakayan through some difficult jungle, forest and repeated boggy streams. The going was very slow and hard work and at times there appeared to be no path and it was my repeated expressed faith in the Dyak/Iban guides that stopped some of our group from wanting to turn back. I had of course seen how good the Dyaks/Ibans were as trackers and guides back in Malaya. The insect variety was also much wider than Malaya and along with the leeches, possibly even more voracious. We did hear what we thought were wild pigs at one stage at the base of the Bakayan mountain but were too intent on our difficult journey to stop and hunt. Even if some of the group had turned back they would have found that our boats had already returned down stream to Malinau so they would have had a long hard wait to get a lift back down themselves. Overall the terrain was about the worst combination I had ever come across in Malaya and it took a full four days to cover the 30 odd miles to Besahan on another river altogether, named the Kayan which in turn runs down to the river port town of Tanjong Selor (tanjong usually means a headland) and then on out to sea about 25 miles south of Tarakan where we had started off from. We had arranged for our schooner to sail down from there and collect us just up river at Selor itself. There were the usual numerous small stilted kampongs along the way with some long houses but the majority of structures were on the smaller side. Mostly we received cheery shouts and waves from the villagers but on the upper reaches it appeared to be only curiosity or even suspicion as I am sure that seeing a group our size of Europeans would be a rarity for them. Again on the Kayan river the military presence was only small outposts, quite incapable of building up to any sort of size or effectiveness through that terrain and over the long high Apokayan mountain range into BNB.

So we could conclude that a serious land invasion from this region was quite impossible. That, then left the outside possibility of those WW2 landing craft being brought up to scratch and in sufficient numbers to travel north from Tarakan (which itself could easily be brought up to a large enough forward military base to support a short distance invasion attempt). So where in BNB could they land and form a beachhead? The nearest possible port and town in BNB would be Tawau about 75 miles up the coast north of Tarakan which apart from being far too far for landing craft and barges to safely travel with reliability is in effect open sea. They could have easily all been sunk by just one British naval vessel unless the Indos. had very strong air and sea support. The Indonesians had neither. Even if a worthwhile landing from the sea was made the long route across the mountains on either of the only two roads could easily be defended by a very small force or just one British aircraft could wipe them out almost before the Indos. even got started on the long hard trek across the top of the island to Jessletown or down to Brunei.

When we all finally got back on board the schooner at Tanjong Selor to head back to Palu on Celebes we had been nearly three weeks up and down rivers and through the jungle. I think by the time we finally retraced our steps back to Surabaya we had been away almost a month. Most of the group stayed on Celebes for a few days of real boar hunting but David and I had to get back to his office in Surabaya on Java. Boar hunting is a very dangerous sport because, often when the animals appear to run off they may actually circle round and come back to attack the hunter from the side, very fast and very low. Since it usually takes more than one bullet to kill a boar, hunters often get seriously injured in the process before the animal can be stopped finally! This whole enterprise would seem to have been financed from the British Embassy in Djakarta through their Consular office in Surabaya. There it had been handled by a quiet and unassuming man named Arthur who it appeared was a mixture of military and trade attaché. He had come along on the hunt and was much older than most of us (at least in his late thirties!). It appeared that he had been some sort of liaison officer between the Australians and the Americans on the lead up to the battle for Mindanou to oust the Japs. He had received a field commission so he must have been much more than a mere messenger!? He was not an easy man to extract any personal (or any other for that matter) information from. But we did gather that the trip had not cost as much as it had appeared since the local Indonesian currency of Rupiahs (Rupes to us) would have been bought on the black market at very favourable rates. In addition some payments would have been in American dollars (for trade in the Philippines) and Straits dollars (for trade in Singapore). I am sure the British authorities would have denied it at the time and may well still do so!

Harping back to the distance thing, I worked out that by the time I had got back to Djakarta I had covered 3,400 miles or the equivalent of going up and down the full length of Malaya three and a half times! Or going from K.L. to Singapore FOURTEEN times! David had been brilliant and his organisation of transport and supplies first class. His rapport with the Dyaks was often very humorous and good as he had picked up on the odd Malay language differences, idiosyncrasies and bit of local dialect too. I learned several useful tips for the future by watching and listening to them. He had also adjusted to the jungle quite well having already been on several boar hunts, which had helped. His shooting with a hunting rifle was good but I was not too sure if he could shoot inhuman communists without hesitating? I think we had all lost at least half a stone in weight, on average and it took the usual couple of weeks to heal up the leech and insect bites. We had not done too badly with cuts, scratches or foot rot on this trip and happily none of us had any septic problems on this occasion.

Back in Djakarta and at the office, I was relieved to see that John had coped with all the marketing transactions, partly due I think to it having turned out to be a fairly quiet period. He did however now quite fancy himself as a marketing man even though he had stuck strictly to the new system, procedures and instructions. He was not impressed by my appearance and suggested that in future I should change my vacation choices! There was, unfortunately more wisdom to his jocular comments than he realised. I was again starting to suffer from the odd mild re-occurrences of my jungle fever which was only lasting for a day or two at a time. Slightly worrying nonetheless. Bruce, at the Embassy, in the mean time had organised everything I had requested plus a few additions which included several military field dressing packs of morphine! Kim Lee had also been in touch with the office just to leave a message that he hoped to entertain me for dinner(?) and a sail within about a month. The time was approaching for me to take life very seriously and prepare accordingly.

61. Borneo-2. (wild man of Borneo?)

That preparation can perhaps be best demonstrated by simply listing the items I wanted to collect together in preparation for the most outlandish escapade and expedition of my life. On the medical side; Iodine, Hydrogen Peroxide (both for wound cleaning and as a disinfectant) Permanganate of Potash (not just as a another disinfectant or to help clarify/purify drinking water but mostly as a skin dye), Tiger Balm, Coconut cream, foot rot talc., kaolin, anti malarial tablets, pep pills (the sort used by pilots on long flights and in my case because being entirely alone it was more than possible that falling asleep in certain circumstances could prove fatal!) I presume they were the forerunner of modern day Benzedrine. Plus cotton wool, plasters, laundry blue bag, strips of crepe rubber bandage, some military field dressings, several syringes of morphine, quinine as well as some cinchona bark to chew, antibiotics in the form of Auromycin and Cloromycin, aspirin and a suture needle and gut set. A small but comprehensive first aid pack which would include strong tweezers, nail clippers and the odd razor blade. Then an item that would be essential for a lone adventurer; a unbreakable mirror. No, not for vanity use but an essential to remove, say a poisonous thorn from one's back or to inspect anywhere just out of sight. It would also serve the possible second task as a signalling method. Two of the latest American cigarette gas lighters (the jet of flame was good for removing leeches) plus salt, in my case for the cleaning of teeth and removal of leeches too. Looking back at the list now it may appear to be a bit hypochondriac-like but in such a wild place with no chance of any real medical attention for days if not weeks and the possibility of no human help either it was very cheap insurance. The load was still going to be a lot less than I had become used to in Malaya since there would be no weapons (apart from the Hart), large amounts of ammo, grenades or booby trap mines and equipment. Not even a heavy radio to share on and off. What relative luxury, or so I thought.

On the clothing side; one spare long-sleeved shirt and multi-pocketed long trousers, several spare pairs of cotton socks, spare under shorts (not tight pants), spare lace-up sandals in addition to normal jungle boots, toe-less plimsolls, sweat towels and head band, hats for sun and rain, poncho and an adequate rucksack with a head band extension to help take the load off one's back on long hauls and up hills - Sherpa like. Then a separate smaller bag to wear in front for camera, films in water proof canisters (so if the camera got wet the films would be ok), binoculars and anything that might be wanted in a hurry. Plus, of course mosquito netting for head and other areas as required. All in addition to the basics already mentioned for my Malayan jungle outings. Finally my own personal fad(?), a couple of pairs of good quality thin ventilated, possibly string backed driving or cycling type gloves or mitts. The mitts were preferable if it became necessary to use one's trigger finger in a hurry! On this occasion that was not a priority but prevention of even small cuts, scratches and anything that could become septic was. I always considered the priorities of health in the jungle were; first the feet then the legs then the hands (hence the gloves or mitts), more important even than a strong back and mental strength in the short term, at least.

On the equipment side; a parang, a kukri, a good army knife on a lanyard, a very strong staff with detachable sliding plate or disc (to stop it sinking into bog or soft ground). A Union Jack and furl, two good fully waterproof and luminous watches, a good field compass and a simple one for the wrist,(all wrist straps have to be cotton linen and have to keep the actual watch out of contact with the skin. Leather straps get mushy and start to rot in days whereas metal corrodes and can cut into softened skin causing poison sores) several small food containers and bags. A very thin sort of money belt with several separate compartments so that only a small amount of money would be on view at any time giving the impression that was all one had! It is unwise anywhere in the world to appear to have a large wad! Then the ubiquitous bum bag which in my case was to be used as a belly-bag with my hidden Hart .38 revolver in it. Two, twenty foot lengths of very strong woven cord or light rope (strong enough to take my weight over a cliff or up a tree) stowed in their own small hooked bags. One of my original Boy Scout home-made filter bottles with fine sand and charcoal granules for filtering out the mud from water which purification tablets alone can not do. Two strong water bottles, one large and one small. A very small French solid fuel tablet cooking stove which folds away into a small mess tin. Although I would expect to eat and drink cold most of the time, there are occasions of long, wet and cold night vigils that really do need a bit of added internal warmth to pick one up quickly and to get going again efficiently!

As I intended to live off the land or more correctly small kampongs whenever conditions or circumstances required, I would have to be able to carry enough food for several days at a time. Mostly rice, hard boiled eggs, dried mushrooms and soya bean curd and similar items. A considerable number of foil sachets of dried and powdered soups. A tin of curry powder and other spices will make almost anything palatable if you are hungry enough! Wild or other fruit would always be available sooner or later. The one luxury I allowed myself was a couple of hermetically sealed tins of glucose boiled sweets. It may be difficult to appreciate the sheer bliss and treat such items can be when alone for long periods in very inhospitable surroundings, with nothing appetising to eat for days, no one to talk to, covered with sores, insects and tired beyond belief. With no obvious light at the end of the tunnel one needs a small reminder that life is worth living after all! (I am sure modern day psychologists will have an answer for that, too?). I would be also carrying identification papers confirming that I was a British citizen (definitely not Dutch) with an interest in the animal varieties of Borneo and a book and notes to help me?! The camera and glasses were for the same purpose, of course! The camera I was provided with was a 35mm Zeiss with a big lens attachment and the binoculars, also German, reputedly from a war time U. Boat? Films, all with their own individual waterproof screw top containers.

The next few weeks were very busy from the work point of view and the social side which included a knock up mixed hockey tournament. Not a game I had ever played before or have any ambition to play again. Not only did I have sores and cuts to heal now some very bruised shins as well! The embassy girls were absolute fiends and seemed to think they would gain their feminist laurels by hacking every male they could on the field and then blithely expect we victims to buy them dinner afterwards. I took Nonnie along the north coast of Java towards Semarang to some very fine coral beaches where the water was so clear that you could see the multi coloured and beautiful coral quite clearly. Unfortunately some local divers were breaking hunks of this remarkable formation off and trying to sell them to the odd passing tourists like us, without much success I am glad to say but there were still heaps of the stuff left lying an the shore all dried out and looking like colourless bones. What a shameful waste! This was to be my last outing with Nonnie, although we still had the odd dinner and dance together at the hotel where she unofficially worked. I forget the name of it but it was one of the big international groups at the time. The slightly strange under manager had his own suite within the hotel which seemed to have no windows or natural light at all. Everything in the large open plan living area was painted bright white including a grand piano and the only lighting was very dim and red. Very effective but rather odd. The man himself was a generous host and had almost permanent open house night and day. He seemed to be always walking about with a bowl of natural yoghurt and drinking/eating it with a rubber tube poked through the apparent skin! Very odd again. I also wrote two or three letters home to my parents with instructions that they should be posted off to them at about monthly intervals. No point in them wondering or worrying as to why my poor and irregular correspondence had suddenly got worse!?

62. *En route*

Finally and roughly as promised Kim Lee returned to Tanjong Priok with his traditional Bugis type trading schooner. These boats I can only describe as the Indonesian equivalent of the Chinese Junk but much smoother and faster and certainly much more manoeuvrable in and out of the islands. It turned out that he actually had a fleet of them dotting all over the archipelago and I was to travel with him on his personal flagship. His cabin which I was to share turned out to be more like a state room with four large bunk beds and room for several hammocks if required. A large table used as either a chart table or for dining if he had guests. A separate toilet and separate shower room with both hot and cold running water, a side chart and instrument storage room. A small ladies room plus an extensive and well stocked bar with a gas run refrigerator for ice and to keep drinks cool. A water bottle/drinking fountain straight out of an American movie. I could finally understand how Kim could transform himself from a wild pirate villain into a dapper city diner and man about town in such a short time, wherever he happened to be. The Schooner had what looked like relatively new main engine and a new auxiliary back up, both with generators big enough to drive winches and derricks for loading and unloading almost anything anywhere. However sails were always the first choice as there was never usually any great hurry and the cost of using fuel unnecessarily would only eat into the profits!

Our first port of call was Banka Island which is about half way north towards Singapore, where we stayed a couple of days before heading north-east towards Pontianak on the west coast of Borneo about 300 miles farther on. At this point it may be of interest to explain that at the fall of Singapore to the Japanese in 1942 and as I have already mentioned, many women and children got away in time but did not all escape to Ceylon or Australia as was intended. Several of the ships carrying these unfortunate refugees were bombed and shot up by the Japanese air force. Several of the ships were sunk with considerable loss of life. The survivors which largely consisted of women, some children and a few male crew members. The women were made up of a large number of individuals, wives etc. groups of nuns and Australian nurses and it may well be that it is thanks in particular to these groups sustained efforts that anyone eventually survived at all! Almost all came ashore on Banka Island and were already in poor state when rounded up by the Japs and interned for about three and a half years in what in effect were death camps. Some of the men were immediately marched off and executed. The women and children initially survived probably because the Nips were confused about how to deal with women in such circumstances and numbers. It was not in their rule book? The survivors from the ship wrecks and assassination all started their imprisonment on Banka Island and were later transferred to Palembang on the mainland of Sumatra, then later back to Banka Island again near the town of Mentok. Hundreds of women and children died there before they were eventually released by the returning Allied troops. These women and children, British, Dutch, Eurasian and others suffered worse privation than the men on the more publicised Burma Death Railway (over the River Kwai and all that!). This particular island and women's prison camp was the basis of the well publicised TV series, *Tenko* (which means roll-call parade) but which could not give more than a hint of the appalling conditions or the abject mental and physical cruelty of their Japanese captors. Reputedly the heaviest woman that survived weighed only six stone! Limbs were so thin that one woman could make her thumb and forefinger meet round her combined upper and lower arm! That's Belsen and Auschwitz standards! Anything like a true simulation for TV was impossible, the series barely even hinted at how bad it really was. At the end of it all most survivors just returned to their former life and adjusted as best as they could to their losses. None of your, largely claptrap, modern counselling for them. Backbones were made of sterner stuff in those days and it was long before such feather-bedding was even thought of. They were largely forgotten as were the hundreds of non survivors. Since they were mostly civilians, the War Graves Commission, who still do such a wonderful job all round the world where service graves are concerned, have no remit where those that died in the camps are concerned. These women's and children's graves therefore remain, for the most part, lost in the jungle!

All that terrible example of man's inhumanity to (wo)man aside and back to my own, in ignorance (then) visit to the island barely ten years later, makes my own harrowing experience still to come pale into insignificance by comparison. It transpired that Kim had laid on this trip largely to accommodate me and the planned incursion into the interior of Borneo closest to the gap in the border mountains. With Kuching the capital of Sarawak not far over the other side as this was the area that Kim was sure the communist supplies were and had been destined for. We would see! He had also arranged for me to use his local manager's home in Pontianak and by the time we arrived should have confirmation that at least one of his interior boats would run me up river to Ngabang where more business friends would take care of me and make whatever ongoing arrangements I wanted or found I required. Kim was almost childishly excited about it all and very happy to be able to do or assist anything that might get back at the mutually hated communists and to poke them in the eye where and whenever possible, to quote him, several Tiger beers later! In this mellow mood and in an almost conspiratorial manner he showed me how to swing his pianola away from the cabin wall exposing a considerable armoury. Most of it was relatively up-to-date but some were collectors items.

This was all more than I had expected or ever hoped for. I remember thinking how strange fate, or life, can appear to be sometimes, as all this had come out of a friendly chance meeting and a drive to a dinner party in K.L. a couple of years before. It certainly pays to be civil and friendly as you never know where it might lead. I was to find this often in life particularly again some years later when I first met Eric Liebman of Fish Canadian Carburettors. My father frequently made comments to the effect that "it was the easiest thing in the world to be rude and courtesy cost nothing!". So many of us do not always appreciate the wisdom of our parents until much later in life when it is hopefully not too late.

63. W. Borneo, itself

What follows will be a bit difficult as originally I was not going to deal with this particular episode and phase of my life. Most of it I had chosen to forget and had largely done so but as I have been writing about people and places a lot of related memories have returned, almost from the unconscious mind. I think any reader will come to understand what I mean as this narrative unfolds. It is almost impossible to put into words the vastness, distances, topography, climate and the environment of Borneo. It is after all, apart from the continental island of Australia, then perhaps New Guinea, the biggest island in the world with the nastiest jungle characteristics anywhere with the possible exception of some of the Amazon, the least developed. with the exception of New Guinea it must have the most primitive and unpredictable interior population (wild man of Borneo plus head-hunters and all that!), anywhere in the world. Its biggest river is about 700 miles long but with all its tributaries probably consists of nearer 2,000 miles of waterways and that's just one river! Even today I believe that it can take well over a month to get up the length of this long river and presumably even longer on up some of the tributaries. On this basis Phineas Fogg would not have got up and down even one long river in the eighty days he took to circumvent the whole globe! The marshes, bogs and mangrove swamps must run into literally thousands of square miles which can expand into hundreds more when it rains, which it frequently does! There are very few roads even of the basic type and these tend to be local and at that time there were none that either cross the country north/south or east/west or even go round the coast. Insect infested river ways are the only roads of any consequence and where most of the varied population live and work.

There are though, a few surprisingly big cities but even they did not have direct communication to each other than by air or very long boat journeys. The world still largely by-passes Borneo which in not on any regular international trade or tourist route (this largely still applies today, fifty years on!). Again, Amazon and New Guinea excepting it must still be world's biggest and most inhospitable backwater. This was what I was entering, virtually alone. I was to be away in the depths of this steamy wilderness for almost three months in the end so it should not be surprising that I really cannot remember just how many nights I slept in this particular tree or that one, hid in river rushes partly submerged, or the number of days I lay up in the jungle observing a communist camp and base, or how many nights I slept in a Dyak long house, or how many nights I spent floating down river clinging to a oil drum raft and then hiding in evil smelling and insect plagued reed beds during the day, or how many days I suffered from the squitters! Or at one stage how many days and nights I spent in a long house being cared for while passing in and out of consciousness (and probably sanity as well!) suffering from a serious bout of fever.

Well we arrived at Pontianak, which is located up the most navigable branch of the many legs of the river delta that I have just referred to, the Kapuas and where it is joined by another slightly smaller river called the Landack which was the river of interest if Kim Lee's information was valid. On arrival it would appear that Kim Lee had virtually his own bit of quayside. The size of this long established city was almost a shock, but although not as big as Makassar or Surabaya, I still found a city of possibly a quarter of a million people in such a relatively remote place surprising.(what do I know about economics?) We were met by Kim's local manager and agent by the name of Cheng Lee, supposedly some sort of relation but it should be remembered the name Lee out there is as common as Smith or Jones back in the U.K. He too was a very brown Chinese of the Straits type and it was obvious that the Chinese had commercially invaded and married local girls in even greater numbers in Borneo than they had in Malaya and Singapore Cheng was, again a very humorous and friendly chap. His office and godown/warehouse was almost on the water front only yards from Kim's usual and almost private berth. We were entertained to a tea party before being driven a few miles to where Cheng lived in a large house set back off the road. It had belonged to a Dutch trader who had departed about three years before! I was not sure whether the inference was six feet under or just back to Holland!?.That night there was the usual dinner party at the house with about twenty other guests for a sort of mixed Javanese and Chinese meal that was as varied at the quests. With very dapper gentlemen in dinner jackets and bow ties sitting down to eat with some wild looking characters wearing sarongs and very ornate bandannas. The next day I spent exploring the vast array of water front scenes and walking out to the edge of town to claim I had sat on the equator at the cairn/obelisk that marks that latitude.

64. Up river

Kim and Cheng had obviously talked of the planned enterprise on some previous occasion because Cheng was able to bring us up to date on the fact that even more Red Chinese supplies had come through the port and been taken up the Landak river by the Indonesian military supply boats! To where exactly was not known but certainly well beyond Ngabang up into the head waters and close to the Sarawak border. Cheng was arranging for me to travel up river within a couple of days in one of his several family type trading boats. These take up essentials and trade and buy local produce from dried fish, chickens, pigs, the odd small deer, monkeys, song birds as well as vegetables, fruit, rice and various spices. Some hardwood timber would be collected and when a large enough raft had been assembled it would be floated down and added to many other rafts until there was a worthwhile ship load. The biggest surprise (only because I had never heard of it before) was that the Kim and Cheng Lee had an interest in diamonds as well. It appeared that there had been a steady supply of them from the area just to the north for a couple of hundred years or so.

Kim, himself was to leave for Singapore, Malacca, Port Swettenham, Penang and back to his base at Medan a day or so after I left. He told me that Cheng would be able to contact him to let him know when I was safely out again and he would then arrange transport for me and set sail himself to Djakarta on which ever of his ships would get there first. To celebrate and then to hear whatever story I had to tell. Before we parted he gave me a handful of pure soft gold discs, tokens or coins. They had Jawi on one side and Chinese characters on the other. Kim said that they would buy anything anywhere and from anybody! I gathered that they were often used for the purchase of unofficial diamonds amongst other transactions. They were worth many, many thousands of the local rupiahs (Rp) and were in effect a hard currency acceptable anywhere. I imagine rather like the South African Kruger Rand that was accepted almost anywhere in the world for its gold value.

Ngabang was up river about 80 to a 100 miles and is the last town of any significance up river. There Cheng had one of his trusted buying and trading agents by the name of Achmed or Achmood (I never found out how it was really pronounced). He was a half Dyak and hated the communists even more than the Javanese soldiers of the Indonesian army who he regarded as invaders of Borneo and considered that they interfered much more in local customs and culture than the Dutch ever had. He in turn would supply me with two motorised canoes with trusted crews, three men in one and two in the canoe I would travel in. To outward appearances they would be in the process of their normal trading and would be flexible enough to ferry me wherever I wanted to go, help with introductions, act as guides, keep me supplied and any other tasks, such as relaying messages etc. It took several days to work our way up to Ngabang through mostly low semi wetlands. Ngabang was in a slightly dryer area but still a bit out back. Achmed was a very short but wiry man with scars cut on his face and body plus a few tattoos to go with them, few teeth and stretched ear lobes. I would sleep easier knowing he was a friend not an enemy particularly when he explained that some of his native relatives still kept the family heirlooms of shrunken heads in their houses. He too lived over the shop but had extended the back of the building, turning part of it into a mock longhouse for his extended family. He also had a concreted and floodlit badminton court and a small garden at the rear to finish it all off. I was given a room to myself with a very potent fan and a veranda that overlooked the badminton court. There was a comfortable bed in the room and a hammock out on the veranda, both with new mosquito nets. To prevent any offence where food was concerned I had to explain that I was a rare mixture of Buddhist and Hindu religions and was therefore a strictly religious vegetarian! In many parts of the Far East and particularly Indonesia any other religions are just lumped together as a form of Hinduism.

65. Even further!

Shortly after arriving I set off again with the two boats and their motley crews up river about 40 miles to the first real confluence and then took the right hand fork. This took about another two days, passing mostly through very small stilted villages in boggy areas on both river banks. Up this right hand or eastern fork was much the same sort of terrain except I could by then see the mountain range to the north that makes up the backbone of the island. More importantly I could also see the relative gap between some peaks in this natural barrier between the two countries of Indo/Borneo and British Sarawak. This gap was about thirty miles wide but still not easily travelled through. It consisted of high rock faces, ravines, very dense jungle and rain forest once into the slightly higher and relatively dryer (less wet!) ground but still with numerous smaller water ways. This right hand leg of the river was heading towards the eastern end of the gap. About ten to fifteen miles up we spotted an army camp with about twenty fair sized huts. Some with corrugated galvanised roofs and others using the local woven and plated palm leaf attap panels. Despite the obvious apprehension of my crew companions I decided on the bold approach and landed at the army's well made jetty.

I climbed ashore to the surprise of a couple of leisurely guards and demanded to be taken to their General or commander. I unfurled my Union Jack and waved it as they quite meekly did so, leading me up to the only hut with a veranda and with a flag pole outside. There I was met by a very handsome Colonel by the name of Yusof something. He was very surprised to see me and spoke very good English. I produced my papers and explained my naturalist expedition to him, he seemed very receptive and promptly invited me to share his accommodation for as long as I wished! My guides/crew would be welcome to stay with the construction staff. This camp or base had been built on ground high enough to avoid flooding from the river when in spate and was on the very edge of the sloping jungle covered foot hills. There were about two hundred and fifty personnel in the camp which looked quite well established.

They received a monthly supply boat which rotated some of the soldiers as well as bringing up building materials and military supplies on an ongoing basis. The base was to more than doubled in size within the next six months and would probably be used as a jungle training base. Yusof, like so many of his kind was very chatty and enjoyed practising his English on me. I stayed with him for nearly a week making mock forays up into the forest each day to search out the wild life and appearing to make copious notes! This, to help establish a plausible alibi with a senior official that might be needed later! I was to be seen taking pictures of hornbills, cockatoos, the odd heron, parakeets, egrets, monkeys, baboons, fruit bats, a fantastic selection of butterflies, dragonflies and anything else I might accidentally come across.

Over the evening meals I would talk a lot of old guff about the fact that these local variations were of potentially scientific interest and he in turn would talk about almost anything. Slowly I got round to venturing the subject of Indonesia taking over North Borneo when the British left in due course. He, like many others took that for granted but did not see any particular hurry. He said that they would have to build a good road through the gap and the present border then on to Kuching and in about this same area! He foresaw that his camp might well be the base for that survey work in due course, as well. All very interesting. He was not particularly enamoured with Bung Karno as a President or some of the elements of the army who were dangerously involved in politics as well and felt that they certainly should not be involved with the communists at all! I asked him about the western branch of the river that we had passed on the way up and he told me that there was a prohibited military area some miles upstream and only military and local native traffic was allowed up that far. It appeared that the regiment based there were one of the type he did not approve of!? Even he would not be allowed up there without a special pass! This was great news since Yusof's base did not have any Chinese packing cases or equipment then it must be this other restricted base that was receiving the shipments. The trail was getting warmer but further access, it appeared was going to be a real problem.

66. *The other tack*

We finally took our leave of Yusof and returned down stream to stop off just short of the 'Y' junction at a local village where my crew obviously had business friends. I had a preliminary plan in my head but was dreading trying to communicate the possible complications to my minders. I started by drawing the 'Y' of the river and marking where we were and where we had come from explaining it all in a sort of pidgin Malay since there are some differences between Malay and Indonesian and there are many different dialects all over Borneo. It may seem strange but in the several days I had been with these chaps we had only conversed in odd words in Malay and a lot of gestures. When listening to most of their conversations, which were rare and brief, I had not understood anything! Now, finally when I was making a comical effort to explain things to them they became much more forthcoming, communicative and humorous too. My conclusion was, that since they claimed that I was, roughly translated; The very brave and distinguished younger brother of the Towkay Besar (a very big and important Chinese business-man) Kim Ling Lee and it would have been in deference to him that they had adopted, what appeared at first sight, as a "only speak when your are spoken to first" policy. Now they became transformed and entered into the comical talking with hands phase with great enthusiasm and amusement. Life suddenly was going to be much easier and bearable.

Out of all this I arranged to send one of our canoes upstream with three on board to find out all they could about distance, layout, numbers, positions of army guards and very importantly, the army's practical policy on passing boats. It appeared that they had all been up river several times before but as a matter of policy had tried to ignore the Javanese soldiers but they now seemed to take an almost a fiendish pleasure in spying on them for me. They were back in four days bursting with information and competing with each other to tell me things that I could not sort into a logical sequence. So back to drawing a map with a stick in the mud to enable me to get into my mind's eye.

The army camp/base was just over two days upstream on the left hand side and consisted (they all argued about the number) of over fifty rumahs (Malay for house, hut or building). There was a large jeti (Malay for jetty) with landing stage and a crane at the beginning of the base area which itself was about a hundred yards away and back from the river on slightly higher ground with minimal stilts.

Behind this again was one of the odd small mountains that do not form part of the backbone chain of Borneo and where the river curved left round the whole area. Partly round the curve were two smaller jetis, one on each side of the river which were used as a passenger ferry rather than cargo. The river bank on the left or base side was high and made visibility of the base difficult. On the other side it was covered with thick reeds with a well used footpath up and along the bank. It was marshy most of the way up to the base and turned into ulu or jungle scrub-land with quite a few large trees starting to appear about a quarter of a mile before hand. The area just across from the camp was fairly dense from the footpath inland. There was a military guard post on the left bank only about half a mile before the main camp jeti. The guards there would stop the larger boats and check under any covers or containers but any of the small local open trading boats that they could see into, they just waved on. My spies had no problems and were waved by several times with barely a glance despite doing it several times. The guards took so little notice of them and appeared not to notice it was the same boat repeatedly! There are several small stilted kampongs on the way up to the base and several after as well so the local traffic is quite high. Estimates of large boats passing were about ten a day and over sixty (thirty each way) small open boats and canoes.

67. Decisions, decisions

I slept on all this information overnight and awoke early with the makings of a plan, as is often the case. The biggest and only real problem was me! How was I to pass myself off as a Dyak, Iban or river mixture? None of the locals even came to my shoulder! To say nothing of me being generally bigger built. The solution was for me to wear a local pyjama top with a large 'coolie' straw hat, rather like an upturned dish. Sit in the middle of the boat and as low as possible. The other two to sit or kneel several inches higher than usual. This coupled with me holding a large round woven fruit basket or display tray out over my lap which should help disguise my build and shape. Finally of course and as anticipated I would dye myself with the Permanganate of Potash over face, neck, arms, legs, feet and anywhere that might get exposed. In fact in the end I covered the whole of my top half in case I may feel the need to strip off in the heat at some stage and would not then want to be happened upon by surprise. So putting my spies in jeopardy.

Assuming I could get past the army check points safely I would be dropped ashore upstream of the base but on the other side, perhaps close to the small jeti on that side or where the jungle looked as if it could absorb me quickly and safely to hide out while I could accurately survey the whole layout. At probably the same landing point we would arrange a well hidden delivery and collection point in the reeds. This for the spies to deliver additional food to me on roughly a bi-weekly basis and to take any used films or messages back down to Achmed in Ngabang, to relay on. The devil takes care of his own, or so they say. We finally timed things so that our two boats would pass the guard post when it was still not quite light, early in the morning. The other boat stayed close to the guard post shore and ours just behind but further out from the shore. Neither boat got more than a glance from the guards but that did not stop me feeling that potential sense of fear and doom in the back of my neck. A bit like the Hash House Harrier run near Cheras when I had fully expected a bullet in the back, on that occasion. The spies description was remarkably accurate. The river did curve left round the army base and the two small jetis were out of sight of the main one and did not appear to be guarded. Rather than run the risk and with daylight coming up fast we paddled slowly close to the reeds on the opposite shore from the camp, found a small inlet in the reeds that almost reached the hard shore. The bow of the canoe fitted in it neatly and I was able to hop off and only finished up waist deep in the muddy water. There was a dry and high bit of reed bed that would serve as our planned pick up and drop off point that was not immediately visible from the bank above or from the river. We jammed in a thick strong cane from the boat to secure things to. I carefully scrambled up the small bank, checked that there was no one about and cut off the tops of some reeds to mark the spot which I could find again from the shore and the spies could also see from the river for future reference. We exchanged whispered, Terima Kasih(s) (Thank You(s)) and Selamat Tingal from them and Selamat Jalan from me. Since both they and I would be travelling it might have been more correct for all of us to say Selamat Jalan, since Jalan is to travel away. It was still not quite fully light as I crawled across the path into the initial scrub which was not too wet underfoot and on into the denser trees. I found a large example of a Kapur tree with the usual buttresses of roots, sat myself into them and just started thinking "what have I talked myself into here, it's all quite mad". No one at home would believe that anyone could be quite so foolhardy and to do it voluntarily. Now that I was alone I did let myself have a bit of an apprehensive moment or two but the potential excitement and anticipation of "biting off more than I could chew" and hopefully succeeding was perhaps what had driven me on before in Malaya as well. I snoozed for an hour or so and had a drink and snack and felt all the better for it. I then left my gear at my adopted tree and returned towards the riverside path remaining in cover about twenty feet from it, spending the rest of the day noting the comings and goings of people and river traffic. Very few people seemed to use the path at all which seemed strange since there were signs of a lot of footprints that I had noticed when I came ashore at dawn. So what were the small and newly made jetties for then?

68. *Very alone*

At dusk I returned to my adopted tree and made a meal of an already stale piece of cheese (kedju keras), a hard boiled egg with curry powder and some rice balls. I then curled up for the night sitting with my back to the tree (as I had done so often in Malaya) a mossie net over my head plus a rain hat and poncho. Boots off, feet dried out and powdered, then lace up sandals put on before putting my feet into a bag to keep them dry and warm for the night. I had already made myself a thick plaited mat with some small springy branches under it to sit on. I slept well and the rain was only light that night. The following morning I woke early (as you always do sleeping rough) had some dried fruit and nuts for breakfast, dressed and packed up everything and headed very quietly and slowly back down parallel to the river path, past the small jeti and almost at the apex of the river bend and obliquely opposite the army base. Then I turned inland in a sort of half circle through the ulu to find a suitable hide for an observation platform and or living base.

Almost at the edge of the secondary undergrowth I found a medium sized variation of the Kapur tree with the usual buttresses that was almost dead due to the parasitical strangler fig tree that had latched onto it and grown round it to its detriment. These huge fig trees surround their victims with a giant, ivy type lattice work of growth. I was able to climb up inside and through this web of shoots until I was about 25 feet above the ground and arrived at the basic tree's first major multi fork or crutch(?) making almost a platform. Peering through the lattice work of the fig tree's tentacles and out, on the river side of the tree, I had a first class view across the river into the camp, of the river itself, in either direction including both the major jeti and the two smaller ones within about 75 yards. It was like peering out through a castle battlement slit. The chance of being spotted in return was almost nil. I pulled up my gear with one of the ropes which later I often left hanging down to aid my climb up and down when the tree was very wet and slippery. It is of course not possible or practical to put knots into such a thin rope to aid climbing so I made up about two dozen wooden toggles and fitted them into a sort of figure of eight knot every eighteen inches or so. They are very easily slipped out again and the rope repacked again in minutes.

The other rope I wound round and round two smaller protruding branches so making a cat's cradle or almost a hammock. These branches were at about 45' enabling me to sleep neither standing up or fully down but at least at full length. A day or so later I wove and plaited some more leafy mats which kept the up-drafts away from my ribs at night. I now even had the option of using the poncho as a fly sheet over my bed or wearing it in bed. It was hopefully a good omen (not that I have ever been that superstitious!) to find such a safe and almost perfectly located base and observation post. I felt that I could snore, cough, sneeze and drop anything without being heard even from the path and certainly not from the camp with the noise of the river and even greater distance between us. As a Backwoodsman I also knew better than to start leaving a regular path from the riverside to my tree, I would constantly vary my route to and from. The very wet nights and days for that matter were horrid and made time pass very slowly and miserably. The only advantage of such wet occasions was that I did not need to climb down to urinate as the rain would wash it and any smell away and insure against additional flies. Where the other department was concerned I was only caught short up the tree twice when I had to use a spare bag when it became urgent because there were several passers-by directly opposite me on the path at the time and were showing no inclination to move on at the critical time. Then later I would climb down and go even deeper into the jungle and bury the contents thoroughly to hide the smell and avoid the potential noise of flies both of which can be detected from quite a distance in the still dank air. No risk, however small, was worth taking.

69. A new home

I spent well over a week mostly residing in my tree, initially watching the camp which as the spies had said consisted of about fifty buildings mostly laid out on three sides of a square with a parade ground in the middle and the red and white Indo. flag flying from a pole. Further building work was going on and some additional ground was being cleared even while I was watching. Several bigger boats had brought supplies and anonymous crates and boxes to the big jeti, which were then mostly just stored away. Some reinforcements or returnees from leave had also come up on the boats. Meantime I had identified the administration block complete with a fair sized radio mast/aerial making this remote outpost not so remote after all which indicated the permanence and importance of it as a forward base. Then there was the canteen and cook house, officers' quarters, the ablutions and the other ranks accommodation. What I did not understand initially was that there was an almost separate smaller camp operating independently of the main base. The big difference being that it had an outdoor classroom with benches that was used every day when dry so I presumed that that there would be an indoor one as well. It did not actually take me long to realise that I had found the communists that were being aided and abetted by the Indos. and which explained the restricted area status of the place. At about the end of this period in my tree I was disturbed late one afternoon by noises and a lot of talking down by the river at the small jeti on my side of the water. There I saw about twenty-five rather scruffy uniformed individuals waiting to be ferried across to the other little jeti on the camp side of the river. This time I could make out the red flashes and stars on some of the communists uniforms and caps. They all crossed over and joined the smaller camp, confirming Kim Lee's and my earlier suspicions and conclusions.

70. Found them!

I celebrated that night and had my first glucose sweet! Nothing seemed to be happening the next day but there was certainly more activity in the commie camp. A Mao refresher course maybe? Over the next few days little changed except that some of the commies strolled down to their little jeti for an evening smoke and then strolled back again but did not leave any guard or sentry. Then, early one morning I thought I spotted one of our spy motorised canoes coming up the river with one of the occupants standing up, which was unusual. I thought I heard its motor fade and then pick up again in the distance. I took the risk in the early morning poor light and part mist to return for the first time to my original landing point. I had trouble finding the cut leaves indication sign because the others had grown longer in the meantime! I climbed down the bank and was delighted to find a woven basket of food, a pair of flip flops, more talc, some soap, a tooth brush and tooth powder in a tin. And a crude note saying "bunya bagus" (very good). It may seem silly but the excitement this incident generated was beyond comprehension and certainly a morale booster. However tough you think you are and however good a loner you are, there is still something inhuman and unnatural in being a total hermit. Some will say it's the sheep or herd instinct in us all. I am sure it's the family tendency which is the ultimate backbone of any decent human society. As far as I am concerned it should always be the antithesis of the 'State' minded and godless communism.

A few days on again and I was awoken very early one morning by a lot of shouting and activity down at the two small jetis. A group of commies were leaving the camp and starting to head back the way they had come. Whether it was the same group or a replacement I did not know but it was about the same number and they were all quite heavily laden. I was a bit surprised that they were not using local porters but concluded that relations were not good or they were being secretive which would be stupid as I was sure that both the Ibans, Dyaks and any other locals would know every inch of their own territory. Perhaps the commies just did not want them to know what was in the camps rather than where they were actually located. I quietly packed up everything and about half an hour after they had left heading up river I followed them. Having checked carefully first that there was no one about I left my tree base and headed slowly and carefully up the path after them. First I stopped and put my exposed films showing quite clearly the obviously Chinese uniformed red starred communist soldiers into the woven basket. This for the spies to pick up and take down to Achmed at Ngabang to be then relayed on down to Cheng at Pontianak and eventually back to Djakarta. I remember that day because it became very hot as the dawn mist cleared and lifted off the water very quickly. The path eventually veered away from the river and started climbing up and over a ridge and down the other side to what I assumed was a smaller side feed river or tributary and which was only just about navigable even in a canoe. As I reached this waterway I noticed a big clearing about a quarter of a mile up stream and several of the usual local type huts and with one long one about sixty feet in length that stretched out over the water. With great caution I crept closer, keeping off the open path as far as possible and when the clearing came into full view I circled inland and up a gentle slope to get a clear view of what might be going on without the risk of someone coming along the path and bumping into me!

71. Typical commies

The group of commies appeared to be just finishing their rest and a refreshment break and were starting to load up again. I noticed that two of them were climbing up a notched pole ladder to the raised walkway on the larger hut. They went inside and I could hear yelling and screaming and saw one bare topped woman trying to escape but being pulled back inside by one of the commies. A few moments later a young man was being thrown out and being beaten by both the commies. Finally he was then thrown off the walkway down into the shallow water below where he let out a terrible shout. The villagers gathered outside were making a mumbling chant and rattling what looked like their spear sticks and the odd blow pipe together in a menacing manner. Some of the remaining commies then threatened them with their rifles and the locals immediately went quiet. I had a distinct sense that this had all happened before. It was like a scene from one of those brutal Japanese war films. This was exactly the sort of communist bandit behaviour that had happened so often in Malaya too. They never seem to believe in the hearts and minds policy which was practised by the British in Malaya and was a important contributing fact in the communists ultimate defeat. Barely five minutes later these two rapists emerged with silly smirks on their faces and still adjusting their clothing. They joined the others and they all set off again together.

72. My good turn

I kept hidden for a while making sure the commies had really gone. I noticed that the young man who had been thrown off the walk way had not emerged back up the river bank and a lot of the inhabitants were now gathering on the bank apparently looking down on him below. Having strangled my earlier impulse to shoot at least a few of the commies I now had a strong urge to see if I could help these people. I broke cover and had almost reached them before I was even noticed. I waved the Union Jack furiously as I had noticed that it tended to confuse people, bought important time and tended to avoid hasty decisions! The group just parted to let me through to see the young man lying in an awkward position over a rotten and broken post sticking out of the mud. I then realised that the outside of his right thigh was impaled on it and he was loosing blood. He was already looking pale and into shock, yet no one was doing much about it apart from two wailing women. I shed my load and slithered down the bank but could only partly lift him off the broken post by myself. Then I shouted like a mad man and gestured for assistance which finally brought some men down to help. We all dragged the poor chap up the slope onto the flat. He had a very deep gash from just above the knee almost to crutch height. I looked around and grabbed a length of plaited material from one of the women and knotted the make shift tourniquet round the top of his thigh. The blood flow slowed considerably and I tried to open up the wound to clear it of dirty splinters but he yelled with the pain. I snatched up my first aid pack and gave him a shot of morphine which quietened him quite quickly. I shouted orders at the audience to get hot water quickly (ayer panas bunya bunya se lekas munkim) plus furious gestures which finally brought results with the supply in a dirty and burnt tin can straight off the fire, I imagined. I added some iodine and literally scraped out the dirt in the wound with a knife. Then released the tourniquet to let the blood flow to do some flushing as well. Tightened the tourniquet again and poured some more iodine into the wound before pulling it all together and using bits of my crepe bandage to hold it all. I then cleaned the outside of the wound with some Peroxide and started stitching with a fair sized curved needle and gut. My stitching was very wide apart and not very close to the wound edges. This seemed to hold things fairly well so I then added smaller and closer stitches in between the original coarse ones making it all slightly and relatively neater, and I mean, only relatively! I released the tourniquet for the last time and waited to see the result which was quite pleasing as very little blood then oozed out between the stitches. It did occur to me that it might be because he did not have much left?! Finally, after mopping off the excess blood I slapped on a couple of field dressings over the wound having removed my bits of crepe bandage which I then used to tie his knees and ankles together before getting him carried into a hut. Wrapping him up and getting some warm soup/gruel into him was next, then leaving him to sleep off the morphine.

73. New friends?

I have no idea how long all this took but I felt quite pleased with myself but a bit emotionally drained. Brazenly and nonchalantly I then parked myself on their veranda walkway and started to feed myself. They all stood at a safe distance gazing at me with what, I wondered, in their minds? Nothing was said but slowly the very young children approached me out of curiosity, I image. I gave two of them a glucose sweet each and with a bit of persuasion got them to put them into their mouths, their faces were a treat. This then seemed to release a mass of chatter that I could not understand and the men all sat down in semi-circle round me and within minutes some women brought me cooked rice all wrapped up in woven leaf parcels in which it had been cooked. Then some sweet corn with a curry sauce and some eggs after I had politely rejected some awful smelling meat dish (it might have been rat for all I knew!). A bowl of roughly chopped fruit followed with strands of sugar cane for extra sweetness. I then thanked them and invited myself to stay the night with them (terima kasih itu makan, nanti saya mau tidor di sini ini malam, boleh? (roughly; thank you for that food, shortly I want to sleep here tonight, ok?) Heads were nodded so my pidgin Malay was at least partly understood. The thought again crossed my mind that had I not, so often been lazy and let local girlfriends like Connie in Malaya and Nonnie in Djakarta do most of the local talking when we were out and about together then my Malay would have been more able to cope with situations like this, when on my own. Local girls or women in such circumstances were often euphemistically referred to as sleeping dictionaries. I was ushered into a spot near the entrance, luckily, as the stink in these long houses is grim and added to which the end over the river having slightly wider slats is used by all and sundry to urinate and defecate through, leaving some dried excrement on the floor boards that had not make it through the gaps!

The following morning for breakfast I added one of my foil sealed dried soups to a well boiled water bowl and had some more sweet corn and a sweet potato. I had a captive or even captivated audience who were even competing to sit nearer me! I took the opportunity to try and converse with them about the communists. They all looked scared and kept muttering mati (death or to be killed). Only one man was prepared to go on with me as a guide but even then not all the way to the commie camp but he would point me in the right direction. All this had taken well over two hours, so after checking on the patient who was looking less pale and after I changed his dressing we headed off after the commies. The path went on through the kampong and along the river and up over another ridge and turned along a deep ravine then down again back into a catchment area which fed the ravine we had just come up. There was a man-made small log type footpath across this boggy ground. The area was very exposed and wisely my guide shook his head when he thought I wanted to cross it. I did not but was grateful to have him to guide me round the edge, which was dryer and in cover most of the way. Being shot by a commie while exposed out in the open was not part of my plans!

We only went about three quarters of the way back to the path where it led into jungle again. Instead he led me around the back of a hill to loop back to the original path about a mile further on. At this point my companion refused to go on any further and repeatedly pointed on along the path saying "Orang Mati Bunya" literally meaning "lots of dead men" but actually trying to say "lots of killer men" (the commies). He told me "Orang mati, jalan satingah hari" or the killers were half a day further on. By this time it was getting dark again so we went back round the hill, found a sheltered spot under some big rocks and lit a fire to stay warm at the higher altitude and to cook even more of the Dyak villager's sweet corn and sweet potatoes, some sago pudding and sugar cane for afters. I slept very well and did not waken very early as under the trees and rocks it did not seem to get light as early as usual!

74. The lion's den?

The next morning I felt very relaxed and almost to the point of laziness. I had another good breakfast and sorted, checked and repacked everything, knowing that I could now be getting into a very serious and dangerous situation. Everything must now be well organised and instantly to hand. I gave myself a good talking to and pointed out that survival would depend on great caution and total lack of emotion, particularly that of my hatred of the commies. "Totally dispassionate" was to be my motto, at least temporarily! Retracing my steps forward again to pick up the track where my companion had refused to go further was easy and he, in the meantime had headed back to his kampong. The track was quite clearly worn and was easy to follow. I stopped every five minutes or so to listen intently for any sounds or signs of my quarry. I passed what was one of their halts or resting spots by a waterfall. The give-away? Lots of cigarette butts. After about two hours of undulating track well up in the hills the path once again opened out onto the side of a deep ravine up to a hundred feet deep. Even from that depth the noise of the water would drown out any early warning sounds of the sort of company I did not want! Progress was very slow while straining eyes and ears for the slightest alien sound or movement ahead of me. It was so slow that I could not even estimate whether it was a mile or three later that I spotted an aerial walkway across the ravine ahead and to my left. With such obvious evidence of human endeavours it was very likely that the risk of meeting human traffic was increasing. I climbed up the banking to my right and continued with some difficulty parallel and above the track.

75. Bingo!

Progress was slow but actually no slower than the way I had been creeping along before. There being almost no risk of unexpectedly bumping into anyone or even being heard up there. Finally I reached the point where I could look down on to a spindly bridge and clearly see any traffic over it coming or going or along the path which also carried on beyond the bridge turn off. I just settled down comfortably as I could with the field glasses for an hour or so and until it started to get dark. It was only then that I finally spotted the glow of a cigarette being smoked on the other side of the bridge. There were a couple of guards on duty. How wise I was to leave the path when I did and make my way higher up and out of sight because they certainly would have easily seen me long before I might have spotted them! Round one to me. Delighted with my discovery I made my way further up the hillside and round a rocky shoulder until I found a fair sized fallen tree which I could almost get under. I made a quick additional shelter wall with branches laid against the trunk and then got inside and scoffed some cold rice and sweet corn for dinner. I awoke a couple of times during the night to hear some animal roaming about nearby. It was on the chilly side and rather wet that night and I knew I would have to find a better bolt-hole or vastly improve that one when I could really see what I was doing in daylight. I woke finally to find myself covered in ants, some of whom had just had their breakfast. Me.

I was glad I had just reorganised my gear so that I was immediately able to lay my hands on one of the blue bags which traditionally was used by our mothers as a water softener in the laundry I believe and it was always the back stop for treatment of insect bites. I assumed that it would work on ant bites as well? In practice it did help. The tree I had found and slept under in the gloom turned out to be better than I thought because the other side gave me a lot more space and shelter when I cleared away the growth and a few rocks and stones The cure for the ant problem was to stretch out two parallel lengths of a rope attached to one of the upended roots at one end a suitable broken branch at the other, about 12 feet apart. I then cut about twenty thick saplings into three foot lengths and attached them to both ropes with the same figure of eight knots that I had used for my tree climbing aid. The result was a sort of sagging horizontal rope ladder with the cross steps only about six inches apart and with the rope ends drawn together. In other words, a hammock with a sapling base. All slightly different from back in Djakarta where we would stick each bed leg into a small tin can or lid and then fill them with paraffin which the ants would not swim across. Next I set about making a simple framework lean-to from the ground up onto the fallen tree. Then wove or plaited the usual attap mat panels and laid then like giant roof tiles on top of the frame work which would keep out the heaviest of rain. Digging a small channel along under the trunk would divert any rain coming in underneath from the other side. A criss-cross, in and out sapling floor mat/cover would ensure much less mud build up on the floor with my constant foot traffic! Finally I collected a good store of dry and reasonably dry kindling and tinder material, including dead twigs, mosses, lichen, peeled bark and dry leaves.

As my new home was about half a mile away from the track, higher and behind a hill, densely covered with trees and bush as well, I considered the chance of the commies spotting any smoke was remote. The other risk but only an outside chance was of them smelling it, I would try and assess that myself at different points of my journey between my observation point and my new home. The previous night had been a bit cold and damp but all this work had warmed me up but had taken most of the morning, so after a hot soup I headed back to my observation point above the bridge. I moved my position into a more comfortable and a slightly better and sheltered spot where I could now clearly see the guards/sentries on the other side. Two of them were just sitting on a bench under an attap roofed shelter smoking continually and with their rifles just lying on a table along with some food and water bottles. Absolutely nothing happened all afternoon apart from their odd call of nature. Then as dusk was descending and I was about to get up and return to my new abode when the guards were relieved by two replacements. The night shift? I returned to my new home in quite high spirits, lit a fire and had a good cook up and then treated myself to another glucose sweet afterwards. I could not help musing on the irony of the situation. Here was I living and hiding in the jungle like the C.T's were doing in Malaya but now it was the communists that were part of the 'establishment' forces to be avoided at all costs. The only real difference was that it would not be politic to start ambushing and killing them, tempted though I might be, I did actually want to get out alive plus the fact that the information I was gathering was far more important than any personal vendetta.

76. Double bingo!

On about the third day of my all day vigils, a party of ten commies came up from the other way and crossed the flimsy bridge, all well spaced out lacking total confidence in the bridge I think. This patrol had been away several days at least and were not carrying any loads or supplies so they had to be part of an ongoing border patrol or incursion policy into Sarawak which I estimated could be only five to ten miles away! The patrol exchanged greeting with the guards and carried on up a path and out of sight but within less than a minute I could hear shouts, even over the water noise which I thought I could safely assume was them reaching their camp less than a couple of hundred yard from the bridge. More potentially useful information. Additional bits of observation were that the commies had reinforced the native bridge with manmade ropes strung across the gorge or ravine for both the hand rails and the very narrow base walkway which would indicate serious long term planned use by them. Their camp or base was obviously meant to be secret and very difficult to approach from any other direction, therefore easily defended at the bridge from any enemy or even just nosy natives? I do remember having the childish urge to go down and cut the bridge away and cause them a lot of inconvenience. Totally irresponsible of course as even in the dark such efforts were likely to be heard. I would have no cover from an automatic rifle fired at me, even in the dark from the other end of the bridge and which would almost certainly hit me. My revolver would be out of range and its flashes in the dark would only pin point me better! It would serve no really useful purpose long term and start the sort of hue and cry I had been trying to avoid in the first place. More importantly, in my mind was the very likely revenge that the commies would take on the Dyaks. They would assume it had been them retaliating for the recent rapes and ill treatment. It was only a silly thought and in effect only a prank and of no real strategic importance, the repercussions though, could have been horrendous. I did venture along and above the path towards Sarawak a mile or so one day and discovered that the water in the ravine below was actually flowing north toward the border not back along the way I had come from on the Indo. side, as I had assumed. My care in keeping up and above the regular path paid off again. Because, as I was returning from this particular recce I would have run into an outgoing commie patrol, consisting of a dozen this time. Then about a week later just when I was thinking that I might start making my return journey, a big group of commies crossed the bridge and headed off back the way I had originally come from, presumably for another supply carrying trip.

I stayed another night before breaking camp and heading back myself and hoping that I might not catch up with them unexpectedly. I was quite pleased with myself, feeling fit and only suffering minimal leech sores, bites, stings and cuts. The slight tendency towards the squitters had been cured by taking kaolin for a couple of days. My urine was pale and not very smelly so the hydration levels were good. I had found in Malaya that my ability to hold my water longer than most seemed to reduce my need for fresh intakes of water. My theory was that as soon as you empty your bladder some of the other retained moisture within the body starts to rush to fill it up again much sooner and quicker than had it not been just emptied? Most important of all though was the fact that my feet were in better condition than expected. The reason was that I would get my boots off at every safe chance and wear the lace up sandals which enabled the feet to breath better and dry out quickly and naturally but still enable me to take off or escape in a hurry should the need arise (you can't run very well in the jungle wearing flip flops!) The addition of the flip flops allowed me to putter about the camp giving more time for the boots to dry out or for me to ablute without the risk to soft bare feet in a steam or the continual wetting of either boots or sandals unnecessarily. I would sleep with dry feet most nights which with the aid of talc as well meant starting each day with much dryer and harder skin than otherwise possible. Plus the fact that the wet footwear could often be almost dried out by the morning.

Early the next morning I headed back along the hillside above the path until I was sure I was well out of sight of the bridge guards. Back down on the path again I made better time and was less hesitant than on my outward journey. The risk of running into an odd commie was still there but knowing the route and terrain helped a lot. I was unlikely to catch the supply group up and even if there was any other returning group I would expect to hear them from some distance away. Twenty to thirty men chattering and shouting at each other when coming toward you and with no concerns about security make a lot of noise. I decided to make the same detour round the open boggy area that my guide and I had used on the way up and stopped early at the same sheltered camp to eat a good meal, turn in early and make an early start the next morning for the relatively straight forward journey back to the kampong where I could replenish my food supply as well.

77. Friends, again

The journey down to the kampong was entirely uneventful and I arrived soon after noon on another very hot day. A series of hooting cries went up as I was spotted and in no time a group of excited children were jumping and dancing round me. As I reached the long-house several adult women just appeared with different little baskets of food. Far too much but I made a diplomatic gesture of taking a little of several items that were recognisable to me. I was ushered to one of the smaller huts that thankfully did not smell too bad. A group of men sat round me to bechara (talk or chat) and so back again to pidgin Malay. The commie supply party had passed through their kampong late the day before and had caused no trouble this time but the men were now going to send the younger women off up to some remote rumah buru (hunting lodge) whenever the commies were thought to be coming by. I suggested that they should arrange some sort of lookout system to which they gleefully said they souda (already had or past tense) I asked to see my patient but they had sent him down river to the rumah sakit (sick house) which I assumed was some little hospital or medical or doctor's house. It appeared he was carried into a canoe and was fit to travel but could not walk yet!

I stayed the night and was well fed and supplied with more food than I really needed when I left in the morning. They seemed reluctant to let me go and repeatedly told me I would always be welcome. I thanked them but explained that I came from many islands away and it may not be possible (because of the commies, of course) for me to ever return. Little did I know!

As I got back to the river area quite early I took cover and waited until dusk before passing the little jeti with no signs of anyone on either side of the river. Finding myself back in very familiar surroundings was almost comforting as I made for my tree with a sense of almost relief. However I did now have to figure and plan how to get back down the river again to Ngabang. I could not sit and wait on the bank for the spies to come past. Nor could I just keep hiding and rush out to them when they next passed or delivered some food.

It was too dangerous and would put them in danger. They, after all had to continue to live here and do business in the area. I thought about leaving a note in our basket-hide-cache to try and pin down a very small time frame for collection but the risk of misunderstandings and the possible long time factor would rule that out as well. It was all a bit of a dilemma but not yet worrying. I had my health, adequate food and I might be able to make my way down river along the boggy shore and bank of the river. My walking staff with its disc had been working well on boggy ground and having a third leg had proved invaluable when crossing rivers by myself, against any current. Then, I thought, when I got down river far enough I could cadge a lift or even steal a boat temporarily. Travelling by foot for short periods at dusk and dawn then hiding up during the day and night until I was far enough downstream to be considered outside the army exclusion zone if I did finally get caught. That night I did not bother to climb up or take my gear up into the tree. I just slept in my often used position, curled up, back to a tree, sitting/squatting on a mat with the poncho covering the gear and me, all under a miniature bell tent.

The next morning I woke, cold stiff, a bit wet and with a few extra insect bites where I had not tucked in my netting properly. Not a good start to any day and having to revert to a cold breakfast did not help either. There was considerable activity on the other side of the river at that small jeti and a few bods on my side as well. I could not figure it out unless it was the commie supply group sorting themselves out ready to head back to their ravine/border camp. Not being up my tree I could not really see what was going on and I decided not to climb it as it was very wet and slippery and I had not yet re-rigged my toggle rope. I was certainly not going to take the risk and further discomfort of crawling through wet and boggy ground just to satisfy my curiosity. A bit more patience after all these weeks was no great problem. By mid afternoon all the noise and activity seemed to have stopped so I did creep forward and looked up and down the path which seemed empty. I waited half an hour and it was still quite clear so I decided to visit the drop-off point in the rushes to see if my films had been collected and to pick up whatever had been delivered. The films were gone and there was a selection of foodstuffs including some tins. A welcome new departure. I collected the food and left the exposed films from my trip up to the commie bridge/camp near the border with Sarawak, to be collected in due course.

78. Disaster?

As I was just about to turn off the path back into the ulu and return to my tree base, a shot rang out and only just missed me. I ducked and turned to see one of the commies running down the path towards me. He was still about a couple of hundred yards away and preparing to fire again while on the run. I turned and fled (no other word for it!) down the path away from him into the wooded bit where the path curves to almost follow the river. Another bullet passed me but nowhere as close this time. Then there was lot of shouting between my pursuer and some voices on the other shore. A few more even wilder shots followed. I did not wait to listen but kept going as fast as I could. The slightly curved semi jungle path quickly hid me as it extended for about a quarter of a mile before it opened up into scrub and marshy ground with no real cover or hiding place. I could possibly have dived back towards the denser area near my tree but I would initially risk becoming a slower and clearer target. I desperately needed some distance and thinking time! As I reached the end of wooded and scrub cover it was obvious and just as I thought, there was no cover or hiding place ahead. Options; (A) I was quite confident that I could move off the track, lay an ambush and just shoot him with my .38 Hart. (B) Again I was quite confident that I could hide and rise up as he passed and stab him before he could turn and bring his rifle into play. The first one I rejected as the noise of another gun would bring reinforcements even quicker and with a sense of urgency. The second I also rejected as it was slightly risky to me and even if it did not bring reinforcements as quickly, when they did arrive, they would mount a massive man hunt to find the enemy who had killed one of theirs.

79. Needs must!

My solution was to turn back towards him and hide behind a reasonably sized tree, which had roots that were half exposed above the ground and ran across the path. I was able to peer round the back of the tree and see up the path through the undergrowth without being seen myself. A couple of minutes later I saw my pursuer almost jogging along with his rifle held forward at waist level. Since I had ruled out using my gun I loosened my kukri as a back up and held my staff by the thinner end at the disk end like a long baseball bat. Then at the instant his rifle drew level with me round the tree and at the moment before he came into view himself I swung my staff with all my strength over his extended rifle and caught him just above the bridge of his nose and across the eye brows. He just wilted to the ground without a sound. I did a quick search and found his papers that showed him to be a member of the Indonesian communist party, the P.K.I., other papers in Chinese and of course his own copy of Mao's little Red Book. Since I now considered my life at serious risk I gave him, what today would be called a Karate chop across the throat so that if he was not dead he would either choke to death or at best not be able to talk to anyone for a long while, if ever! Then the enterprising thought came to me that if I placed him face down with his head/face wound lined up and resting on one of the tree roots it MIGHT look as if he had tripped and knocked himself out, badly. I placed his rifle to give the same impression. Since there was unlikely to be post mortem the chopped throat was unlikely to be noticed which might maintain the illusion that he died alone and of his own volition! It would certainly give and leave room for doubt.

Quick note at this point, as having recalled a survival course I had attended in Malaya where a Korean had been employed to give hints! on survival. Not the usual living off the land and backwoodsman type of thing but survival in dirty personal combat. We were not there to earn coloured belts but to learn about lethal pressure points or areas of the body and how to deal with all sorts of attack, martial arts or otherwise. I had remembered that we should never, when using a baton or stick or staff, strike downwards at the head because as a target it's the easiest part of the body to move quickly to avoid any blow which may only then skim the head and at best only cripple a shoulder leaving the other side to counter attack lethally before the stick could be lifted and used again with unlikely success! Such weapons should be used initially to wind or cripple the attacker rendering them incapable of retaliating, at least temporarily so enabling one's second blow to be an un-resisted fatal one, if needs be. After a lot of waving bluff a straight prod though one's opponent's guard, like a snooker cue was very effective! These same lethal points can be applicable to some punches, be they straight finger or single knuckle. As to the throat chop I only ever used that again, twice, in anger, once some years later in Canada when a man was unwise enough to threaten me at gunpoint! Now back to the past.....

By now I could hear others, presumably having crossed the river, coming along the path leaving me no time to go back towards them and dive into the undergrowth without being at least heard. How I wished for real jungle where within three or four steps you could just disappear. Even today I would deny feeling desperate at this stage, even though my options were disappearing fast, as worrying only confuses and clouds the mind. I imagined that I had only about two to three minutes in which to disappear. My new pursuers did not know that and might well think I was well away in several possible directions already, including the ulu they had just come through themselves, and by the time they found their prone friend. They also certainly did not know who or what they may be looking for. As I was sure that any shouted conversation across the river would have been a bit garbled and certainly not specific. Decision time. I ran only a few yards into the open and exposed area with no cover. The boggy water on the inland side of the path was stagnant and had a bit of an oily film. It would certainly show up any recent disturbances. So it was down the bank into the rushes and reeds at the river's edge without leaving any evidence of sliding or slithering down. Again my staff assisted by enabling me to pole vault clear of any surface that would show tracks. I lowered myself into the river and squeezed quietly through the virulent growth until, at about fifteen feet out I reached some clear water. Then I swam a few feet along the edge of the reeds until I found a small inlet into them but with very dense growth back towards the shore/bank itself. All I had to do then was to loosen some of the reeds and close the reed 'door' behind me so that I could not be seen from the river, either from passing boats or from the other riverbank. Then I jammed my staff into the reed roots, which gave me an anchor and a perch to hang onto for what might be a long wait.

80. Water baby

Luckily darkness was by now falling rapidly and I could hear quite a lot of shouting, which indicated to me that they had found the commie's body. Several times I heard people passing up and down the path. After a quiet pause it started again with torches flashing up and down the bank. Then I heard a motor boat start up and head to my side of the river, it passed so close that I had trouble not to choke on its wash. The occupants of the boat were shining their light high up onto the shore about fifty yards up at about the point where I had left the commie. The boat then patrolled up and down the river several times over the next few hours shining its lights now and again on to some imagined sighting and almost always well above my head height. On the shore there seemed to be regular patrolling, judging by the hum of voices that came and went. After about four hours in the water and bearing in mind I was quite chilled, even in a tropical river. I had to make up my mind as to whether I should stay in the water, well hidden as I was or risk coming out and running into a patrol before I could get back up the path to a point where I could escape into the ulu, quietly, which is not too easy in the dark anyway.

I had just made the decision to stay put when a patrol with torches passed above me. I had used my staff as a step and eased myself largely up out of the water to half sit and half lie on the rhizomes or root clumps of the reeds. The air was cool though not as cold as the water had been but I still put my hand over my mouth because I was worried that the patrol might hear my shivering and teeth chattering! First signs of paranoia I asked myself? It was an awful night, probably the lowest point in my life. The insects were worse than ever but I got some relief by caking myself in as much mud and slime as I could scrape up and smear on myself. Hair, ears and everywhere I could reach. I really did miss my head net. At dawn I lowered myself back into the water quickly as the heat from the early morning sun was drying out the mud, making steam rise from me which at that stage of paranoia did not help. In practice even if it had been spotted it would have looked like the morning mist rising. There were several patrols up and down the bank on my side and I could make out the odd individual guard on the other bank spaced out at intervals. The normal boat traffic was going up and down but each and every one was stopped and searched, even the smaller canoes! On several occasions I was strangling choking noises caused by their bow waves and wakes. About mid-day it all went quiet and the guards and patrols seemed to cease operations, at least in my proximity. I stayed still all that very hot afternoon with my head protected by mud and a large lily leaf.

As daylight was fading I came out of my hide swam back the few yards to the cut or inlet in the reeds towards the shore. For several minutes I could not even stand up or even take my own weight other than on hands a knees. I had decided to wade and crawl back along the bank below the path at the water's edge This should enable me, if I crawled, to stay out of sight from the other bank, screened by the reeds and below the path and hopefully out of immediate sight of anyone walking along the path above. If I heard a patrol coming I might be able to slide back into the water again amongst the reeds, in time to avoid detection. By the time it was fully dark I had got back into the beginning of the wooded area. Climbing the bank I listened very carefully before crossing the path into the ulu. Being now quite dark I worked my way very slowly and watching every step to avoid noise as far as was possible. About two hours later I found my tree and could not believe my luck. The area must have been searched. I thought but my gear and sleeping mat that I had secreted between the roots of the strangler fig tree and its victim had not been found. Everything was safe, so having had nothing to drink for over twenty-four hours, I downed a couple of pints gratefully. I had eaten though, since I had the rice (but no tin opener for the tins) and other items I had just collected from the riverbank only minutes before I was first shot at. The rice was very damp and it was only later that I realised that it may have been contaminate by muddy river water!

I slept that night at the foot of the tree but was too exhausted to change, clean up and had an awful headache which I put down to lack of enough food and water the previous day and night. At least I could sleep warm now but I woke several times during the night not even sure where I was and each time had to go through a long mental process to remind myself. I was also feeling uncomfortably warm, even hot but when I lifted the poncho to cool off I immediately started shivering.

81. Not funny

Came the dawn, as they say and I still felt terrible when I got up. I had a quick drink, as I seemed to have developed a great thirst. I was not hungry but I made myself eat well knowing that I was going to need a lot of strength and stamina. I gathered everything and set off, heading further and further, deeper into the jungle and away from the river by a compass bearing which was slightly north of right angles from the river. I remember nothing of the journey except feeling very strange and suffering a sort of feeling of illness I had never felt before. Later in the day I came out of the jungle's edge to face what looked like a half mile of bog and swamp before being able to reach a wooded hillside and with the mountains to the east of the gap now showing up clearly behind. I was at least still compos mentis enough to realise that I would not be able to cross this barrier before dark.

So in what, looking back I can only describe as a sort of daze, I stripped and washed in the rather dank swamp water, spread out my clothing in the late afternoon sunshine to dry, then lit a fire and cooked a meal that I still did not feel like eating, took my first antibiotic capsule and drank a lot. The squitters were showing signs of returning so for afters I took a couple of spoonfulls of kaolin. I burnt off quite a few leeches as I knew I was due for more of them during the crossing of the marshes, they would be sitting just waiting to almost pounce on me everytime I just brushed against a leaf or shrub. Iodine was applied to as many of the scratches, cuts, bites and stings that I could find. My feet were the worst they had been all trip and I trimmed off some perished or rotten skin dried them with talc, added some Tiger Balm and put on a pair of clean cotton socks. Finally I took the trouble, in a sort of slow motion, almost out of body state to methodically and laboriously make myself a very cosy bed of springy branches and a lot of dried reed and other leaves. Put my feet into a bag draped myself in the poncho and covered everything I could in netting. I either passed out or dropped off to sleep like a log.

The next thing I knew was waking up feeling grossly overheated but again when I let some cool air in I started shivering uncontrollably. I think this happened several times during the night. At dawn I woke again feeling very weak and like death warmed up but I knew I had to force myself to make a huge but seemingly now impossible effort to wade through and across the marsh land to those foot hills. I packed up and set off with only a drink, an antibiotic capsule and a glucose sweet to sustain me.

Luckily I still had the presence of mind to take a compass bearing on the bit of hillside I was aiming for in the distance. Barely had I started off than I was over waist deep and shortly thereafter very, very heavy rain started which wiped out visibility beyond about twenty feet. I remember constantly checking the compass and using my staff as a third leg one minute and then horizontally like a double ended canoe paddle to help pull me through some very resistant plant growth. Having been over chest high on occasion it was suddenly a surprise to find myself only knee deep and climbing out of the morass at last. The rain was still heavy but letting up slightly. I just sat down and fell asleep leaning forward with head in my hands, for how long I do not know. I woke to find that the rain had stopped and I could make out the hillside ahead of me clearly. With the greatest difficulty I got to my feet and plodded off up the hill on the same compass bearing. I slipped, slid and crawled up to the top and did the same down the other side. Then up another hill and when I stopped for a rest I was not too sure if I could go any further or not and had a long, almost remote debate with myself as to whether I should stop to rest and then not be able to get going again or just to keep plodding on until I dropped. A difficult decision but I was feeling so ill I almost did not care anymore, anyway.

At this point I remember I imagined that could smell smoke, which made up my mind for me, I would plod on regardless. After a few more undulations I was looking down on a familiar Dyak kampong. Either by chance or instinct I had completed the two other sides of the triangle to the direct path from my river tree home to the Dyak's village where I had patched up the victim of the commie rapists. I do not remember even bothering to check if it was clear and safe as I staggered towards the longhouse and collapsed.

82. 9-10 & out!

The next thing I knew was waking up surrounded by young women in a hut that did not smell terrible. It transpired that the villagers had carried me on a sort of litter/stretcher to their secret (from the commies) hunting lodge where they now hid the younger women when the commies were passing through. I could not glean the information as to how long I had been there. The nearest I got was "bunya jam". Bunya generally meaning much, more or lots and jam meaning hour(s) or just time. So I was not much wiser. I had been stripped and washed, I imagined that I had been soiled by my own squitters. My clothing was roughly washed and laid out and I was starkers and lying on a thick woven mat and covered with several layers of coarse sarong material. I was sane enough to realise that I was going through the worst bout of fever yet! The young women were wiping and mopping me frequently also insisting that I drink some very peculiar tasting brew. I even remember that I hoped it was safer than their usual drinking water? I came and went several times and could only guess at the passage of time by it being dark one time and bright daylight the next. A few days I think.

Finally early one morning I woke up feeling very weak but not as bad as usual. Had the usual strange drink which had become an acquired taste in that it was no longer revolting. I was so weak that I could not lift my head up without help and even lifting an arm or hand was a concentrated effort. But I could finally face some food which initially consisted of a sago pudding with lots of crushed sugar cane. (come back school dinners, all is forgiven.). In a few days I was onto baked sweet potato, some onion/leek type of vegetable and a bean/dall mix and egg coated, almost a veggie burger! I was taking short walks within a week of waking up full time. I was back on the kaolin and antibiotics and most of my cuts and scratches were healing quite well but my feet were taking longer. One of what I assumed was the remains of a leech attachment point on the inside of my thigh had gone septic. I scraped out as much of the puss as possible then put some iodine on it and made up a kaolin poultice. This cleaned it up/

out overnight and it started to dry and heal over the very next day. A hopeful sign of health and resistance building up again at last. I was even putting a little weight back on. My physical jerks and exercising caused considerable mirth. I wore only a loin cloth and went bare footed to enable the sun and fresh air to dry and heal up as many cuts and sores as possible. Even my feet were improving rapidly, a great relief.

I was almost reluctant to turn my mind to the still major problem of getting past the Indo. and commie camps to escape down river which surely was going to be that much more difficult now. I was still a bit light headed and had silly thoughts like "it will all come out in the wash". "It" being me and the "wash", the river I had to pass along. Another was the old question? What is worse than raining cats and dogs? Answer; hailing taxis in the blackout! So I was to be heard, sort of singing during a very heavy rain storm (of which there were many and sometimes more than one a day!) a silly made-up version of *Singing In The Rain* which included "raining taxis"! When I thought I was well and strong enough we all (the women and I) returned to the kampong to hear that the commies had passed through back up into the border camp only a couple of days before so the coast should be clear for about a week at least. Lookouts were now permanently posted in any case.

83. Brain into gear

My latest scheme was to lash together a couple of 5 gallon oil drums within a framework to act as a raft of sorts. From the several to choose from I found the best two with reliable screw tops to keep out the water. I seemed to remember from my school days, that each gallon of displaced water would support about 10lbs in weight, so the two drums would support 100lbs which was more than enough for my gear and some of my own weight if I just used the raft for some support and as a buoyancy aid. The kampong had several bolts of cloth and I was given about 3 yards of black material which was attached over the raft and covering my gear in the vee between the two drums and leaving a good overlap at one end to pull over my head as a camouflaged hood if I was hanging on to the raft at that end. A head band or bandanna (to hide my rather distinctive long wavy and relatively light coloured hair) and a cross between a cape and pyjama top completed my disguise. A short cord was to be tied to one of the drum handles and the other end to my wrist to ensure that we would not drift apart in the river currents. It might not be possible or even feasible to hang on by hand hour after hour and for continued survival I would require this lifeline to my gear and food etc. The black cover/hood was then daubed with mud making quite a good night time camouflage of black and reddish brown. On my last evening I sat round to a special meal with the group of elders or heads of families. I was never able to identify which of the very old ones might have been the chief. I bypassed most of the feast foods diplomatically as usual. They presented me with a neck chain of odd teeth, beaks, small skulls and some very colourful feathers. In return I presented them with the now water and mud contaminated Zeiss camera, which was completely useless. They could still have great fun opening and closing it. It was almost ceremoniously placed up on a special shelf with some old ancestral bones and sculls. The amusing thought crossed my mind that one day in the future some intrepid anthropologist might have considerable trouble sorting out the history and customs involved that had led to this incongruous collection of exhibits! The most rewarding part of my last few days was the return to the stilted kampong of my patient with a well-healed thigh but a rather wide, jagged and blue/black scar as a badge of honour which he seemed very proud of. (rightly so in my opinion!). He insisted on repeatedly demonstrating while standing on one foot his re-found ability to bend the knee of the injured leg and wiggle his toes despite still having some difficulty in even limping. Apart from being forever in their debt, I was going to miss these rather strange and in some ways almost childishly happy and friendly but still very smelly people (they could not tell me if they were Dyaks, Ibans or one of the others. They just used what I assumed was a local description of themselves, a bit like "river people with muddy feet").

So late one afternoon a small group of us set off back down to the river path towards the area of the Indo. and commie camps. Eight of them made very light work of carrying my raft on a long pole litter or stretcher. A couple of scouts had gone ahead to check for the odd commie but we reached the river safely, unloaded the raft and launched it into shallow water at a gap in the reeds. This was about half a mile before or upstream of the camps and my erstwhile tree home. I had to be quite insistent about them returning home and leaving me alone. I feared that a group, even of locals chattering away might draw attention to the spot. Soon after midnight when there should be the least movement on the shore and no more normal river traffic to contend with, I pushed the raft out into the midstream where the flow was fastest and then drifted along at what seemed a painfully slow rate. Luckily it was a dark night and on occasion it was not possible to even make out the difference in shade between the bank and skyline, even from so low in the water. I thought or imagined that I saw the odd cigarette glow but no challenge, sudden searchlights or bullets! An hour or so later I knew I was past and clear of the camps because on the left hand side the sky above the bank was now distinctly lighter as we flowed past the last of the trees, where I had left the hopefully dead commie in what seemed like a lifetime ago, and on into the strictly boggy areas.

At the very first signs of daybreak I kicked and paddled out of the mainstream into the much slower moving water close to the left bank. I am not entirely sure why the left bank. Was it because it was still on the opposite side to the Indo. and commie camps or because that was the side I had been living and operating on for several weeks and it had become instinctive or a habit? I started worrying a bit about my thought process or lack of it! I need not have, as I found a shallow muddy little tributary that I swam and pushed up, about fifty feet into. Waded ashore and pulled the raft partly up out of the water and well hidden from the main river. I had picked a spot where the bank was about ten feet high and had been undercut by flood water at some time so even if (when) it rained I would have some shelter. I had not suffered from too much cold in the drizzly hours in the water but it was nice to be out of it. When the dawn mist lifted it was a hot sunny day so I stripped off and dried everything out on the nest or platform of reeds which was well out of sight of the river although I could see the passing traffic over the top of the reeds. I climbed the bank and saw no kampongs or any sign of human activity but still did not risk lighting a fire. The smoke would be seen from the river and by who knows who? Soon after dusk I did light a fire and cooked a big meal. The flames could not be seen from the river or surrounding countryside and at night the smoke would not be noticed. The smell, if it was noticed I did not worry about as with luck I would be long gone down river by the next day in the very unlikely event of my temporary camp even being found. As usual I would cover my tracks as far as possible, anyway.

Once again and towards midnight, when the last of the evening river traffic had stopped. I retraced my way back to the river and drifted out to the middle and got into a slow doggy paddle routine with my legs to speed up the progress of the raft and be faster than the natural flow speed of the water. I would go through this routine for maybe twenty minutes, rest awhile and then start all over again. It is impossible to remember if it was the second lay-up or the third or even the fourth day that I crept ashore early in the dawn onto a small hummock or hillock which in effect was an island at the edge of the river, when in flood but just surrounded by a reed covered muddy ditch when not. I find the memory cannot always keep these monotonous memories in the correct order without milestone incidents to indelibly inscribe themselves on it. This little raised island covered with scrub and on which I scratched out a bit of a hollow and then covered myself with vegetation while watching passing river traffic all day. It was a place to put my sanity back on track. I was busy playing silly mind games as usual, which included betting with my other self, as to whether more boats would go down stream than up in the next hour. I was also wondering if I should give up my surreptitious behaviour and risk coming out into the open and getting a lift downstream in the hope that I was now well out of the area of interest to the Indos. I still felt almost instinctively apprehensive but was starting to doubt my judgement when (luckily?) an army patrol boat stopped a small launch almost opposite me and did a thorough search before letting it proceed. It also dawned on me then that there were definitely more army patrol boats about than I had remembered on our journey upstream. A moment of great elation because I suddenly realised that I was not being paranoid at all, they were! This was the sort of mental boost and strength I needed to talk myself into keeping going and to overcome the physical pain, discomfort and generally feeling so weak and rotten.

84. Disaster, almost

Very early one morning when I was about to head for the shore to hide up for the day as usual the current picked up speed and swept me into a wider bit of river which is not what I expected since wider rivers flow slower not faster! Suddenly there was the sound of a motorboat behind me, and then a dreadful bang as it hit my raft on one side as I was swamped by the boat's bow wave. I went well under and struggled to surface which I managed to do thanks to the wrist line still being attached to me. Conversely if the raft had sunk it would have taken me down as well! My raft however was still floating but looked a bit askew in the gloom. The boat continued on its way oblivious of the chaos it had caused me. While looking around to re-orientate myself after being spun about I realised that I had finally reached the confluence or river junction which is why it was suddenly wider and flowing faster. The boat must have been coming down the other river leg possibly from Yusof's military camp? and I had been swept into the mainstream ahead of it. Well they had not killed me and presumable not thought the slight impact (to them) of anymore importance than any other bit of flotsam or jetsam that they might regularly bump into during their river journeys. After coughing, spluttering and spitting out the filthy river water, hoping I had not swallowed too much, I swam and pushed towards the shore with perhaps fear driving me on. The water flow was much slower close in and after about a mile or so and having passed a stilted group of huts, a decent gap appeared in the reeds with, what looked like, some likely cover up on the bank above it. So once again I climbed out of the muddy and dank water as dawn was breaking.

Before climbing up the bank to hide for the day and secreting my raft I could see that one of the drums was badly dented and the extra effort to pull it ashore was caused by it being heavier, having leaked some water, hence the askew appearance of the raft when floating in the river. There was nothing I could immediately do as it was getting light quite quickly and my priority was to find cover for the day for myself and to sort out my gear, checking for damage, loss and dwindling food supply. There were no obvious losses or damage with the exception of my parang, which was not strapped down tightly enough and presumably now lay at the bottom of the river. There was still enough food for a couple of days, if I was not too hungry! I actually did not feel like eating again but knew I must. My homemade water filter was now clogged and took about three hours to filter just one cup full of drinking water. The stock of purification tablets was now very low. I started adding a small pinch of Permanganate of Potash to drinking water as an added or imagined form of insurance. Although, bearing in mind the amount of water I had probably swallowed that morning it was probably too late anyway. Things were starting to look a bit bleak as the longest part of the river still had to be navigated and bearing in mind all the circumstances I was going to have to move much faster. Certainly I was now well clear of the exclusion zone but those more frequent army checks bothered me. If I sought help it might backfire badly and being a coward at heart I decided to risk starvation and illness rather than finish up even temporarily in an Indonesian jail, where I would probably stay ill and go hungry anyway.

 I took a bit of a risk and went down to my raft slightly earlier and lighter that evening, than usual to assess the damage. The split drum was more dented than open. So I rotated the split portion round so that it was above the water level. I tilted the raft up and the opened screw top allowed most of the water to drain out of the damaged drum. So I was almost back to normal but lacking some confidence in the now suspect drum. The river from there on was wider, much more populated and with numerous kampongs along the way, which in turn would mean many more curious eyes and risk of patrol boats. Clearly much faster transport was essential and the stark choice was risking stopping a local boat for a lift and hope they would not be stopped in turn and searched, even assuming they would want to take me in the first place with the army activity going on. My cover would then be blown for good and all my secretive efforts would possibly have been for nothing! The only real answer was to steal some sort of boat and make my own way down stream under cover of night, again. The added advantage was that it would be much faster than drifting with the raft and I would not have to stay wet so long and so often plus my bathtub skin might have a better chance of improving a bit. There were places where it appeared to be about to rot and peel or fall off!

Not a pretty sight.

So once again I pushed off and floated downstream but staying closer to the shore this time in the slower water looking for some sort of boat to steal. At the first stilted group of huts all boats were pulled well up on the shore so I drifted on to the next one to find several canoes of different sizes floating and just secured to the house piles. I selected one that was on the outside of the group, undid my wrist cord and attached it to the canoe's prow. Swimming round the stern it was easy to just flip off the two loops that secured it to the next canoe and then suddenly we were drifting off slowly having hardly made a sound in the process. I made the mistake and exhausted myself as I tried to push the bow of the canoe in towards the shore but with the raft attached to it and the current acting on it as well it would not turn in as I wanted. So I gave up and pushed the stern in instead, which worked and then towed the raft behind it like a sea anchor. When it all got to the shore and shallow water I could make an inspection. It appeared to be a two man vessel with a lot of space in the middle for carrying produce and goods. It also had three paddles that were not very well matched but I now at least had motive power as well as the current to speed up my journey.

All my gear was transferred into the canoe including the drums which I thought might give the impression of a working cargo to at least a casual glance. This with my black top, head dress and liberal applications of mud to my exposed bits hopefully would not attract too much attention in gloomy conditions but certainly not work in broad daylight. So once again as dawn started coming up I found a suitable parking spot. I did not hide the canoe as it would appear, an everyday sight along the river banks. I just hid myself for the day where I could keep an eye on my new found transport. I did remove my gear from the boat just in case it attracted personal attention from a nosy passer by. No one took a blind bit of notice all day and my skin was noticeably better for having finally spent a night out of the river and relatively dry. I was convinced that I had already covered several times more distance during that night than before but such optimism must not lead to carelessness or over confidence as there were still several patrol boats passing up and down during the daylight hours.

The next night's journey also covered a lot of ground (water) and traffic was getting heavier all the time with even a few travelling by night by spot lights being switched on and off as required and presumably to save battery power in some cases. By keeping in close to the shore the potential danger from these boats could be avoided and they in turn seemed to ignore or not even notice a small craft creeping along. The only possible worry was that one of these boats with the intermittent lights might turn out to be a patrol boat, but my luck held. Towards dawn the river opened up into a small lake with literally dozens of stilted hutments and many of them joined to each other by the most precarious and decrepit walkways. I cut off the main channel and paddled under several of them, even bumping into several of the stilts as I headed on and away from the them to the far shore past some poles with fishing nets that had to be avoided. Finally I had found a non boggy shore line where I could get away from the river into forest and be relatively dry except for the rain that now seemed to appear at some time each day as well as most nights. Most of the really heavy rain and thunder storms seemed to have been left behind towards the mountains. I was feeling like hell with a permanent headache but did now have a very optimistic attitude. I forced myself to eat virtually the last of my food including the last sachet of soup, heated over a fire that I risked, being well away from the river and that would only possibly be spotted by disinterested locals. There was very little life left in my one remaining American gas lighter but I still had some salt left even after I had given my teeth a good clean. My gums were bleeding but they would have been a lot worse if I had not used the salt to clean my teeth on a fairly regular basis. My fever was back but either I was just getting used to working through it or it was only a mild attack. My kaolin and both antibiotics were finished and my quinine tablets were down to three so I took another and finished up the strange meal with a couple of glucose sweets. I laughed at myself as there were several still left, such self-control, I congratulated myself again as I drifted into further silly mind games. There were very few septic cuts or scratches that I could see or find and none of the leech wounds had got out of hand. My skin in several places was in the worst state with excessively soft white and wrinkly bits in several places with the feet, as always, being the biggest worry. After washing them in warm permanganate of potash water and very careful drying I applied some Tiger Balm and put on the last of my semi clean cotton socks to protect them from anymore, river mud and dirt.

    That evening feeling instinctively, almost geared up I started out earlier than usual to pass back under the stilted huts, which were illuminated by dozens of hurricane lamps. Once back into the river flow with the heavier water traffic and despite keeping into the shore, good progress was being made. About 3am a mass of lights on both sides of the river came into view. Street and other electric lights appeared, so it was obviously a town. It had to be Ngabang at last and to say I was relieved and a bit emotional would not be an exaggeration. They were the first I had seen for a couple of months! I nudged into a small jetty and tied up. Loaded my gear and climbed up the rickety ladders to an equally rickety walkway and zigzagged along them until I reached the first actual street. When I found an area I could recognise and confirm that it was indeed Ngabang I returned to my stolen canoe and set it adrift, to float off wherever it wished, downstream. My thinking was that if it was found and identified as having been stolen then it might set off a search for the thief in the area wherever it was found, particularly if moored safely. Then I set off back into town and a mile long walk to Achmed's establishment.

85. Escape, Stage 1. Completed

When I got there the place was in darkness but the old Sikh jaga was sitting on his charpoy smoking at the front door. He rose to challenge me as I approached with his nightstick at the ready. Not surprisingly he did not recognise me at first, even by the rather dim street light. The moment I spoke he did and said Tuan mati, dari mana? Which literally is, "Mr. dead, where (have you come) from?" He sat me down on his charpoy and poured me a large strong tea from his simmering night urn. I then fell asleep on his charpoy and woke in the dawn light to find Achmed and several other members of his household gathered round me. They helped me into the house and up the stairs to the room I had used before that overlooked the badminton court. First I was given a large hot tea "lima bintang" which referred to the 5 star brandy it was well laced with. Then I was helped to strip right off and within minutes, it seemed, several of the old-fashioned zinc plated clothes washing baths with warm water were brought in. I stood but not very steadily (the special brandy laced tea, on an empty stomach may have been a contributing factor) in one of them while two of my hosts repeatedly washed and scrubbed me down in the non-sensitive areas. Where my skin was on the verge of peeling off very delicate and repeated rinsing was used instead. Great hunks of my mud (and worse) matted hair was cut off. The whole process seemed to have a weakening effect on me as I had to be assisted to dress again and to even sit down! Food appeared in what seemed a very short time and consisted of at least two huge mushroom omelettes, some coconut rice, a selection of vegetables and some fresh hot bread and hot curry paste, plus a large jug of ayer djeruk to drink. Someone had been to the local Chinese apothecary and returned with a brown paper cone funnel of some mixed powder that I swallowed obediently! I was barely allowed to speak and told that whatever I had to say could wait. The most sobering memory of that morning was catching sight of myself in a mirror. Even with my strong beard growth, my cheeks appeared sunken which certainly matched my eyes! My skin was sallow, sickly and had that jaundiced yellow look that quinine was notorious for at the time. Bodily I was the nearest to a bean pole that I would ever be. My weight I can only guess at because even after a couple of weeks being well fed I was still two-stone lighter than usual!

I slept right through the rest of that day and the following night, waking at dawn again. Had a good breakfast and found my head was clearer than it had been for weeks. After that I was subjected to a 'pidgit' which appeared to be a pretty vigorous massage with oils and movement. A sort of kill or cure in my case, I thought. This word 'pidgit' I have never found in any Malay dictionary and when I had heard it before I had assumed it had certain sexual overtones? In this case it certainly did not, it was quite tough going. About noon it was conference time. The first thing I learnt was that Achmed had already despatched a messenger down river to Cheng Lee at Pontianak to inform him I was alive and would join him there as soon as possible. I had been presumed dead as my spies, who had dropped off my last food supply had gone on upstream and on their return had heard the shots being fired at me and witnessed the frantic crossing of the river between the two small jetis by quite a number of commies and Indo. troops. The spies wisely kept going on down stream but had been stopped and checked by the army on each journey since!

The river rumour mill had stories about a mad Dutch hermit, a leftover Japanese soldier that may not even now know that the Second World War was over. A small invasion force that had crossed over from Sarawak, composed of what? no one seemed to know. (perhaps the Indos. had a guilty conscience and thought that the British were playing them at their own game. As of course they did some years later!). The stories were apparently endless. A General had flown in from Djakarta and had torn through the local military establishment for their inefficiency and poor security. Hence, their over reaction of more patrol boats and regular searches which did not amuse the lazy Indos. The locals were delighted, despite the small added inconvenience to them, to see the hated Javanese occupying (to them) forces having been made to look foolish and loose face. The Indos. had, as far as anyone knew come up with nothing and had no explanation to offer. The death toll stories from a supposed pitched battle varied from one to dozens! I was right to have been verging on the paranoid! If I had been caught in these supposed circumstances and atmosphere it would have been a very tough and uncomfortable time for me. My exposed films had all been collected and thought to have been already delivered to a Mr. Bruce at the British Embassy in Djakarta, via and thanks to the auspices of Kim Lee's organisation. A great relief and pleasure on my part because although they may need a bit of explanation as to actual map reference locations the gist would be almost self explanatory and very convincing evidence in itself.

In the meantime I was to be fattened up, rested and healed as far as possible before being smuggled out of Ngabang down to Cheng Lee's home at Pontianak. The Indos were apparently still checking and inspecting most boats going either way, at and through Ngabang but not afterwards, down river. It would be necessary for me to get onto a boat after it left town, a few miles down stream. The chance came about a week later when a family boat was due to leave. It had suitable coverings and hidden lockers on board. I got the impression that smuggling of other things was not unusual among these people. Achmed promised me that he would either get the stolen canoe back to its owner up stream, with some recompense or just good compensation that could never be traced back to him. For Achmed, with grateful thanks and because I could never repay him for his help, support and the fact he wanted nothing anyway, I therefore felt obliged to give him my binoculars as a good-bye present. He was so, almost childishly pleased with the gift that he finally showed some emotion for the first time. It was so unlike his usual matter-of-fact and efficient demeanour. He also promised to see that all the spies got some sort of bonus to be added to my kukri and my army knife that I had already given to them to share on each boat as a thank you memento.

My spies had all appeared a few days after my arrival at Achmed's establishment, dancing around me with apparent glee and humming, a bit like a bunch of North American Indians. I feel slightly ashamed that I do not remember even a single one of their names, not that I think I ever knew them all anyway. There I was, so relieved to be relatively and nearly safe that I was giving Her Majesty's property away again. First the Zeiss camera to the Dyaks and now the binos' to Achmed. The thought did occur to me that perhaps Her Majesty had not obtained them in an entirely legal manner in the first place from the Germans. Spoils of war no doubt, so I was hardly going to worry about being sued for their return by perhaps a non rightful owner anyway!?

The early morning of my departure came and Achmed drove me in his ex army American Jeep, suitably covered up in the back until we left town, along a riverside road for about six miles to an old timber loading pier where the boat was already waiting. They had been the subject of a cursory check and inspection as they left Ngabang, so the continued caution was a wise move. The two-day trip down to Pontianak was entirely uneventful. I donned my original disguise complete with coolie hat any time a patrol or army supply boat was spotted. We slept and cooked on board and I still remember the overbaked sweet potatoes split open with some wickedly hot fillings. There was an icebox with a choice of cooled drinks or the usual strong tea or gritty coffee to choose from. The family crew were nice enough but not very communicative and I felt that they were a little afraid of me (or the trouble I might bring on them?) or just in awe of the large wild looking foreigner.

86. Escape, Stage 2. Completed

On arrival at Pontianak I hid on board until dark when Cheng Lee himself appeared to collect and take me out of town to his grand (former Dutchman's) house. Several hours were spent exchanging news and information before retiring to bed. One of the first things I did was to divest myself of Kim Lee's gold tokens that I had not had to spend, luckily! I was obviously now, a well trusted fellow rogue as Cheng with no effort at surreptitiousness, just got up, lifted his seat cushion and unlocked a very old fashioned and heavy looking safe which in turn was welded to robust brackets and chain that were buried into a large concrete block beneath. I got the impression that in that safe was as much value as the small local banks might hold! It appeared that Kim Ling was on his way back from some activity near Siam (Thailand) and in the meantime had suggested that I did not return directly to Djakarta by any official route since I had not arrived in Borneo that way! Whether it was only a coincidence or not but it had transpired that recently there were closer checks on non locals travelling between the larger islands and a sort of visa or travel carnet was being asked for now. Of course I did not have one! The best answer seemed for me to head for Sumatra on Kim Lee's next boat to Palembang. It would be a lot easier to explain my presence there than in Borneo. I then discovered, at least partly, the reason for such good and relatively quick communications around the Kim Ling Empire. The answer, simple, a short wave radio.

A couple of days later, I was off to Palembang, which was the nearest big city in 1883 (although in the lee of Sumatra did not suffer as much as the towns on the South West coast of the island) when the Krakatau volcanic explosion that had blown itself, as an island into almost non existence at the time (I believe it was the largest volcanic eruption ever and recorded at least halfway round the world!?). This trip to Palembang was on one of the smaller boats that Kim used for shallower, more inland and small island ports and waterway as a feeder to his bigger boats. It was therefore a rougher passage than would have been the case usually. The crossing took just over two days and

I was nearly driven mad when a couple of the crew constantly kept practising their Gamelan (a local style of music) drums and gongs, perhaps my nerves were a little strained already? There were many Europeans working in and around Palembang so my presence, when I got there was not going to arouse any interest. The city, apart from being the main port in Sumatra apart from Medan in the north and was the biggest exporter of produce and the main oil city in the area which meant there were quite a lot of scruffy Americans about who worked for Caltex in various capacities. Kim's man in Palembang was one of the largest Towkays I had ever met or even seen. His name was Ho, a white skinned Chinese weighing nearly twenty stone! When in town he lived and worked from above the usual Chinese open fronted shop just a few streets away from the waterfront where the organisation had two fair sized Godowns in the port itself. Ho's flat or apartment was large and airy but sparsely furnished with what today would be called minimalist furniture and all the usual pictures on the walls with often more Chinese character writing than actual picture itself. Lucky slogans and prayers, usually.

87. Palembang

On my second day I was finally able to get a phone call through to Bruce at the British Embassy in Djakarta who told me to stay where I was and he would collect me from the local British Consul/agents home (not office) two days hence. He would drive up via the Java to Sumatra ferry leaving from Merak near Semarang at the North West tip of Java over to Bahauheni on Sumatra and then on by road to Palembang. He duly arrived wearing an impressive naval uniform complete with gold bits on his hat in a Cyse driven Humber Saloon car, complete with British Embassy regalia. This enabled a form of diplomatic insurance against being stopped and asked any questions about say, an extra passenger without a ticket on the return journey although I would be in the boot for the actual crossing, which only took about three hours. I was able to discern that there were a couple of craftily hidden compartments with access through to the back seats of the car as well, I did not ask why! Once a few miles down the road and clear of Semarang I transferred to a small private car for the rest of the journey back to Djakarta and at which point I felt great relief and lost the tension that I had not really been aware of until then. It did then occur to me that I should have been a nervous wreck, but no, just a feeling of overdue, home coming, without the jubilation bit to go with it. I was just delivered (dumped) at my (the company's) Garden City flat at Kebayoran and told to get a good night's sleep as I had a lot of explaining to do the next day!? Ubah, one of the servants just greeted me as if I had just returned from the office as usual at the end of a normal day. John came home about an hour later with his usual sort of grunted greeting but a added comment to the effect that I looked like death warmed up. Great, I did not know what to expect and had not even given a thought, as to how it all might appear to other people. I had been away or missing for three months, give or take the odd day or two. Without any explanation, which would seem totally irresponsible, thoughtless, selfish and many other things as well.

88. Djakarta, at last

I had my good night's sleep and the next morning just after John had left for the office, Bruce arrived with a trusted Indian doctor who spent over an hour going over me. Then with a stenographer who filled several pages of my replies to some very searching questions from Bruce. This went on til lunch time and again into the afternoon. It was not a grilling I enjoyed and to this day I resent that sort of de-briefing treatment, but of course it was essential and I had earned and deserved it, too. Late in the afternoon another, but nameless chap arrived armed with several maps at different scales of the western end of Borneo showing both the British side of Sarawak and the Indo. side where I had been. These maps had considerable blank-ish areas and were nothing like the Ordnance Survey maps we are all familiar with at home. With some difficulty we managed to pin point the salient points and areas of interest such as the military camps and the commie hideout. Some of the shapes of ravines and rivers I did not agree with and with the aid of transparent lay-overs and wax crayons I marked my impression of the curve on the river and its relation to the individual mountain that was the background to the combined Indo. army and commie camp. The ravine where the communist forward base was I could pin down quite accurately even if the ravine itself was not shaped correctly. It appeared to be even closer to the Sarawak border than I had imagined.

As will be obvious, it is very difficult in such terrain to be very accurate about just where a border may run. It's easy with a coast line, a river, roads or high ground points that can be linked up. In thick rain forest one cannot just establish a trig point on each hill or mountain as they would have to be up to a hundred feet high to be seen above the trees from another similar structure. It would also be quite impossible most times to walk or survey the route between, so rather vague compass headings have to be relied on mostly. When you are there it is easy to see how errors could be at least a mile or two! When the cartographer left us it was to catch a plane back to London, having flown in only the day before. He was a very skilled ex-war time RAF map and aerial photo reader and interpretation expert. I am not sure if I was surprised or flattered but it was obvious that someone back home took my findings very seriously. Then a miracle, Bruce took me out to dinner to a hotel that I had never visited before, just off the main road into the city and that had been a long established residence of some Dutch official or businessman in pre-war days. It had also been used, during the occupation as an officer's recreation club (brothel?), by the Japanese. During this meal Bruce said that when they (presumably Major Smythe) had my health report in full some serious decisions may have to be made but in the meantime London had no idea as to what to do with me next. I had a premonition that I was not going to like the outcome, whatever it was.

The gist of my second report and assessment was roughly as follows;

Firstly, unlike eastern Borneo the situation in the west was potentially very serious indeed as it was very clear that the Indonesians had aggressive intentions when and if they thought they could get away with it. There was even less chance of them mounting a sea invasion than in the east and they still had no potential air cover and would have to mount any sort of air invasion and backup supply from somewhere like Palembang on Sumatra. It did not seem likely from a distance and a logistical point of view and such preparations would be quickly spotted. They were committed to a land invasion through the gap area towards Kuching. They could move several thousand troops through the gap using, perhaps several (I only knew of one) routes. Forming up secretly in the jungle to launch an attack on Kuching within two days travel. Their disadvantage would be that they would only be lightly armed, as they could not easily transport even medium field guns or vehicles along these routes.

Secondly, the Indos would probe into Sarawak to test the reaction and response using the communists as a front while denying any government responsibility. The chance of having enough men and resources to mount an attack up most of the length of the island towards Brunei was less likely. Therefore with the communists being so well backed up and supplied it was almost certain that the communists would set up jungle bandit camps in just the same way as Malaya. Adopt the usual hit and run tactics, intimidate the locals for food and support. In addition they would certainly set up the Malayan pattern of Min Yuen cells for support from the towns, to recruit, to foster unrest and riots as and when they could. This was of course, to first weaken any British argument and to possibly justify an Indo invasion at some time in the future.

Thirdly; The Indonesian government and/or army (or at least certain sections of it) were taking a huge risk encouraging and supporting the communists (they clearly had not learnt the British lesson from Malaya) as the communist political party was already one of the biggest in the country (Indonesia). These uncontrolled forces with support from both Russia and China could very easily become uncontrollable and take over the whole country. As I have already mentioned the other political parties and a large section of the army were already alarmed at the possible prospect. But President Sukarnoe (Bung Karno) having got away with "supping with the devil"(the Japs.) thought he could get away with it again. Apparently ignoring the fact that this time there would be no massive Allied war effort to beat his, then enemies(?) for him! Indonesia could become a Communist state, almost overnight!

My recommendations were;

1. Establish a large garrison in the Kuching area, which should feed and back up numerous jungle patrols over a wide enough area to cover the full width of the gap. A fan of about 30 to 40 miles. Smaller garrisons near Brunei and Jesseltown (modern day Kota Kinabalu).

2. Train up even more Dyaks, Ibans etc. as used in Malaya but this time to stay at home and integrate into the hundreds of remote border communities as spies, liaison contacts and even the setting up of little home guard units. Build up the 'hearts and minds' policy with these people as in Malaya ensuring thousands of additional eyes and ears at work. Small kindnesses, some medical help and a bit of education works wonders. I'd already proved it and after all these people hated the communists too!

3. Increase the Special Branch activities in the urban areas.

AND 4. It must be assumed that the much larger river Kapuas that also flowed out at Pontianak and of which my river, the Landak, was but a large tributary may also have more potential Chinese Communist garrison forces. The river Kapuas itself, as I have already mentioned, was many hundreds of miles long and had perhaps dozens of tributaries feeding it all along the mountainous border with Sarawak and almost up to B.N.B. It must also be assumed that most of these will have emanated from and through the border mountains via valleys, ravines and a variety of water eroded possible passes. In much the same way that my exploration had found. These gaps feeding the Sugai (river) Kapuas were not anywhere as wide as the one south of Kuching but could be regarded as more than possible, smaller back doors into British (later Malaysian) territory. NEEDLESS TO SAY I DID NOT VOLUNTEER TO GO AND FIND OUT!

A BIT OF EXPLANATORY HISTORY

After his treacherous association with the Japanese, Sukarnoe manoeuvred and inveigled his way into the presidency on his 'kick the Dutch out' propaganda and policy. He had grandiose ideas of being the saviour of Asia from all the imperialists while acting rather like his Japanese imperialist heroes in suppressing any and all opposition in some of the remoter areas among even his own people. Under the postwar United Nations arrangements the former Dutch East Indies were supposed to have been divided into an Eastern Indies and a separate Western Indies but Sukarnoe was successful in spoiling that idea. He was not nicknamed the political puppet master for nothing! He then kept pushing to get the Dutch out of Papua or Irian Jaya and with the Americans interfering again applying financial blackmail to the Dutch, forced them to leave, so making Papua a separate province of Indonesia. If the Americans had had their way the rest of Papua New Guinea (the eastern half) would have gone to them as well. Happily the Australians are or were not so easily bullied and/or financially blackmailed. The Indonesian greed for territory has never subsided and still goes on today. Every time any area wants to retain some local autonomy the central government will try to crush it. Be it for the oil, other produce or just to repress the Hindus or Christians. When I originally wrote this there was a virtual war going on at the northern tip of Sumatra called Aceh to retain its oil and gas.

Since writing this some months ago the world has been shocked by the tsunami which has devastated almost all of the northern tip of Sumatra and totally wiped out the main city of Banda Aceh. Already there are ominous signs that the cynical central Govt. in Djakarta want to get rid of the foreign aid workers and take full control themselves! I would suspect that they see this tragedy as an ideal opportunity to finally crush all opposition and the local people's aspirations once and for all! In its usual cynical, ruthlessly cruel and oppressive way the central government will, I am sure take full advantage of the situation with little real regard for the suffering of their own people.

The central government regularly use Militias to kill off problem Christians in places like Central Celebes (now known as Sulawesi) and in the Moluccas Islands. I have already mentioned the semi no-go area of southern Java where we had to buy a car visa before even approaching Yogyakarta itself. This is but one of the many indication of areas that had and often still have little wish to be loyal to the central government back in Djakarta. There is also clear evidence that the central government also support the Muslim terrorist activities in the southern parts of the Philippines since the vast majority of Philippineoes are Roman Catholics.

Then there is the much more publicised example of East Timor where the Indonesian Government hid behind murderous Militias as usual while their army of occupation just stood by and let it go on, often with witnessed support! When the Portuguese left the country that had already voted over 80% to be independent (even while being intimidated). This still did not stop the Indonesians in 1975, invading and murdering great numbers of Christians (Roman Catholics)! Of course our cowardly and excessively liberal Press did not dare to make such a point. Which is why I would suggest that the Muslims have got away with too much for too long! It was only after many years of what was amounting to a systematic genocide that the timorous United Nation finally intervened. Then, after 24 or so years these unfortunate people finally got their independence in 1999. Even now, ten years on there is still overt Indonesian pressure and influence being exerted on the East Timorese. It is perhaps worth noting that the President of Indonesia today is Megawati Soekarnoputri, Bung Karno's daughter! We can only hope that she has not inherited any of her father's unpleasant genes. I will be very surprised if, despite the token trial of the Bali and other bombers history does not show that she and any future President does not continue to play footsy with the mad Muslims in the same way her father did with, first the Japs and then the communists! I think my contention is adequately born out by the fact that the Indonesian Government have not yet outlawed the Islamist terrorist group Jamaah Islamiya who are known to have been responsible for the Bali bombings. Only a token number of arrests have been made of some indirect members of the group and who after trial have been sentenced to nominal periods of time. This will be quietly reduced when the world's media is no longer focused on them and moves on somewhere else. The real culprits are unlikely to be caught and tried!? Since the Balinese are staunch Hindus the largely Muslim Govt. will not be unduly concerned about the victims, only the loss of foreign currency from the tourists. Already the Govt. only mounts proper security on a regular basis when the media are present such as at the second anniversary of the bombing. Then back to only a token gesture! Hardly enough to prevent it happening again (and again?). Since writing this it has happened again!

Again and since writing this many months ago Bung Karno's daughter has been ousted in an election and is now replaced by a army General by the name of Susilo Bambang Yudhoyono! Deja vou? Remembering that her father was superseded by a General (Suharto). Is history now repeating itself? Now, again some months later (Sept.2005) sadly there has been another bombing on Bali exposing just the points I have already made and we shall wait and see if the evil terrorist group Jamaah Islamiya is now outlawed or not!? I doubt it anymore than I believe that the real culprits will ever face serious trial either.

Bung Sukarno's superficial reign continued until about 1966, but in the meantime some of his generals had been engineering a series of cooked up coups, which had enabled the army to largely regain their power and influence. The leading General was a man named Suharto who slowly increased his own power while reducing President Sukarno's. The Muslim and other Generals led by Suharto in 1965 then, instigated a huge purge of the communists and well nigh a civil war ensued. Reputedly at least a minimum of 150,000 and possibly up to half a million communists were murdered/killed (other sources since have put the figure at close to 1,200,000.!?). Little international coverage was given to this huge event. So, as not to upset the Muslims? So once again we have seen fundamentalist Muslims literally getting away with murder. While any reader will by now know I would shed little in the way of tears over dead communists the more important point is that, again, and largely without notice or comment, is the fact that it took many, many thousands of Muslims, not just a few extremists to carry out all these murders. They being the normally mild mannered and law abiding citizens but if they are told that their religion is threatened or insulted then they are duty bound to kill the named perpetrators. The, not so long ago, Salman Rushti affair is but one example. The world needs to wake up to the fact that Muslims, when their religion can be utilised as a stimulant and an excuse then almost everyone of them is capable of murder and/or terrorism in one form or another, either physically or spiritually, directly or indirectly! In such circumstances they will feel entirely justified and feel no remorse. A sobering thought! I first noticed this very unpredictable and dangerous Muslim characteristic in Singapore when a group of very mild mannered and tolerant Malay trishaw riders got the idea that their religion had been slurred, which in turn led them to grab their screwdrivers and try to stab anyone and everyone who they thought might be responsible directly or even indirectly! The riots continued for several days and all over next to nothing.

Digression enough, now back to Indonesia. General Suharto finally became the President in 1968 and while not so inherently evil as Sukarno, he, his family and friends were very corrupt. He was however less fanatical and more pragmatic than Sukarno. Malaya had become independent in 1957 and in 1962 the British mooted the idea that all of their territories in Borneo should be included in the new Malaysia, which then happened in about 1963 with the exception of Brunei. This of course infuriated Sukarno who had always laid claim to the whole island of Borneo (Kalimantan) himself and he then dramatically stepped up his efforts to de-stabilize the ex British sections. He even coined the term 'Konfrontasi' while denying he had started a war. But nevertheless he pushed more and more infiltrators over the border, mostly into Sarawak and to a much lesser extent into B.N.B., now known as Sabah. They did not succeed. Then later with the total destroying of the Communist party in Indonesia, policies changed. The about to be new President Suharto and his now entirely non communistic army stopped the 'Konfrontasi' in 1966. Then, reputedly the Indonesians actually cooperated with the British forces in mopping up the odd remnants of communist forces in the border areas!

From my personal point of view I noted that over 80% of all the 'Konfrontasi' actions were in or near the gap area that I had visited and reported on. At one stage well over 50,000 troops were deployed to defend Sarawak, Brunei and B.N.B.(Sabah) and included my old friends the Gurkhas, Brits, New Zealanders, Rhodesians, Australians and some of the old Malayan Scouts who were by then part of the re-formed S.A.S., not to forget the locals whose jungle skills and knowledge saved many lives on our side. Interestingly I saw recently, that there is now a road from Kuching to Pontianak, that passes through the gap and being the only official border crossing point at a place named, Entikong near Tebedu on the Sarawak side. I naturally wonder if this was the road that my friendly Indonesian and non-communist Colonel Yusof planned to build and had talked of? Despite all these apparent reservations I still concluded that I preferred to live and work in Djakarta than the more, snobbish Singapore. But my real, for want of a better word, spiritual (Asian) home remained, Kuala Lumpur, with Penang still my favourite resort. Finally, being fair and also excepting my Borneo brush with the communists the only real violence while I was there was the huge volcanic eruption of Gunung (mount) Merapi in central Java which engulfed several small kampongs, with the usual loss of life!

Right, back to the actual narrative and away from the boring history and geography bit!? Some sort of reaction was taking place within me that I could not explain or understand. I was repairing quite rapidly, my No.2's were almost normal. My yellow pale face was starting to fade but no sign of rosy cheeks yet. I felt rather strange but could not pin it down other than to dismiss it as reaction and the weakening from so much fever, which was still coming and going on an irregular pattern that I did not like. I insisted on going into the office within a week of being back in Djakarta, much to John's annoyance, particularly when I found that he had mistakenly unwound one of my long-term straddles, leaving the company or our clients several hundred tons short on a market moving away from them and unnoticed, it appeared. It took me several very tiring days to rescue and save the situation, reducing the risk down to only about twenty tons that I could not cover either in Singapore, London or even New York. It would just have to await market developments over the next six months and possibly tie it into some other hedge nearer the time. I should have obtained great satisfaction from this dramatic and expensive rescue but I found myself totally lacking in any enthusiasm. This was possibly the point in my life that I started to realise that being a King Rat in the rat race of commerce was not what life should be all about. I wrote to my parents a very non-committal and belated letter home with no real explanation as to why I was coming home a bit ahead of schedule! If I remember rightly this was about the time my younger but taller brother Clifford had started his career in fine arts and antiques through an aunt by marriage. Aunt Winnie who was very much a career woman herself and was, I think, Picture Editor for *London Calling*, the overseas version of the *Radio Times*.

89. Sick again

In my second week back the fever returned and flattened me for several days. Marion Thomson from upstairs appointed herself as my personal Florence Nightingale and constantly forced me to drink, then mopped off the constant eruptions of sweat and applying ice bags to my head. One hour I would be only wearing a sarong and the next several soggy sheets and a blanket (actually a car rug) to try and keep warm when the temperature was over 90*C outside. I believe, looking back, that the scandal tongues had started wagging again and when I ventured the point, her husband Jim just dismissed it and said it was not their business but his and he had given his blessing to the situation. The medical opinion was that I should be shipped back home as soon as possible and to seek the assistance of the Tropical Diseases Hospital in U.K. as soon as possible. Because locally they could not pin down which of the recurring local jungle fevers it might be. I refused point blank to make any instant decision as I had several priorities in my mind to deal with first. I wanted to see Kim Ling Lee (or Lee. K. Ling, I'm still not sure!). I wanted to go back down to Surabaya again and most importantly I was not going home before I had visited Bali. So there!

Kim Ling appeared unexpectedly one day when I was able to sit up for a while. He, having left his ship in Tanjong Priok the moment he landed. On this occasion he was far from the usual inscrutable Chinese when we talked and I was able to confirm his original prognoses where the hated communists were concerned. In the meantime I had borrowed a small electric engraving machine and had worked onto my Hart .38 revolver; XK-BOB on one side of the trigger guard and a star with a heart in the middle and in turn with a bullet piercing it, on the other. Signifying the Red Star of Communism and that we had shared a mutual effort to attack the (local at least) heart of the hated creed. This very wealthy and worldly Asian was more than overwhelmed with my gift or perhaps the idea and sentiment of it. So that is why today I have only my Asian shed sweat stained gun belt left as a souvenir of my trusty SIX GUN. I was clearly not going to get another chance to use it in Asia and it would be foolish to try and smuggle it back into Britain, even if back in the Jaguar's sump!

I flew back to Surabaya as soon as I felt well enough again and rather weakly enjoyed my friend's company and the social life there which included meeting Miriam's husband who turned out to be a very efficient local (Dutch of course) lawyer. Miriam panicked when she saw me arrive at her home for a party and frantically took me on one side to promise not to breath a word of her activities on board the *Willem Ruys*, during her journey out. I was able to reassure her, not that I would have been so tactless anyway. I danced a few evenings with Anastasia who kept insisting that I should marry her and take a good job in the family hotel business, "just pick which country you would prefer", she kept saying. I did little work in the office with David and refused the chance of a boar shooting trip to the Celebes jungle. I wonder why? After a couple of such weeks I booked my flight to Denpasar on Bali and, as a thank you, I phoned Jim to see if he objected to his wife Marion flying down to join me. He thought it a splendid idea and she duly did just that and arrived on the same plane from Djakarta that I had booked onwards to Bali for myself. I had long since decided to ignore any possible gossip since I would be leaving soon and neither Marion of her husband seemed to be concerned about it. Up to them!

90. Bali

Well Bali was all I imagined and more. Looking back after all these years it is still the most wonderful place I have ever visited, that is, as it was back then I might add, being long before the world's surfers descended on the place in their droves and the millions were spent on huge hotel complexes ruining the lovely reef protected beaches that I knew. We had booked into the Bali Hotel (what else) in Denpasar, the sole, real town at that time and quite close to the airport. In those days it was the only recognised western hotel on the island. The first morning dawned beautifully and I was out to breakfast first, enjoying the cool breeze before the very hot sun rose too far. The outdoor dining area was rather like a Victorian Band Stand which protruded out from the main building like an island connected by a causeway. It protruded out so far that the main road had to circle round it before continuing on its way. Rather like half a roundabout. The traffic consisted of only the very occasional slow moving car or van and mostly very colourful people either cycling or pushing or dragging carts. The trees were all a mass of flowers, more flowers than leaves despite the huge number that were picked at dawn each day and spread all over as decorations These were placed as multi headed displays floating in bowls of all sizes, almost anywhere there was a flat surface. The food was delicious and the fruit in particular was memorable, particularly the small local bananas, which I would have sworn were liqueurs.

After breakfast I just wandered round the open and remarkably quiet streets bearing in mind the actual amount of bustle and general activity that went on. The people were all smiling, friendly and content with life, a complete contrast to the rest of Indonesia that I had seen. Balinese are of course largely Hindus as against mainly Muslims elsewhere in the archipelago. They dress colourfully and seem to carry themselves proudly but not arrogantly. I was there at a time to see the first signs of the Muslim government back in Djakarta interfering in other cultures and customs.(yes the writing was on the wall, as they say!). Traditionally the Bali women went about topless and the Muslims were bullying them to stop this age-old habit or custom so in town they had to cover up. Out in the countryside however they did not until a stranger was spotted or a vehicle came along when they would temporarily cover themselves just in case it was some Muslim official. The older women were more defiant and only bothered to cover up one shoulder and breast! Being a gullible male I did not find even one unattractive woman the whole time I was there. Ironically this bullying from the Muslims had the opposite effect than they had wanted, instead of suppressing the Hindu culture it actually gave it a boost. Since the interference began the Balinese had built more new temples than they had in the previous fifty years, coupled with much bigger turnouts to each and every festival (plus a few new ones I suspect).

Half the shops seemed to have the traditional Balinese heads carved in wood for sale. These were to be seen in almost every household that had ever had anyone visit the island and many that had not. They consisted of a male and female with local head dresses on in a bust form, almost like a pair of bookends. Because they were so common as to be almost corny I was determined NOT to get a pair. I was to search out much more interesting and original examples of their loving handicrafts and in one case illegal! I returned to the hotel to find Marion had finally surfaced (at about 8.30) and was enjoying her breakfast too. The whole place was so calm and relaxing that it almost took a mental effort to get going and do something. So I went and hired a car, a great big American convertible one, which turned out to be wider than some of the roads! We spent the next few days just tootling round the island stopping frequently to admire the quiet industriousness of the population. Their complex tiered and irrigated rice/paddy fields that often ran quite well up the mountainsides. The large variety of the local lantern topped temples in some very inaccessible places, up mountains, set into the side of them and out on picturesque promontories into the sea. The beautiful long sandy beaches were often protected by reefs that kept the wild looking surf under control and at a safe distance from the shore. Watching the local fishermen negotiate the small gaps in the reefs in such wild conditions was a spectacular spectator sport to us but an every day occurence to them.

One day when we were just strolling along a particularly remote and deserted beach at Sanur Bay, we were hailed by a voice emanating from a small group of local huts/houses that had a distinctly European accent and that I assumed to be Dutch (naturally). We strolled up the beach to join him and were invited to have a pleasant but innocuous local drink with him. Of course we were happy to join him in such a wonderful place, sitting on his veranda looking out to a colourful and entertaining sea one way and towards attractive looking mountains the other. I forget the name of the drink but imagine it was related to a strong Sake rice brew. This middle-aged man introduced himself as something - something - Lemeyeur (I have no idea if that is the correct spelling). He was a Belgian artist who had married a world famous Balinese dancer when her troupe had been touring Europe back in the Thirties. He had returned to Bali with her and lived there ever since, even during the Japanese occupation. He had not been interned, because he was the husband of such a famous Asian cultural icon.

One more coincidence! Almost two years after writing this bit about Bali I happened to be looking at a modern tourist guide book on the island and came across a mention of an art museum on Sanur beach. And to quote;

> *"Museum Le Mayeur, built in the 1930's by Adrien Jean le Mayeur, Belgian painter and one of Sanur's first European residents, on his death in 1958 the house became a museum and gallery which has seen better days. Some of the buildings are wooden, with carven decorations. The courtyard garden features in Le Mayeur's work. Le Myeur's wife, the famous Balinese dancer Ni Polok, is the subject of several of the painting on show".*

Adrien Le Myeur therefore died less than five years after I had met him. I also wonder what became of his wife and daughters. They do not appear to have sold off all his paintings to New York! Unfortunately right next door to his old home they have built a large multi-storey Grand Bali Beach Hotel and further south on Sanur beach is now the Bali Hyatt Hotel which coincidently again is where my daughter Laura and my grand daughter Bellin stayed with a school friend of Laura's about thirteen years ago! Again almost eerie that we should have walked the same beach almost forty years apart but in dramatically different guise. Almost totally deserted in my day and now an international resort. However the wonderful beach protected from the thundering surf appears to be the same and to quote again,

"Offshore, enormous breakers crash into the reef. The calm water between the reef and the white sands are good for swimming". So, in general it appears that my fond memories did not deceive me. Perhaps I should have become an enthusiastic publicist or opened a tourist agency for the island. I think I would have qualified.

The Nipponese during their occupation promoted anything culturally Asian they could, in their efforts to denigrate anything colonial and imperial, meaning British or Dutch and of course totally ignoring the fact that they were probably the cruellest imperialists of the century themselves. Le Mayeur's wife and two daughters (who had inherited her looks, not his), were, even to this day, the three most picturesquely beautiful women I have ever seen. The wife looked barely thirty years old and the daughters late teens. Impossible to tell! They gave the impression of being three close sisters. No, it was not a sake induced illusion either. He clearly enjoyed our European? company and was insistent that we stayed for a wonderful lunch served on banana leaves by his daughters and having been cooked by his wife. We curiously asked how he sustained himself with his art. After lunch he took us into one of the larger rooms to show us several quite large examples of his work. It was the sort of art/painting done with a pallet knife leaving the sweeps quite raised. They were either local scenes or mostly very good portrayals of the wife and daughters going about their domestic life right there in the home. I am no artist but I was very impressed! He had some business arrangement that every now and again he would send one to a New York art gallery for sale. He said quite nonchalantly, that, "they usually give me about U.S.$10,000. (a lot of money in those days!) each and there is a waiting list". Amazing. I can only liken his work and circumstances to the famous artist who had lived on South Sea Islands and painted similar sorts of scenes by the name of Paul Gauguin the French post-Impressionist. This work by Le Mayeur I found much more attractive and very realistic with almost the accurate touch of a Pre-Raphaelite! At the end of this idyllic day he was reluctant to let us go and left us feeling we had made a friend for life.

The Balinese food continued to impress us even down to the rice being so tasty that I would have been quite happy to have eaten it on its own if I had to. The dusk continued our euphoria with the fragrance of the masses of flowering trees in the still evening air. What a fantastic contrast to Borneo of only a very few weeks before!

Relatively heaven and hell! Everywhere we went was just so nice, entertaining too and I found the local ducks highly amusing. They would be penned up at night and let out in the morning when their owner would give a piercing whistle and set off down the road with a pole over his shoulder and simple white flag/cloth attached to the top. He never looked back the see if his charges were following, marching almost in step and in a regimented two by two formation. Then when he got to the grazing paddy field the farmer would just plant the flag and go off for the day to work elsewhere and the ducks would never stray away from their imprinted flag. At the end of the day the farmer would return barely giving the ducks a glance, give another piercing whistle and march off home. The ducks rushed to follow, often falling over each other in their efforts to get into the same formation for their march home to their nocturnal quarters. Again the farmer never once looked back to check on the birds. Hilarious and almost Disney like.

Having sworn not to buy the usual tourist Bali heads, we went up country to a remote village where a master craftsman reputedly lived, taught and worked, we found him, much to his surprise I think. The variety of his work and quality was very impressive. I fell for, to me, a very beautiful wooden carving of a naked Bali girl. It turned out to be a personal piece, as he was not allowed to do that sort of work any more because the hypocritical prudish Muslim officials had banned them. Because I admired it so much he gave it to me and made me promise not to let it be seen, as he would get into serious trouble with the authorities. He refused to take any payment for it, which was very embarrassing, however I overcame that by also buying a build up set of a typical Balinese temple which again was not really for sale but I persuaded him to part with it, this time for money which of course I simply doubled, to save his face and my conscience over the girl. Marion bought a few examples of his pupils work so they did not do too badly out of us and we in return had almost unique examples of Balinese wood carving which even today I still value over most other personal possessions.

Finally, as they say, all good things must come to an end. We flew out of Depasar and I stopped off at Surabaya and Marion carried on back to Djakarta. About a week later when I got into the office David handed me the phone with a strange look on his face. It was Marion, in tears as it appeared that the wives had been ganging up on her at the club for her disgraceful conduct of having gone to Bali with me and un-chaperoned as well! Her husband Jim was now upset as well as the bitchy wives had cajoled their husbands to get at him as well. I know two wrongs do not make a right but I think after all I had been through I just could not accept the petty and small mindedness of people who contributed little to life and being so hypocritical (two of the women I knew had been unfaithful to their husbands when they were away) and allowing their dirty minds to be so erroneously wrong.

Ni Polok. The famous International Bali dancer and wife of Belgian artist Adrien Le Myeur. Bali 1954

91. Post Bali

I caught the next plane back to Djakarta, stormed into the office, roared at the weak men concerned and deliberately embarrassed them in front of the Asian staff. Something that should never happen! I then went to the club to find most of the guilty bitches gossiping over their afternoon tea and scones. I doubt that, if any of them are still alive today, they will have forgotten the names and insults I hurled at them. They included reminding them, in a very loud voice, of incidents that they were going to have a hard time explaining satisfactorily to their husbands! All very wrong of me I know but I did feel better for it. They in turn had all turned ashen faced and silent for a change. At the office the next day nothing was said about my outburst but certain people were very polite and picked their words to me very carefully. Jim, being a nice chap apologised for putting me in such a position. I was a bit short with him and suggested that if he wore the trousers a bit more often and sorted his marriage out this sort of thing would not happen. I think he was worried that I had risked my job for him and his wife so I let him off the hook and told him I was not likely to be returning to Djakarta after I left in about three weeks time.

The best part of my unscheduled return was that the engineering exam results had arrived and I had done well! I think I also took the opportunity to write to my pen pal, Prue to let her know we were likely to meet about two years early! My next job was to book the shipping for my beloved Jaguar back to Southampton from Tanjong Priok on a ship that left a couple of days after I was due to fly home. So it would be a full six weeks before we would be re-united again on English soil for the first time.

92. Homeward bound

I flew home First Class on a K.L.M. Super Constellation, a large long nosed four engined aircraft, still propeller driven in those days. By modern standards it was very noisy and went through some very rough vibration periods. K.L.M. gave each first class passenger a very good quality, small attaché case that just fitted snugly beneath the flight seat. I still have it today and it is still robust but looking a bit tatty and with a repaired handle but perfectly serviceable except by snobs! John and one of the directors saw me off and I think I detected the signs of relief on their part. I had discouraged both Jim and Marion from coming as well. I had done none of the usual round of goodbyes. I had not contacted Nonnie since my return from Borneo but I did phone David in Surabaya, who promised to look me up when next home on leave. We left Djakarta very early in the morning and stopped to refuel and have breakfast in Singapore where I spotted the banned book (in the UK) called the Kinsey Report on the sexual habits of all types and classes of men and beside it a companion volume on women too! So I bought both for the shear devilment of it, fully expecting them to be confiscated on arrival in the UK. I still have them to this day but never got round to reading them properly, historic comic-reading by today's standards anyway. After Singapore it was a stop at Bangkok for an excellent Siamese Curry tiffin and so on to Calcutta for afternoon tea. Next stop was Karachi at midnight. When they opened the cabin door it was stifling and I am sure nearer 100* than 90* outside AND at midnight. Then overnight to Beirut for breakfast at the brand new international airport that had only been open for five days, yet every single toilet was blocked as the Arabs did not or could not grasp the innovation of flushing lavatories! The desperate passengers from both our flight and others were led over the runway and down to the beach to pick their own spot in the sand. I often wondered how long it took to clean up that swimming beach? We flew over Greece which looked very parched and then had lunch at the Rome stop. Last leg was to Amsterdam for afternoon tea again. A short wait and a flight across the channel to London where it was raining and the first I'd seen all the way back. I was only wearing a short-sleeved white shirt and shorts but with my tan build up I did not feel cold whereas everyone near me was looking miserable. The customs did not seem to notice the books so they were not confiscated and repose today somewhere among all my clutter of many years.

93. Home?

Was I glad to be back? A very difficult question to answer. I was permanently sick of swampy jungle but still loved trees. The Casuarinas and the always impressive Kapur trees coupled with the wonderful smell of Sandal and Camphor wood (especially at night) are probably still my favourites, even today. I had met, worked and even lived with some wonderful people but others were absolutely despicable. I had seen and experienced so much and so many cultures. Had seen death, politics, total incompetence and extreme bravery, in fact, the lowest and the highest of human endeavour. I was almost uniquely privileged and did remember to count my blessings, sometimes! The real question was how was I going to leave all the adventure behind and settle down to the relatively mundane and drab existence at home. I was in some demand to renew my marketing and business ability in the City but I knew I had lost the zeal. I am sure I would have done well but the prospect of becoming a nine-to-five bowler hatted gent was never ever a starter. So I missed the chance of becoming the stereotype and an early Yuppie. In any case mechanical things were interesting me more and more so what could I do in that line then? Nothing obvious came to mind or presented itself initially. I had lots of time and with six month's pay and bonuses in the bank I could actually live for several years in retirement before I would need to worry about money. I had one meeting at the Pall Mall Club with the Major who was very kind and complimentary about my exploits which had produced some priceless information (his words not mine) and that I could feel free to call on him for any help, references or even money if I wished. In all the circumstances he said I could consider myself, from their point of view, semi-retired, on sick leave or just on a reserved list. Big deal! The tropical diseases people could be no more specific about what fever I was suffering from again confirming that it was not Malaria but I could expect it to rear its ugly head from time to time but at hopefully diminishing levels of severity. They proved to be quite correct in their prognosis but it took nearly thirty years before I could say finally that I was no longer aware of the problem. The occasional bouts of feverishness just got less severe and with longer gaps in between them.

94. Prue.. in person

The Singer sports car that I had left behind in the UK for my friends to sell after I left for Java, had now, unfortunately finally just been sold so I was without transport until my Jaguar arrived. My oldest friend Barry Davison was almost as excited about its arrival as I was and insisted on taking the day off work to go down to Southampton docks with me to collect it. He was keen to be the first of the gang to have a ride in it. On our way back from Southampton I did a bit of naughty showing off and I think he was amazed. His only complaint was that at the speed we were doing (no speed limits in those days!) his cigarettes were burning down in less than half the usual time.

I had finally met Prue and we got along very well. I liked her a lot. She was of course very young and innocent, the total opposite to the worldly women I had been meeting and associating with abroad. It was genuinely a nice and refreshing contrast. I was not so enamoured with her mother or elder sister though and anticipated future problems but had no idea how they would manifest themselves. Time would tell!?

Particularly after my XK120 arrived I started taking Prue out and about, which in those days would have seemed quite long trips. One time we set off down to see old friends at Combe Martin in North Devon for lunch stayed longer than originally planned so were some hours behind schedule in getting down to South Devon for what had intended to be afternoon tea but which finished up as late dinner. When we finally got under way back to Surrey we encountered no end of 20mph lorries on most of the journey back. Even in those days the infamous Exeter by-pass was a major problem. So instead of being late back at about 1 to 2am which would have been pushing my luck as it was, we finally got back nearer 5am! I was fully expecting an irate parent confrontation the next day which would have been fully justified in my opinion, at least before they knew the circumstances? But no they did not seem at all concerned about their young daughter's reputation. I was more than a little surprised, to say the least. It also came out over these weeks that they were actually bragging about their daughter being taken out by this very wealthy young businessman from abroad who had a huge car with a bonnet from here to here apparently emulating the sort of gesture that a fisherman demonstrating the one that got away might make. It appeared that I could do no wrong and was clearly the catch of the year as far as they were concerned.

95. Unemployed?

However that all changed very dramatically one day when I happened to mention that I was not planning to return to the Far East in the foreseeable future and I must have seemed a bit too nonchalant about what I might do instead. It transpired that as soon as I had left, Prue's mother rounded on her to the effect that "I hope you are not thinking of marrying him now. He's unemployed and might be penniless". Funny, since as far as I remember neither Prue or I had ever even ventured the idea ourselves. Making it even more ridiculous was the fact that two months of my leave pay was more than her father earned at his bank job in a year! Whether what bothered this awful social climbing woman was my possible lack of money, prospects or the image of being unemployed, or just the combination of all three, I do not know. The net result was a distinctly frosty reception each time after that, which could not have made Prue's life any easier. And of course being me, I made a point of seeing Prue more often than before! No, not just to annoy her unpleasant mother (and sister) but out of a sort of, perhaps misplaced loyalty to reduce the time she had to suffer her mother's nagging about the situation and the fact she was prepared to endure it for the sake of whatever our relationship might turn out to be!? In the meantime I had received a letter from Anistasia telling me she was returning to Holland. She would love to see me again and could I meet her when the ship arrived in Southampton? I presumed she had got my address from David in Surabaya or through the firm. I did not take her up on the invitation and that was the last I ever heard of her. A little later Marion Thomson also returned to the UK and was staying with her parents having parted from her husband Jim. I declined to get involved, even remotely, in her situation and although grateful and beholden to her for nursing me, I decided that taking her to Bali had been more than enough to even things up! I was fond of both of these girls and had had some great times in their company but I was nowhere as fond of them, as say Nonnie. Apart from the fact that I have always regarded myself as a reasonably loyal and faithful person (a principle, often to my cost!) I was now in a semi or potentially serious relationship (an awful modern word that has since changed its meaning) with Prue. This, in retrospect is perhaps why I did not make any effort to look up Connie either and to this day I have no idea what evolved in her life but hope it was of the very best. She deserved it.

96. Out of...comes life!

Then another of those amazing coincidences or bit of fate occurred within about a couple of months or so of my return and before I had got too bored. The solicitor who was handling my case against the lying and dishonest insurance company over my near fatal accident as a passenger in Tony van Beugen Bik's XK120, claimed that he had an important client who was in the aviation business and who was looking for a Personal Assistant that also had good mechanical knowledge, not a common combination I gathered. It appeared that this client who had the reputation as being a bit of a wide boy had bought about seventy ex-Naval Mosquito aircraft (my ears more than pricked up!) which were spread about the British Isles, so he had the problem of not being able to be in more than one place at a time. Enter Robert (Bob) A. Short the boss of Short Aviation and who it was claimed was the Black Sheep of the Short part of the Short and Harland aircraft family, mostly in Northern Ireland. They of course were famous for the large flying boats that did such marvellous work during the war and were then used for luxury air travel out to the Far East and I think even on to Australia. We duly met and agreed to have a trial period to see if our rather different personalities would not clash too much. I think his reputation may have been as a result of some of his regular member/customers that frequented his night club somewhere out in Kent. In the time I spent as his P.A. and while in his aviation office at Whyteleafe (not far from the famous war time and Battle of Britain airfield of Kenley, up the Caterham valley between Purley and Caterham. I saw or heard nothing amiss about him or his business which was certainly open and legitimate and included being the sole concessionaire for the, then, presumably defunct Miles Magister (affectionately known as the Maggi) aircraft and spares. All contrary to stories and the odd rumours circulating at the time.

97. Mosquito reunion

My first meeting with his Mosquitoes was at the old airfield, R.N.A.S. (Royal Naval Air Station) Culham in Oxfordshire and just up the road from RAF Benson where the Queen's Flight was based (and may well still be?). If I remember rightly there were only about half a dozen Mossies there of which only a couple were to be flown out with the others being stripped for spares. Flying them out was going to be a problem as the Atomic Energy people (I presume from nearby Brightwell or even Aldermaston) had posts and cables draped all round the place including across the runways doing some metering or measuring of radioactivity. The already shortish runways had got even shorter making any planned take-offs very tricky indeed. It would take a very brave and experienced pilot and a howling gale from the right direction to make it just possible. Robert A. Short (R.A.S. from now on) left me for a few days with his resident airframe fitter who had been RAF ground crew during the war. He certainly knew his way round and inside a Mossie and taught me almost everything on the airframe side of things very quickly. The hydraulics, the pneumatics, the cable controls, the instrument systems and the main electrical circuits. R.A.S. also had a few Mosquitoes at Stretton outside Liverpool, which I never visited, plus quite a few at Abbotsinch near Paisley just outside Glasgow. In those days Abbotsinch was still a Naval Air Station and Renfrew was Glasgow's civil airport. When the Navy gave up Abbotsinch and because it was further out of the city and much larger it became the natural choice for expansion and is still Glasgow's civil airport today. Renfrew was then relegated to become a housing estate and a supermarket site. All the aircraft at Abbotsinch were stripped for spares and I will make further comments about that site later! The majority of Short's aircraft were located at Lossiemouth on the Moray Firth where there were about fifty Mosquitoes and almost all potentially airworthy.

Back at Culham and on the mechanical side I largely educated myself where the wonderful Rolls Royce Merlin engines were concerned. The components were all pretty obvious to me but the overall design and layout was of course new. All logical and fairly simple from the outside! So days at Culham were spent on the airframes and in the evenings I researched and studied everything I could on the power-plant side of things. In addition to that I familiarised myself with the basic inspection schedules which included learning the number of hours any given component was allowed to do before being changed whether there was anything wrong with it of not! Any changed part or component including even spark plugs have to be released, a term that means tested and certified (with documentation to prove it) by a licensed or approved establishment or company. Some things have to be done daily whether the plane was flying or not, like draining the overnight water condensation out of each fuel tank and often again shortly before take off as well! Checking that the flying control locks were secure. Undercarriage lock pins in and secure, indicated by long flapping flags. Wheel chocks in place and pitot head covered (usually with an indicator flag as well) to ensure that weather and /or insects had not got in to potentially block the passage to the air speed indicator (A.S.I.) instrument!

Although I had flown a Mosquito I had never actually had to go through the routine of pre-flight checking and procedures, apart from the usual taxiing tests and checking the brakes and their differential function. Then of course the mag. (magneto) test at full power against the brakes. On aircraft most functional items like pumps etc. are duplicated for obvious safety reasons and in the case of the ignition the magnetos and whole ignition system including the spark plugs are duplicated on each individual cylinder. In the case of the Merlin engine, being a V12 cylinder with two spark plugs to each cylinder and each full set being fired by a separate magneto. Almost the last check before take off is to run the engine up to full power against the brakes and switch off each magneto in turn and check that the engine speed under power and load does not drop back more than 50 RPM on either of them. This is usually referred to as a "mag. drop".

Lossiemouth

By Syd Guthrie, Melbourne, Australia

Syd Guthrie a fellow aviator and lifelong friend comes from that all but forgotten era when flying was still a hands-on activity and when personal responsibility was inbred or even instinctively inherent. Syd went off to Australia (1955) with a view to marriage a year before I went to Canada so he missed some of the wildest Lossie escapades. Syd, apart from being a more than competent pilot/nagivator/ observer and maintenance man, is also an accomplished violin player along with other projects such as building of one of the first reinforced concrete boats and the planned building of a flyable scale Spitfire in his Melbourne back yard!! He is still very active in the Arts and music world and particularly so in his local yacht club. His professional medical background included haematology, which led him into administration with the Australian Red Cross Blood donation/transfusion service. He was also involved in the designing and building of their latest self contained mobile "Blood Wagons."   Bob Henderson

Syd: I originally met Bob Henderson during the early nineteen fifties in a hanger full of De Haviland Mosquitoes at Lossiemouth. At the time I was winding down my Scottish/Inverness life, as I was due to depart for Australia for a then planned marriage. One day a pilot named Pen Collins, whom I knew from his Air Traffic Control days at Dalcross Airport, Inverness, phoned me and asked if I would act as co-test-pilot and observer on a series of ex-Naval Mosquitoes that were due to go to Israel. I had had the odd dodgy flying experience with Pen Collins already, so expected some more! My first impressions of Bob Henderson were that he was very young to have such responsibilities. It did not seem to worry him one iota. I was immediately impressed by his confidence and leadership qualities. We were all young at heart, thought that life was a great adventure and we soon became a very close knit team and life long friends. We developed a total trust in his engineering skills and abilities, even his unconventional ones! Peter Nock, whom I also had the privilege to fly with, continued to praise him fifty years later. Bob was the only engineer that he had ever entrusted his life to, 101%.

Bob has covered adequately and accurately most of my remembered experiences of those times. These include the hairy take-off from Culham, where we had to wait for a strong enough wind from the right direction plus only half a fuel load and pacing out the runway, to give us a small envelope of opportunity for a relatively safe take-off. I had arranged that the Control Tower would, in an emergency, turn off the multi thousand volt cables should we have an 'incident'! Then there is the amusing, all but international incident. On arriving at Blackbushe, Pen and I parked our Mossie outside Eagle Airways hanger to fix a small hydraulic leak in the CSU unit. It never occurred to us that parking an aircraft emblazoned with the Israeli star of David beside an Egyptian diplomatic aircraft would set off such a security fuss. Then again, later when Pen and I had to divert into Brough airfield during a serious hailstorm, with very limited visibility and barely 20 minutes of fuel left. Skimming up the Wash at a very low level, looking for an unmarked airfield in such conditions is not an experience I enjoyed and to this day I cannot explain how a mass of still frozen hailstones came to be inside the cockpit beside me! Outside the hailstones had largely stripped off the aircraft's paintwork. Two days work later we took off again in another dodgy envelope of wind direction, fuel load, grass runway length and various obstructions to complete our trip to Blackbushe.

One incident however that Bob has not 'remembered' was inside the hanger at Lossiemouth when he was insisting that wet petrol did not burn because it requires oxygen as well. No one seemed to believe him so he just lit a match and plunged it into a full fuel tank and closed the lid. Not only did he prove his point but demonstrated that it is possible to empty a hanger in five seconds flat! I mention this advisedly since it personifies Bob's confidence, competence and courage in his own convictions. It certainly put the frighteners on me, never mind that the rest of us all but had heart attacks! Now at age 85 I find it is interesting to look back, but find that it is becoming more difficult to find anyone that knows (understands) what the heck

I'm talking about. The Lossie saga or story was a memorable part of my life and Bob Henderson stands out as an extraordinary man even amongst extraordinary men and times.

98. Lossiemouth

My next trip with R.A.S. was up to Lossiemouth in the County of Moray (the Scottish Riviera, the Moray Firth and where the least number of flying days were lost during the winter training period) on the North coast (not the Far North!) of Scotland or *H.M.S. Fulmer* as it was at that time (much later, and again when the Navy gave the base up it was taken over by the RAF and run in conjunction with Kinloss just a few miles away to the west at Findhorn. There, at Lossie resided the majority of Short Aviation's 70 odd Mosquito aircraft and often with the lowest hours on them. I remember that some had less than ten hours flying time in total! Of course contracts had had to be fulfilled so some aircraft were delivered new (by air!), then an acceptance flight, a later test flight, then later again a ferry flight to their final destination, possibly a final acceptance flight and then inhibited and cocooned before storage. At some period later they would become obsolete or surplus to requirements and be sold off which is when the astute R.A.S., in this case stepped in and presumably got a bargain. Such aircraft and other military equipment could only be sold abroad to acceptable destinations and would require an export licence as well. Short Aviation had obtained such a licence for at least 20 Mosquito aircraft to be exported to Israel. This licence specifically excluded guns and armaments so any aircraft requiring them would stop off at Nice in France and have the arms refitted! Having recently found copies of the aircraft inspection schedules I will quote the final lines; NOTE; "Aircraft will not be equipped with any armament but will have the existing armament installation left in situ"!!?? The French have always taken an independent line in who to deal in arms with! They often seem to have some funny friends and never hesitate to deal through any back door if it is to their advantage or to steal a jealous march on the victors of Waterloo!? The Falklands war and more recently the Iraq situation, are but two examples! Back stabbing historically seems to be their favourite hobby and has clearly been seen in recent times towards America and ourselves from De Gaulle onwards.

On arrival at Lossie., R.A.S. was not at all happy with the progress of de-inhibiting the chosen aircraft and working them up to airworthiness again. He had arranged to employ the on camp Naval personnel who were only working in the evenings and spare time at weekends. Surprisingly he had permission to employ them from the C.O. who I think resented the fact that he was not in full charge of his ship with at least two of his A.H.S. (aircraft holding section) hangars being entirely out of his control and coupled with all these outsiders coming and going and flying almost as and when they wanted. The Navy had no option unless the aircraft had all been scrapped and taken off in bits. Even then they might have had to put up with even less responsible and certainly more unsavoury characters than us. The Navy were not happy but cooperated fully with a view to getting rid of us all as soon as possible! The problem was that with very few full time staff and the majority of the work only being carried out part time by Naval personnel, it was costing a fortune and taking far too long. I don't think that R.A.S. had anticipated that the part time sailor workers would be working to the traditional Naval routine and systems. Which meant that a couple of erks would do any particular job, supervised by a Petty Officer and then have it all inspected by a Chief (a Chief Petty Officer) who then would add his signature to the long list to finally pass or clear the possibly very minor task. Time was in effect being almost totally wasted. R.A.S. justifiably blew his top and called a stop and then after a considerable amount of negotiation got the Chiefs to agree to actually do the work themselves (for a price!) since it was only their signatures that ultimately mattered. They were of course skilled men but had not got their hands dirty for possibly over five years or more! All this got the work done quicker and cut the labour costs to about a third!

99. Instant Promotion

The next thunderbolt from R.A.S. was for him turning to me and saying "I'm leaving you here in total charge. You will collect the wage money each week from the Post Office in Elgin and pay the men accordingly. You will organise all the work schedules and documentation on each and every aircraft as and when required. You will give me your engineer's report on quality, progress and schedule test flying in each case as soon as possible. You have my full authority to order anything and everything you think that will expedite matters to my satisfaction. Is that understood?" I was quietly stunned and flattered but quite confidently and nonchalantly said "of course Mr. Short". "Good" he said "you've been dying to get your hands on my Mosquitoes ever since you've known me, haven't you?" I admitted it and added "do I take it that I am finally on your payroll then?" It appeared that I was, although I got the impression that the thought had not even crossed his mind before! It seemed that I was already regarded as part of the team and that he had full confidence in me, which I should have known or at least taken for granted! Quite a compliment I thought.

A week later R.A.S. phoned me up to announce that the Israeli buyers were sending their own acceptance engineer to work with me. His name was (I doubt if I ever knew the correct spelling!) Ari Benz Zvi. He turned out to be a very pleasant and slightly swarthy chap of medium height who knew his stuff and was almost fanatically conscientious about his work. Nothing that would affect his loyalty to Israel would get passed him. We were to get on fine, not one argument or dispute ever arose between us. His standards were of the highest order and he missed nothing. Well almost nothing! I did manage to get two items passed him though, but which of course had nothing to do with safety or reliability. The first was to do with the very small gaps that open up or close at the wood joints (the Mosquito's airframe being almost entirely a wooden construction.) particularly high up in the wheel arches or at the top of the nacelles where the main wing spars joint into the undercarriage and engine reinforcement areas.

Wood being what it is will swell slightly in damp climates tightening the joints and dry out and shrink in dry atmospheres opening up any joints slightly. Ari, I noticed seemed to have a thing about these gaps in the joints and I had visions of him rejecting a perfectly airworthy aircraft that had cost a lot of money to raise up to that level and readiness. I decided to check with De Havillands at Hatfield. They were very helpful and pleased that some of their favourite aircraft were being put to use again. They gave me the official limits for both hot dry and cold damp climates, which of course varied quite a lot. It appeared that Ari had the cold damp figures, presumably because Scotland was just that, more often than not. However, since the Lossie aircraft had all been sealed up with a desiccant and in a heated A.H.S. hangars they thought they were in another country altogether! Hence the slightly wider gaps, but which were still well inside the tolerances allowed by De Havillands.

100. Skulduggery?

After Ari had gone off for the day I spent one evening with a torch and several tubes of model aircraft glue (balsa cement?) which I squirted into all the debateable joint gaps high up in the top corners or the wheel nacelles on either side of the engine oil tanks. The second item that I doctored was at one end of a riveted laminated bracket at the tail wheel mounting. I should explain that all Naval Mossies had the hydraulics to the tail wheel blanked off so that the wheel stayed down and locked all the time so therefore could not be retracted on take off, or at any time. It was fixed and locked permanently in the down position. There are no indicator lights in the cockpit for the tail wheel anyway, only the two for the main undercarriage which sometimes meant that although the main wheels were locked safely down the tail wheel may not have been. It had been known for the tail wheel to slowly retract halfway down the runway when landing, dragging the rear end on the ground with embarrassing damage! The Navy had decided that some loss of speed in the air was a small price to pay for avoiding such occurrences on a small and congested flight deck with other aircraft following very closely behind. They therefore fitted two small blanking cones into the tail wheel hydraulic pipes at the two couplings just up inside the back hatch to the left and close to the mass of copper bonding (earthing) strips that run all over the aircraft. (being a largely wooded airframe there is no common and uninterrupted metal earth return path for the electrics). I do not remember quite how it happened but I think that a jack had slipped and slightly damaged the laminated mounting bracket, which was really only an aesthetic matter when modified as just described. I replaced the outer lamination strip with an undamaged one but had to doctor one of the rivets to look as though it had never been touched. The doctoring was actually stronger than the original rivet but illegal as it was not faithfully recorded on the Form 700, the universal replacement and service schedules. Just to add to the possible paperwork confusion, the Israeli Form 700s were in Hebrew and were laid out, unlike ours, right to left so great care had to be taken to fill out the correct sections and boxes! This particular part of the bracket actually did nothing unless the hydraulic retraction and lowering ram was operated, which of course it could not in this modified Naval version. While writing this I have just remembered another unrecorded change that was a bit of an entrepreneurial decision at the time but as any reader will see in due course was in fact a great compliment to the quality and consistency of the Rolls Royce aero engine production standards.

Ari Benz Vie

101. Fun Mossies

The fifty or so aircraft at Lossie included possibly up to twenty of the aircraft carrier versions of the Mossie, designated the Sea Mosquito TR 33. These varied considerably from all the land based versions (and there were many of them) in as much as they had folding wings which were hinged and locked but had to be folded by hand with a long beam with hooks and catches and required several strong Matelots to lift and lever the wings up and over, to finish almost wing tip to wing tip just above and behind the cockpit cover and above the dinghy box used for any emergency water ditching situation. These TR 33 aircraft were fitted with the fairly basic Merlin 25 engines but more importantly with De Havilland's own four bladed propellers which being narrower revved up much faster and were much quicker to respond to the engine throttles, both on and off. Whereas the usual three and almost paddle bladed Hamilton props seemed sometimes only to reach their maximum revs halfway down the runway. In an aircraft carrier situation any such delay would almost always be fatal! Another difference was the wheels and landing gear. The land based Mossies all had multi cone rubber suspension with very few inches of travel and a lot of the landing stress was absorbed by their fairly large tyres. The carrier versions had much smaller wheels and tyres but much longer travel struts, using air and oil 'oleo' legs to absorb very hard, quick and uneven landings on a deck. The load transfer to the front wheels was greatly increased when the arrester hook was caught and pulled the aircraft up in a fraction of the usual runway length. To help take the huge strain of the arrester hook the fuselage had additional long reinforcement strips down each side to stop the plane breaking into two on landing!

 The next few weeks were very busy as might be expected. Getting to know everyone and employing a few additional, full time local men. The two most important were a chap by the name of Davie Souter who lived at Sea Town in the sand dunes on the other side of the river Lossie from Lossiemouth itself. He was always reliable, honest and willing to do anything from plain labouring to humping heavy parts about, pushing a seven ton aircraft about the hanger and always willing to lend a hand to anyone - salt of the earth type. He was also a very good duck hunter and often took Ari out with him who rapidly became proficient with a shotgun too! Ari's military training had been with only rifles and the odd machine gun. The other man, who became a life long friend, was Bob Stewart who was also from a local fishing family but had been in the Air Force and done his training in Canada during the war as a navigator. He was also a very good mechanic having done that sort of work on fishing boats and cars as well.

Ari Benz Vie - duck shooting. Lossiemouth 1955

Bob became my right hand man and unofficially took over when ever I was away. In our spare time we took up lobster fishing and split the earnings three ways. One third, to his boat's cost and maintenance and a third each to us. Bob's father who was retired kept our pots or creels in good repair, which saved a lot of time and enabled us to become the most successful boat in the area, which did not always go down with the longer established fishing crews. We experimented with all sorts of methods, creels, baits and even saved time by using cut up inner tubes as rubber bands to hold the claws together instead of the traditional laborious way of having to tie each one up. We tried different ways of storing them and various methods of packing to send to Billingsgate Fish Market in London with the least loss. (reputable fish merchants will not accept dead lobsters as within a very short time the internal dead man's fingers break down and allow the often deadly poison to seep back into the flesh.).

The helicopter crews from the airfield found a novel way of pick up training, they too became lobster fishermen by hovering over the floats and picking up the pots which required some very tight and accurate manoeuvring. They even had the advantage of being able to fish on rough days when the rest of us could not even get out of the harbour for the large waves and winds, usually from the north-east. We had reason to believe that the chopper lads would then poach from the unattended local pots and presumably also kept the officers' mess in lobsters. Their other local training method was to chase rabbits back and forth about the golf course and local cliffs. Good training for them but it was not appreciated by the odd sailor out with his girlfriend in the long grass or bushes! They in turn would hide their identity and keep the draught off by pulling their jack tar collars up over their heads. The local rabbits at this time were being decimated by myxomatosis inland and on the airfield but the rabbits beyond this double fencing on the golf course seemed to keep clear of it. A sort of quarantine zone?

In the meantime I had found a very nice flat to rent on the first floor of Amor Villa in Commerce Street and which had a good view straight out to sea and even the mountains to the far north west around Helmsdale across the Moray Firth and well up north from Inverness. The flat had been done up as a demonstration for bathroom suites by the owner who was the local plumber by the name of Smith. He had later built a separate show room so the show flat became available, very conveniently for me! He and his very large wife were very staunch Plymouth Brethren and had a delightful young blonde daughter who was made to repeatedly sing "Jesus wants me for a sunbeam" for any and all visitors. The flat was not very well heated and on exceptionally cold and very windy mornings it was not unknown for the lino to actually lift off the floor despite being a solid stone building! It could be so cold in the mornings that I had worked out a system with a kettle on my bedside table which I could switch on and make tea and boil an egg with one hand only exposed until I got my hot tea. I was never in the flat long enough to light the coal fire until Prue came up and lived in the flat later. I also managed to get a lock-up garage less than a block away to house my Jaguar, which I was missing. In the meantime I was stuck with a very ponderous old Humber station wagon, which had no shock absorbers and required almost half a turn of steering wheel movement before anything happened. Hardly the precision steering and handling I had become used to.

102. Mother-in-law trouble already!

It was perhaps a month on before I could travel south by train, which in itself was a chore. First the local train from Lossiemouth to Elgin and only if lucky catch the night train from Inverness via Aberdeen, Edinburgh and finally on down to London (our lobsters had to do it all the time!). I had certainly missed Prue and it appeared she, me, which was heartening and probably helped us both to strengthen our long-term intent. Her mother was still a pain but could hardy claim I was unemployed anymore. I got the impression that my new job was not anything she felt she could boast about and clearly hoped I would be away, "all the way up there", for as long as possible and that Prue would then lose her enthusiasm for me. Within a few days I was driving back north again in the Jag loaded down with aircraft radios and all sorts of valuable spares including a fortunes worth of platinum spark plugs all freshly released for the first flights of our Mosquitoes. R.A.S. had appeared to be more than satisfied with the way I was running things for him at Lossiemouth but was a bit on edge in anticipation of the first test flights. He had distinct reservations about the pilot he had employed for this task. A supposed Canadian (who turned out to have possibly originally come from Cornwall) by the name of Penn Collins and who R.A.S. thought was more of a talker than a do-er but that was the best he could dig up at the time and circumstances. Most pilots did not want to be hanging about the north of Scotland but Penn had a wife from Perth so there were family advantages in his case.

103. Penn, a third rate pilot

Penn turned out to be the blowhard that R.A.S. had thought. It was difficult to pin him down for test work and he never turned up when he said he would and was living the life of Riley at the best hotel in Elgin; The Gordon Arms. He was not only unreliable, reluctant but a liar and a thief as well. He had inherited the lumbering old Humber Estate or Shooting Brake, as I now had my XK120 with me again. I happened to go out to our K type hangar one evening only to meet Penn about to leave with a 40 gallon drum in the back of the Estate full of 130 octane aviation fuel! When I asked him what he thought he was doing with it he flannelled about and claimed it was contaminated and he was going to store it separately in our small store for valuables in Elgin. First he had no authority to even go there. Secondly it was illegal to store fuel other than in proper screw-top cans of no more than 2 gallon capacity anyway. He was not very pleased when I insisted he unload it again and assured me he would not go out to the hangar outside working hours without advising me first. He tried to bluff his way out of it all by saying that my authority did not cover flying crew as well. I, tongue in cheek, agreed that he might be right but in this particular instance if he wanted to make an issue of it I would phone the police and R.A.S. and let them decide. He very quickly climbed down and took the 'old boy' and misunderstanding tack. It appeared that I had spoilt his weekend off as he had been getting ready to go down to Perth to visit his wife and children who were staying with her mother there. He now had to buy his own petrol for the gas guzzler instead of using stolen fuel. The 130 octane fuel was not a good idea anyway, in normal car engines it was inclined to burn out the valves unless it was drastically diluted to bring down the octane rating to something into the 90's only. This could be done with kerosene or even engine oil but it made the exhaust a bit smoky! I later discovered that he had stolen some oil and hydraulic fluid for that very purpose. This pilot was getting to be real problem and I discussed the matter with R.A.S. He agreed with me about the difficulty of the situation but said there was no immediate alternative to Penn and to play him along as best as I could but to watch him like a hawk.

We had worked up three aircraft ready for test flying but day after day Penn would find almost any excuse to delay the testing, from feeling unwell to imaginary weather changes. Luckily a very nice young (old to me) navigator/observer from Inverness by the name of Syd Guthrie joined the team and was to accompany Penn on his test flights. Syd's influence (encouragement?), plus taunts of laziness and even cowardliness from others finally got Penn into the air for some rather short test flights. They all went well mechanically with the exception of one that landed again hurriedly with some genuine difficulty. It appeared that the plane was 'porpoising', in that it would not fly straight and flat and as soon as any elevator was applied to correct either a tendency to climb or dive, it would over correct and do the other. Penn was shaken to the core and to this day I am convinced that Syd was the one that got them down safely taking over some of the controls, like under carriage, flaps and fuel selection and advising Penn what to do next. Penn was convinced that the plane had been sabotaged, probably by Egyptian Arabs and was all for calling in the Police.

The real cause was rather different though and not the work of visiting Arab potential buyers. The first aircraft to be readied had all been worked on and supposedly finished and signed off by the former naval personnel. Anything after that on those planes should have been a relatively superficial D.I. (daily inspection) and pre flight and post flight checks unless anything showed up while in the air or say a mag. drop before take off. On thorough inspection this porpoising plane had nothing obviously wrong or amiss with the elevator cable controls or mechanisms. So we did a back to basics routine major inspection only to find when we applied a tension-meter to the second stage of control cables in the rear fuselage we barely got a reading! They were only just taught and under full flying load would stretch and become slack. The adjustable turn-buckles were all wired up and correct but obviously someone had taken something for granted (often fatal on an aircraft). My guess was that it was the fault of the early on Naval too many cooks syndrome, where one person had screwed them up roughly while awaiting a meter for accurate setting up and someone else had come along and assumed that the tension had been checked and gone ahead and wire locked them up without double checking first.

One of the few test flights in lighter vein that Penn did with Syd was I think when they went off to beat up Inverness and flyover Syd's family home on the corner of Maxwell Drive. We concluded that they had flown a bit low when we discovered on their return some green leaves and small twigs in the air intakes to the radiators! Visiting the area later myself I concluded that what had happened was that since there was a sharply rising hill to the south side of Maxwell Drive which is in part a cemetery as well covered by some fair sized trees. It appeared that the lower tips of the propellers must have just clipped the tops of them! Afterwards in Inverness there was reputedly a bit of a furore over it and complaints that led the police phoning American air bases to protest. They and most observers had luckily mistaken the Israeli markings of the blue Star of David on a white background for the American white star on a blue background combination? Again, if I remember rightly, it was a Thursday because that was when Syd went through to Inverness to give his regular evening lectures on navigation to the lads in the local ATC (Air Training Corps.). They too were all very excited about the American Mosquito that had buzzed the town earlier in the day. Luckily the authorities never found out the truth of the matter. It was with some merriment that we envisaged the sort of conversations between various police organisations and several very widespread American Air Force bases all over Britain and maybe even on the Continent as well!?

This was the only really chuckle-worthy memory that I have of Penn Collins, otherwise he was totally incorrigible. We carried out a few flour bombing raids on the odd occasion for just sheer fun and devilment. On one roof where we scored a direct hit it took nearly three years for the weather to finally wash off the then glutinous remains of the splattered flour bomb. The bomb bay on a Mosquito could alternatively carry a couple of long range fuel tanks adding a further 150 gallons and if then added to a couple of outer located wing drop tanks of between 50 to a 100 gallons extra each, you will see that it tremendously extended the long range photo/reconnaissance potential. On such missions the total fuel carried would be about 800 (+/- depending on the type of drop tanks used) gallons. So at about 300 miles an hour they could have a range of over two thousand miles! Quite exceptional in its day. As an alternative to the usual 500lb bombs the Mosquito carried a wide selection of alternative ordinance. Any readers will have seen the various movie films depicting the wartime Mossies at work including the bouncing bomb, a la Dambusters. Other variations had multi-rockets for staffing convoys and trains. The Naval T33 versions could carry a torpedo and in some cases a single huge cannon to shoot up U Boat submarines. All in addition to the standard cannons and machine guns, therefore it can be claimed that the Mosquito was by far the most versatile aircraft ever produced.

T33 Israeli Mosquito at Lossiemouth

104. A salient lesson

That lesson of the slack but locked control cables has never left me in all the, now many, years of engineering and preparation I've been involved in since both aircraft and automobile. As far as I'm concerned the same standards and criteria should be applied to cars too, even if they do not fall out of the sky when they conk out. My engineering policy priorities have been, first; always be prepared to go back to basics. Second; KISS (keep it simple, stupid). Third; always check and check again and get a different checker to check the first one. When checking one's own work it is all too easy to make the original mistake again. No one should take this requirement personally or to heart as the best of us can, and do, repeat our own mistakes. Fourth; after reading Nevil Shute's book *Round The Bend*, I took very much to heart the aero mechanic who regarded his job as an almost sacred responsibility and thought, taught and practised that any job should be regarded as a responsible vocation and done religiously (a much stronger version of the usual idiom of 'if a jobs worth doing its worth doing well'). Now back to the offending 'porpoise'. In addition to the control cables being relatively slack we found several desiccant tins still taped in their original storage points, including the radiator ducts which if they had come un-taped could have damaged a radiator or jammed the adjustable duct flaps. Penn continued his almost hysterical paranoid delusions by claiming that the Arabs had planted these tins as a test run to see if they would be spotted as a prelude to replacing them with a bomb or bombs later. While I am sure the Arabs would have loved to get up to such antics there was no possibility whatsoever with the evidence in this particular set of circumstances. Penn was rather jeered at and again it was suggested that he was funking getting on with his test-flying job. The plane was flown again shortly after and was fine. I did however instigate a recheck of all the other aircraft that the Naval bods had worked on but happily all were ok. However even only ONE such incidence is TWO too many to my way of thinking (one of my pet cliché(s), usually referring to the use or dealing in drugs).

105. Penn, the regular thief

The next episode in Penn's thieving career was after I had been tipped off by a man who had become a very good friend. Albert Bonicci who ran or owned the Park Café on the edge of Cooper Park that in turn was close to the ancient cathedral ruins in Elgin. We all took our lunches, and most evening meals as well, at his cafe. Albert apart from being a good cook was a graduate of Aberdeen University with an expertise in metallurgy. He was also an entrepreneur and all round businessman. One of his sidelines was dealing in semi precious metals so the platinum from old aircraft spark plugs was a regular turnover for him in that area. Kinloss and Lossiemouth airfields were both potential sources. Another was a local farmer who had got his land back after the war, complete with a hangar, which was now a large barn. More to the point was the fact that it had been a dispersal point and where plug changes had taken place. At the time they were all just dumped into a hole in the ground and had been bulldozed over and filled in. Now, all those years later and whenever the farmer needed some extra pocket money, he would go excavating to find a few old plugs and sell them off for their platinum. Reputedly there could have been literally thousands of old plugs to be dug up. Our Penn however was never prepared to put any effort into anything that he could avoid. In this case he was sneaking back to our hangars (we had the use of two. One was a large 'K' type, which was a big steel and corrugated building with four massive sliding doors at each end. The other one, an 'L' type which are partly sunken concrete buildings with a curved concrete roof covered with grass and again the four sliding doors. Late at night bluffing his way past the gate police, he was removing the engine cowlings from some aircraft that he knew we may not be even looking at for many months, taking out the spark plugs (24 per engine) and replacing the cowling to hide any trace of his activities.

These were of course fully serviceable plugs worth a lot of money, even in themselves (much more than the platinum content) to have to be replaced later. Possibly even more important was the fact that these engines were then open to uncontrolled atmosphere and corrosion despite the rest of them still being fully inhibited. If, after even a fairly short period of this exposure, the Israelis or any other customer would be within their right to reject the whole engine. This in turn would be very costly as the engine may have to be written off or at least returned to the factory for a very, very expensive rebuild and overhaul. Plus the cost of labour, time, inconvenience and all the involved paperwork. I was absolutely furious. I phoned R.A.S. who was perhaps even more annoyed and agreed that I should have Penn banned from the airfield and instruct the police at both main gates that he was only to be allowed on the base when accompanied by one of a select number of escorts. I confronted Penn the next morning, who, of course just lied and still tried to bluff his way out of it, as usual. Finally, the silly and over confident smirk on his face was too much for me and I did something I have very, very rarely done in my life before or since. With a fist that I think started somewhere behind my right knee and which came up and round before landing on the side of his jaw with such force that he staggered back several paces before falling flat on his barely conscious back about ten feet away. He did not get up for several minutes. I was not proud of this lack of self-control on my part but I did feel much better for it! Needless to say Penn never tried to lie or flannel me again and actually became more amenable about test flying after the incident!

106. To marry or?

I cannot be sure of the exact time scale but it would have been about this time, when I was back down south to consult R.A.S. about Penn and other matters plus collecting a few valuable aircraft parts, that Prue and I decided, despite the opposition from her mother in particular, to get married. We all had a meeting which included both sets of parents and it was finally agreed that if Prue and I both felt the same in six months time then no one would then stand in our way, even though Prue would still not be 21. Well, the six months were more than up when I went south again at Christmas time. Unsurprisingly Prue's mother had gone back on her word and now attempted to forbid the marriage altogether. Prue's father was clearly very embarrassed by the situation as he was inherently an honourable but weak man and was sheepishly embarrassed by the situation. It all came to a head when, after Prue had had a furious row with her mother, she ran out of the house to come to me at Court Echo about half a mile away. She then collapsed into a frozen and snowy ditch at the side of the road and the first we knew was the police bringing her to us as she had refused to return to her mother. My parents phoned her father and said that she would stay with us overnight.

A day or so later when Prue had come up to London to see me off on the train at Kings Cross Station she looked so forlorn and unhappy that I decided on the spur of the moment that she should come with me. I really could not bear the thought of her being alone and continually got at for weeks on end in my absence. What sort of potential husband would that have made me? Her only concern was that she did not have a ticket! When the ticket collector came round later I just bought a single one. When we arrived in the early morning at Waverley Station in Edinburgh, I sent a telegram to her parents to the effect that, "I am quite safe and happy and have decided to take a holiday in Scotland and will be in touch later. Please advise work (Covent Garden Opera House) that I will not be back in time after the New Year break!" We had a bit of a chuckle at breakfast and mooted the idea that her parents might at that very moment be driving north in their Morris Minor to frantically stop a Gretna Green marriage. (at that time anyone sixteen and over could be married in Scotland without parental permission. Whereas in England it was still twenty-one). We caught the train up to Aberdeen and on to Elgin where we did some shopping for Prue as all she had was what she stood up in. One of the lads collected us and delivered us to my flat in Commerce Street, Lossiemouth where I sought permission from the Smiths to let Prue stay in my flat and I would stay in a large caravan on the airfield that belonged to black bearded Ray and his wife. This caravan was parked beside another 'K' type hanger next to ours that was the Naval M.T. (Motor Transport) dept. Ray was one of the few Naval types that I had kept on and he sorted all our radio and electrical work on the Mossies. He was later to be our best man when Prue and I finally got married about six weeks later on the 14th of February 1955 (St. Valentine's Day which I thought appropriate?!) at Lossiemouth Registrry Office in the Parish of Branderburgh (not a lot of people know that!). The Lapworths, needless to say, had not rushed up north to rescue their daughter but decided to take their (her) fury and frustration out very rudely on my father when he innocently phoned them, to keep in touch with Prue knowing the undue pressure she had been continually subjected to and as an excuse to nonchalantly ask if she had heard from me recently. Dad was verbally abused and accused of being involved in a plot. He of course was genuinely taken aback as he had no idea that I had whisked Prue off north with me, as usual I was not that good at keeping in regular touch and in any case I was only a mere 600 miles away on the same island not 7,000 and halfway round the world! Thoughtless boy. I believe I did finally ring home to let them know we were getting married, about a week or so beforehand. Prue, I think just wrote to advise her parents.

Prue, my recently eloped bride in her Glynebourne dress. 1955

107. Enter Peter Nock, Pilot Extrordinaire

Peter Nock

The first of the planes had left for Israel, having been collected by a wonderful man and pilot by the name of Peter Nock who had his own ferry service company called West London Air Charter Ltd, based, I think, in Richmond, Surrey. He really was very experienced, skilled and meticulous about his inspection of the aircraft and his initial acceptance flight. At first I think he thought I was a bit young for the job of Chief Engineer, for that is what I had become, but he was fair-minded and regularly complimented me on the standard of preparation I insisted on. On the occasion that he took Prue with him in a Mosquito down to Blackbushe, outside London, to enable her to visit her family soon after we had been married, Peter for the first time in his career did not bother to inspect the Mosquito and said with a laugh, "If you trust me with your new wife I will assume that I can trust you with my life". Peter had not got back from the last trip to Israel in time to have been best man at our wedding. another possible had been Syd Guthrie but I do not recall now where he was at the time. However Peter Nock brought us back a wonderful wedding present of a deep ruby red and gold coffee set that he picked up passing through Turkey on his way back. Our best man in the end was that certain black bearded Ray, a Naval sparks and radioman who worked for us in his spare time. We were particularly pleased to have him in the end as he and his wife had really put themselves out to support us, particularly Prue in her first few weeks, so far north in a strange country. It was all so new and different to her but she just adapted, settled in and everyone loved her and admired her placid and artistic temperament. Not at all like me!

108. and Penn the liar

The ensuing spring and summer were very happy and busy times. The weather was exceptionally good, even for the Moray Firth, which boasts a generally good, mild and clear climate. I believe that the main reason that both Kinloss for the RAF and Lossiemouth for the Navy used these airfields for training was because hardly ever was a flying day lost because of weather, even in the winter! We got a few more flights out of Penn Collins with no more dramatic incidents. Although I had no more personal problems with him he continued his confidence tricksters blarney and guff. One day when phoning the control tower to check on the weather for take-off, he introduced himself as Captain Collins. When I questioned him about it he stated that in the Navy anyone who was in charge of a ship was a Captain and as he was in charge of a (air/plane) ship he was therefore technically a Captain and anyway, the Navy were mugs for rank and much less likely to question him about anything he might not want to answer! His absolute gall has never been equalled in my experience since. Just before he was due to finally leave us he was filling in his log book on his flights, duration, type of plane and destination etc. etc. I discovered that he was faking entries (just something any honest and honourable pilot would never, ever do) and was including hours of different helicopter experience that he had never had. He'd never even been in one! All this was to get a job with the Mexican Government, as some sort of helicopter advisor. Years later I heard that he may well have got the job! A couple of years or so later when I was working for Spartan Air Services at Ottawa, Canada I happened to mention the name Penn Collins as I understood that he had also worked for them in the past. The reaction was very rude as it appeared that he had been an even bigger crook and con man over there than in Scotland. Plus he had been deported TWICE, for his dishonest activities! Need I say more? Game, set and match.

109. Another Con. Man (boy)

Another con man that arrived at Lossiemouth was the son of a friend of R.A.S. who I was told to put to work on anything, as he was a very useful lad with experience as a development engineer at De Havillands on the wonderful Comet aircraft. He appeared to know nothing, less even than an apprentice bicycle mechanic! Every tea break he asked a lot of foolish and ignorant questions and made copious notes in a thick black book. I had to report to R.A.S. that he was useless and could not be trusted or relied on for anything that mattered. So R.A.S. told me to just keep him amused for the sake of his friendship with the boy's father, reluctantly I did. The matter was resolved some weeks later when he left his black book on the tearoom table. One of the others picked it up, initially only out of mild curiosity, to see what sort of notes on our work he had been making. It was clear that he understood very little but then when the reader went back to the early pages, which referred to his time at De Havilland, it turned out that his sole development, but hardly engineering experience, was testing the different grades of Bostick adhesive to be used on the upholstery! When confronted with his lies and inexperience later he at least had the good grace to be embarrassed and promptly caught the next train south back to mummy and daddy. My decision not to trust or rely on him for anything was more than justified. Lives would certainly have been at stake!

110. More Peter N.

Some of my best times were when flying with Peter Nock on his acceptance flights. He demonstrated an absolute mastery I had never encountered before (or since). He obviously enjoyed demonstrating some of the Mosquito's abilities and potential. We went wave hopping along the coast throwing up a spray according to some fishermen we met later! We climbed, turned and dived at 'G' loadings I had never experienced before. We were certainly reaching speeds approaching 350 knots (getting on for 400mph) on shallow diving runs. The fuel consumption on average flights on a Mossie was about 90 to 120 gallons per hour. On one occasion Peter had got that up to almost 300 gallons per hour. "The sort of consumption you can expect in an active combat situation", I was told! The thought crossed my mind that the Israelis were likely to need a lot of high-octane aviation fuel! On another occasion when I was not up with him but standing on the top of our L type hangar with some of the others watching Peter take off and head off along the coast until he was out of our hearing. We just stood about waiting for him to return within a few minutes only to suddenly be aware of a deep roar from behind but before we could even turn round to see the cause we were all sucked or blown off our feet and went tumbling and rolling down the grass sided hangar. Peter had headed out to sea, then flown very low to stay out of our sight and hearing and attacked us from behind at very high speed to such an extent that he was on us before we could even turn or react in any way. The thought did occur to me that he and many other skilled low flying Mossie pilots must have put the wind up many, many Germans during the war! The draught as he had passed over us can only be imagined unless actually experienced! My conservative estimate was that he could only have been about 15ft above us at about 300mph!

On another occasion when Peter was flying alone and after I had collected him from Inverness railway station where he had arrived at dawn, having travelled up on the overnight sleeper from London. It was a beautiful bright sunny winter morning with a very heavy snow fall overnight. The Jaguar and I were one of only two vehicles that got through from Elgin to Inverness and back. At one cutting near Forres the drifts were so hard and deep that as we rallied over them we looked down on some fencing instead of up! The car was open with just the side screens on and I think Peter was finding the draught a bit on the cool side! We had a slap up breakfast back at the Park Café in Elgin and went on out to the airfield. After a quick check over and removing the snow from the Mossie concerned, Peter took off alone. He had only climbed a few hundred feet out West over Duffus but had kept full power on and was lowering the undercarriage again instead of continuing to raise it, even as he was turning, flatter and lower than usual, to come back in again. He landed perfectly and taxied in towards us.

When we opened the hatch we were greeted by a Peter with chattering teeth and not able to communicate too well other than to indicate something above him. We were initially mystified and did not notice the absence of the cockpit canopy top! It transpired that it had come off within a few seconds of take-off and as the undercarriage was being retracted. It must have been very cold and draughty and quite alarming even for such an experienced pilot as Peter. He was absolutely frozen, almost stiff and we had quite a job getting him out. I'm not sure now, but I think we had to pull him out through the now open cockpit top and slide him down the wing and catch him as he reached the trailing edge of the port flap before crashing to the ground. The sequel to this story was that some months later we heard about a mysterious incident from a farmer who had lost an animal that was grazing beside the ruins of Duffus Castle. It appeared that a piece of aircraft had fallen from the sky and completely decapitated one of his cows! It had died instantly, happily, which hardly seems the right word?

We took Peter back into Elgin to the Park Café for a few hot drinks, which initially we had to hold for him, to warm his fingers as well as his inside. The slowly returning circulation was obviously quite painful. We always put Peter up at the best hotel in Elgin, The Gordon Arms but when we went along there the place was open, cold and we were told that they never lit the big fire until late afternoon and that there was no central heating working either. So we wrapped Peter up with a woolly hat and scarf a couple of hot water bottles hung under his long heavy tweed overcoat, a full bottle of whiskey or brandy, I forget which and settled him down in the local cinema for the afternoon. It being probably the only, and certainly the warmest building in town. Again, if I remember correctly he had chosen to fly wearing his hill walking/climbing boots so I think he borrowed my nice and loose lambs wool lined flying boots to thaw out in! That evening Peter was fully recovered and he was able to join several of us at a very nice dinner. To celebrate what I'm not too sure! Perhaps the best value cinema ticket ever? My historic memory does not recall how much of the whiskey or brandy was consumed, if any or even what was left in the bottle after that afternoon!

111. Another Israeli!

On one occasion, when Peter was I think involved with flying one of the relatively inferior RAF Mossies across the Atlantic to Spartans Air Services in Ottawa. We also had a Mossie ready to go to Israel so a very pleasant Israeli pilot turned up to do the ferrying for Peter. His name was Hugo Meisl or Marom, as at this time the Jewish names seemed to be all changing into Hebrew, which caused a bit of confusion on occasion. He was of Czech origins and had flow with the RAF during the war but I'm not sure whether it was with Peter or not. He was known to have been a night fighter pilot with a Mosquito Squadron but whether they ever crossed paths with Peter's Pathfinder activities I do not know. Either way they obviously knew each other by then. Hugo was an active Israeli Air Force pilot of varying ranks, it would appear. At that time he was or had been a Captain and a Squadron Commander of the very famous Knights of the North. He was also acting as an Air Attache in London and attending University for an engineering degree, from there as well. Like Ari Benz Zvi and all the other Israelis I met, Hugo was dedicated and quite happy to help out on anything that may assist his country's security. He left us for his long weekend to fly to either Haifa or Hatzor, via Nice, Rome, Nicosia and was due back in London for university classes by the following Tuesday - that's dedication for you. The additional story that involved this particular ferry flight was that, and as I have already mentioned we were not licensed to supply arms, only serviceable planes. So on the flight out to Israel some planes would stop off in Nice. Not only for fuel but to refit the guns and ammunition that we could not be associated with and which then enabled the Israeli planes to arrive home fully armed and ready to fight. Nice was the place that a larger number of Mossies had been resurrected from to go to Israel earlier than ours. So we assumed that they had not only large stocks of spares but armaments as well. The story goes that Hugo arrived at his destination during an air raid by two Egyptian jets and having been warned by radio Hugo caught the first one off guard and promptly shot him down. The downed plane actually crashed within the airfield perimeter. The second one got the wind up and promptly dived off and away in a wide spiral to avoid Hugo, who with the much more manoeuvrable but slower Mossie took the short cut down the middle and caught up with the second jet almost at ground level and shot him out of the air as well. The second Egyptian pilot presumably still looking behind for Hugo only to find him unexpectedly in front! Often, what was not realised was the fact that although jets were much faster they are nowhere near as manoeuvrable in a dogfight. Hugo was my first, apart from Ari Benz Vzi, but not last passing contact with Israeli Intelligence, more often these days referred to as Mossad!

112. Musings

Since writing this I have had the pleasure and privilege of starting to read Peter Nock's own memoirs. On coming to the day of the freezing incident I notice that he makes no mention of the alarming few minutes in the air or his suffering which tends to confirm my long held opinion that he was a pilot that would never make a drama out of even a potential disaster. His exact comments in the memoirs read as follows;

"All things being considered these (20) aircraft were in pretty good shape and starting in mid Oct. I had done (delivered to Israel) 5 by Christmas and another 5 by early in the New Year. There were NO UNDUE EXCITEMENTS or even INCIDENTS and the most hair-raising event of the six months was in a car. Getting to Lossiemouth meant the night train to Inverness from where Bob Henderson always collected me in his XJ120 (actually an XK 120!). On one occasion the roads were solid snow and we still made the journey of 40 miles in not much over the hour. Luckily I happened to have my parachute bag on my lap and it was very comforting to have this solid object between me and the windscreen".

Peter's comments about the hairiest, or riskiest, part of that trip to Lossiemouth was travelling with me in the open XK120 from Inverness to Elgin in under the hour on snowy roads that were not officially open. I take that as an oblique compliment in his faith in our mechanical standards of preparation for him. If the brisk drive was the only risk he thought he faced, then it is one of his many complimentary and supportive statements he was to make on my behalf. I remain very grateful. This risk question is always very subjective and in this case mirrored by me and my feelings about some of the hairy mountain climbs that he took almost for granted, they would frighten me silly. These things therefore always depend on where you are standing, personal inclinations and specialised experiences. In all cases a different point of view is reached depending on personal skills and proven ability. It will always be slightly debatable as to where bravery changes to plain stupidity and it will vary from person to person and even then change in the same individual with age, wisdom, responsibilities and hopefully not too many bitter experiences.

Peter's recollection of some of the Lossie happenings does not always quite tie in with mine. For instance he states that the reason the Penn Collins would not get on with his test flying was because he (Penn) claimed that RAS had not paid him and in turn that RAS stated that he would not pay him until he did fly. My version, since I was living and working there full time is, I think, more accurate but there is certainly truth in that both parties were also doing some bargaining at the time. So Peter would be just repeating what he had been told by them both. In addition, of course RAS was in no mood or hurry to pay Penn due to his constant thieving! The other slight mystery in Peter's writings was the fact that he seemed to think that Syd Guthrie was one of the mechanics. While it is true that Syd, like the rest of us was always prepared to pitch in and help with anything. He was primarily there to fly and I thought that Syd had flown with Peter as observer/navigator on the odd occasion at Lossie but I cannot be sure of that. I may well be wrong! (again). Bob Stewart was of course also an R.A.F. trained navigator (Canada, during the war) so apart from Peter, on his visits we often could have mustered up to four potential flyers on the airfield at any one time, if we had to. Syd of course flew with Penn but also assisted Ray on the electrical and radio work. Bob Stewart spent most of his time on the ground, as did I, attending to the engine and airframe work. We all really did (except Penn) muck in and it worked as a very loose but surprisingly efficient team.

113. Lossie. Madness?

One of the last of our (my) capers was supposedly flying through the hangar, which was then reported to the Naval authorities by one of the gate police. The Navy would or could not really believe it since there were very few feet clearance between the wing tips and the big sliding doors of the 'K' type hangar, even when they were fully open. Coupled with the fact that there was only about ten feet above and below the Mossie to play with as well! Despite not wanting to believe it, they did threaten dire consequences if they heard of any further similar incidents. They were not worried about my life or the possible damage to our aircraft only any mess or damage we might do to their hangar! However, the major, wildest and probably most irresponsible (for a recently married man) escapade that I got up to was to extract one of the PRU34 (Photo Reconnaissance Unit and high altitude version) Mossies that was going to be stripped for spares. Even though there was nothing wrong with it and was in as good basic condition as any other of the stored planes. As mentioned these models were fitted with the Merlin 113 and 114 two stage, two speed supercharged engines, potentially capable of several hundred horsepower more than the others, to help compensate for the higher altitude. The extra boost was not intended for use at lower levels! To cope with the extra boost and warming of the intake air these engines were also fitted with an inter-cooler, which brought the general engine mass forward a foot or so making the nose of the aircraft inherently heavier. Needless to say I had better (other) ideas on the subject. This particular plane was brought up to scratch, modified so that the full boost could be brought in at any altitude and to be on the safe side I did my wind blown trick of richening up the full throttle fuel supply setting to the injector carburettor. The next thing was perhaps even more illegal as we painted this aircraft up with the Israeli Star of David and borrowed the serial numbers from one of the Mossies due to go off to Israel very shortly. In other words we had two aircraft with the same registration numbers on them! We made sure that at least one of them was always in the hangar, largely out of sight, at any one time! The planes that shared the same numbers were not even the same model but I doubted that anyone outside our team would even notice. Luckily the Naval Air Traffic Control personnel in the control tower certainly did not.

So, a couple of weeks after I had made my irresponsible plan and decision, the duplicate aircraft was made ready for its first test flight. The flight went perfectly but I did find that the more powerful but (nose) heavier PRU model was nowhere near as responsive as the ordinary models and certainly not as good as the TR33s. The PRU had the speed and straight line stability but was definitely slightly reluctant to change direction in a hurry and it was while doing a fairly shallow dive that the heaviness of the controls must have subconsciously warned me to take a precaution that was almost certainly to save my life about a week later. These high altitude versions had a double handed control column in the shape of a W instead of the usual single joy stick so one could apply the strength of both hands/arms when the controls got a bit heavy. This heaviness I noticed got worse as the diving speed got higher and higher so I thought I would try and apply more elevator trim. This seemed to have a disproportional effect and made the pulling out of a fast decent much easier. Even at about 350 MPH. I did not detect any obvious loss of speed due to the extra drag from the adjustment either. This lesson was internalised as they say today! If it had not been for this, one of Peter Nock's tips that he had passed on to me, I may not have survived to be writing this now! I am sure though that he never imagined that I might ever push my situation in the air in the way he obviously did with his mountain climbing?

What now follows is almost the sort of thing that nightmares could be made of. The sort of experience that changes time and its relation to one's brain, whether the worst of it was something that lasted many seconds or a couple of minutes, it is impossible to be sure. It was a situational experience that would forever be burned into my psyche and perhaps even re-programmed my risk taking mental ratios in subsequent flights and later in motor racing. I really do not know but I certainly did sense a change within me that day. A bullet can be quick and a car crash is a few seconds but this was a lot longer to have to face and adjust to the infinite possibilities. Whether I suffered much fear I am not sure but if I did then it did not make me freeze either mentally of physically because I remember vividly now that I was determined that I was going down with the brain still trying to figure out the exceptional combination of uncontrollable circumstances, situations and then, hopefully, the solutions to them all.

114. Entering the valley of D.........

The initial part of the flight went well on a wonderful Moray Firth cold crisp and cloudless sunny winter's day. I batted up, almost due north towards the Shetland Isles with a view to descending quite rapidly from about 25,000ft after turning back south again towards Lossie. As I cut the second stage of the superchargers in there was a more violent surge and vibration than usual but it certainly increased the speed of my decent! Since I had rigged them manually they remained 'in' instead of cutting off as we reached lower altitudes enabling sustained very high boost and higher power output than officially allowed at lower altitudes. The A.S.I. read well over 380 knots which is close to 440 MPH and it then started reading erratically as sometimes happens also at take off. The speed continued to climb and the needle wavered well beyond the 420 knots (off the clock!) or heading for about 500 MPH when I decided to pull out of the dive having had my fun, in the sense of probably having equalled if not exceeded the existing maximum speed the plane was meant to be capable of?

The problem was that the aircraft would not pull out of the relatively gentle dive however much strength I applied with both hands to the control column. Early in the dive it had felt tail heavy but now it felt dead. At this point the engines were over speeding and not immediately reacting to throttling back on the boost. It almost appeared the plane had reached, with the aid of gravity, such a high speed in that the wind was still turning the props, like a windmill, rather than just the power of the engines. Disconcerting to say the least. I remember hearing that some propellers could go into surge or a form of cavitation at speeds above 375 MPH and where the blades no longer cut the airflow properly. I tried a gentle turn in the vain hope that descending in a long spiral, which, would increase the distance and time before the ground/sea was reached! Thinking time for alternative actions and strategies was appearing rapidly to be required but running out! Any slightly off line manoeuvre was reluctant and caused more violent vibrations that gave thought to wings being torn off. In semi desperation I cranked on even more elevator upward or nose up trim and pulled the pitch levers back a bit which in normal flight then take a bigger bite through the air absorb more power and drop the engine revs accordingly. In my circumstances though I was a bit worried that, instead of reducing the revolutions due to extra drag with the bigger spoonfuls of air it might have the other effect while diving of going even faster! I just did not know and I am not sure that even a very experienced test pilot (which I was not) could have told me with any certainty. I really was in a set of circumstances that might just have well been, from an experience point of view, on another planet!

Well I'm still here so miracles do happen! Apart from the hand of Big G.., which I have come to accept more and more in my life. My logical and practical theory, and it is only a theory, was that as I descended at a sort of balanced maximum terminal speed through the higher thin air, the drag or wind resistance would increase in the lower denser air then slowing the plane down by maybe 30 to 40 knots bringing the air flow over the control surfaces to a point where they responded properly again? Painfully slowly the weight on the control column eased and I was able to pull the plane steadily out of its wish to meet the ground. The G loading was quite high and I sensed that my parachute/seat cushion was a bit compressed but at least I had not soiled it! The plane finally levelled out quite close to the long deserted beach near Spey Bay at well under a thousand feet. I even remember being able to pick out the individual fishermen on their Seine fishing boats a mile or two off the coast, I was that low! A few more seconds and sand castles might have been part of the day's activities. As I then headed inland towards the Grampians I slowly climbed a couple of thousand feet, which still left me close to some of the peaks. I turned to port slowly and in a flattish turn as I had a feeling that the plane might not welcome too much more strain. The starboard engine in the meantime was coughing, misfiring and rapidly loosing boost and therefore power. We crossed the coast, out to sea again near Portsoy and then headed west along the coast back toward Lossie. Well knowing that I might need most of the long operational runway on this occasion. I called up the control tower early. I was only too aware that my voice was unreal and emotional from reaction as I sought clearance to land, which was luckily immediately granted.

I did not have long to try and plan a landing that as far as I know is still not in the book. As I have already mentioned I had absolutely no experience of one engine flying or landings with Mosquitoes and did not think this was the time to practice one! I was not sure whether the power had dropped enough on the ailing starboard engine to warrant shutting down and feathering to reduce the drag or to limp on with much reduced and erratic power that might then fail fatally on final approach to landing? So on the basis of rather the devil you (almost) know etc., I kept the dodgy engine running but had to have the good port engine at full power which meant considerable effort to keep the aircraft anything like straight with some trim, rudder and ailerons to prevent the full power, port engine turning the plane slightly crab-wise to starboard on its approach to the airfield. Too much power from the good engine and it was more crab-wise but not enough power would drop vital speed and altitude. A bit of a juggle! I came in higher than usual in a sort of bomber style approach rather than the usual lower, almost fighter plane, method I would usually use on a very long runway. I had lowered the undercarriage safely, well in advance, just in case the lack of hydraulics from the dodgy engine meant they had to be pumped down by hand at the last minute and which was not a prospect I would welcome after everything else that had occurred.

I need not have worried, it came down and locked with no problems but dramatically slowed the plane due to lack of the usual two good engines/hydraulic pumps. Instinctively, (as a rebel) I lifted the throttle gate/stop catch and pushed the port engine into normal over-boost, as in emergency or limited combat mode. It did not help the crabbing but controlled to decent rate just in time to allow selection of full flaps down, which to this day I am not sure was the right thing to do as it noticeably slowed the aircraft further but it did at least mean that I could land at a slightly lower speed, which I did, but not far from stalling I think (I had long stopped looking at the instruments and had clean forgotten to select gravity fuel tanks as well. Nor had I made anything like the right trim adjustments). I finally dropped her in very hard having landed from too high and very heavily on the left hand side of the runway only to then veer over to the right and onto the grass. I just did not care, I was down, in one piece after which, in retrospect seemed like an eternity. I nonchalantly drove along the grass and back onto the runway with no problem and happened to notice a fire engine racing alongside me on the perri track. Since I had not announces an emergency to control I assumed they had spotted the smoke trailing out of the very sick starboard engine. I was wrong again it was only one of the MT boys testing the emergency speed of the fire engine after its full service!

115. Postscript

After taxiing into the open hangar (strictly illegal, again) with the starboard engine still smoking badly, I decided to push the fire extinguisher button for that engine, just in case and then promptly climbed out through the top canopy or escape hatch, instead of squeezing out through the small double skinned opening set in the lower part of the fuselage and cockpit floor. Apart from wanting to keep clear of the smoke, steam and extinguisher fumes from the wounded engine, I also, for some reason, did not feel like waiting for the ground crew to open up and fix the very flimsy ladder for me. I just sat down on the wing behind the good and valiant port engine, allowing me to slide down and off the back of the port nacelle onto the hangar floor, trying to be as nonchalant as I could but finding that my legs were barely able to support me. The poor plane was in a mess, almost all the illegal paint work had been blown or stripped off. Oil had been blown out of both engines and all down the nacelles and was now dripping onto the floor in puddles. The starboard undercarriage was distorted and partially collapsed due to the heavy landing and the wheel was out of alignment which had accounted for the reluctance to turn left while taxiing that I had assumed was due to lack of power on the starboard engine or uneven brakes. There was barely a pint of oil left in either tank or reservoir, the starboard being the worst which may have caused the apparent lack of pitch control in that propeller, if the CSU (constant speed unit which controls and adjusts the pitch of the propeller) was being starved of enough oil to work properly. A lot of oil had spread over the engine and was still smoking and I wondered why there had not been a bad oil fire? In some ways even more serious was the fact that while looking up into the wheel bay at the oil situation it was noticed that a large gap had opened up at the critical point high up where the main spa (of the wing) links up with the power plant and undercarriage mounting points. I had a sneaking suspicion that I may have cracked the main spa or at least torn/split it at these mounting points. Either way the aircraft was a write off! Not a lot was said by the others but I did seem to get more than the usual funny, strange looks.

After a good mug of tea and the proverbial Chelsea bun, I regained my mental and physical composure and promptly made out urgent work schedules. FIRST, to scrape off any remnants of the illegal painted markings. TWO; to remove both engines and propellers and to clearly label them as "scrap or for major factory overhaul". Then to duplicate the information in their respective log-books. THIRDLY; to strip and gut the airframe of everything, from fuel tanks to instruments. For good measure I took a big fire axe and smashed a few holes in the fuselage and wings so there could be no mistake in the future! I felt very bad about it from an almost sentimental point of view. After all, this wonderful plane may well have saved my undeserving life and we had certainly had an exceptionally intimate but very brief relationship. It was a truly remarkable aircraft and my life was saved with only one important contribution from me, which had been that extra elevator trim adjustment but even then it was the plane that told me about it in the first place! I tried to rationalise the situation by comparing it with having to put down a very old, sick but brave rescue dog. It helped a bit! The remains were towed to the far side of the airfield a week or so later for it to become the first of several stripped fuselages to be burnt over the next few months as we finally finished up at H.M.S. Fulmer and much to the Navy's relief, no doubt. The end of a remarkable era.

116. Some further technicalities

Perhaps a few potentially boring comments about the great oily mess that the plane was in when I landed. It may be of interest to aircraft and/or Rolls Royce Merlin engine fans and historians. One of the characteristics of the Merlin was the fact that its crankcase breathing was rather heavy. This was because the 27 litre V12 engine was a dry sump type with rather limited expansion and contraction space below the reciprocating large pistons. Unlike a car, which has a relatively large wet sump but with plenty of breathing space above the oil. The engine oil on the Mossie was stored up high in the wheel arch and was fed by gravity to assist the oil pump. After passing through the engine, another (scavenge) pump picks it up and returns it to the tank again via its oil cooler which resides in the leading edge of the wing between the fuselage and the engine itself. This is located alongside the normal coolant radiators (in our case 70%/30% glycol/water mix. This strength of antifreeze is required because of the very cold temperatures met at high altitudes). This returned oil retaining some of the crankcase pressure as well. The top of the oil tank acts as an expansion, separator and buffer area venting any excess pressure and some oil to the outside of the aircraft. On take off, landing and in extreme combat mode when using maximum engine revs. and high boost pressures, some of which escape past the piston rings causing the pressure in the dry sump to build up excessively and is then transferred back to the oil tank where the short term extra pressure tended to blow out quite a bit of oil with it! This coupled with a reasonable normal oil consumption always meant that after a flight the oil level would drop by several pints! Trying to start a flight with a bit more oil in the tank (therefore less breathing space) just meant that even more oil got blown out on take off and the result was back to the same messy square one! In my case I had used excessive boost which would have partially leaked past the pistons and added to the crankcase pressure and blown even more oil out. And certainly not helped by the lower ambient pressure outside at higher altitudes, so making the pressure differential even greater. Then and since the engines had also over-speeded the pumping action from the underside of the pistons at the higher revs. would have increased the problem even more!

Because of all this, known situation, Mossies on long distance flights that were fitted with additional fuel tanks (wing, drop tanks and sometimes a larger extra tank in the bomb bay) would also be fitted with an additional long-range oil tank. This being located high up in the fuselage and just behind the dinghy box and the contents would then be transferred to the running short standard tanks, late on in the flight to replace the used or blown off amounts of oil, so preventing the engines running short of oil in the basic systems before returning to base and blowing the last of the remaining oil out during the full power landing and risking engine failure! Another oil safety point was that at the bottom of the normal oil tanks or reservoirs were hoppers or a spare, separate reserve of oil. This was so that, if there was an engine failure that also led to total oil loss there would still be this separate, in effect supply for the required propeller feathering pump. Without it the propeller would not have enough oil left in the system to be feathered which would be the cause of wind-milling and apart from the tremendous wind resistance or drag from the unit and which could and did lead to engine fires! 30,000 ft up and a wooden airframe!? No joke. It was just this, to some a contentious, emergency provision that a year or two later led me to my falling out with one of Spartan Air Services directors when lives were likely to be lost! That particular story will emerge in due course.

117. More musings

As I've said before, I have found since I started these ramblings that I begin by thinking that there is not much to cover here but once staring into section memory starts bringing things back. Things that I had honestly not given a second thought to for 40 to 50 years. Lossiemouth is no exception, suddenly I am remembering so many incidents and aspects of life that perhaps had a great influence on me, even if unconsciously. The problem is putting them down in any sort of cohesive manner let alone in any chronological sequence. So they will just have to go down as I remember them and if I live long enough I'll maybe get round to organising the events better in due course. So in the meantime please look on all this as a series of notes, as I have already indicated.

Once Prue had joined me in Scotland life was generally very pleasant, even relaxed between periods of serious activity. One of the very nice breaks was when my Uncle George and Aunt Nancy drove up to join Prue and me for the odd weekend at Tomintoul, a sort of halfway meeting between us and Windygates. Tomintoul is probably the highest village in the country and is laid out in a very attractive square, nestling in a surround of mountains. Beautiful walks and excellent food at the Gordon Arms (another one?).The winter though, is another matter! Originally when Prue had first met my Uncle George some months before at their house, Laggan, on the edge of Windygates she had not been able to understand a single word he said, not even an 'and' or an 'if' or even a 'but'- nothing. He had only ever been south of the border to England twice in his whole life and that was only to see Scotland play rugby at Twickenham. He did not have much of an accent, more a Fife monotone mumble. I was however particularly pleased to have been able to spend these times with Uncle George because within a very few years he had died, I think while Prue and I were in Canada so he never saw his nephew and niece, Laird and Laura. Of course his widow, Aunt Nancy did as we frequently visited her at Laggan on our many pilgrimages to Scotland after our return from Canada. Uncle George, as I remember was a heavy smoker and liked his drink as well plus not taking much care of himself, despite Aunt Nancy's best efforts. I can imagine he might have not have been an easy man to live with. I owed him a lot as it was probably my work experiences from the age of eight with him and the men in the George Henderson yard behind Edna May at Windygates and out on sites in the Ochil Hills that got me interested in many practical skills, from blacksmith onwards.

118. Some neighbourly and local activities

Reverting to our good friend Albert Bonicce of the Park Café in Elgin. As I have already mentioned he was a graduate and very much the all round entrepreneur. One of his bright ideas was to produce a large quantity of Highland Heather perfume to be shipped out to Australia to be marketed in conjunction with Princess Elisabeth's visit. Unfortunately her father the King died when she was in Africa at the beginning of her tour so had to curtail the rest of it. The Australian contract fell through and poor Albert was left with several lock-up garages full of unwanted perfume. He went out of business as a result of it all, returning to the family café business to make a living again. When we first met him he was fed up with routine cooking but was delighted to go back to it and produce my first experience of such a wide choice of British/European vegetarian dishes. He, himself pecked away at his own cooking for years, all day at the food and was grossly over weight as a result of it. In his entrepreneur guise he ran local dances and booked bands which led him into becoming a sort of impresario promoting concerts along the north of Scotland and managing some of the turns. One of these was a very gifted local chap who seemed to be able to play anything and did most of his own composing as well. The name Henry Roberts(on) sticks in my mind but I do not remember if this was his own name or the one he adopted later as a quite famous pop star.

On one occasion Henry was due to be playing his double base at a theatre in Inverness that evening and suddenly he was going to be very late for some reason or other. Albert asked me if I would be kind enough to run him through to Inverness. I agreed and it will need little imagination to visualise Henry sitting in my open XK 120 with him frantically and blindly clutching his double base round its middle and it, in turn sticking upright, way above the windscreen, totally blinding him. It was a nice evening with the setting sun in my face for most of the journey. It took barely thirty minutes to do the almost forty miles, touching well over 100 mph every chance I got. There were no speed limits in those days outside the 30 mph limit in towns and villages.

The setting sun was a bit of a problem though but I still got Henry there with three minutes to spare. This he certainly needed to regain his composure, calm down and cover up the physical ravages of the windy journey! He looked a stunned wreck having been unable to see or do anything behind his double base but to frantically hang on to it as best he could. We remained good friends despite the wildest and hairiest experience of his life.

One of Albert's other enterprises was to build a hotel on the approaches to Elgin from the west. Henry and I , among several others had been helping Albert design this hotel on the back of newspapers and envelopes for months. I do not remember all the ins and outs of the financial package but he reached a situation that if he did not get a token bit of wall up in time he would lose some financial grant or backing. So one weekend just before his time ran out a gang of his noshing clients gathered at the site and about ten hours later we had a wall about fifteen feet long and six feet high looking very lonely in what at that point was the middle of a grassy field. Today as you approach Elgin from the west at roughly the fork in the main road which splits some local turn off from the main road you will find the completed hotel/centre on the left called I believe Eight Acres(?) It was completed long after Prue and I had gone off to Canada or even later but it was finally there and run by Albert's widow Betty when I returned on a visit some ten years later.

Another local and incongruous job that cropped up one cold winter spell that required our gang from the airfield to turn out to help, as good neighbours, was when my landlord, Mr. Smith got into a flap and panic. It appeared that as the leading plumber in the town he had the responsibility for some of the empty hotels during the winter. In this case it was the main one, The Stotfield. Mr. Smith had forgotten to drain all the cast iron radiators on all the floors. Then, unfortunately one night during an exceptionally cold spell dozens of these radiators had burst and exploded like bombs. Bits of shrapnel had stuck into the bedroom walls and stuck in the curtains! All we could really do was to disconnect them all and throw as many as possible out of the windows to the lawn below. Where this was not feasible we put them into the many baths, wrapped in bedding to avoid scratching the enamel. Our many hours of voluntary work helped Mr. Smith from a bankrupting liability situation. Because, if all those radiators had thawed out and flooded the whole hotel the damage would have been enormous. Almost next door to the Stotfield Hotel was a grand house with similar views out over the Moray Firth. This belonged to one of the directors of Players cigarettes and it is the view from his house, across the sandy bay, the skerries and on over to the lighthouse showing the often wonderful colours of the sea and sky in that area that you will find set into an oval picture on the back of a packet of Players cigarettes (not a lot know that). The other rather amusing situation was Mr. Smith (who was a plumber, remember?) asking me to design a heated baptismal tank or pool for his less hardy Plymouth Brethren converts.

119. The hated Paisley bit!

By far the worst situation that arose working for Short Aviation was when R.A.S. asked me to go down to Paisley to take on that project as well and work for a couple of months at Abbotsinch air field which was still a naval air station at the time (I forget H.M.S. what?). There were a dozen or so rather older (although serviceable) Mosquitoes there that he decided to strip for spares, engines, instruments etc. Prue and I duly went down having arranged to hire a caravan to live in, right on site within the secure perimeter fence and next to the aircraft to be worked on. The unexpected problems arose when I went along to the local labour exchange to hire about a dozen labouring men with mechanical leanings! I was told that there were none! I said "but there is very high unemployment in this area". To which I was told, "yes, but they are all unemployable". I could not believe it. However the upshot of it was that he would go through his long list and send along any that he though might be of some use but was not very optimistic. The initial problem was that the first few were rejected by the Air Field Police due to known criminal records. Finally a very few were cleared and given passes. Only one was any real use and honest. He was a regular Merchant Navy man whose mother was dying of cancer and he planned to stay at home with her until the end before then going back to sea. The rest were skivers, drunks and thieves. Not a very nice atmosphere at all. I made them all sign an agreement that they were joint and severally responsible for all tools and that losses would come off their wages. They made the mistake of thinking that this young fellow was still wet behind the ears, so to speak and clearly they did not take the situation or their responsibilities seriously.

Come the first pay day and I can remember, even now, that there was £63 worth of tools and equipment missing. I said nothing and just deducted equal amounts from each pay packet. They were astounded and had cod like expressions on their faces with disbelief that I would dare to do it. After about ten minutes they came to the caravan with a deputation demanding that they be paid in full and that the bit of paper they had signed was worthless. I was very quiet and patient and suggested that if they could find the missing tools and equipment they would be immediately paid in full. I made the mistake of going over to one of the aircraft and finding a couple of tools (I had noticed them planking (hiding) them earlier). They were not amused and went into a huddle about it. My next mistake was to walk off to leave them to discuss the matter further. I became aware of one of them coming up behind me fast so I ducked, crouched and turned in time to get under him, get up and lift him off his feet and his momentum took him on over the top of me. I had also punched up just below his rib cage with a straight all fingered jab which would be enough to render him useless for some time but just to make sure I dived for the crow bar in his hand that he had been carrying with obvious intent. I snatched it and struck one of his knee caps with it with a view to impairing his ability to stand up and retaliate. A form of self defence, of course! I then challenged the rest, and perhaps with and because of the rather unnerving cries from their crippled hero on the floor they all thought better of it, at least temporarily. Luckily the police at the back gate at the St.Mirrens road end had seen what was afoot and arrived on the scene very quickly which certainly prevented the rest of the heroes from having any second thoughts about attacking me in numbers.

An ambulance was called and the police calmed the situation down. They backed me over the tool deduction and the workers all asked to be allowed extra time to hunt for the missing tools. Prue and I watched through the windows of the caravan as each and every one of them went and found tool after tool in some very strange places. Within half an hour every single one had been accounted for and the men got their money in full. I heard later that the one with the crippled knee was not even able to pretend to work for several months. The gate police did suggest that in view of the situation that it might be wise for us not to go into Paisley by the usual direct route, past the St. Mirrens football ground. We took their advice.

The rest of the miscreants all turned up, bang on time, on the following Monday morning and seemed to work rather better than before. No more tools ever went missing but they did continue to steal bits of scrap copper and brass and would hide items just inside the fence so that after they had checked out through the gate they would put their hands through the fence and grab whatever they had planked earlier. We complain about the parasites living on the State today but even then and particularly in the case of one Alex Crossan, it was nothing new. The men were paid well above the usual hourly rate plus a bonus (Prue and I were anxious to get back to Lossie). Despite this Alex was heard to complain that he was working long hours for next to nothing!? It appeared that with all his allowances he was getting nearly £50 a week from the State! (a lot of money back then). So he saw working long hours for only another £10 as not a good deal. All the others were more than pleased with the hourly rate. Alex, it seemed made a habit of just working long enough to get his stamp and then retire on the State until the stamp was due to run out again. The biggest problem was trying to get him to understand that the bonus (or any bonus payment) was only due if earned in excess of the basic. He turned up one Friday to collect less than one days payment and had no argument about that but insisted that he should still get the bonus as well! He got very heated about it and I finally fired him and got the police to eject him and rescind his pass. He then went to the newspapers in an attempt to make trouble. This led to them trying to get pictures of these illegal aircraft that were going to Israel. One, they were not illegal and two, all the Abbotsinch ones were being stripped anyway. The matter became a bit of an ongoing problem because at one stage one of the reporter/photographer types followed me all the way down south to Whyteleafe in Surrey to Short Aviation's office and took a picture of me standing on the office door step with RAS. It was published prominently in, I think, the Daily Mirror. The title being something like "Red bearded Robert Henderson..." and so on. They tried to link the also perfectly legal sale of tanks from Belgium with us. All under the totally unfair and untrue heading of "Illegal Arms Sales". It all died down and was the usual 24 hour wonder and to our chagrin even the picture of us was far from flattering! Although the 'Red Beard' was quite a good disguise, in as much as they would not have recognised me without it.

There was one otherwise apparently reasonable young chap at Paisley that I spent some time talking to in an effort to understand the local work culture. He lived at home with his parents but liked to drink and watch St. Mirrens play football. I naively suggested that a bit of extra money would come in handy to watch football. Oh no he said "if I'm broke I've got a mate that gives me a hand to get over the fence". I then suggested that he needed money to buy his weekend drinks? Oh no, he said again, "if I'm broke I steal an old wife's bottle of milk off a doorstep and run the coal gas from the poker through it. It produces a hell of a kick but leaves me with a headache for days" (but he still did it). I gave up. How can you reason with that sort of mentality? Many, many years later a good friend of Fay's and mine, one Elma Meredith who hailed originally from Paisley told me that this gassing of drinks was not unusual, to such an extent that the council/gas board had to change all the gas outlets on the street lights from curved down to only vertical to stop people just plugging in their potential booze into the gas mantles! There were others miscreants all in much the same vein. One in particular kept smashing the compasses just to drink the alcohol in them. I even offered to buy him booze if he would stop doing it but to no avail so he had to be fired as well. We also discovered that he had been drinking what was left of the de-icing fluid as well in several of the aircraft. On, I think, his last day I heard a weird noise, so rushed out in time to see this man writhing about on the ground in agony and turning some strange and very unhealthy colours. We called an ambulance but he was dead before they got to us. It turned out that be had been drinking the highly toxic Ethyl Bromide out of an aircraft fire extinguisher bottle, thinking it was also alcohol. It must have been a terrible death but by this time my patience had run out and I found myself feeling absolutely no sorrow or compassion for him.

The only good thing we found in Paisley at that time was an excellent tool shop located under the railway arches. We were also at Abbotsinch when the large explosion occurred at the ordnance depot at Inchinnon only a couple of miles away and which put up a very impressive mushroom cloud. I think that there were some casualties but I do not recall just how bad it really was. It was certainly about the biggest bang I had ever heard and felt at such a distance. After all this any reader will not be surprised at my utter amazement, when a very few years later, while in Canada, I read that the government had spent millions of pounds on building a car factory at Linwood (just outside Paisley) It was obviously doomed from the start with such a dregs of a labour pool to call on. The taxpayer could have been saved a fortune if the powers-that-be had had the same conversation with the local Labour Exchange manager that I originally had!? And to quote, "All totally unemployable".

120. Relief, Lossie. again

So back to Lossiemouth with some relief and where everything had been ticking over with only the odd day trip from me every couple of weeks. Working and almost living on an active Naval airfield meant that Naval flying was going on most days and even at nights when the training schedules called for it. The Navy's carrier plane of choice at that time was the Sea Hawk and the majority of the months long training was done on them. It seemed in retrospect that there was a loss or dramatic incident on average about every month. The out and out fatal crashes, numerous belly or to be more correct at that stage one leg landings as it appeared that less damage financially was done to the aircraft if it landed on one leg of a faulty undercarriage and the plane cart-wheeled in an alarming way tearing off its wings etc., than doing a good old fashioned relatively smooth belly landing. It appeared that this grinding away at the fuselage, which along with the engine and all the early electronics, cost a relative fortune to replace or rebuild compared to just bolting on a couple of new wings and other relatively cheap bits. It was claimed that the fire risk was about equal with either method! I got the impression that the young and green student pilots did not relish the cart wheel stuff but had to follow standing orders and laid down procedures. In one case as the aircraft had hit the ground and was still cart-wheeling/spinning in the air the ejector seat went off and fired the unfortunate young pilot down into the ground and in effect almost buried his remains along with the rocket aided seat a foot or so down!

The Sea Hawks being essentially carrier planes had folding wings and they were usually set to fold away on landing. The system was of course basically hydraulic and the pumps had to be switched on by the pilot but they would not actually start until the weight of the plane had compressed the undercarriage after landing which in turn would energise a micro switch which then completed the electrical circuit to the pumps and the wings would then start fold up on their own. Some of the pilots would select wings up in advance, along with their other finals and rely on the undercarriage micro switch to make the final actuating connection once down and the weight was on the under cart. So one would see the wings starting to fold up while the aircraft may still be doing a 100 mph down the runway. Unfortunately on one occasion the undercarriage switch was faulty or wrongly connected and the wings started to fold up even before the plane was anywhere near down. The plane was largely a write off but the pilot got away with relatively minor injuries. In those days such a low emergency ejection was not recommended so either way the pilot was at serious risk. Not a decision I would want to make so I make no judgemental comments. The other nasty ejection seat incident that I recall was when one of these rocket seats went off inside a hangar with a fitter sitting on it at the time. He was flattened to a pulp on the concrete roof and witnesses claimed that he seemed to stick there for some seconds before the mess returned to the floor.

The vast majority of flying was the Sea Hawks which were about to be superseded by Buccaneers which must have been a very good all round aircraft since thirty years later they were desperately sent for to assist in the first Gulf War. By far the noisiest Naval aircraft were the Wyverns and the Gannets I am not sure which was which now but they were stubby and very deep bodied planes that served as radar and anti-submarine torpedo workhorses. The engine was huge and drove a double propeller arrangement with one just in front of the other rotating in opposite directions. The appalling noise was I think a combination of the prop arrangement as well as the engine. They looked very ungainly but did an excellent job that they were designed for. On the lighter side, I am not sure now whether it was Commander Air or Engineering that had his own pet (private?) two seater De Havilland Vampire painted blue which he reputedly used for weekends off.

The most dramatic and impressive aircraft was a visiting English Electric Lightning that was either just about to come into service or the factory were on a sales assessment tour. The factory test pilot flew about giving a quite good demonstration of the planes abilities. After landing and again I'm not sure, but I think it was Commander Air that after a phone call consultation with the factory was given permission to fly it as well. He was reputedly only one of three holding either a blue or green pilots ticket at the time. After the usual, getting the feel of the thing he started to beat up the airfield barely ten feet off the runway. He then did the same on the short runway that heads toward the coastal hills/cliffs and tall radio masts at Covesea (pronounced locally as Cowsea). It appeared that a crash was inevitable and that no aircraft at close to the speed of sound could pull up (as in climb, not to stop) in time. Halfway down the runway and with total disaster only seconds away he was able to suddenly change direction and climb almost vertically with us all looking up what looked like a flaming dustbin, with our mouths open. The pilot was obviously using reheat (after burner) for what looked more like a rocket climbing than a mere aeroplane. The noise, again had to he heard to be believed. The plane landed with a very nonchalant pilot stepping out to a flabbergasted audience. That was by far the most impressive and dramatic flight I have ever witnessed. Modern Air Shows would not allow it, I imagine?

121. Naval clangers

In the meantime the mortality rate of the Sea Hawks seemed to keep climbing and was at its worst at the beginning of each new batch of young pilots. One lunch time Prue and I were driving into Elgin for lunch when a Sea Hawk crash landed on the flat ground to the left of the main road just short of Spynie Palace. It then tobogganed across the road ahead of us and kept going over the field to our right and finally stopped with the aid of a grassy bank about a hundred yards from the road. We stopped and rushed over to see if we could help but a helicopter arrived from nowhere behind the bank and the rescue team beat me to it by a few feet. The emergency was obviously known about and the helicopter must have been hovering and waiting for the down. The pilot was ok, having suffered a flame out and had been doing his best to glide it down with no power, not easy in a jet. By the time we returned to Lossiemouth after lunch the crashed plane had gone and the only evidence was broken fences and long muddy tracks. This flame out seemed to be a regular problem with these planes as only a month or two later two Sea Hawks touched wings while flying in close formation. One pilot was a tutor and the other a student. Both planes had flame outs which always meant a crash. The student baled out correctly and the plane crashed into the Dornoch Firth but the tutor managed to glide his plane with no power, the 30 odd miles back to Lossie. An unheard of accomplishment. He had glided and nursed a brick over, what was thought of as potential world record distance. I do not recall the height that it all started at, presumable very high?

Another classic clanger was also a Sea Hawk coming in to land. As it turned out round the town and over the sea and to head towards the golf course before crossing the perimeter fence and onto the long runway. His flame also went out and he crash landed into the sea only half a mile from the harbour wall. When they fished the plane out later it was found that the dozy young pilot had switched the fuel off instead of selecting flaps down on his final approach. Watching this same young pilot trying to drive his Triumph TR2 sports car about like a clown did make me speculate as to how he ever got off the ground in the first place! Another Sea Hawk that went down on a long approach but much further out, the pilot did not manage to get out. So, when they finally found and lifted the plane up and out of the water, the pilot was still sitting in the cockpit but was already a skeleton after only a few days. The answer was of course crabs and lobsters which were still inside the flying suit moving about which the rescuers found a bit disconcerting, to say the least. There were quite a few others which went down miles away, often over Sutherland which could take weeks to find on occasion as the terrain is so vast and bare. When searching for a recent crash, the rescuers, on one occasion, found a missing plane from World War 2! It really can be that remote.

As part of their attack training the planes would use a beach site near the Black Isle for rocket practice and also a beach just a few miles east of Lossiemouth towards Spey Bay where the long and high sand dunes made a good butt. Some rather brave locals would go out there and dig up the practice shells for the lead content which was used instead of explosives for practice purposes (just as well with some of those pilots). Lossiemouth also had a satellite air field a few miles across the Lossie river, set deep in the woods that was called Milltown (I have no idea why). No longer required for its war time diversionary purposes it was being used for carrier training. The planes would land, extend the arrester hooks to catch the cables laid across the runway which were in turn attached to very heavy anchor chains. This slowed the planes down dramatically and was to get them used to the short and relatively violent deceleration on an aircraft carrier. Cheap, simple and effective.

122. Personal flying & clangers?

This bit is clearly out of order and sequence since I have inserted the worst experiences already and do not know how to rearrange the order on the computer!

Having dealt with everyone else's flying, a few memorable examples of my own fantastic and exciting experiences may now give the impression in retrospect of someone deranged or obsessed or both! It was all in another age and almost now, looking back, another planet, well worlds anyway. The chronological order I cannot vouch for but the individual incidents are clear and memorable. I think Syd went off to Australia at least a year before Prue and I went to Canada and Penn had already disappeared off into the possible Mexican helicopter woodwork. Peter Nock was then in effect the Chief Test Pilot, Acceptance Pilot and the then the Ferry Pilot as well. His time was therefore obviously at a premium and we could not waste his time coming up to test fly and risk the possible failing of an aircraft and then to either hang about for days on end or go off south again until we might be ready for the next test. By this time I was doing all the high speed taxiing and brake tests myself. We had arranged to use almost the whole length of the perri track on our side (south) of the airfield which was not a problem for control because the Navy always used their own side (north) both before take off and after landing so we were well segregated. We had a long enough straight to be able to reach nearly 90 knots (not that far off an un-laden take off speed with full flaps down) and even just getting the tail wheel off the ground, leaving just room to cut back engines, brake and slow down again with a couple of hundred yards of grass as well if required. The perimeter and taxiing track is much narrower than the main runways so great care and precision was required to stay on it during these tests. I had no problems and got far too confident in the circumstances so one day I just contacted the control tower gave them our call sign and decided to take off for a test flight of my own.

Everything went well on take off and I climbed to about 3,000 ft as I skirted, on the seaside, R.A.F. Kinloss at Findhorn. Then proceeded out over the Moray Firth in a north-westerly direction towards Wick. I went through all the procedures and controls from trim adjustments on all three surfaces, to instrument reactions to turn and banking, yaw and rate of climb etc., tried both engines at different speeds and boosts and the propellers at different pitches. I was not brave enough to try cutting an engine and feathering it, just in case, since I had no experience of flying, let alone trying to land on one engine. I knew how and that it could be done but decided not to tempt providence that far. I then climbed up to about 10,000 ft., turned to starboard to do a full power turn and side slip and promptly nearly frightened my self silly but I need not have worried as the Mossie pulled out of it quite smoothly about a couple of thousand feet lower! Heading then back across the Firth towards Spey Bay and again turning back west again along the coast tried to keep my voice steady as I called up the tower for permission to land. It was granted and I made a very long and gentle approach over the beach and golf course, staying quite high before landing on the main long runway nearly halfway along it. Slowed in good time for a very leisurely turn off onto the perri track and taxi back our 'K' type hangar. I climbed out as nonchalantly as I could be but actually on the verge of the shakes. Not because of any frightening experience but more to do with the belated realisation of the responsibility implications. One of the lads said almost casually "I did not realise that you flew, too?". To which I replied equally casually, "of course, I used to fly Mosquitoes in Malaya, didn't you know?" No one ever even raised the point or questioned me again on the matter despite the further dozen of so test flights I was to make over the next few months.

My new work system worked flawlessly and there was not a single aircraft that Peter Nock came up to ferry away that was not accepted first trip (not always first time!) by him. He must have been more than pleased because a couple of years before he had been ferrying out quite a number of French Mosquitoes to Israel and most of them had required up to six test flights from Peter before he could risk ferrying them out to Ekron in Israel. I, of course was having a wonderful time of it, flying off over greater distances, almost like an airborne tourist but not always of the most responsible type. The odd friend had his house flour bombed, which then took months of rain to wash it off again! On one test run I turned inland, but not too low, over Inverness and on down Loch Ness at quite a high speed and very low. So low that I had to climb up above the trees around Fort Augustus to avoid collecting leaves! Then on, following the Caledonian Canal past Fort William off to port and on down Loch Linnhe, past Oban climbing up as I then turned to starboard above the Corryvreckan Whirlpool between the islands of Jura and Scarba where I was met with one of the greatest sights of my life. The sea was almost mill pond calm and it was possible to see the shape of all the swirling sea currents, both in the Sound of Jura, out towards Colonsay and out in the open sea, showing clearly the influence of differences in water levels and that the tides made. This quite dramatic picture of patterns spread for about fifteen miles in all directions. Fantastic, the picture remains in my mind's eye to this day.

On the ground side of things everything seemed to progress very well although nothing ever happened quite fast enough for R.A.S.! Probably to do with cash flow, would be my guess. We did not have an aircraft towing tractor or tug and often had to wait hours for the Navy to send one over to us along with the special spring loaded solid attachment to hook up to the Mossies tail wheel. They were always towed from the tail. Being me, I got a bit impatient and impetuous and started towing the odd Mossie out of a hanger or just about the hard standings with my Jaguar which had no problem with the weight at all. I just had to slow down carefully so that the plane would not keep rolling on to the Jag doing damage to both! An illegal possibility was to start the engines up inside the hangar (strictly illegal and against all rules and regulations) and simply drive or taxi it out! The alternative was for up to half a dozen men straining away with difficulty. This method also produced dramatic and entirely unexpected results that had us scratching out heads for some time.

123. Learning experience

It first came to light after I had taken up a four fine bladed propeller equipped TR33 Sea Mossie. These were the most fun to fly as they react quicker to the controls and are faster on acceleration and take off sooner. This particular aircraft had a terrible vibration on the starboard engine, which varied with prop speed and brought my test flight to an abrupt end with a tense landing. This was a new and worrying experience for me. It was cured however, by simply changing the propeller on that engine. A few weeks later the same thing happened again on another aircraft, which had been perfectly serviceable the day before. This new phenomenon, which apart from being a nuisance and time consuming, needed to be investigated thoroughly! Anything that cannot be explained on an aircraft should always be a reason for concern and a potential worry. Eventually it dawned on someone or it may have been just one of many, often wild theories being bandied about. In the process of us man-handling the odd aircraft about someone had pushed or lent too much weight/ strength on a prop blade and had very slightly bent it. Only about half an inch out at the tip but that was enough to cause the violent problem. It had only happened on the thinner bladed four blade De Havilland props and not on the usual heavier three blade Hamilton versions. Needless to say this did not go down in any of my reports!

    The next sequence circulates around Merlin engine exhausts. Being a V12 configuration, the normal layout was six stubby individual exhaust pipes about a foot long, sticking out, down and back on either side of each engine. Unfortunately the Mosquito being a largely wooden aircraft, it was thought the rearmost or no.6 exhaust with its often foot long open flame was a bit close to the woodwork! So this rear exhaust port was fed forward and Siamese-ed into the no.5 exhaust stub keeping it far enough forward to avoid any scorched wood! The later high altitude photo reconnaissance (P.R.) Mosquitoes were fitted with more powerful engines with two speed/ two stage superchargers. These required fairly bulky intercoolers (which cool the, now hotter, higher pressure inlet charge), which in turn moved the whole engine forward a couple of feet enabling the exhaust system to revert back to six exhaust stubs, now well clear of the woodwork. Obviously these open and flaming exhausts can be seen from the ground at night. So when the Night Fighter/Bomber/Pathfinder versions were produced these open pipes were fed into bulging cowls which covered all the pipes and the individual exhaust flames became combined and then emanated from one large aperture with no flames now being visible from below.

124. Specialised Mossies

These high altitude (over 30,000 ft) P.R. (Photo Reconnaissance) models could also be identified by the clear astral dome let into the cockpit roof/canopy to enable the navigator to navigate by the stars when cloud cover made it impossible to take a fix back on earth. This bulge also helped an observer to spot enemy planes approaching as well! The more important differences were not so obvious The cockpit area was all double skinned and sealed to enable it to be pressurised as obviously relying on oxygen only at that height was far from satisfactory. The more powerful engines also now included cabin blowers for the pressurisation of the cabin and I think the heater was up-rated too. It should be explained that the more powerful engines were to replace the lost power at altitude. In the same way that pilots suffer oxygen loss at altitude so do engines as it is the oxygen content in the air that gives the power, not the fuel. That is only used to extract the power from the oxygen present in the air. So obviously the thinner the air or less dense the less oxygen content and therefore less power. The loss of atmospheric pressure and corresponding drop in oxygen level is about 25% for every 10,000 ft of altitude (passenger planes start to use oxygen at about 12.000 ft., if not pressurised). At 30,000 ft. (already higher than Mt.Everest) 75% of the power of an engine has been lost which then may not even be enough to keep the aircraft in the air anymore. So supercharging has to be used to pump in enough additional thin air to build up the pressure and air density so that the engine thinks its flying at a much lower altitude and produces the power accordingly. Therefore a UN supercharged 1,000 BHP engine taking off at sea level or ground level will only be capable of still producing 250 BHP at 30,000ft!

I have covered this aspect merely as a sort of introduction and part explanation of the following acts of perhaps madness, in retrospect. The extra stage and or speed of the up-rated supercharging was normally operated by aneroid switch which could cut in automatically at higher altitudes. The considerable extra power available was not for use at normal altitudes or circumstances. Rolls Royce, as everyone knows are a very conservative manufacturer with reliability much more important than performance. Even on their road cars they always refused to get in to the horse power advertising/exaggeration game, which in most cases is a pack of lies anyway. Rolls contented themselves, where BHP was concerned, with the comment adequate with no actual figure ever published. Even in the normal Mosquitoes there was the ability to get a bit of extra, short term boost in an emergency (possible one engined manoeuvres, landings or combat). This was enabled by twisting and pulling the red 'T' handle high up on the left hand side of the instrument/control panels to break the lock wire and enable a short burst of additional supercharger boost and therefore power. This red 'T' handle was always checked on landing and if the seal was broken it became an automatic engine change in the interests of reliability and safety. There would almost always be absolutely nothing wrong with the engine but as far as Rolls Royce were concerned the guaranteed length of life MAY have been shortened!?

My rather labouring of the exhaust and extra supercharger boost details was for an explanatory reason as will become clear from the coming escapades. I should also add that all this was part of a long term educational curve for me but which seemed to just go over most heads. When we ran up one of the aircraft for the first time at maximum power against wheel chocks, the tail tied down and the control column fully back, it was noticed that the starboard engine was slightly miss-firing and instead of the usual shades of blue the exhaust flames had intermittent flecks of orange and puffs of black smoke (sign of unburnt fuel). Usual indication of faulty or dirty spark plugs. Unfortunately it was not, so we changed the ignition harness (leads) but no again, so we then changed the whole magneto. Still no cure then it was off with the camshaft cover to check valve clearances and compression. Still no joy! The only other theory was wrong fuel mixture strength but this is set at the factory, sealed and wire locked and not an allowed field service adjustment. The official procedure was then a full engine change, very costly in time and money.

125. To some a gamble?

Being me, young, stupid and impetuous (or in a vain manner, I probably kidded myself it was a good entrepreneurial decision!) I decided to break the seal and try changing the critical maximum fuel adjustment (only to satisfy my curiosity of course!) but instead of making a small adjustment and then starting up and running each time I thought I'd be smart and do it with the engine running at full bore! We took the top engine cowling off so I could reach down into the area of the injector carburettor and supercharger. I then lay face down on the top of the wing above the nacelle and hung on to some rigid pipes with one hand while making the adjustment with the other. We tried the first run with anything up to 1,500 BHP worth of air blasting over me from the engine's propeller at full bore and only about eight feet away. It promptly blew off my goggles, broke the straps and blew my tight cap (to keep my hair out of my eyes) off as well. To say nothing of almost blowing me off the back of the wing as well! Next try was with my cap taped on, over the top and under my chin with masking tape making me look a bit like a cartoon toothache patient. I hooked my belt to the rear of the engine framework that then gave me two free hands. No goggles this time but eyes turned down and away as far as practical, then barely seeing anything but adjusting largely by feel alone. I could still just see the colour of the roaring exhaust flames out of the corner of my eye and after a little juggling back and forth I got the ideal varied blue tongue of flame on all cylinders. We shut down the engine which was also getting a bit hot by now. Replaced the top cowling after re-wire locking the adjuster and had a cup of tea. I had to bathe my eyes with Optrex and they remained very bloodshot for well over a week.

An hour or so later and after temperatures had stabilised I took the plane for a long taxi and a couple of full power taxi runs up to about 80 knots. Both engines were almost perfectly synchronised and certainly an operational pair. The next day I took the plane up for an extensive test flight and found the culprit engine now working perfectly throughout the whole range of speed and load. This aircraft went off to Israel and Peter had not a moments problem with it! This of course was not the only time that I have failed to do everything according to the book during my life. Another example at Lossiemouth was when someone had badly damaged some external casting on one cylinder head, which, while not affecting the engine's function or safety, would not be atheistically acceptable to the client! Again I was reluctant to change the whole engine and face all that paperwork. As luck would have it we already had a spare engine sitting in a corner that had had to be changed because of a sheared supercharger drive. (about the only thing that seemed to ever go wrong with the Merlin engines). The rest of the engine was perfect and had almost the same number of hours use as the damaged one. What we then did, apart from being strictly illegal has to my knowledge never ever been done in the field (even during the war) before or since. Since we did not have any major engine gaskets and would not be allowed to use them anyway, we could NOT just swop the cylinder heads. I considered the only option was to swop the whole head and block assembly! The only seals or gaskets then concerned were the ones between the bottom of the cylinders as they spigot-ed into the crankcase and these looked as if they could be saved and reused.

The task was very touchy and quite delicate. I mikked up each piston and mating cylinder bore to find that the Rolls Royce reputation was more than justified as there was never more than 2/10th of a thousandths of an inch difference between any of them! In effect a 100% match! The five hour operation was fraught with difficulty and precision. The head and block assembly have to be pulled up at an angle and off the very long multi waisted studs that run up from the crankcase through the block and cylinder head. Taking it off was easy but gently lowering the new one on was another story, since each of the six, four inch diameter pistons were at different heights and positions so the pistons had to be fed up into the lowering cylinders a fraction of an inch at a time, held square for initial entry and then compressing each piston ring until it too was engaged. This meant keeping a sharp eye out and hopping from piston to piston in an almost frantic permutation of order to avoid pinching or breaking even one of the rings! Eighteen in all I think and not very favourable odds even in ideal working conditions and facilities. We used cut down Jubilee clips and a variety of soft copper wire clamps to compress the rings in turn. No special Roll Royce tool, number so and so, on this occasion!

We finally got the whole assembly seated properly down into the crank case and visually sealed. The next and last tricky bit was getting the camshaft timed accurately. This is done with a vertical, geared (at each end) shaft. The lower gear engages into the crankcase and is related to the crankshaft position and the top gear engages with the camshaft in what could be almost called a vernier system. One tooth out would be disastrous, as we had no basic timing specification to fall back on! We could hardy phone up Rolls Royce either! After torquing (by finding out what some of the spare parts engines were torqued down to!) down the head, connecting up all the coolant pipes, wiring, ignition harness and resealing the cam cover we turned the engine over a few times using the propeller. All seemed ok so after priming we started up the engine which coughed and spluttered and blew out some smoke but then settled down and appeared to run perfectly for several minutes. No initial leaks of oil or any other fluids. Close down and do a compression test. All perfect! Bob Stewart and I were extremely tired, both mentally and physically and decided to knocked off for the day (actually about 8 in the evening). We thought we had earned it, morally if not legally?

126. Put your money……

The next day the engine started up perfectly, did all its taxiing tests, still no leaks so I decided to fly it. Take off was fine, although I did use more runway than usual in case our cam timing was slightly out and the power down a bit making it difficult to balance the two engines. I need not have worried because it was another matched pair. I spent about an hour nipping up to John O'Groats and back with no problems at all. Well, with one exception, I lost all radio channels including the emergency one so on arrival back at Lossie. when not one of the radio selector buttons had responded. I flew twice in over the airfield wobbling the planes wings to indicate a problem and after checking again that the skies were clear of other traffic I came in on final approach with flaps and undercarriage down hoping that it was permissible to land. Almost at the last moment and when I was about to apply full power, retract undercarriage and go round again, the more than welcome green flare went up for me from the mobile traffic control at the approach end of the runway giving me permission to land! After returning to the hangar I phoned the control tower to thank them and to apologise. To which a very jovial voice replied "that's all right Captain, this sort of thing is happening all the time with our own traffic". Captain, I thought, little did they know!? All the post flight checks were fine and still not an engine leak to be found. Another great sense of illegal accomplishment. This aircraft too went off to Israel within a month. The delivery flight was also totally incident free.

As the work on the last of the twenty Mossies to Israel was approaching the end it was going to be necessary to find a new home for the rest of the aircraft as the Navy would not allow us to remain indefinitely on HMS Fulmer on the off chance of future sales and besides they wanted the use of their own hangars back! Also at Lossie were a few De Havilland Hornets which were due to come up for sale as well and RAS was intending to buy them if possible and if successful they had to be flown out as the Navy would not allow another prepare on site situation to arise! These Hornets were the logical development of the Mosquito, smaller, single seater versatile fighters, faster, even more manoeuvrable and combined aluminium and wood construction. With the later powerful Merlin 130 and 131 engines and with the propellers that turned in opposite directions so now, no more nasty torque swing to port on take off. They steered straight as a die with no obvious vices that I could detect on a couple of assessment pre purchasing flights. They drove beautifully, off down the runway like a very fast car. I loved them and was so looking forward to working and flying them in due course. Where to move to was a big question and I think it was Bob Stewart that suggested that we should go and look at Banff airfield which was now back in the hands of either the Gordon or Seafield Estates, I've forgotten which now. This airfield I thought was ideal as it was only about thirty miles along the Moray coast from Lossiemouth to the East. Right on the coast again and quite high up. In fact one of the runways is slightly downhill and finishes almost at a cliff edge making take offs a bit like an aircraft carrier. Quite appropriate for ex Naval planes, I thought and potentially great fun! There was a bit of hangar space although probably not enough for long term use on such an exposed coast in winter. The control tower and surrounding buildings were all in reasonable condition and Prue and I quite fancied a self contained flat in the control tower with its great views. As far as I was then aware RAS was concluding a lease or even a purchase which would take a few months and it looked as though we would be moving over to Banff by the spring of 1956.

127. Hopes dashed

However it was not to be and for whatever reason I was never able to discover. When RAS finally broke the news to me I was a bit upset and even more so when he said he wanted me, in due course, to take over the travelling engineering job of running all over the place fixing his Miles Magister clients problems. I'm not a snob but to go from the exciting and very responsible job with Mosquitoes to servicing, what to me would appear mere toys did not appeal at all. However and luckily I was talking to Peter Nock about it on one of his later ferry trips to Israel when he volunteered the information that the firm in Canada that he was also ferrying some, not so brilliant ex RAF Mosquitoes to in Ottawa, were looking for engineers with Mossie and particularly Rolls Royce Merlin engine experience to work for them on these same aircraft. He promised to speak to them on my behalf on his next Mossie ferry trip to Spartan Air Services. As ever, Peter was always as good as his word and when he next came up to Lossie, he, I thought indicated that there was a possibility of a job with them and I should go to see them when I got there. In the meantime Prue and I had discussed the matter and decided to emigrate to Canada anyway and until we got settled we could always stay with her favourite aunt Ron (her mother's sister) in Toronto and who did not share Prue's mother's animosity towards me. So plans were made to go off to Canada, later that same Spring.(1956).

128. Self employed!?

But again I get ahead of myself. While the Banff situation was all up in the air a bit RAS had been in one of his "it's all costing too much" moaning phases and I had been a bit impatient with him and had told him it was all his fault for keep changing his mind about which plane was to be finished first and the order of the following ones. This had led to constant duplication and repetition of work and the relative extra costs involved. His reaction was predictable and when asked if I thought I could organise his end better as well as my own? Impetuously, again I said, "yes, of course" and since he had just stated what it had been costing for each aircraft I said I would undertake to do it for THREE QUARTERS of that price. He immediately said "DONE!". I think I'd, unexpectedly, called his bluff and he possibly impulsively was hoisted on his own petard? RAS was, at least to me, a man of his word and he kept to the deal to the absolute letter and never ever complained about anything to me again! Oh, except my leaving for Canada, later on. So I supposed I ceased to be Chief Engineer for Short Aviation at that point and became my own independent sub contractor. It all worked very well. I paid the lads a bit more, made quite a lot of money myself and got all the aircraft up to scratch and away to Israel ahead of the original schedule. RAS was delighted but still did his usual moaning bit, that he had still paid me too much and so on! In all conscience I can say that everything was done to the highest standards regardless of my new financial self interest. Every Mossie got to Israel in almost pristine condition and continued to operate with no problems emanating from us at Lossie. (we were not responsible for the later odd bullet holes!) The one and only slight incident was a change of an Avimo coolant hose in Rome which was more a form of insurance, anyway. It was discovered later that there was a tiny production flaw in the rubber moulding, from new!

129. The other Lossie

Another good Lossiemouth friend was a garage owner and first class mechanic by the name of Gordon Leslie. I entrusted my Jag to him for servicing and any odd jobs. He was the old fashioned type that never did only half a job. He would frequently just take out the whole engine from a customer's car to do even a simple but awkward task. Often saving time and money in the end, also being able to check over other things at the same time. I owe at least some of my modern day garage policies and practices to him. There was at that time in town a wonderful Police Sergeant by the name of Anderson who came from Aberdeen. At one stage the powers-that-be decided that he did not have a good enough arrest rate and planned to transfer him. Choosing to ignore the fact that Lossie was one of the most trouble free towns in the area, despite having a large number of drunken Naval types each weekend. Typical. Everyone respected him and they all sobered up almost miraculously when he appeared over the horizon with his usual "here noo lads what going on then?" A petition was got up and he stayed! The locals saw no advantage in having a change of policeman with an increase in convictions PLUS an increase in offences and crime as well!? Sgt. Anderson was a large strong man yet when a drunken sailor stole his beloved vintage Austin car from outside the police station and house one night and then drove off down one of Lossie's famous dead straight streets the Sergeant could not have been very pleased. With the large policeman running/plodding in a rather ungainly fashion after the culprit, only to see his car crash into a lamppost at the end of the street. The amazing thing was that the good Sergeant did not kill the joyrider on the spot, when he finally puffed up to him. Instead, he was more concerned with the thief's fairly minor injuries! What a gentleman giant in the truest sense. We were all frankly staggered by his example, which has not been wasted, since here I am telling the complimentary story a full 50 years later! The other story was when Sgt. Anderson came into Gordon's garage late one evening (it was a bit of a gathering place in the evenings for car fans) apologised in advance before he announced that everyone would have to pay their car tax next month, or else. This startling announcement left most speechless until he then added, "I'm having to do so, as well". It appeared that the Duke of Edinburgh was due to arrive by helicopter from Balmoral to open one of his sponsored sports fields and that there were bound to be a lot of nosy outsider policemen in the area for security reasons. With such a good explanation and reason everyone rushed out and became legal, if only for a very short while! Perhaps just one last motoring tale. Along Commerce Street, where Prue and I lived, there was a particularly nasty barking dog that ran out frightening and barking at every cycle and car that passed. This caused several people to fall off their bikes and cars to swerve dangerously. The owner would do nothing about it. This ugly mutt had done it do me several times until one day I thought it was time for it to be educated. As usual it ran out alongside me barking and snapping at my arm over the Jag's door. I grabbed its collar without being bitten and promptly accelerated off down the street somewhat faster than even a greyhound could run. After two blocks I released the hound and watched it creep and slouch back up the road home, obviously with red hot and sore feet. The next time I passed all I got was a dirty look from the ugly beast and it appeared that it never ever ran out or chased anything again. Cruelty to animals? I think not but of course it was really the owners fault but I could hardly do the same to him, even with an understanding local policeman like Sgt. Anderson. Or could I?

Well, unless I remember any other interesting stories or experience that just about wraps up Lossiemouth. It was a wonderful time, the place, the area, the friends and all the illicit and other experiences. Prue had settled in and we both did manage to spend a lot of time together. Partly helped of course by our two main meals a day together, not always alone of course, at the Park Café. Prue, herself was always very busy artistically, embroidering things and making beautiful butterflies out of copper wire and dyed nylon. She did some seamstress work locally for good causes. In retrospect and memorably were the wonderful and enduring images of Prue working away or just reading while sitting on the sea and harbour wall all that long summer and the last spring. She would be happily and contentedly waving to me as I flew by coming into land (I could not wave back as my hands were always full with finals and could only afford thebriefest of glances!) and again when Bob Stewart and I were out in his lobster fishing boat. The grandest sight in nature was at night when the Northern Lights often displayed, night after night for almost months at a time. Finally, and to crown it all, Prue was pregnant about a year after we had been married. I was to have a son, conceived in Scotland and to be born later in Canada.

129a Lossie, confirmed. June 2005

I write this insert many months after the rest and after a visit from Syd Guthrie and his wife Norma. Of course we had many hours reminiscing about the old days and Syd spent some hours looking through Peter Nock's memoirs since they mention him as well. Syd also confirmed that everything I had written as regards our Lossiemouth experiences was correct and accurate to his memory of things. He was also able to fill me in on a few points and situations that I was not fully aware of at the time. Firstly, Syd told me that Penn Collins had flannelled his way into being an air traffic controller at Inverness airport known as Dalcross at that time. On one classic occasion Penn has cleared an aircraft to land on a given runway and from a given direction. A few minutes later the wind had switched round 180' and he then cleared another aircraft to land on the same runway but from the opposite end! Luckily one of the pilots spotted the impending crash and took last minute evasive action but was not very amused. This pilot stormed up into the control tower demanding to know who the (clever?).........person was that had nearly cost several lives? He then went up to Penn and asked "and what other clever little trick would you like me to perform for you?" I think that is one of the best understatements I have ever heard. About this time Penn had been helping Syd to restore an old Delage motor car. Then one weekend when Syd was meant to have gone off somewhere but luckily did not because a group of Penn's pals had come up from Scone (Perth airport) to collect the Delage which Penn had apparently sold to them! Syd was not amused and sent them packing and never did get a satisfactory explanation from Penn when he next appeared. The man was an incorrigible serial thief and all round rogue.

I had not realised that Syd and Penn had been associated so much before they worked for R.A.Short Aviation and I had forgotten that they were the ones that had flown out the odd Mossies from Culham in Oxfordshire with the sort of difficulty, that I have already mentioned. The only runway available was a short one and it required almost a gale from the right direction coupled with a minimum fuel load to get off and up high enough to miss the trees that had grown somewhat since the Mossies had last flown in and out of there. It appears that it was only the fast revving T33 carrier versions that could accelerate fast enough to get up to take off speed in time. On one of these occasions Syd noticed that one of the inspection panels had not been fastened and was flapping about alarmingly which got Penn into a bit of a panic, he then asking Syd what had we better do? Syd quite rightly said "land again as soon as you can". The nearest airfield and almost adjacent was RAF Benson (the Queen's Flight and all that) so they lobbed in there without permission or clearance barely a couple of minutes after taking off from Culham. No time for even an emergency radio call. They landed safely and taxied off the runway and stopped close to the control tower from where a very senior officer, who turned out to be the Commanding Officer, strode purposefully towards them. Penn was in a blind panic and insisted that poor Syd should get out first and face the music, which he did. The officer did not react badly at all and was in fact very understanding, about rules being only for NON emergencies! He invited them to the officers mess for a drink to settle their nerves (bars are always opened during emergencies) while he arranged for one of his RAF erks to secure the errant panel before they took off again within about half an hour to complete the short flight to Blackbushe where Peter Nock would take over the plane for the ongoing ferry flight to Israel.

On another occasion when the pair of them had flown into Blackbushe they had taxied up to a hangar and parked the Mossie beside an Egyptian diplomatic aircraft. After they had left there was a major security flap and all but a serious diplomatic incident! The Egyptians panicked and overreacted when they saw an aircraft with Israeli military markings on it, parked right beside their special diplomatic aircraft. Guilty consciences, I should not wonder? I was aware of course, of the very touchy situation between the two countries but not as over concerned as they obviously were. It appears that Shorty, as I have just discovered is what Syd called R.A.S., was attempting to do business with both countries at the same time and was often having to juggle business meetings to keep them apart. On one occasion Syd was asked to drive an Egyptian client round the countryside and take him out to lunch until RAS had finished dealing with an Israeli. Syd must have smoked in those days as the Egyptian offered him a cigarette and as Syd had run out he put the rest of the packet into the car's glove box, for later. A few days later Syd was again doing his taxi bit and had the Israeli inspection engineer Ari Benz Vie with him just before Ari came up to join me at Lossie, remember? Ari was a heavy smoker and asked Syd for a fag and Syd absentmindedly told Ari that there should be some in the glove box. There were, a packet of Egyptian cigarettes! Ari was not amused and Syd must have had a very difficult time trying to explain that one away!? Now that I know all this it makes the Penn Collins overreaction to the supposed and imagined Egyptian sabotage on one of our Israeli Mossies at Lossie and particularly after a frightening flight, almost understandable?

Another frightening flight that Syd shared with Penn Collins was when they took one of our Lossie Mossies down to Blackbushe to save Peter a trip. They were heading down the east coast of England and as they approached the Humber river they ran into a very severe hail storm which knocked out the odd instrument and some radio channels which meant it was too dangerous to risk entering London's air space so they decided to land as soon as possible at the nearest airfield which was Brough (not in Yorkshire, this one is up river from Kingston-on-Hull and on the northern river shore). They landed in difficult weather conditions only to find that almost all the paintwork had been blasted off the aircraft by the severity of the hailstones! When the weather cleared a bit they realised how lucky they had been as at the other end of the only serviceable runway was a paint factory screened by very tall poplar trees, which were not going to make getting off and out again very easy! It took several days to get the aircraft repainted and required legal marking reinstalled for the onward flight to Blackbushe. Syd and Penn then had to wait for a strong wind from the right direction before they could get airborne again. They reckoned that the undercarriage clipped the tops of the Poplar trees and were not looking forward to crashing into the paint factory. Of course when the airfield had been operational during the war the trees were not that tall and there was no factory building as a potential hazard either.

Finally and I thought worth recording are some salient thoughts and comments from Syd, at the end of our recent happy reminiscing, which were; A. "we were lucky, we both came though it all, too many others did not!" and B. "It's great to be able to talk to an old friend and one that knows what the ...I'm talking about"! That comment from Syd clearly indicates the quite dramatic change in our national character and abilities. In barely two generations since the end of the Second World War (The third one we will not win!) and with the growth of a nanny state that stifles and discourages all the things that originally made Britain 'Great', such as initiative, enterprise, inventiveness and most important of all, commonsense. With the advent of our so called health and safety, liberalism, feminism, homosexuality, drugs and political correctness, often driven by the faceless axis of Nazi Germany and the Vatican, are all leading to the prophetic statement that we and America will loose the "pride in their power". Call it what you will, The Fourth Reich or the Seventh Holy Roman Empire, the result will be the same, terrible and deserved subjugation. My mother was quite right and with only a small amount of German blood in her she saw what was coming. She knew they would be back and, in fact, of course they never went away. They were already preparing, with the Vatican's help, for the next war before that one was even over!

Syd and I both agreed that Penn was exceptional, had had a presence that was hard to resist and also that he had certainly a constructive influence on both our lives?! Certainly he was the most adroit and convincing con man I ever encountered coupled with the ability to charm the birds out of the trees, as they say. Hence my frustrated anger, almost loss of control and verging on despair with him on occasion.

To finish this insert perhaps an excerpt from Peter Nock's widow, Sara might be of interest. This from a letter she sent me after I had sent her a condolence card for the second anniversary of Peter's death.; *Dear Bob,....but which unnerves me. Did Peter too. We belong to another age. Funny that, isn't it? The pull of the primitive mountains was more insistent with Peter than the amazing abilities of, say, aeroplanes and other more modern inventions. Anyhow, I wanted to thank you very much for remembering the anniversary and sending me a card of sympathy. However sad I am, I have to remind myself that I am actually luckier than any other person I know; we had such a lovely life together, and he even left me a beautiful letter, from beyond the grave. I am so glad you have gone apace with your own memoirs and was delighted to read them along with the stories of my dear* (in fact I had only sent the pages that included Peter and the family have now included them into his memoirs, which I take as quite a compliment). *So like him not to have mentioned the freezing incident. Very naughty of him to have attacked you from behind* with a monstrous wind-what is 15 feet! Nothing between you and decapitation! He was not at all like that later, thank goodness; when I knew him his days of flying under bridges were over and he took a very sober view of danger, didn't fear it, but wasn't going to let it in through carelessness. That was how I managed to be as relaxed as I was about his absences; I knew that no one could influence his judgement if he thought it time not to fly, or not to climb. I've been looking, so far without success, for a cutting from a Canadian newspaper of long ago: Peter is being interviewed prior to a rather epic flight he was to make. One of the journalists asked him about his war experiences and Path Finders and raids over Berlin; "Did you ever get shot down?" "No" said Peter, "Nothing exciting happened." Typical. ....Thank you so much again....PS; Not surprised Peter remembered that car ride!

Well I think that just about sums it up and says it all in fond memory of a great man. One that influenced my life a lot and to whom I owe so much in retrospect.

130. Off to a new life

I don't recall anything special about the transitional period up to our sailing out of Liverpool to Montreal on a Greek ship by the name of *Olympus*. It was a rusty tub and only one stage short of being a total disgrace. From the safety, hygiene and facilities one got the impression that as 'immigrants' we only qualified as superior cattle. I am not normally a complaining type but I was more than sympathetic to those that did. They were told, "very sorry but this is the last voyage and the ship was then to be scrapped". So most people did not bother to pursue their legitimate complaints after we all landed, if the ship was going to cease to exist anyway. Some time later in Canada we met other people who had come over on the same ship and they had been told the same lies and it had been going on for years! We were all conned. The food was just about bearable which did not interest Prue as she was definitely off hers anyway and with the usual morning sickness to add to it. The only advantage to me was that I got to eat her black olives which I am not that fond of but I was not going to waste them, on principle!

Our arrival at Quebec was in good but cool weather and the city which is right on the river seemed to have a lot of attractive building with their wonderful aged, green copper roofs that were very impressive. The last of the ice on the St Lawrence river was drifting downstream in relatively small chunks. At this time in history, ships could not get up to Montreal in the winter, the port was iced up. The St. Lawrence Seaway, a mammoth project, was already under construction which would dramatically change that situation within a few years. On arrival at Montreal we disembarked but had a few hours to kill before our train on to Ottawa. We wandered about doing the almost tourist bit and found that although it was supposed to be a French city in practice it was very cosmopolitan and a surprising number of English speaking people about. The French influence was a bit contrived and disproportionate we thought. A lot of it was just trying to be awkward and ill mannered about as many things as they could. Typically French of course and even worse than the Welsh and their ill mannered nonsense we see in the UK. After an hour or two of window shopping and doing some of the sights including walking up to the top of Mount Royal for the wonderful view out over the river to the south and the mountains away to the north we went into a large department store and upstairs to the very English tea room where we ordered a pot of tea and scones. The tea was foul and consisted of a teabag hanging over the cup and a pot of only lukewarm water. The scones were not much better! We were suddenly very unimpressed and wondered what sort of place we had come to? We need not have worried as everything else that day was quite impressive, even the huge railway train that was to take us on to Ottawa. The countryside was nothing out of the ordinary but the grand looking Ottawa railway station we emerged from was. It was part of one of the group of grand green copper roofed buildings, including the National Parliament, that makes that part of Ottawa distinctive and almost picturesque. Most of this part of Ottawa is Federal property and is policed by the Mounties in their distinct uniforms. The rest of the city by a separate city police force that had a much lower standard of entry! Then as soon as you leave the city limits there is a third police force covering the whole of the rural areas of the province (Ontario). They too were of an inferior calibre!

Prue and I found ourselves a rather cramped bed and breakfast within a few blocks of the station. Only later when we returned from a meal did we discover that half our room had been let out to another couple with only a semblance of a temporary screen erected between us. Once again we were not too impressed! The next morning we made several phone calls from our landlady's private phone for which she charged us a dime (10cents) each for. Only weeks later did we discover that all local calls were free! The old bat was an opportunist, to say the least! We found several quite nice flats available to rent and settled for one on Bronson Avenue, a quiet and well tree-ed avenue only a few blocks from the main streets. It was on the second (third in North America) floor with a very pleasant big balcony to sit out on. Actually a flat roof of the floor below. The family were a very nice, partly French Canadian with, I think, eight children. The father was the local representative of the American Bradings beer concern marketing *Cincinnati Cream*. The family were most hospitable and always invited us down to join them for supper on Thursday evenings when a mountain of steamed sweet corn on the cob was served. We were expected to eat half a dozen at they probably had to watch their family budget. We both liked the family and were more than happy with them which makes it even more shameful that I cannot remember their names, either.

131. Work, Canadian style!

The next morning, having phoned in advance, I took the local bus out past Mooney's Bay to Uplands Airport to visit Spartan Air Services. I was met by a Bill Dougherty, the engineering director who was quite abrupt and demanded, "where were you yesterday? We had expected you to start work then!" I was a bit taken aback as I only thought that I had a good chance of getting a job but it appeared that as far as they were concerned the job was mine and it had been understood for weeks! It appeared that once again I was more than beholden to Peter Nock who had told them that not only was I a wizard on Rolls Royce Merlin engines but that I had a natural feel for them and the Mossie aircraft as well. Spartans were desperate as they had several of those rather tatty ex RAF Mossies that Peter had bravely ferried over the Atlantic but they had literally no one who knew anything about them when they had got there. The hangar floor foreman was a tall friendly Englishman by the name of Harry, a former RAF sergeant and ground crew. He too was more than pleased to see me and we spent the rest of the day going through each Mossie's documents to work out schedules on four aircraft in relation to their planned duties. I was to set the programme and he would supervise it and call me from aircraft to aircraft as required on those that only needed guidance and advice dragging me away from the jobs that only I could do at that stage. I was given two quite experienced mechanics to work with me to learn and then run their own maintenance crews. One was a recent arrival from Hungary and had got out just in time, from under the Russians tanks as they entered his country in 1956. The other was a strange but amiable and conscientious chap from the Lebanon. They were both quick learners and within a month I could leave them to a job with only a minimum of help, guidance and supervision. Some of the Canadian fitters and mechanics were not so hot and a bit too casual for my liking, some even telling me how to best do a job! They, already having become experts on everything after only a couple of weeks with Mossies! Again I was not impressed, for while I admired the Canadian attitude reflected in the popular national saying, "the difficult we do all the time but the impossible takes a little longer". Fine but not when lives in aircraft are involved. Another admirable one was "the best way to kill time is to work it to death". Both are as true today as they ever were, although it seems, NOT in 'great' Britain today.

Other worries were developing and not being an airframe structural engineer I was not in a strong position to do more than politely question the wisdom of cutting out various bits of fuselage and internal ribbing. This was to allow room for a third person to fly in the rear to take photos through the large window they cut into the bottom or underside of the fuselage. This window weakened the floor structure near the bomb bay rear bulkhead. They then did away with the emergency ditching dingy and its box and so making an opening but limited space from the cockpit back to the, now rear camera operator. It was not big enough to crawl through and when flying contact would still have to be by intercom. It probably helped the poor fellow to not feel so cut off and remote, though I still thought it would be very claustrophobic. In this opened up space was also where the long range oil top-up tank was normally situated which was essential when the long range bomb bay or wing drop tanks were being used to dramatically increase the range of the aircraft. I warned the powers-that-be, including the big boss "Weldy" Phipps, that they would loose engines. This because with the long range consumption and with the blow out at take off and full power they would run too low on oil in the standard tanks. I was not listened to and told it was only a limey theory! Unfortunately I was right and several engines were lost and some very dodgy single engine landings had to be indulged in. More on this saga later on when matters got very serious.

Prue and I settled into a reasonably active social life. When we arrived we were approached by an organisation called the Independent Order of Foresters which organised regular meetings and dances for we new starving immigrants. In fact it was just a nice way of selling, we newcomers some insurance. At these events we met some couples that were to become regular acquaintances if not close friends. There were the families of my workmates and we joined the local Motor Club. I rapidly became in demand for help to tune the quite wide variety of British and European cars that the members owned but could not get even serviced locally with any satisfaction. The only exception to this was the ubiquitous VW Beetle, (Hitler's revenge?). That was sold from an exclusive dealership organisation with great emphasis on service and executed with German efficiency. This was run by a local Jewish family by the name of Morton, which struck me as slightly ironic. The Ottawa Motor Club ran regular local car rallies but they were of the rather tame, stop watch and almost treasure hunt style with average speeds of barely 30 mph! They were so boring that as a diversion we would turn off onto a wrong road and drive until we reached, say a phone box or some common land mark and then turn round and drive like mad to get back on schedule having often done twice the mileage actually required! Since these events were often timed to the nearest second we never won any! It could hardly be called fun but we met a lot of people that we would not have done otherwise. The winners of these events were often little old women civil servants (Ottawa was full of them, being the nation's administrative capital). They would often sit in the back seat doing their frantic calculations and corrections with the dutiful driver obeying instructions. Seeing some very powerful and sporty cars creeping about the countryside and town, often being passed by regular traffic, seemed rather ridiculous to me and certainly did not come under the heading of motor sport or even fun in itself.

132. Transition?

Among the office staff at Spartans was a young English draughtsman by the name of Michael Holt who owned a bright red Triumph TR2 sports car. Having a common interest in aircraft engines and sports cars in general we struck up a long lasting friendship which led to a business partnership early on. We started a small part time business/club, working out of a large private garage in a back garden just off one of the main streets. One of the first customers, outside our immediate club and friendly circle was the Commercial Attaché from the French Embassy. He had a little Renault 4CV and being pragmatic he much preferred to use it around town. He must have been impressed with our efforts because he offered us the full Renault franchise for the Ottawa city and valley area! There was a new model recently announced that they hoped would compete with the VW Beetle. It was called the Dauphine, certainly a much prettier car than the Beetle. Our biggest and immediate problem was premises, not so much on the service side but prestigious enough for sales and promotion. Our, at least temporary, solution was to rent an empty corner plot at 1149 Bank Street, one of the main streets but out at the residential edge of the city near the Rideau Canal. It was right beside a good café so if it was raining or worse we could retreat into it and keep an eye on the site through the windows for potential customers. We covered the plot with clean gravel and made up a timber stand for the car to sit up on and a ramp up the back to drive it up and down. The first demonstrator car we took home at night and used it on an everyday basis, to and from work, to demonstrate to potential clients and parked up on the ramp/stand on show every evening and all day at weekends. We took it in turns to man the site and drank a lot of coffee in the café. Michael was not only a good aero draughtsman, he was a good artist as well and did a very professional job of colour sign painting of the exhibition ramp. So good in fact that we kept it for use on the forecourt of the brand new garage and service station that we moved into later on. This, out at 1868 Carling Avenue, on the corner with

Maitland Avenue. Carling Avenue was and may still be the main western route in and out of Ottawa! We sold several cars which was not easy as the vast majority of potential clients wanted to trade in their old vehicles. Had we been in a position to get involved in that side of the business as well, we could have sold ten times more Dauphines than we did! At about this time the neighbour of the house whose back garden we had our workshop in, starting blackmailing us into doing free servicing and repairs on their large Canadian (American) car or else they would report us to the council since it was a residential zone. No one else was bothered and it was all private vehicles that we were working on we were not even breaking any bye-laws. Not taking too kindly to blackmail and since we were starting to need much more space we moved the garage side of things down to 55 Caruthers Street just off Scott Street, alongside the railway, down near the river and not far off the Federal Parkway where it crosses the Ottawa river via a couple of islands and bridges. It was a bit of a dump but was cheap, had a very good heater and had all the space we needed. We retained the more prestigious sales site which was used as a collect and pick up point as well. The café became our waiting room and the owner was quite happy about this as his passing business certainly improved as well.

Also about this time Prue and I were travelling in a bus along one of the main streets into the city centre when we spotted some remarkable looking cars in a large showroom window. They did not look anything like the run of the mill American cars that generally prevailed at the time. The most obvious and dramatic difference on this Coupe shape was a large front or radiator grill of the sort of multi square egg box design that one would expect from a Ferrari! Curiosity aroused, we made a point of visiting the showroom within a very few days. We were amazed to find that these cars were Studebakers and there were very few left as the dealership was desperate to sell them off as soon as possible as they were switching to a Ford franchise. What a happy coincidence as we already knew we would have to get a local car with space for a baby (due that November) for not only space but a good heater for Ottawa's regular −20odd degrees or more of frost. The XK120 did not even have the vestige of a heater so was not too practical for use in semi arctic conditions with a new baby. The Studebaker came with two heaters, the usual type set in and behind the dashboard and a second one under the driver's seat which blasted hot air both under the driver's legs and to the legs of any rear seat passengers. The shortcomings if shortcoming they were, were that it had a bench seat in front that took three with no problem and two more but sitting lower in the back. On close examination the front grill was a bit flamboyant but on the Power Hawk model we settled for only had the relative vestiges of rear fins compared with the top of the range, the Golden Hawk! The Power Hawk had the smallest and lightest of the three V8 engine options and was therefore less inclined to go straight on at the corners! The other heavier options demonstrated massive under-steer, to say the least. The biggest engine in the Golden Hawk was the 6+ litre Packard (same company), out of their large limousine! Unfortunately all these bargain basement cars had automatic gearboxes handy for city driving and a great help to Prue, with her very limited driving experience and now on the wrong side of the road as well. In practice and despite only being three speeds I could hang on to each gear to maximum revs. and the car was almost as fast as the Jag up to 90mph. It also returned about 28mpg against the Jag's 18-20 in similar circumstances. After 90mph the Jag. just kept going whereas the Hawk struggled, even down hill! I insisted that they take off the white walled tyres and put proper tyres on plus inner tubes. They also agreed to fit the optional Stewart Warner instruments, including a tachometer. The silly speed limits were I think, about 55 mph in Ontario on even the major roads but marginally better at 60mph over in Quebec. I anticipated some problems in this department?! This Hawk coupe was finished in two tone green and was not unattractive by even European standards and it certainly served us very well.

Spartan Air Services Mosquito 1956

133. Motor sport?

Late on that first summer in Canada we even used the Hawk for local car rallies. Prue was of course very pregnant and absolutely blooming. The most amusing bit of these tame events was the other women who kept rushing up to see if Prue was still ok at every check point, particularly on forest and rough country roads. It transpired that North American, both U.S. and Canadian women seemed to think they automatically became invalids as soon as they even thought they might be pregnant and clearly considered us madly irresponsible! One of the local Motor Club members was a chap by the name of Bob Potter who appeared to be a bit on the impecunious side and could only boast a very basic and bottom of the range Chevrolet, fitted with the relatively small six cylinder, side valve and pretty gutless engine. Bob was born with a club foot and had the most amazing set of large, almost horse like teeth with considerable gaps between them all! They were always on show as he was always happy and smiling. The snobby elements of the club clearly looked down their noses at him and criticised his choice of an entirely unsuitable car for club events. The snobbiest member was a Naval Lieutenant Commander (yes one of them again!). who was a frightful poser in his immaculate Chevy. Corvette Sports car fitted with all the latest navigation equipment and a two way radio. He would turn up at events, hardly say a word to anyone, collect his route card, instructions and set off alone. He used the two way radio to speak to his wife at home in an attic control room, she then acted as his navigator and did all the calculations and radioed instructions back to him. At the finish he would only wait long enough to see if he had won anything and then drive off almost without saying a word to anyone else. Not a very sociable chap but worse he had been very unkind and rude to Bob and went out of his way to humiliate him, every chance he got on the road. Some of the other members were not much better. I do not remember quite how it came about but I do remember Bob all but begging me to drive his car in one of the out of town events to try to reverse the situation. Bob with the best will in the world would never be a sporting driver and this coupled with his ungainly and heavy boot for his club foot was never going to be a winning combination. I agreed against my better judgement but warned him that his car may never be the same again. He did not care, in his desperation to see his mundane car show the much more expensive and suitable cars that his was not just an "ugly duckling". I am not a fan of large American cars with their sloppy steering and suspension plus ungainly weight distribution and tyres that seem to want to roll off the rims at the slightest provocation! Prue was not with me and Bob on this occasion and was travelling with friends in a more suitable vehicle. We chucked everything out of Bob's car we could and secured anything we could not! The tyres (sorry in Canada now, so its TIRES) were pumped up at least another 10 PSI in the vain and only hope of improving things a bit. It really had become a David and multiple Goliaths situation.

We set off near the back of the field in what in truth was a frightful vehicle. When we got onto the country dirt roads at well over the legal speed limits I was having to almost turn the steering from lock to lock to keep it in an almost straight line. The dust trail behind us was like those American desert movies. After a while we caught up with other competitors who were not pleased and even less so when we got past them with a car that must have looked completely out of control, to say nothing of the dust we covered them in. We caught up with a Sunbeam Rapier sporty saloon (sedan) who was reluctant to move over downhill on a forest track. He thought that there was not enough room. There was when I put one wheel onto the verge and squeezed past them. Their fright resulted in lots of flashing lights and horn blowing at us. They then got an even bigger fright when Bob's exhaust system tore off and sailed through the air bouncing over their bonnet (hood) and then their roof only just avoiding going through their windscreen! We soon lost them in the dust with a car that was now sounding like a tractor. A mile or two further on the engine started misfiring badly so I pulled over and lifted the bonnet (hood) only to find that the metal air cleaner canister had jumped off the carburettor and had dropped down on to the plugs shorting them out. Solution, yank it off and throw it into the boot (trunk).

The Sunbeam had then passed us again with a lot of jeering. Within a mile or so we had caught them and as we came up behind they pulled right over and almost stopped! Bob while all this was going on was almost hysterical with delight and jumping up and down shouting loudly over the exhaust noise, things like "that'll show them etc. etc." He seemed to be totally unconcerned that his car was falling apart just as long as it showed them. A few more miles and several pass-ings later we had just been using full lock on the steering to get round a very tight corner when the steering seized solid on full lock. We ground to a halt luckily only half off the road and in our own dust cloud. We jacked up the front of the car, took the wheel off and I noticed a side plate on the steering box itself which I took off only to find that with the violent steering the peg had come off the end of the turning worm! With the aid of a hammer, screwdriver and a tyre lever we managed to re-engage them and put the cover back on again, now minus most of its grease. Once again off we went re-passing all the cars that had passed us while we were effecting repairs and half off the road. I was a bit apprehensive about it happening again in a much less "lucky" place this time. I avoided using full lock and hoped for the best?

An hour or so later when we were dusty, dirty and almost deafened we caught up with the snooty Lieutenant Commander in his immaculate Chevvy Corvette who was clearly not amused and refused to move over for us. So we just played with him for a bit pretending to pass on one side and then the other. He got angrier and angrier and his driving got more and more erratic and Bob was all but screaming with delight and shouting, "get him", "get him". Well, in truth a rather less polite version (children may eventually read this!?). Finally on a downhill stretch and it had to be a downhill bit as he was much faster than us on the flat so we could only catch him again on corners or downhill when HIS skills ran out! On this occasion there was shallow ditch which we used to good avail to get the width we needed, a move he clearly had not anticipated or been able to block until it was too late! It was becoming a huge laugh as I never ever thought I would have had such great fun in the most basic and unpretentious of "yank tanks", and certainly never have again. Dear Bob Potter would be able to die happy and I honestly do not remember now if his car ever recovered?

134. Up a gear?

The snooty Corvette driver on arrival at the finish just checked in and flounced off home like a spoilt child. I do hope he never made Admiral? Bob's self confidence improved no end and he repeatedly rubbed in the point that his car was not so inferior after all. Of course he did not exactly make himself popular over it but he was more than happy within himself. No one seemed concerned about my part in it all, which surprised me a bit but I think that this was because no one from the Ottawa Motor Club had ever done well in the country's only International Winter Rally. I was suddenly their promising candidate for the next one! It appeared that they had never seen any car driven the way Bob's was that day and assumed that I might be able to accomplish something worthwhile in a proper car for their rather inexperienced and amateurish club. No one from Ottawa had managed to do so yet. This Winter Rally started from two cities at the same time. The majority started from Toronto and a lesser number from Montreal, which is where the Ottawa club members usually started from, being closer to get to for the start and to get home again afterwards! The two separate starts meant that the two groups were up to a day apart and could get entirely different weather conditions when they got round to the same part of the route. A bit of a gamble and I gathered that no starter from Montreal had yet won the event. Not being superstitious and enjoying a challenge that fact did not bother or deter me.

This big event was named the British Empire Motor Club's International Winter Rally. I found the continued use of the word Empire faintly quaint! This old established and salubrious club was based in Toronto and initially I was a bit reluctant to enter the event as the Studebaker Hawk with its automatic gear box was hardly suitable for a serious attempt but the Jaguar which was, in most respects but did not even have a heater etc., was a right hand drive, rather draughty side screens and very basic stick-on electric windscreen de-icer/de-frosters that plugged into the cigar lighter. Not much stowage space for even a snow shovel, de-ditching gear and traction mats and chains or spare snow tyre equipped wheels. We would have to operate down around the lakes, St. Lawrence river near the American border on cleared roads at only about −20* and on up into the far northern parts of Ontario and the Laurentian mountains in northern Quebec where it was likely to be closer to −40*. I had no doubt about either me or the car's ability from the straight driving point of view but had to consider the possibility of meeting likely problems without the independent ability to sort them out ourselves.

The word 'ourselves' then took me on to the next problem as the rules called for two drivers with competition licences although there was no possibility, of me ever letting anyone else drive my XK120! If I went then I would do all the driving myself, an unheard of situation on a tough event lasting at least two full days and nights. The other hazard was the rumour that, if you went off the road anywhere in Quebec no farmer with a tractor or anyone else would help unless you spoke French (yes, them again). So as a form of insurance to cover this eventuality I would take along one Tim Plottier another recently arrived immigrant, a French lad who was married to a very nice English girl named Jean and who had become Prue's best friend in the motor club. Unfortunately Tim had only just passed his driving licence test so was hardly qualified for a Competition Licence. I had a very hard time talking and bluffing the authorities into issuing him with one. I told no lies and only finally clinched it when I said I would hardly even consider the possibility of letting anyone who was not very skilled and in whom I had every confidence, drive my precious XK120. Would I? They, of course took the inference that he would be driving but I was careful not to say so! Since no one had ever even considered driving the rally solo it never even occurred to them that that was what I intended!

They granted Tim his Competition Licence on a provisional basis and intended to instruct the Marshals to report any infringements on his part, which would lead to our disqualification. Needless to say it would never happen as there was no chance that I would even let Tim drive round a car park in my Jaguar. He was there only as a French interpreter when and if required. I even doubted his ability to be any use as a navigator. While we were away on the rally Jean would stay with Prue and help look after our new baby son Robert Laird who had arrived on November the 30th 1956, St.Andrew's Day and Winston Churchill's birthday as well. Tim's total driving experience was driving his new little Standard Ten (with overdrive) about seven miles to and from work on almost empty roads and had probably not even driven more than a couple of hundred miles in total!!

Once again I am getting ahead of myself. So back to our first summer and autumn in Ottawa.

135. The writing on the wall?

Where the car business side of things were concerned we seemed to get busier and busier and apart from the word of mouth increase in business we were getting more and more involved with club members cars as well. We had to take on a part time salesman to help man our street corner sales site and a young mechanic who was called "Titch". I am not sure if I ever actually knew his real name despite him being Michael Holt's younger brother and of whom the whole family despaired, as he would not stay on at school or do any form of further education. It was cars, cars and more cars, nothing else interested him and he was already very knowledgeable, enthusiastic and a good motor fitter for his age. Another influential and good friend from the Motor Club was a chap by the name of Gerry Bisson who was mad keen on all aspects of motoring. He regretted that he could not run a British or European sports car as well but his very full time job was selling Fords, in the form of the slightly upmarket varieties entitled, Meteor and Mercury plus the odd Lincoln as well. He also ran and promoted the local Stock Car Racing at the Lansdowne Stadium, which was still well within the city limits. Gerry would join in our local events with whatever he could 'borrow' from the used car and trade in lot at work! He never seemed to stop and his energy was phenomenal. Just to show how enthusiastic or daft he was, he entered the B.E.M.C winter rally with a Ford Ranchero. In fact a new model idea at the time and in reality was a Ford pickup truck that had lots of padding and fancy car type upholstery and other embellishments and did look relatively smart. He did not last long on the rally and had gone straight on at a tight corner just after a hump. The nose of the vehicle was well buried into a snow bank and the tailgate was well up in the air. He was sitting on it waving a torch (sorry, flash light) to warn the rest of us of his hazardous presence in good time. I stopped to see if we could help but he said no, it was too far into the ditch and would require a hefty breakdown truck to get him out. He said he was not too bothered as he had a good heater, plenty of food, hot drinks and a radio which he would enjoy after he made sure no one else joined him in the ditch and snow bank, too!

136. Americans cheat, too!

Gerry inveigled me into becoming his official scrutineer and responsible for measuring the winning stock car's engines at the end of an event at Lansdown Park. Having absolutely no personal interest either directly or indirectly he saw me as an unassailable and totally independent judge in such matters. Such strip downs are always a bit of an irritation at the very least and it was not unknown for furious rows and arguments to break out over the accuracy of the measurements and the calculations required to arrive at the engine's total cubic capacity. It's really quite simple, as are most things when you know how. The formula is; pi. R*2 which gives you the area of one piston which is multiplied by the length of the stroke giving then the total swept volume of that single cylinder. This is then multiplied by the number of cylinders in the engine concerned. In the case of these stock cars it was always eight, in V formation. Four cylinders each side and with separate cylinder head each bank. So in that way you finish up with the engine's total cubic capacity. There had been mutterings about some of the American cars that came up over the border, which always won on these regular visits. Cheating was suspected but they had never been caught out, yet! At the very first race meeting I was to officiate at I was watching the racing from very high up in the stands and noticed that some of these American cars had no problem in passing the others on the far back straight but then just dropped in front of the others and never pulled away despite the much greater power that they must have to be able to pass so easily when almost out of sight on the back straight. They never managed to do it in front of the spectators on the front straight! These cars, as well, had a very distinct and even rougher and uneven exhaust note than the usual V8s do. I smelled a rat and wondered why this discrepancy had not been noticed and commented on before? Perhaps it had but on stripping the winner's engine if it was found to be legal and with no signs of special fuel etc. there was not much anyone could do about it but swallow pride gracefully.

At the end of this race meeting and by the time I had got down from my eyrie and slightly eerie vantage point high up in the grandstand and arrived at the paddock and pits for the winner's measuring session. The winning car's mechanics had already almost stripped and removed the left hand cylinder head for me to measure the internals. They stuck me are being too anxious, somehow. On only an instinctive whim I requested that the other head should be removed as well so that I could measure the whole engine. I was furiously told that the established and agreed custom was to strip only one side and then just double the result from the measured 4 cylinders to make the total for the 8. They refused to do it so I refused to certify their engine. This led to a bigger row from the Americans claiming that they were not prepared to be messed about and they would never come back to Ottawa to race again and further they would not claim their winning and cup in protest, supposedly on principle! Poor Gerry as promoter and organiser was stuck in the middle.

By now there was a large audience of the Canadian drivers as well, who outnumbered the Americans and who were not going to let them get away with anything. One mature and quietly spoken Canadian said to Gerry, "I back your man and think that, if only on this one occasion, we should insist on the Americans stripping both banks for measuring". He was immediately supported by the rest of the Canadian drivers, who would not physically let the Americans leave until they complied. Finally the very unhappy and angry American crew stripped off the other head. All was finally revealed, as the other bank was nearly a litre bigger than the first one! In other words if the engine limit for that class was, say 5 litres then the winner had a very uneven 6 litres! Which accounted for the dramatic increase in power output and the rather strange and uneven exhaust note I had noticed. I say, 5 or 6 litres but in reality the classes were, as is the usual American habit, actually classed in cubic inches rather than litres as we do in Britain and Europe and most other international venues. There, being roughly 61 cu.ins. to the litre. Before the measuring was completed the cheating driver was suddenly nowhere to be found, conveniently. He never returned to Ottawa as far as I know to drive but in reality the whole team must have been guilty and known what was going on as the driver himself, was not the machinist or builder of the illegal engine. The Americans continued to come up and compete but, surprise, surprise, they were never as clearly successful again! I can only conclude that there must have been more than one American cheat?

137. Gerry Bisson, the ongoing friendship

Gerry continued to be a good and loyal friend and certainly not typical of most French Canadians. I tactfully never asked but I did wonder if his name had crept into his family a few generations back by an unfortunate mistake? He phoned me one day with a generous proposition. How would I/we like to move out of town? Our answer was yes, despite Prue's impending motherhood. We had no shortage of transport and I could be contacted by phone and whether I was at the airfield or the garage, could be home within twenty minutes! The offer was for a wonderful, almost new mobile home situated in a grassy and partly wooded park by the name of Nine Pines. It was just off one of the main roads south and just outside the city limits in Carlton County. Compared to caravans, as we knew them, this was a palace. In practice, about 45 feet long and about 10 foot wide. Double glazed, skinned and insulated. Complete with oil burning hot air central heating which was ducted through the floor and up into each room. Full sized bath and shower, the main bedroom was roomy enough that the double bed stayed down all the time with plenty of room round it with wardrobe and dressing table. The second bedroom had two fixed bunks with one that could be turned into another double! The full kitchen, dining and sitting area was very spacious and had a large refrigerator with a TV on top which could be watched by those in the sitting room which then, in turn had a row of mirrors above the full width end windows allowing anyone still in the kitchen or dining area to watch the box via the mirrors. Simple, clever stuff. The cooker, oven and sinks were household size and all in immaculate condition.

We could have all this by just taking over the existing H.P. payments and with no deposit. This was to come from a friend of Gerry's who had some problems and was having to move. Naturally we jumped at the chance, gave in our notice to Bronson Avenue and moved out within a couple of weeks. We had most of the late summer out there at Nine Pines and Prue much preferred being left there all day (and often evenings as well) in the fresher air than in an upstairs flat in town. The mobile home was well away from the few others on the site, in a sheltered and very sunny corner. We had some regular and amusing nocturnal neighbours, from skunks to raccoons (my favourites) who would attack everyone's dustbins (sorry garbage bins) most evenings and nights or as soon as they knew any dogs were safely inside. The raccoons would sort out their spoil and then take any food, like, say an apple core away and wash it first before eating it. The skunks were less fastidious and certainly less intelligent as I can vouch for, from actually owning one that had been de-ponged. Although an amusing pet it was a bit on the dim side but with great tenacity of purpose. A bit like McGinty's goat that attacked the dam and did not seem to know that its task was impossible. So it kept on going until eventually succeeding!

138. Spartans, a growing unease

Work at Spartans settled into a fairly regular routine but I was getting more and more concerned about the question of the Mosquito fuselage and particularly the oil reserve modifications. These were being put forward and implemented without first being fully thought out. There was also a plan to coat some of the operational wood surfaces with a new type of epoxy resin which certainly could be made to produce a very smooth finish compared to the fine linen or Medapalin (a sort of Irish linen I believe?) and 'dope' that was usually used. The dope and linen can be removed without damage to the wood surface for inspection of the plywood's condition. Once covered in Epoxy it would no longer be possible to strip it off for inspection without serious damage to the base surface! So how were they going to regularly check all the structure properly? I was not very popular when I raised the question with management! One of the upstairs staff in the hangar, which consisted of management, traffic control and drawing office, was a woman by the name of Kathy de Corcurea (the spelling is only guess work again). I say woman rather than girl as she must have been at least thirty and so much older than me! She was German and had married a U.S. or Canadian serviceman to get a passport to escape the grim conditions in immediate post war Germany. Many thousands of German women had taken this escape route. Needless to say and as in so many similar cases the marriage did not last. Kathy was a very efficient and hardworking woman and was dating one of Spartan's Mossie pilots by the name of Rocky. I'm not sure if I ever knew his real name despite us becoming good and trusted friends over the ensuing months. I think it was Kathy and Rocky between them that arranged for me to go up into the communications room whenever there was some sort of problem or emergency as it appeared that my 'limey' English was much clearer and understandable over the airwaves when poor reception was encountered. It seemed slightly strange to be talking to pilots from the ground instead of as a pilot, talking back to base. Kathy was also always the announcer over the hanger Tanoy loudspeaker system, so on the 30th November 1956 and having just taken the phone call from the Graces Hospital that Prue had given birth to a baby boy, she proceeded to make a very long winded and public announcement to that effect. To my slight embarrassment and a chorus of cheers from everyone on the hangar floor who all seemed to rushed over to carry me out to my car for my rush back into the city to see mother and the baby boy who was to become one Robert Laird. When I got to the hospital Prue looked tired but otherwise blooming and quite rightly proud of herself.

Rocky, a bit like Peter Nock seemed to develop a great faith in my mechanical and diagnostic abilities. He even asked my advice about the flying characteristics of the Mossie as well, which was a bit ridiculous in retrospect since he had probably dozens more flying hours on them than I did. I think it was my ability to relate the mechanical side to the flying that helped me a lot. I found it strange and incongruous, and still do, that a lot of very good pilots have only the minimum of practical engineering knowledge! More and more often Rocky would ask me to do his pre-flight checks and frequently do the taxiing, high speed brake testing and the mag. drops "while you are out there". Of course it was inevitable that after I had flown with him on the odd test flights as his observer Rocky said one day, "take it up yourself and use my call sign". All very illegal but hardly a new experience for me! The longest trip I got to fly a Mossie was up to the town/city of Churchill on the Hudson Bay. A pretty bleak and frontier type of place but I at least got my first sighting of polar bears in the wild on my approach to the far from smooth runway. This was partly made up of those linked metal strips since the ground below was often unpredictably soggy depending on how hard the permafrost was at the time!

Spartan Air Services had a fair selection of aircraft apart from the growing number of de Havilland Mosquitoes and included a couple of Avro Lancaster bombers, several Lockheed P38 Lightnings, several Douglas DC3 Dakotas and run as a separate entity of about seventeen little two-man Bell helicopters. They had contracts and commitments from all over northern Canada to do with the far from top secret DEW (Distant Early Warning) line, which was the paranoid American way of getting a couple of extra minutes warning IF the Ruskies should lob the odd atomic or hydrogen missile over the North Pole at them! The Americans ploughed so much money into Canada during this period that for the only time in history the Canadian dollar was worth several cents more than the American! Visiting Americans were not amused to be charged a premium on the their almost sacred dollar but had been only too happy to charge visiting Canadians the same in the past and now again to this very day. Spartan's work up north was survey and supply/cargo hauling. Some of the survey work was by photographs that had used the P38 Lightnings until the arrival of the Mosquitoes but because the P38 was a single seater the pilot was often trying to do the impossible three jobs at the same time. The Mossies were now, after adaptation and modification, a three man aircraft! The pilot, the navigator/observer and the camera man who could concentrate on the photo work full time making the majority of photo flights successful. Thanks also of course, to the now new windows in the Mossies that still worried me. The other method of surveying was by magnetometer which consisted of a torpedo like object being towed below the plane (usually one of the Lancasters) on a long cable to measure the changes in the magnetic fields below. An aerial geological survey over vast areas. When finished the cable was wound up and the torpedo stored on the bomb bay

.

139. At large with Spartans

Another area of Spartan's operations was in South America, mostly in Colombia and usually operating out of Bogotar. In retrospect it seems strange that I did not even think to try and look up or try to find anything related to my mother's childhood either in Bogotar itself or in Cartagena (pronounced, I believe Carta-henna!) where I know she lived as a very young girl. I have a photo of the family car outside their house with the chauffeur by the name of Alphonse posing beside it. Cartagena is down on the Caribbean coast looking west towards Panama. Bogotar on the other hand is well up into the local Cordillera Oriental mountain range which is in effect the northern limits of the Andes mountains. Some very unpredictable weather could delay work for days at a time. Once out of the city it was mostly jungle, which was why the magnetometer survey work was essential as the jungle and mountainsides made a ground survey about 90% impossible apart from taking far too long. Maintenance and servicing aircraft in remote places can be feast or famine. Days of doing nothing but minor checks and refuelling every few hours or suddenly an all night engine change. Assuming, of course that you had a spare one ready and did not have to wait days for another one to be flown in and then have to deal with the usual bribery and corruption inherent in the officialdom at Bogotar at the time. I was glad to have gone and experienced the place but I have had no burning desire to ever go back! Apart from the fact that I did not want to be away for more than a few days at a time, potentially neglecting my wife and young son at home and my rapidly growing motor business.

One place that we could visit and fly down to with our families was Havana the capital of Cuba. We were able to get in a couple of enjoyable trips while Castro was still fighting in the surrounding hills. A very few months later he had taken over and that was the last of the Cuban visits. Again I did not think of looking out for my mother's birth place while there. I quite liked Havana's suburbs with their grand houses and walled, shaded, attractive but slightly decrepit courtyards and gardens. The sort of place my mother and her family would have been living in was much more attractive than the city centre which was like Bogotar but bigger and best described as very Faded Spanish. (Who says I'm not a diplomat?). Cuba's beaches were good and the Brazilian frenetic type sporting activities were almost continuous. The food was very good, quite varied and cheap as were the cigars and booze, which were of no interest to me but most visitors stocked up with plenty for their friends back home. With my continued hatred of communism I quite often think of the over fifty odd years the majority of those poor likeable people have had to suffer the almost hysterical pontifications of Castro's communist regime. I am sure the ghost of Ernest Hemmingway would join me in wishing for the early departure or demise of Fidel Castro and his lot! The Cubans in general are very friendly, quite industriously innovative and deserve much better.

The work sites we were involved with in northern Canada could not have been a bigger contrast. Often very bare and with areas of strewn boulders. In some places, even when the ice had gone the actual permafrost may only thaw out for a bare month when the concrete like surface became a horrid bog. The insects that then emerged often made my experience of the tropics in this regard seem almost mild. I saw mosquitoes appear that were much bigger than anything I had ever seen in Malaya or even Borneo. Amongst the flies was one called an eye fly which dive bombed anything wet and shiny which included the eyes of many unfortunate workers. Their eyes then got very badly inflamed and red which took up to a couple of weeks to clear up even with medical help! On balance I think I preferred the colder part of the year despite having to work outside at 30* to 40* below freezing in the shade! Often though in brilliant sunshine which made things dangerously deceptive. For instance ear tips were always prone to frostbite and should be covered at all times along with our mouths covered to stop the risk of suddenly inhaling a gulp of very cold fresh air which could damage one's lungs. I had visions of tiny sharp icicles puncturing them. In the coldest weather our tools had to be heated as the steel could turn very brittle and break quite easily. It had been known for spanners to shatter like glass when being dropped. That's cold!.

When an aircraft landed in such cold conditions is was usual to keep the engine(s) running if it was due to depart again within a few hours. It would be allowed to idle for say twenty minutes and then revved up to stop the spark plugs from fouling up and misfiring. If for some reason the aircraft was not flying again for days then a tedious procedure had to be gone through. It was not possible to turn the engine over with its own starter from cold as at such low temperatures the crankshaft having got relatively brittle could snap! Engine oil would have become almost as thick as tar and certainly not flow and lubricate as it should. It would probably snap the oil pump drive in its efforts. This coupled with the fact that batteries tend to lose about 10% of their capacity for every 10* below freezing. So, all else being equal the battery would be incapable of turning and starting the engine even under normal temperature conditions.

Most Arctic aircraft had fittings on their engine cowlings for attaching large hot air heater pipes. These would be used for several hours before the propeller(s) would be turned by hand gently for some time. this to check that the engine had freed off to normal. The lubricating oil would then be diluted with a measured amount of fuel which would later boil off via a flame trap as engine temperature reached normal. The battery(s) would be preheated to bring them up to normal operating capacity. The reluctant engine(s) would then be started but only kept running if oil pressure showed on the gauge almost immediately! Ice build up on wings is usually fatal and our DC3s all had air expanding rubber panels on the leading edges of the wings which could be inflated from the cockpit individually to break off the forming ice on take off and initial climbing. The Mossies had no such equipment and had to be painted with a grease or paste with a high glycol content in the hope that the ice would not stick to the wings. This gunge was applied with a long handled broom - very technical. On the fluid cooled engines (Mossies, P38s and the Lancs.) the coolant (antifreeze) was between 70 and 90% glycol because not only was the air temperature at ground level well below freezing it got much colder at any altitude plus the wind chill factor as well. The Pratt and Witney air cooled engines on the DC3s did not have the coolant problems but still had to thin down the oil with fuel and go through all the other pre-heating and freeing-off operations and preparation.

The extreme cold did have some (not many) advantages though. For instance if an extension to a runway or perri track was required often some quite large boulders may have to be removed first. The ground was often too soggy for a bulldozer even if one was available so a lot of boulder removal had to be done by hand. The procedure was to drill a deep hole into the centre, pack it with explosives and blow it apart. The last few of the day would be drilled as normal and then filled with water and just enough antifreeze to let it still flow without instantly turning to ice and blocking the hole! A wooden bung would be hammered into the hole as a cork or plug. Then later that night quite a noisy crack or report would be heard as the boulder split apart. A dramatic and graphic example of the power of the expansion of water as it freezes. In the morning the bits, which had much cleaner surfaces than the explosive ones, could then be removed.

140. American security!

The next bit reminded me of the situation at Crail airfield in Fife during the Second World War when my Uncle George had told me that the nosy submarine watching us was a German U-Boat and that Berlin would know sooner than London the state of progress!? Then may years later at one DEW site close to the Hudson Bay area and where as usual the Americans were paranoid about security, having double checked we visitors repeatedly despite knowing full well who we were and our clearance from previous trips. The Americans, in their wisdom had a policy of employing locals to work for them (very democratic!?). These would often include Eskimos, some hardy Indians and even French Canadian hunters and trappers who could make good money compared to their usual precarious fur hunting and trapping. In fact they would employ anyone who just turned up from the wilds around about the site with of course no identification or pretence of a security check. They would drift in and out to suit themselves with no organisation at all. Some of the Eskimo looking types I was told were actually Russians from the Mongolian end of the USSR and had just strolled into the site having walked a few miles from a Russian submarine that had just popped up through the ice to drop them off. So, just like wartime Fife, but on this occasion it would be Moscow knowing more about what was secretly going on in Northern Canada than Washington did! So much for secrets and security, American style.

One of the encouraging pluses or perks of the work so far north in the cold and very inhospitable land was that no expense was spared where food and possible comfort was concerned. So the cooks were very well paid as well and it had happened that a long term crew refused to go north unless it was with a well known and exceptionally good cook. This I knew about and often heard mention of the point. In my case I was not bothered as I was only ever on short trips. Days, rather than weeks and months. On one occasion I heard the discussion about which cook was preferable to be horrified to gather that it was not the relative merits of their cooking that was being discussed but their sexual services and the charges they made to further supplement their already large wages! I thought I was worldly and broad minded but clearly still naïve where apparently the remote normal North American sex lives were concerned! What I found even more confusing was that the men concerned were heterosexuals not even homosexuals. I had no idea that such perversions existed then and to this day I am still appalled by such behaviour.

141. Police matters!

This was just one more of the growing bits of disillusionment I was to suffer. Some of the others were to do with the police, both city and provincial which as I have already mentioned who were a far cry from the RCMP (Mounties) standards. Two very disillusioning events will illustrate my point and explain my feelings. Both occurred while Prue and I were still living out at Nine Pines, during our second spring and early summer there. The first one was in broad daylight while on my way home for a quick lunch with Prue and baby Laird. I was driving at my usual ambling gait when I spotted a provincial police car trying to follow me round corners with some difficulty despite the fact I had slowed to stay within the speed limit before they had caught up. So I knew they could not charge me and was therefore rather surprised when the lights and sirens went on for me to stop. One of the policemen rushed up to the car as though there was some sort of emergency and ordered me out of the Volvo 544 I was driving. He started to push me about and prod me with his revolver, ordering me to face the car in a voice that can only be called hysterical. The second policeman was standing back and appeared to be slightly embarrassed and not wanting to be involved in the farce. Farce or not I did not fancy being under the control of this apparent maniac. As I appeared to be obligingly turning to face the car and slightly brushing his gun to one side first I stepped back and then cropped my arm to clamp his gun arm tight to my side with the gun then protruding safely past me. Quickly I dropped to one knee while turning abruptly which dragged the clown off his feet to the ground and forced him to release his grip on the gun, which I of course assisted! Leaping up with his gun now in my hand and stepping quickly back over his body I had both policemen covered before the second one could even think of drawing his gun, not that he showed any sign of doing so.

The rage and abuse from the undignified grounded policeman could not be repeated in civilised company! He screamed that I was really in the worst sort of trouble now and they would throw the book at me.

The second policeman, relatively calmly confirmed that it (the situation) was now becoming a much more serious matter and agreed to keep his hand off his own gun as long as I did not threaten him with the one I was holding at his partner still on the ground. Being quick witted or inspired, I'm not really sure which, I agreed that the matter was very serious since they were obviously NOT real policemen at all! and I was going to take them back into the city and turn them over to the city police or maybe the RCMP. I claimed, tongue in cheek and with as straight a face as possible, that no decent well trained professional policemen would have stopped a perfectly innocent motorist, roust them out of the car at gun point unless they, themselves were the crooks and trying to steal my rare car! The audacity of my allegations almost left them at a loss for words. I continued to claim that I was convinced that they had stolen the police car and uniforms and were using them all as a front to commit crimes of who knows what and in my case to steal an unusual and rare car. The calm one wanted to reason with me and he eventually told the floored one to "shut up and let me deal with it". He almost pleaded with me to believe him that they were real policemen and after a period of ongoing grovelling and attempts to justify his partner's over reactions I pretended to half believe him but since I was not prepared to put my life at risk by releasing the clown on the ground and even if they were just rogue policemen as I put it, I was still going to turn them in and file a very serious complaint at the highest level.

I told them that they were to handcuff themselves together and climb into the car boot (sorry, trunk). If it turned out that they were, just possibly real policemen I laughed at them and said they were going to have a lot of embarrassing explaining to do to their colleagues! The calm one looked appalled at that prospect and asked if there was not some other way the matter could be resolved? Eventually and pretending mock reticence and after being told by the calm one that his partner who I still had one foot on and with his gun pointing at his head, had wrongly over reacted on this occasion. This was supposedly because he had developed a warped attitude to suspected speeding motorists after a nasty and fairly recent incident. This being that, he (the one on the ground) and another partner had stopped a group of drunken kids, initially to just warn them and to then have a shotgun stuck out of the car and to well nigh blow the well meaning policeman's head off! I then used this explanation to, still tongue in cheek, express my sympathy and at least partial understanding to the extent that I would now condescendingly take a huge gamble and let them go free. Conditions being that the mad cop on the ground was handcuffed and put into the police car's boot. That the civilised one would then drive off with his mate in the boot and not stop for at least twenty minutes or try to return to that spot for at least an hour when they could then retrieve the first one's revolver from just behind an adjacent road sign. The moron was not amused but had become a little calmer but still furious (with me or himself?). The sensible one almost sheepishly agreed, looked more than relieved and was heard to tell his problem partner that the best thing he could do was to shut up forget the whole incident rather than be seen as an embarrassed fool and laughed at by all their mates back at headquarters! So, finally they drove off, with an almost cheery or embarrassed wave? I left the revolver where I had agreed and went home to lunch! I avoided using that particular route to and from work for sometime and did not use the same car again either. Luckily, nothing of the matter was ever heard of by me again.

The next silly (dodgy) police experience. Funnily again in one of the Volvo demonstrator cars. This time rather late at night on my way home at about 2 am when I was using one of the southern minor roads before turning off towards Nine Pines. Just before I left the city speed limit a young chap stepped out and thumbed a lift. I think I must have been tired and not really thinking properly because I was due to turn off this road within about two miles so it did not realistically make sense to pick someone up and then drop them off again shortly afterwards where a lift would be more difficult to get? I stopped he got in and I was explaining just that, when he stated that I was going to take him all the way to Kingston. Being somewhat tired and irritable I said that he was not to be so B.... stupid and I was dropping him off at my planned turn off or he could get out now! He then had the cheek to draw a gun on me and say "this gun says that you will take US all the way". I was caught by surprise and suddenly worried as he then told me move off and then to slow down and pick up his mate who suddenly appeared in the headlights on the side of the road, literally at the city speed limit end. I woke up rather rapidly as I realised that with two of then in the car and with possibly two guns I would have more of a problem than I wanted. I pretended to comply and agree and as I slowed down to pick the other one up I dropped into second gear and at the last moment accelerated hard and deliberately ran into the waiting hitch-hiker and knocked him into the ditch. The one already on board turned to see what had happened to his mate and took his attention off me for an instant in which I was able to swing my right hand across from the steering wheel and over the gun to give him a karate chop across his temporarily exposed throat. This made him choke and wheeze and drop his gun as he put both hands up to his neck as he was having great difficulty in breathing which was now in noisy gasps or whoops. Not a pretty sound!

    I stopped, reversed back and got out of the car having retrieved the gun. The second hitcher was lying in a rather distorted position in the ditch moaning and almost crying being obviously in great pain. I did seriously consider leaving the pair of them on the side of the road to whatever fate or help that might or might not come along at that time of night. The possibility of being later charged with a hit and run or leaving the scene of an accident was not a hassle I wanted even if it could all possibly have been justified in the circumstances. This coupled with the dangerous and laborious breathing of the first one which looked as if he was going to need oxygen very soon or a tube stuck down his now, almost closed throat, if not a full tracheotomy. The vague thoughts about self defence versus attempted manslaughter problems did cross my mind though. The final and quite quick decision was to drag and stuff the second hitcher into the car boot and leave the horrid gasping first one in the car as he was quite incapable of doing anything but fight desperately for breath and I had the gun now anyway. I turned the car round and drove back into the city down town to I think it was Wellington Street police station where I pulled up outside dragged them both out of the car and dumped them on the police station steps outside and went in and up to the duty officer behind his fenced off desk. I slammed the revolver on the desk told him I had been held up at gun point and the two villains concerned were outside and in need of medical if not hospital treatment!? I left my business card and said I would be in at some stage later in the day to prefer charges. I then just walked out despite the officers almost speechless and confused protests.

    I finally got home very tired at about 3 am, had a very late supper and went to bed. In the morning I slept in and had a leisurely breakfast before driving off to work at the garage/service station on Carling Avenue. It may seem ridiculous but the previous night's activities were not even on my mind. I got to work late at about 10 am to be greeted by several of the staff, all with very concerned faces. It appeared that the police had called in three times already with a warrant to arrest me for attempted murder! They had all loyally and conveniently not known where I lived so the police would have to wait until I got to work! Jim Hardy, one of my salesmen who was the son of a retired Senator and lived out in the wealthy area of Rockcliffe Village, claimed to have the best up and coming lawyer as a friend from their college days together. He phoned him and it was arranged that we would meet immediately and this young lawyer would accompany me to the police station as I turned myself in.

The scenes, the shouting and general carry-on was to me unbelievable. The police really did seem to want to charge me with attempted murder! The police attitude to the hitch-hikers and the gun question was almost, "boys will be boys". It was to me surreal. Without this young lawyer I would have been subjected to a lot of serious bullying and intimidation as all their interest and questioning was to get ME convicted. Possibly because of the way it appeared that I had taken the law into my own hands. They did not want to even consider the question of my right to self defence. I should not really have been so surprised since I had long discovered that the north American insurance culture was that no one should fight back or even resist a robbery as the cost of possible injury compensation might be much greater than, say the wages being snatched. This was NOT my culture I'm afraid! After about two hours and more senior police officers being brought in they decided not to charge me yet! But had to be assured that I would not leave town in the near future. This young and very persuasive lawyer stood no nonsense from the police and put them in their place several times along with serious counter threats for exceeding their brief and false charges, threatened arrest, pointing out that I had come in voluntarily. Anyway we all left in time for a late lunch and to talk the matter over and discuss any future possible ramifications. I do not remember what the legal fees were but it was probably the only time in my life that I though they were value for money.

142. Justice?

Many months later the two hitch-hikers appeared in court where I had to give evidence. Unusually (so I was told) the judge commended me for resisting their hold up and even said that it was a pity a few more citizens did not do the same thing as it might act as a deterrent to the rising number of related cases coming up before him. The second hitch-hiker got a suspended sentence since it could not be proved that he knew his mate had a gun or his intention to hi-jack a lift. It appeared that when I had run him down I had smashed his leg and hip and he would limp badly for the rest of his life. So the judge, in his wisdom considered that carrying his punishment with him for the rest of his life was adequate in the circumstances. The first one, with the gun got a two year jail sentence and again the judge said that since my chop had permanently damaged his voice box and was still painful, that too was a deserved punishment and why he was getting away with only two years. Finally, a satisfactory outcome but I did reflect that for someone else it could have all turned out very differently. The villains had, unluckily for them, picked on someone who was able to take care of themselves and was not easily frightened or intimidated. And again was not in awe of the police and finally had a loyal friend with an exceptional young and energetic lawyer - college pal. Justice should not have to depend on any of these things. So summing up it is largely an indictment of the local legal system.

The only other police incident involved the RCMP this time. One very pleasant sunny afternoon I was driving along the Federal Parkway and heading over the Champlain bridge towards the Quebec (Province) side when I noticed a RCMP car chasing after me but far too late to prove a speeding charge! He signalled me over and leaped out of his car looking exceptionally smart with all the highly polished leather belting and gun holster absolutely gleaming with polish. When driving, the Red Coats (RCMPs) do not wear their red dress tunics or boy scout hats but do still drive about wearing their horse riding jodhpurs but with flat caps and yellow bands. He obviously knew I had been speeding but was too late to prove it but decided to give me a hard time anyway. I listened politely but I thought he was never going to stop nagging on about it. Perhaps, unwisely I finally stopped him in mid flow since I was in a bit of a hurry and claimed that he was trying to bully and intimidate me just because I was in an unusual car and a timorous new immigrant. I further added "and I thought this was meant to be a FREE country". He stopped immediately and went to great pains then to repeatedly claim that it was indeed a free country and that I was not to get any sort of idea that it was not! Did I now understand that and agree with him? I said yes I had already thought that until he had stopped me, an entirely innocent motorist and then him acting as though it was a police state! He went on and on about it being a misunderstanding and did not want me to proceed until I reassured him that I did now (again) accept that Canada was a free country. And I was never, ever to forget it! We parted on good terms and shook hands. All rather funny in retrospect but slightly pathetic but it did again demonstrate to me another chink in the new world's physiological and immature confidence armour? The very few other occasions that I had any dealings with the Mounties demonstrated clearly that the vast majority were hard working, efficient, dedicated and a fine body of men whose selection and training was vastly superior to the other ordinary police forces in the country.

143. More nonsense

On our way over to Canada Prue and I had struck up a good friendship with another couple on board who were going on down to Hamilton, a smaller city beyond Toronto. He was an experienced plumber and thought he would have no problem getting a job. There was a shortage of them there, or so his brother, who had emigrated several years before, told him. They would also be able to stay with the brother and his wife until they got settled in properly. Prue had kept in touch with this couple as arranged and we made the effort to go down to visit them one long weekend. We found them and had a very enjoyable time with them including the inevitable trip on down to Niagra and the Falls, of course. All quite spectacular but because the falls, particularly the Horseshoe (the Canadian falls as against the American section) ones are so wide you do not fully appreciate the height until you are in the tourist boat called, I think *The Lady of the Mist* when underneath and looking up into the wettest mist you can imagine you really finally and fully grasp the grandeur of it all. Most of the countryside between Hamilton and Niagra was agricultural with lots of fruit orchards and named locally as the Banana Belt. The climate being so relatively mild for that latitude. I've since heard that most of these orchards are gone and a massive amount of housing has replaced them in a form of commuter belt. A great shame.

This couple were not entirely happy with their situation as he had not been able to get a job commensurate with his experience and he was told his time served in England as a plumber did not count! He was expected to start off and serve time over again as an apprentice for the usual number of years before he could sit his exams and become a qualified plumber again. In the meantime he could only earn the union rate for a young apprentice which was hardly enough to keep a married man in a new country. Luckily his wife managed to get a job which helped them through the situation. Even better he had just got a job with a firm that appreciated his experience and was prepared to bend the union rules and pay him a more reasonable wage while he served his apprenticeship again.

My own experience along the same sort of lines came to light after some official came into the garage one evening and wanted to see my garage repair licence which, of course I did not have and did not even know about! Further I could not even apply for one unless I had at least one designated and certified mechanic. I suggested that I was experienced enough to qualify as a certified mechanic. I was told no and that I would have to go and serve my apprenticeship for, I think three years, before I would be even allowed to sit my exams. I kept the ball in the air, so to speak initially by claiming, quite truthfully that I was not repairing cars only tuning them and their requirements were therefore not valid since their so called licence specifically said repair. And that I therefore did not come under whatever jurisdiction they thought they may have had. It all went to a higher level of management where reluctantly they finally agreed to make an exception in my case and count my years of mechanical experience on aircraft as an equivalent apprenticeship. But I would still have to sit the final exams to which I agreed, much to their relief, I think.

Officialdom is never happy or comfortable with things they feel slightly out of control of and beyond their limited logic and book experience. Some weeks later I went to sit my exam along with a bunch of spotty and not very bright young individuals. The exam papers were of the multiple choice type but with a series of windows in which to write yes or no as we thought the case might be. On one page the questions were all about the float height and settings on Carter (as used on Chryslers) or Rochester (as used on G.M. cars) carburettors. I had not the faintest idea of the answers. My next dilemma was the wording or phrasing of the questions which were hardly in the English language that I thought I knew! The one classic that I do remember was something to the effect, "is a charged up battery full of electricity" I did not know if it was a sort of inane question pitched to the basest of educational abilities to find out if a battery was ready for use or function if it had been charged up first? In which case to such a moronic level the answer would be YES. On the other hand and as far as I was concerned a fully charged up battery is not full of electricity, only a potential when connected and in which case the academically correct or educated answer would be NO.

I never did find out what THEY thought the correct answer should have been! With the yes or no choices I could not even qualify the answer or give any reasoning. I left the examination room feeling distinctly short of respect for some Canadian officialdom. A few weeks later my certificate or diploma or whatever it was supposed to be arrived much to my surprise. I hung it on the office wall upside down, deliberately, to show my feelings of contempt for the whole system. This was the only qualification or certificate I have ever displayed or even produced in my life. It also appeared that I was the only student or examinee that was not told his qualifying percentage gained. My conclusion was that I had failed miserably and they just gave me the certificate to get rid of an embarrassment. I still do not know or even care to this very day but considered that I had beaten the(ir) system!?

144. That winter rally!

As usual I have got a bit ahead of myself again, so returning to our first winter and before the police episodes just mentioned which would have been several months later in the following or second spring and summer. Having rather reluctantly agreed to enter Canada's only International Rally some serious thought had to be put into preparing for it. The only luxury was to rig up and I mean only rig up an old Land Rover heater jammed on top of the gearbox tunnel with a couple of crude holes through the bulkhead for hoses to be connected up to the engines cooling/heating system. The Jag engine ran very cool, too cool and there was no warmer thermostat available to help. So I carried out several weekend trials with a different amount of thick carpet blocking off the radiator until I had the ideal average but could still raise it or lower it a bit using some lead covered electrical cable to bend and adjust as required quickly. Space remained a major problem so I had to make the decision just to run on my normal Michelin X tyres and rely on skill and the weatherman rather than try and take spare wheels with snow tyres fitted. No support and back up in those days. You took everything with you or did without! I found a good folding snow shovel and made up some traction mats out of some of the Mosquito bullet proof fuel tank covering which we had removed at Spartans. One surface of this laminated material was almost like sand paper and not too thick, so four strips did not take up much space. Since in such cold weather the side screens would be in use all the time so we had a wide but fairly narrow compartment behind the seats for essential storage. (where I hid my gun and ammo while in Indonesia, remember?) Since the car's two 6 volt batteries were behind the seats and well boxed and after removing the normal fold up hood (soft top) we could stow extra clothing above them too. The limited boot was just enough to carry a couple of spare cans of petrol, some oil, tools and an assortment of sundry wire, tape clips a small hand winch, some steel pegs, a few shackles, wire cable loops and odd lengths of fine woven and strong rope. Any last minute or emergency items would just have to go inside on the floor under the passenger/ navigators legs!

I had quickly gained a bit of winter confidence after driving home from Uplands airport one evening just after a very light snow fall. All the local drivers were sliding and skidding sideways on the very small incline beside Mooney's Bay. Literally dozens of cars were having problems. I was in the Jag and just put it into top gear at a bit over 20 mph and had no problem just bumbling past them all. They could not believe it, nor I, despite the fact that I had already decided that most North Americans were hopelessly unskilled drivers in their Yank Tanks, their poor tyres, automatic transmissions, too much power/ torque and unrealistic speed limits which almost guaranteed that most drivers would never learn to drive properly and certainly never how to control, say, an even medium speed problem skid. I had thought that "at least they will know how to drive in snowy and winter conditions". I was wrong again, they were hopeless, as were even the police, who were frequently to be seen travelling sideways, even in town on their useless knobbly, so called winter tyres which in practice are useless except in fresh snow. On snow-packed or icy roads they would have been better off to have kept their normal tyres on and just put on chains every now and then, as really required. The other daft local belief was that if they kept spinning their wheels and digging in deeper, they would eventually dig down to the ground and get grip? There was some truth in that but hardly when they only moved forward inches before starting the wheel spinning all over again and again and again. I did have to admit that, on occasion the automatic transmissions had an advantage if one did get stuck in a rut. The technique is to rock the car forward and back repeatedly until the car climbed up and out of the rut and carefully kept moving. The automatic having an in-line gear change it is easy to go from forward to reverse and back again very smoothly whereas with a manual gear box one often had to cross over the gate and through two right angles from one gear to the other so loosing momentum plus poor clutch control with winter shoes or boots on! After witnessing all this repeatedly, almost day after day I decided that the odds in any winter rally, were not stacked against me so badly after all! I should perhaps add that the standards of the basic Canadian driving licence were very low and it was called an operator's licence. Any sort of commercial driver would take the slightly more advanced test (particularly if he drove a stick shift), which was known as a chauffeurs licence, which sounds a bit incongruous to us. The other advantage of the more advanced licence was that it could lower insurance premiums.

Well, we finally set off up to our chosen starting point at Montreal, arrived in good time to sign in and get all the guff. Most of the Montreal starters were far from friendly or sociable and we almost wished that we had taken the much longer option and gone down to Toronto where the majority would have been more our sort of people. We were looked at and spoken to like aliens and even with Tim's ability to speak French did not seem to help any! Our starting number was quite late on and about an hour down the list. Gerry turned up at the last minute in his Ford Ranchero and set off with a wave and before we could even greet him. We started off back the way we had come, on the very slushy main roads. Then about fifteen miles on out of Montreal we turned off and north into the hills and back roads of provincial Quebec. Soon it was solid hard packed snow with high snowploughed banks but a bit on the narrow side which did not make passing very easy although we could brush along the snow banks without fear of rocks or other hazards. As we got into what we might term the foothills, the roads got quite undulating and of a bendy nature making it very difficult to maintain any speed, not really knowing what would be round the next corner or over the next hump. Any sort of braking when almost off the ground would just lead to locked up brakes and a straight-on skid to disaster. Choice, to drive at about 20 mph slower, just in case or drop a gear and rely on the engine to do most of the braking which is then through the rear wheels which makes it all much more controllable and stable.

Within a couple of hours from the start I had just come over a small hump and the headlights while still up in the air showed a gap in the trees indicating that the road carried straight on but as the lights lowered again the straight-on bit was a farm road and the proper road swerved left at its entrance. So down a gear and lift off the throttle for engine braking. Instant disaster, the throttle decided to stick open so no worthwhile braking at all. Straight into the snow bank between the farm entrance and the road. Bale out and light a flare to warn the next car that there was a hazard over the hump - us. My first thought was "this is why I brought Tim, to go and find and persuade a local French farmer to pull us out with his tractor". Luckily though only a small amount of digging was required and the Mossie fuel tank bullet sealing mats were enough to enable us to reverse out again. The flare worked and the following cars were able to creep round us safely. The cause of the sticking throttle turned out to be a tiny bit of rock salt grit stuck under one of the carburettor's throttle stops so preventing it from closing properly and causing the engine to race. It was then only a few miles on and coming over a big hump that we found Gerry in his Ranchero in the incident that I have already mentioned earlier. He had put a flare out well before the hump and was sitting on his tailboard waving a torch as well. As I've already stated he did not want any assistance and was anxious that we should not be delayed on his behalf. He seemed to think we were doing very well but I was not very confident at that stage. Where Gerry had gone off and straight into a snow bank was on a sharp right hand bend with a bad and downhill camber. Coming with no visible warning. I think the majority of cars would have come unstuck there so I think it was Gerry's mistake and subsequent warning that many of us have to thank for even completing the first night's stages. "Greater sacrifice hath no man-----", and all that.

The rest of the night became a blur of hairy, constantly sliding, bouncing off snow banks and riding other peoples ruts cut into the packed snow a bit like tram lines and hoping that none of them led off the road! This riding the ruts was a new technique to me but I warmed to it and found myself going faster and faster round these corners at speeds that appeared to defy the laws of physics. I developed a new feeling of being "at one" with the car, full of confidence and optimism. It appeared that more and more cars were collecting time penalties at these stages but we were managing to stay clean. On the last night stage and just at dawn we were descending a very winding and icy road rut riding and bouncing off snow banks into a town where there was a check point. The roads were clearly quite slippery but we were still doing over 70 mph on occasions! We pulled up outside the checkpoint with the car still sliding-on a bit even with the hand brake on, which should have warned me? I got out to get our documents recorded and stamped only to slip over and find that it was so slippery that it was impossible to walk upright on the slight slope. I literally had to walk on all fours up this slight, almost camber-like slope to check in. Wearing my flying boots with very thin and rather smooth soles did not help either. Good news though, we were one of only three Montreal starters that still had a clean sheet.

I do not recall much of the following daylight hours other than it was a beautiful sunny day. One incident which seemed a bit trivial at the time (but crucial later!) was a check point or way point that was supposed to be passed. Some of these way points were manned some were not and there were also a few secret check points which did not figure on our stage point sheets. These were usually to ensure that someone did not take some ridiculously easy alternative route so avoiding a testing bit of terrain. We arrived at a map reference that we had been given to pass through only to find it was on a country bridge joining the relatively main road that we were already on to a smaller parallel one on the other side of a small frozen-over stream. I took the map from Tim and very carefully pinpointed the reference which was definitely on our side of the bridge. So we checked it off on our route sheet and thought no more about it until the next manned check point when someone mentioned the manned way point that was on the other side of the bridge and on the smaller parallel side road. Which it appeared both we and the majority of others had missed. I double checked the map and reference again and along with several others put in a protest that the marshal was not at the correct point and therefore the route check should be cancelled. I was a bit naughty by laying it on that I was a pilot and was not in the habit of making navigational errors!? The importance of this move instigated by others was only really supported by me as a moral backing for them but turned out later to have massive significance on the final result. This beautiful sunny morning that I've mentioned found us on almost entirely empty roads up in northern Ontario in the region of Sudbury. The roads were thick packed snow and with larger build up and almost continuous snow banks. We were driving along, over relaxed taking a slice of snow bank off the apex on every curve or corner instead of bothering to slow or even brake, just letting the snow bank do the slowing! The rest of the time we would ride the ruts and use the full width of the empty road going into and coming out of the corners. While happily swinging along like this, perhaps not fully concentrating and getting a bit blase we came round a corner in a flurry of snow as usual only to be confronted by the first car we had seen in over an hour (Canada is a big country). This happened to be a police car coming towards us in the middle of the road and equally lacking concentration in the sunshine. The police driver's face was one of absolute horror. We were closing in on each other for a monumental head on smash. I swerved and half mounting the snow bank at quite a speed and angle managed to only just squeeze past. Since we had not touched I did not bother to stop but did worry a bit (not like me) that he may feel aggrieved for some unknown reason and radio in a complaint to the next town. However, we need not have worried and we concluded later that he must have been so relieved that he decided to count his blessings instead and ignore the incident. While pondering these matters some miles after it had happened, it suddenly dawned on me that I had instinctively passed him on the wrong side! Not entirely surprising while driving a right hand steering car on the right hand or other side of the road and in a dozy state of mind and tiredness? So we had passed him on his inside!

We had a partial night rest at a lodge complex outside Sudbury, for a shower, a civilised breakfast and a snooze which was very welcome. It was so cold that several of the cars had great difficulty getting started again after the, only few hours stop. At about first light that morning, Tim had sent us up a road that after a few miles did not seem to have the sun generally on the correct side if from what I remembered from the map that I had looked at before we set off, was right. It is often difficult on a windy road to judge the average direction one is heading on. I have a very good sense of direction from my Boy Scout and flying days and almost subconsciously I concluded that the sun was too often on the wrong side of us. So we stopped and I grabbed the paperwork from Tim and concluded that we had headed up the wrong slot and turned back and it helped to keep awake by driving quite fast to make up the lost time, about twenty minutes if I remember correctly. When we finally came south again and arrived in Toronto at the point that the other half had started from well over a day earlier we heard that they had all got through the country roads to Montreal before a very heavy snow fall had closed off many roads behind them, but of course in front of us! So it was with a bit of grim determination that we all set off again.

An hour or two after leaving Toronto, but still on occasion, near the edge of suburbia we came up a small rise to find that the whole area had been dug out a bit like a saucer, a hundred yards wide. The ongoing road no longer existed and was diverted very suddenly to circle this crater. There was no warning but it is possible that any sign had got hidden by the night's heavy snow fall? At the speed I was driving and if I had even attempted to turn onto the rudiments of the circle road I considered that rolling the car was more than a possibility!

So I drove straight down the bank keeping the power on so as not to loose momentum and across the bottom of the snowy crater looking frantically for the easiest bit of banking to charge up again at an angle and hopefully back onto the road. I picked a slope that looked promising but still rather steep. I got about halfway up when the car started sliding sideways and back down again but when all seemed lost the side of the car hit a post of some sort which stopped the sideways slide just enough to give some grip and we were up out of the hole and back on the road again at the other side. Had I not kept the speed up when first leaving the road we would never have made it. It was a lesson that I retained in other forms of motor competition in the years to come! Brands Hatch circuit in particular

The snow had dramatically got worse and when we came to a turn off into a village to a supposed checkpoint no one had got through and no sign of an imminent plough either. Having come that far clean I was not going to let an unploughed road stop me from at least trying because I thought that the marshals may have got into the check point from another direction and would be there. So with great difficulty and repeated efforts we managed to battle through, only to find that the checkpoint was unmanned. So I left a note to the effect that "Kilroy" and a certain Bob Henderson with car no .... had been there at such and such a time! It transpired later that the marshals could not get into the village even in their Land Rover so the stage was cancelled. This decision irritated us a bit but was very good news for the majority of Montreal starters. Our next and almost last dramatic escapade on this rally was some hours later when again dozing along, enjoying the sunshine on a very easy bit of well ploughed and gritted dirt road. The area was a mass of small lakes and low ground, to such an extent that all the roads were artificially raised to keep clear of any rising water and it was a bit like driving along the top of a series of banked up dams. You would drive along one with water (ice at that time of year) on either side and then suddenly come to another frozen lake right in front of you with the road literally at a sharp right angles to left and right and so onto the next similar T junction. I was very tired by now and should have anticipated the situation arising. But tiredness, the soporific and almost blinding effect of the sunshine coupled with the fact that I had my right leg and foot out of my flying boot and across the other (left) one that was on the throttle (instead of clutch and brake) trying to thaw out a bit from the mediocre warmth from the jury-rigged Land Rover heater mounted under the dash and on the gearbox tunnel. Tim was of course able to rotate his feet and hands for warmth on a continuous basis without the problem of working any controls at the same time.

Well it all went horribly wrong, as, on a curve and as we passed under a tree that had thawed its load of snow in the sunshine and dropped it onto the road where it had frozen again in the shade and into a very wide and raised platform of smooth sheet ice. At the same moment I spotted the fact that, straight on the road led into a frozen lake and we were going too fast to even think of slowing to negotiate another T junction. Even without the extra icy surface it would not have been possible to slow sufficiently for a sharp right angles, left or right at the junction! So here we go again, accelerate hard and keep the car straight, over and down the six to eight foot banking and onto the ice, hoping to spot a suitable place to drive out and back onto the road again, a-la, the previous excavated roundabout episode outside Toronto earlier. But no, the car broke through the ice and started sinking so I yelled at Tim to get the side screens undone and be ready to bale out quick as I expected the freezing water to come rushing in very quickly! But no again, because after the lake had frozen over the water below had drained away. This had left a hollow and bone dry leafy bottom on which the Jag sat happily with the surrounding broken ice at almost windscreen or top of wing height, also making it impossible to open the doors! A curious sight indeed but coupled with huge relief as well. The lake could have be much deeper and still with water under the ice although obviously the ice had only broken because there was no water to support it.

As we both scrambled out amazed, relieved and surveyed the disaster several of the other Montreal starters arrived on the scene and stopped to see if they could help. This rather surprised us, as until now we seemed to be regarded as alien interlopers. Of course what had happened was the fact that it appeared that we were now the only Montreal crew to have a clean sheet and they were desperate that even outsiders like us should carry the Montreal banner for them. Three or four cars stopped including one Jaguar saloon who thought we had a common bond after all!? The dozen or so people along with a vast array of winches, cables, ropes and a variety of big hammers and ground spikes assembled to help get us back up on the road, backwards. Initially the ropes and cables were attached to a convenient telegraph pole as an anchor. Unfortunately the pole snapped and was left dangling on its wires! So the anchors were run over the road and hammered into the far side of the embankment. With two winches, a few fence posts as levers and many willing hands the car was dragged backwards up and back onto the road looking a real mess. The rear bumper-ette irons had taken all that load and drag without distorting very much. These being the same bumper-ettes that had towed 7 ton Mosquito aircraft about at Lossiemouth. Tim and I cleared everything off the car and it started up fine after blowing a lot of detritus out of the exhaust and seemed to drive ok so all our helpers drove off to try and make up for their lost time and with assurances that when we caught up with them they would immediately let us go by. Very patriotic! I asked for an update from my navigator, no, I asked Tim, there is an obvious and growing difference and I don't mean it too unkindly. I had completely lost any sense of time during all the exertions and excitement? Tim stated that we had 'X' miles to go to the next check point and 'Y' hours and minutes to do it in. My recent bitter experience of these zig zag back rural roads told me we could never make it in time. But looking at the map I reckoned that if we went the wrong but much longer way we could. Why? Because within only a few miles we could be on a main road that would take us to just beyond our next checkpoint which was not far off the main road again. Therefore if I could drive at probably twice the speed on the main road I might just make it and loose no time or points. Going the official route I could not.

The only problem was that we knew that there was one more secret route check and if we missed that the points penalty would mean it was all over anyway. But if we stuck to the official route we were going to be late anyway so the gamble was the only option. We made the main road within a few minutes and found that it was largely clear of snow and ice but had patches of very fine drifting powdery snow. I should mention that in the various incidents some snow or ice or mud had got into one of the front brakes where the winter blanking plate for the air-cooling duct had got knocked off and allowed something to get in and impair the brakes performance a bit which meant that any braking was dangerously unbalanced and pulled the car off to one side rather badly! Again I was going to be a bit dependent on engine braking to help. So up to about ninety miles an hour I stayed in third gear instead of top which gave me just enough smooth engine braking when I had to slow to say sixty or seventy mile an hour situations! Soon after we had passed one of the recently retired competitors on the same route we entered a small village with about twenty to thirty people all walking in single file at the side of the road on their way to church on this bright sunny but cold morning. They were all dressed in black, coats, hats, everything. We must have passed them from behind in the region of eighty miles an hour and towing a vast cloud of this fine powdered snow behind us. The Arctic equivalent of the dust clouds you see made by cars in the dusty desert conditions. The crew of the recently passed retired car told us later that the church-goers had all but disappeared having been completely covered in our snow storm and it was almost impossible to know that they were originally clothed in black! They had become like,white flour men. We thought this hilarious but I doubt if they did?

Well we made good time but we still did not know if the gamble had paid off, yet. We should make it in time with a few minutes in hand or so I thought. In the meantime I had been going through the various calculations in my head which started not to add up and initially I put it down to tiredness. Finally and suddenly I said to Tim, "what were the exact times that we left the last main checkpoint and the intermediate ones and how long should that give us now to reach the next one on time". He gave me the intermediate times from the schedule and I suddenly realised that we were about to, almost rush into the checkpoint an hour early, not possibly late at all! Somehow in the lake and ice incident and in our fatigued state we had lost sense of time and assumed we had lost more time than we had in reality. In effect gaining an hour over our erroneous minds by going the very fast route and despite our icy off. Some how we mistakenly thought in effect that we had only four hours to complete the long section instead of five! So as we entered the small town from the wrong direction and after getting some funny looks from fellow competitors going in the right direction, we found a café to have a warm-up, to hide and kill time well off the rally route. We then found a back street way round, which enabled us to get to the correct side of town and drive into the checkpoint bang on time and from the right direction! We had done it and were still clean. The only question was had we missed that last secret check on the route we had by-passed? I very nonchalantly asked the marshals where the secret check was as I had not noticed it.

To which I was told that there was no secret check on that section as any alternative route was so much longer and would take even more time (I assumed he meant at legal speed limits?) therefore there would have been no point in it! So the last secret checkpoint was still to come and we were therefore still in the running with a good chance.

The next few hours driving back towards Montreal all seemed easy going by comparison, there were no more frights and we did pass the last secret checkpoint, correctly! The finish then all seemed a bit of an anti-climax. As expected we were the only Montreal finishers with a clean sheet but due to the protests about the early-on and incorrect map reference it was going to have to go to arbitration to decide whether that checkpoint should be scrubbed as well. I was too tired to care much anymore and only wanted to drive on back to Ottawa and go to bed. I did come to appreciate the wisdom of why they insisted on two competition drivers on this rally though. Regardless of the result in the end I felt like a winner anyway having done the whole thing solo, as it were and in a far from comfortable or warm car. I think it is safe to assume that it has never been done again!? To this day I retain a sense of accomplishment and would rate it as my motoring Borneo. I had been on the go for sixty-eight hours, almost three full days and nights with only a short couple of hours rest but hardly slept at the night rest point. I say my Borneo because the rally had its risks, required excessive stamina, willpower to fight sleep and general fatigue, mental and physical tenacity and quite a lot of mental activity since I was my own navigator most of the time as well as being BOTH drivers. I am not trying to blow my own trumpet but it must have been rather like driving TWO 24 hours Le Mans races with only a very short break and doing both of them single handed which of course is not allowed either! Some may say that the speeds on the rally are much slower than Le Mans but I would maintain that up to speeds of 110mph on snowy and unpredictable icy roads is much dodgier than 150mph on well known and practised roads or track. The nervous tension at every unknown slippery corner has to be much greater!? (so, ends my commercial). The Jaguar was (is) a wonderful car and never gave me a moments concern throughout the whole rally and being so strong and tough it obviously saved us from possible injury as well. The car arrived home running just as if it had only been on a local shopping trip. The body work did have a very few minor battle scars that precipitated a new colour paint job later and then changed to the mid metallic blue that it was to remain until the turn of the century, forty five years later. Some weeks or even months later my winners silver rose bowl suitably engraved arrived to acknowledge my efforts. I was told it was a bit grudgingly presented since it was the first time it had gone to a Montreal starter. Another slight disillusionment, and one which I still find today, is that north Americans are not terribly good losers. The winning seems to be more important than the actual sport itself. A pity. The Canadian Rose Bowl I have kept along with very few of the other pots that I collected over the years from various forms of motor sport. It is still a bit special to me, even today, fifty odd years on and writing all this has sharpened up the memory too!

B.E.M.C. Canadian Winter Rally Trophy 1957

145. A bit of flying

The last rally chapter is a bit out of sequence and should be inserted back a bit. Meanwhile back at Spartans I was able to do more and more mobile testing and on a growing number and types of aircraft. When I first started working on the Lockheed P38 Lightnings which were fitted with Allison V12 engines (a bit like the Rolls Royce Merlins and close to the same size and power), I found that these were not supercharged in the usual way but by what then was called an exhaust driven supercharger which is what we would call a Turbocharger today. Both the Allison engines and the rather ingenious supercharging were by a branch of General Motors (not a lot of people know that!), The largest car maker in the world from Chevrolet to Cadillac in America, Vauxhall in U.K., Opel in Germany and Holden down in Australia. As many will know today the turbocharger is driven by the engine's exhaust and utilises both the exhaust pressure and waste heat energy, which in turn absorbs a lot of the noise energy so reducing the amount of exhaust muffling or silencing that is normally required. When the Allison engines start up the predominant noise is not open crackly exhausts as on the Merlins but more like a powerful vacuum cleaner as the exhaust turbines wind up to very high revs. It was strange and uncanny at first but very pleasant and relatively restful for a pilot. Flying the P38 was easier than the Mossie, first because its engines rotate opposite to each other so negating the powerful torque reaction of the Mossie and like the Hornet it could be driven down the runway in a straight line with no problems and almost like a car! The next and most obvious difference which initially takes a bit of getting used to is that the plane has no normal fuselage but twin booms (a bit like the De Havilland Vampire jet plane) running back from the engines and joining up again at the common tail plane. The cockpit is then mounted almost as a separate pod perched alone up front between the engines on the main plane (wing). Initially it felt a bit strange and gives a feeling of one being a bit exposed and not part of the rest of the aircraft. This impression passes very quickly once on the move! The other most obvious difference is that the P38 has a tricycle undercarriage arrangement, which means it has a nose wheel instead of the more usual tail wheel. So unlike the Mossie where on take off initially a little nose down is used with care to get the tail off the ground and then stick back for the actual lift off. On the Lightning there was no concern about keeping the control column back to avoid tilting nose down with disastrous results to the propellers. The stick needed less pull back on the runway until take off speed was reached. On landing again and as the plane slowed and as the weight transferred to the front end less stick was required again because the front wheel would stop the usual risk of the nose going down. I did enjoy my limited flying time on the P38s. The power and performance were broadly similar to the Mossie but I think the P38 was potentially more manoeuvrable but the slight skittishness would take many hours to get used to in combat situations. The Mossie instilled a lot more confidence and seemed inherently much more stable and predictable, at least to me, a mere novice. The big initial difference was that one's first flight in a P38 (being a single seater) is entirely solo, unlike the Mossie when one can take another pilot for advice and help if required! Flying the DC3s was largely routine for me but I did get a bit alarmed when the cargo weight distribution was not done correctly and even more so on one flight when a couple of 40 gallon oil drums moved about a bit making the handling rather erratic to say the least. But, in general the old Dak. really is a forgiving and reliable workhorse.

    Perhaps the short term highlight was getting my hands on the controls of one of the Lancaster bombers. I had expected it to be a bit of a lumbering and hard to control monster. It was nothing of the sort and very biddable and manoeuvrable in a slightly reluctant sort of way once in the air. In the air one felt high up in the pilot's seat but on the ground one had the impression of being even higher, at the sort of height of a two-storey building. You certainly would not want to jump out of the window! The aircraft is very noisy, not very fast and I imagined that all those very brave pilots that drove them night after night over Germany must have suffered boredom when they were not scared stiff! My admiration and respect for them shot up no end. The Lanc. is remarkably gentle in its landing, particularly for its massive size and can be made to almost float down with the use of plenty of flap. On take off it again almost lifts itself up in a most willing manner. However all these impressions are with, in effect an unladen aircraft. Our usual supplies and the magnetometer weighted literally many tons less than a full bomb load! Naturally impressive to me were the four Merlin engines which seemed to remain remarkable in sync despite the long linkage involved in the controls for them. To have four of these engines to control was a lifetime experience for me. Just image having control of about 7,000 BHP with just one hand! I only managed three drives in these now very rare aircraft but testament to their overall greatness was the fact that with different engines they continued to serve Britain's Coastal Command up to about fifty years after their initial introduction, latterly in the form of the Shakleton. Then only superseded by the wonderful De Havilland Comet in non-pressurised form called the Nimrod. The question of the Lanc's four Merlin engines will be the subject of comment later as they were not real Rolls Royce engines but made by Packard. Packard whose cars, pre-war were reputedly the nearest the Americans came to their equivalent to a Roll Royce. After the war they rather faded away to become part of the Studebaker group whose Power Hawk model I was driving at the time on an ever day basis. On the American luxury car market the Packard became eclipsed by Cadillac, which is the top of the range by General Motors.

The only other fixed wing aircraft that Spartans had, were a couple of Canso sea planes which were a variation of the famous Catalina flying boat (on one the propeller pushed the plane and on the other it pulled) that rescued and saved lives of many downed pilots during the war and as air sea rescue afterwards as well. Spartan often used them as supply boats to projects that were near sea coasts or even the thousands of lakes that make up parts of Canada too. I never got to drive one but had the odd delivery run in them. Landing and taking off on water is one of the flying experiences I do regret not experiencing! For some reason I never had or got any sort of experiences on or with Spartan's seventeen Bell helicopters. It seems strange in retrospect and I do not understand it as it was completely out of character for me. Perhaps I was more a practical realist than I thought and had faced the fact that I was already living at least two lives and should not get diverted further into a third! I don't know, well psycho-babblers what do you think? That, I feel, just about winds up my breadth of experience in the flying field and in practice was also the end to my personal flying career, if that was what it really was?

146. Carling Av

I had reached the stage at Spartans that I would only go in a couple of days a week except in desperate need and the rest of my time was more than taken up by the rapidly expanding car business. In the end I had no option but to leave and just be on call in what today would be referred to as a consultative basis. The motor business now required a suitable front, if not an actual showroom, to display the new cars that we were getting more agencies for. The Renault with its Dauphine was soon to be joined by another French car, the Peugeot in the form of the modern looking and slab-sided 403. This was shortly followed by a German car make by the name of Borgward and its Isabella model. This was very much the quality car in the 1.5 litre saloon (sedan) class. It was the fastest and most economical for its size with the, then very modern independent rear suspension (for rear wheel drive). Volvo followed shortly after that with their robust and very well finished saloon 544 model and a very roomy estate version that went down well as it was not so dated to look at as the 544 saloons which were thought of as a bit old fashioned in appearance and only likely to sell to real enthusiasts and knowledgeable buffs. These cars were winning all their class races at the time, the only modifications being, taking off the bumpers, the air cleaners and disconnecting the automatic front brake adjusters. This was because while racing and after very hard braking the front drums expanded with the heat allowing the brakes to adjust up a notch but then as they cooled off again the drums shrank back and the brakes would start to bind so slowing the car down! The lack of glamour and looks of the car were constantly being supported by Volvo's almost weekly promotional pictures of the most attractive Swedish girlie models. They never seemed to run out of them! The Volvo people were not too bothered by the sales resistance to their old shape and when I told them that one critic said they reminded him of an eight year old American Ford Coupe he just said "good, that means they are talking about the car and that is what matters most at the start of a sales campaign". In retrospect he was wiser than I gave him credit for at the time and it is something I've remembered and used myself in business later in life! Other legal agencies that our growing reputation for proper service brought in were Aston Martin, A.C. and Alfa Romeo. In fact I was also approached by the Alfa Concessionaires to build up and run their official works team to compete seriously in the following year's B.E.M.C International Winter Rally! Compliment indeed. I have never really considered myself a snob but wanting to appear more than just another garage or motors we adopted the term, Specialists. So was born European Car Specialists Ltd., later of 1868 Carling Avenue, Ottawa, Canada.

We had also been approached by the Jaguar, Rolls Royce and Bentley Importers to undertake the servicing of their cars sold in our area since the existing agents all had poor reputations for service work but could not be changed for contractual reasons, soon enough to save the car's local reputations! Again, a great compliment to our standards as we would also be allowed to sell or bootleg these cars ourselves with the paperwork still in the importers name in Montreal to give the semblance of legality? It was clearly becoming essential to move into a more prestigious site to do these famous makes justice. There were no obvious sites or existing showrooms or even time to build anything. So against all the professional advice I leased a Fina service station at 1868, Carling Avenue, the main dual carriageway west out of the city. Just a mile further out had been built a new shopping centre as well so there would be an even bigger flow of passing traffic than already existed. This service station was on the approach corner at Maitland Av. and shared the other corners at this suburban cross roads with three other oil company petrol stations. This Fina station had been lying empty for many months as Fina in general had got a reputation as a sort of kiss of death outfit. I had no idea why but ask anyone and they did not have a good word to say about the company or their fuel. Nothing traceable but somehow they had got a frightful image.

After we moved in I did a count on several occasions at our station and at two other Fina establishments to find that in a given period of time when fifty cars would stop for fuel at the typical block of four stations, out of those fifty cars only three would go into the Fina one, even if it meant queuing at the others! These Fina stations were finished in white and blue tiles, looked very smart, bright, clean and could be spotted at a distance. Ideal on the face of it. However I began to understand the problem when negotiating our lease with Fina's local area manager. The initial rent was low but rapidly became geared to the gallons of fuel sold (it may seem funny now but at that time petrol was almost regarded as a waste product. So much so that the refineries and the chemical extractors were desperate to get rid of the petrol after they had extracted all the chemicals and by-products, from plastic onwards!). If we did not sell enough petrol the rent went up automatically in stages. In our case we were not even remotely interested in becoming a successful petrol sales outlet and I calculated that even if we were penalised to the highest level of rent it was still more than worth it, to us, for the site alone. We also had to take on the cost of the high pressure lubrication and fixed service equipment. Again fine, because we would be bringing in our own servicing work from our own agency cars. Ideal for us as we were not looking for any ordinary local servicing and routine work anyway.

They were not too happy about the number of cars we might have on the open forecourt as they thought it might discourage potential petrol customers from buying if they had to negotiate an obstacle course! A bit of a joke in their circumstances. Apart from the pumps on a twin island we had a large glass fronted office/shop, a lot of inside storage space and two large fully tiled service bays with a giant hot air central heating system to warm everything. There was also an undeveloped space which in some cases Fina could build on another four service bays. Of course it never happened due to their universal lack of business. So I managed to get a separate letter signed by the local manager that we had the option to build a showroom on the space as long as it matched and tied in with their existing blue and white façade. I think he agreed to this in desperation to get the prestige site occupied. Probably never thinking it would happen. He was very conscious that to keep having a site of that magnitude constantly closed gave an even worse image to their Belgian national icon, FINA.

It was the nearest I ever got to playing poker but I won on all the bits that mattered to us and I do not think he fully grasped what we would do with his station in practice. Plus the fact I was the only other player anyway and he was under pressure from head office. What I found out later was that the unpleasant people at Fina were working some sort of tax dodge and were often using the hapless and well meaning tenants as a unwitting cats paw. If a tenant was not profitable to them on the petrol sales front they kept putting up the rent until he quit and it appeared that if the site was then empty for six months, then they saved at least a years rates on that site and could claim some corporate and write down tax back as well. What was even worse they then sued the unlucky ex-tenant for the balance of the value of the servicing and expensive lubrication equipment. He having thought that it was a safe deal originally as it had appeared that he had five years to pay it off. In practice the poor chap might go broke in the process and Fina would keep the disputed equipment and start the whole process again with the next unfortunate mug! Well it was not going to happen to us and with the separate agreement letter it would mean that we had them over a barrel for a change just as long as we paid the ceiling basic rent. Plus, in due course with the next door site being wholly owned we could find all sorts of ways NOT to enhance their business approach if they really got stupid about it. Our new signs might obscure theirs!? Today Fina do not seem to exist as a separate entity anymore and appear to be just part of the Total/Elf, now mostly French oil conglomerate.

The next plot to the service station had been a rural small holding which kept bees and I started negotiating for its purchase which would then give us a full block and more than double the frontage of the service station but even more importantly it would face the incoming traffic to the city, so exposing us for even better public sales promotion and a prestigious image. That was for the future and in the meantime we moved all we could out to Carling Av. The ramp/stand that Michael Holt had sign written was moved from its original site beside the café and sales waiting room out there as well and placed on the front corner of the lot and with a car up on top could be seen from a quarter of a mile away from either direction. Michael's young brother Titch had been working for us for some months full time and some others, part time and they now quit their full time jobs to join us full time. My chief mechanic was a chap by the name of Eddie who had been the foreman at English Motors who were meant to be the Rolls Royce agents for Ottawa but failed miserably as a company to provide any worthwhile service and backup much to the disillusionment of Eddie who was very happy to join us. Some, roughly twenty years later and after he had also returned to Britain with his wife, we were to meet again and had we got the Argyll Turbo G.T. car project into a bigger factory outside Glasgow he was very keen to come and work for me again as production/ factory foreman. Another employee of English Motors was a good friend by the name of Patrick Faithful who had been treated rather badly with his good nature grossly taken advantage of and treated like a second class go-for. In addition he was still expected to run and organise their hopeless stores dept. Pat would be my right hand man and could be trusted to do anything for me, the way I would want it. He attended to all the day to day problems, organised the stores or parts dept for all the different makes we now had to contend with and with his more than personable manner and demeanour more than capable of selling the odd car as well. He was truly, Faithful by name and by nature too. There were many occasions that I could not have dealt with without his long hours of support and work. They broke the mould where he was concerned! Many years later he also came to see me in Scotland and would like to have come back to work for me again but had family problems back in Devon which is why they had to return from Canada in the first place.

That second summer saw other changes as well. The Nine Pines site had new owners who wanted to shift us out of our nice sunny corner location and put us too near the road for our liking so we decided to try and find an alternative site.

It turned out not to be that easy but Bob Potter's brother who was a builder and had been doing some odd jobs for us arranged for us to move out to a farm just outside Stittsville a small town or large village a few miles outside Ottawa. The site was a bit exposed for winter but during that summer it was very pleasant. Two problems showed up soon after we moved out there. The first was that Prue's frightful mother wanted to come over and visit us, ostentatiously to see the baby grandson, Robert Laird, now eight month old. She came and stayed and behaved herself and true to her snobbish form was all over me when she saw the size of our organisation and what we had accomplished in just over a year. She was overly impressed and verging on bragging about how well her daughter and son-in-law had done for themselves. It was quite sickening to witness, the two faced treacherous old bat! However at least the family diplomacy situation had drastically improved and I was very pleased, if only for Prue's sake as it had never been easy for her to deal with or accept the situation. Blood, water and all that. Prue's mother's sister, Aunt Ronn, could not have been more different. A wonderful, charming and generous spinster who was also the chief of all the Toronto school libraries. She had welcomed me whole heartedly when we first met on a visit down to Toronto and had certainly not pre-judged me on anything her sister may have had to say. Back at the new site on the mobile home front, the other problem was that the rather lightweight power line from one of the farm's barns out to us would not take our load in addition to some machinery and their commercial washing machine, all at the same time! The result was that the power cut out repeatedly at the most awkward times. This would make it imperative to move again and before winter set in.

147. Financial matters

When Prue and I first arrived in Canada we had a reasonable amount of money that would have tided us over for a few months even if I had not got a job straightaway. Spartans paid well and having built up a very good credit rating with the world's biggest Credit Bureau, Dunn and Bradstreet thanks to making the HP payments on the Studebaker Hawk and later on the mobile home regularly and on time. The first garage tools and equipment I had also bought on credit (at their insistence) from a firm called Canadian Tires, the Canadian equivalent to our Halfords. All this coupled with a couple of good references shot us up the credit rating ladder exceptionally fast. Despite this however when I approached the leading car credit company for wholesale finance to enable us to stock enough cars, particularly over the winter periods they messed me about for a couple of weeks which did not build any confidence for the future. They were too negative and I was not prepared to have to pull teeth or almost beg at any time in the expanding future. They did have the cheek though to say that they would welcome any and almost all retail finance I could put their way!

I then managed to find a small, almost local, finance company who would take on up to at least 50 cars wholesale and possibly more within six months if our track record warranted it. Great, we were in serious business. Needless to say they also got all our retail business as well. Some many months later when Carling Avenue was seen to be booming, the manager of the first finance company came, almost cap in hand, to ask for some of our business and even tried to bribe with special deals and slightly lower interest rates. Any reader will now know me well enough and my attitude to loyalty, to be able to guess what he was told as he was shown to the door!

The finance companies take the full financial responsibility for most normal good credit deals. Those that are debatable they will take on but with a higher interest charged of which a part gets credited back to the dealer on satisfactory completion many months or a couple of years later. These deals are call redress and I was caught out a couple of times because I had not realised that the conditions are different. When the Finance Co. repossess the vehicle it is returned to the dealer concerned who is immediately responsible to pay up the whole balance due. A couple of those a month can really muck up one's cash flow projections! Even so I had started off with next to nothing and selling an almost totally unknown make of car on a street corner in my spare time plus a bit of tuning work on friends' cars to a turnover, within the first eighteen months, of well over half a million dollars (in today's money it would be well over 5 million dollars!?) .

An invaluable bit of advice that I got from our accountant when I had made some comment about how well one of our petrol rivals was doing just across the road has stuck with me ever since and stood me in good stead. His comment was to the effect that "a hive of industry and even a large turnover is not always a sign of a profitable business!" I've always related to that as well to S.P.Q.R. (small profits & quick returns). To this day I still largely look on money as only a tool to do a job with, in itself it has no interest to me at all.

The greedy banks however seem to always be impressed by large financial turnovers presumably assuming that the more money turns over the greater chance there is of some of it rubbing off and sticking. This, despite the number of times they seem to get ripped off by an age-old ploy. One example of this occurred in Ottawa at the time we were there. This bright lad opened a bank account with, say a thousand dollars then drew most of it out again within a few days and re-deposited it again a day or so later plus an increase which made it look as though he had done some very profitable deal. He did this a few times to build up confidence with the bank and then one day approached the manager and asked to temporarily overdraw for a bigger than usual transaction and that the money, with profit would be back within a week. The manager agreed (probably worried he might loose a growing and good regular customer if he did not!?) and the apparently profitable proceeds were banked as promised so building up the greedy bank manager's confidence. This profitable client had in the meantime done exactly the same thing with several other banks using the same money in and out of them all! Eventually the day came when the rogue drew out all the overdrafts from all the bank at the same time and had left the country with way over ten times his original 'seed' or stake money before they woke up to the situation or even started worrying about it!

While mentioning finance or just money the lying thieving insurance company had finally largely accepted my claim from the Tony van Beugen Bik's XK120 car accident at Catterick, those several years before. My solicitor advised me that they would finally pay the original claimed amount but not my costs. My reply was to the effect that I would not settle on their terms and was looking forward to exposing them in court with their lying letter trying to claim that Tony Bik was not even covered for passengers. This made them think again and reluctantly they agreed to pay all my costs as well. Knowing that I now had them on the run and the case was finally coming to court very shortly I demanded interest on the money as well and if they did not agree I would go for inflation also. Further, that if I had to leave my business and fly back for the case these expenses would be added to by my air fares and London hotel bills etc. plus things like my wife having to move into the city to a hotel etc. before our soon due second baby was to be born. I really piled it on and continued to give the impression that the money no longer mattered and that it was a matter of principle to expose them publicly and that I even had a Press release all ready for the occasion! Mr.Curtis (I finally remembered his name!) my solicitor phoned just three days before I was booked to fly back to UK for the case to say that they had finally agreed to pay everything, much even to his surprise? The reader will have gathered that I am not very insurance minded and have always been prepared to carry and be responsible for such risks myself with the possible exceptions of things like, third party motor insurance and on one's house/home.

Another but only remotely related to money episode was when the whole front of the Jackson Building in Ottawa on, I think, Spark Street, was blown out by a massive natural gas explosion early one Saturday morning. Luckily it was a Saturday so there were not the usual several thousand people at work. The street outside was covered with glass and debris plus dozens of broken open metal filing cabinets with the contents blowing all over the place and much of it lost. The real significance was that the Jackson Building was the headquarters of the Federal Income Tax dept.! It reputedly took nearly two years to get everything sorted out correctly. The gas explosion had occurred across the street from the tax building in the basement of a car showroom. The only death was the showroom's night watchman who, on smelling gas had decided to go down into the basement to investigate the source but failed to realise that as he switched on the light he had signed his own death warrant! The poor fellow lived a day or two and was able to report what had happened. All the cars in the showroom were blown up and out into the street along with the other debris. The explosion was so great that it had completely destroyed three quarters of the building next door to the showroom as well, which was a cinema with its entrance round the corner on another street. That wall had survived and it was strange to look along, past all the major damage and just see the cinema's balcony facing one in almost mid air with no auditorium, stage or screen still in existence.

This natural gas was a major problem for Ottawa and in other places. There were numerous explosions and even more serious leaks that were fixed without explosions. In fact for a mile or so Carling Avenue there seemed to be dozens of patches all along the road where repairs had had to be carried out. It appeared that the over educated experts had failed to realise that the new natural gas was a very dry gas and as it flowed through the old town or coal gas pipes it dried out the joints allowing the new gas to percolated up through the ground and even through the asphalt! It proved to be a very expensive and false economy. This was dramatically demonstrated one day when a car was parked at the red lights almost outside the Graces Hospital on Carling Avenue as he started his stalled engine again there was a big bang that blew him into the air like a football. The ignition spark had set off the gas that had gathered under his car while waiting barely a minute. All very disconcerting. When I returned to the UK I warned as many friends and acquaintances as I could but I fear that I was thought a scaremonger. However history tells the story though, with several examples of several floors being blown out of blocks of flats and even complete houses totally demolished as well. I would not have the stuff in any home of mine unless it was bottled and I could control everything related to it myself. I rate the risk even higher than that of living in a house at the bottom of a steep hill on a 'T' junction with the house being in direct line for a lorry or tanker to run into when the brakes fail! Or even living in a house directly under a canal bank. But as is usually the case there is no credit given to a prophet in his own life time. For a supposed bright species we do seem to take a long time to learn, even from history.

148. Exit Spartans

During my last weeks at Spartans I grew more and more concerned about the lack of oil reserve in the modified Mosquitoes to enable the propellers on the Merlin engines to be feathered after an engine failure, this had led to several dodgy incidents and one crash already. In one case when the prop could not be feathered the dead engine was kept turning and apart from the tremendous drag and load on the other one, and great difficulty to keep the aircraft orientated, plus it caused a fire to break out which was not entirely extinguished by the inbuilt system. Engine fires on a Mossie were never to be taken lightly as reputedly they could lead to the main spar of the wing (wooden main plane) burning right through in about five minutes! Finishing up with one engine and only one wing! Since parachutes were not usually carried the option of baling out was not an inviting one and the faster the pilot then tried to descend to a lower altitude with a view to possibly crash landing somewhere, the faster the main spar of the wing would burn through!

I thought that the whole situation was getting very dangerous and out of hand so I reluctantly went to the Civil Aviation Authorities only to be told that since the aircraft concerned were not carrying fare paying passengers they had no interest in the matter. I was shocked and horrified at such an attitude for while it was true that all the incidents so far had been over unpopulated territory but one still has to wonder what if it all happened over a town or city? They did not even want to consider that at all! This was all making me far from popular with management and I in turn was feeling more and more that I really did not want to be associated with such policies anymore. The final break, when it came, I can only describe as a form of armed neutrality. There was no general animosity from the staff or aircrew, many of whom, agreed with me and even became car customers as well. Art Smail for instance, one of the navigators bought the first Aston Martin DB2-4 that we sold after becoming the official agents. Michael Holt remained at his job in their drawing office and continued as our part time salesman, which certainly boosted his salary.

The terrible sequel to the dangerous modifications carried out on the Mossies came about a year later. Kathy and Rocky had remained good friends of ours and customers/clients after I finally left Spartans, as had several others. Late one evening a taxi pulled up at Carling Avenue and out got Kathy very much the worse for wear with drink, which was not like her. She was in tears and badly broken up about something but in such an incoherent state it took some while to find out the problem. Basically it appeared that poor Rocky was either dead or terminally injured and she had come from either the funeral or some church/memorial service but we could not be sure which. Kathy kept crying and collapsing with the combination of drink and sorrow. She repeatedly said to me, in effect, "you told them, you warned them and they would not listen would they? It took about an hour with the aid of lots of strong coffee and pacifying before we could calm her enough to even think of taking her home. Eventually Mike Holt and I got her into a car and took her home to the other side of the city where she lived on the fourth or top floor of an old building in an attic/studio or penthouse flat. Mike and I had a hard physical job getting her up all those stairs to her abode.

We thought we had her settled in and were just leaving when she called me back, then sneakily locked the door, secreted the key about her person and then challenged me to find it! It appeared that it was not just sympathy she was seeking but some form of consolation that was hardly decorous or appropriate in all the circumstances. I finally escaped through her fanlight window in the bathroom and had to climb across a roof and down all those floors on a very suspect fire escape in the dark. Mike was back in the car waiting for me, laughing like a drain and said he was not sure if he should have called out the fire brigade and or the police to rescue me? Poor Kathy, she looked very dispirited and sad, not surprisingly for many months afterwards. Neither of us ever spoke of my fire escape episode again perhaps she was too drunk to even remember? I was hardly going to embarrass her over it was I?

This episode of Rocky's death did not seem to upset me as much as I would have thought. Perhaps I half expected it sooner or later? In retrospect though it was the point when I finally turned my back and walked away from personal flying with out a backward glance, so to speak. In much the same way as I did from motor racing nearly fifteen years later when I moved our business up to Scotland. The only regret, in retrospect was that I tended to loose contact with some wonderful people. Peter Nock and Syd Guthrie to name but two. Happily Syd tracked me down and just arrived in Lochgilphead many years later when I instantly recognised his voice without, even having to look up. I was so pleased to see him again and as a result even phoned Peter Nock who was more than pleased to hear from me and appeared to have never stopped singing my praises in all those years. He was, of course by now retired and seemed keen for me to visit him. He, of course did not think to tell me he was already dying of cancer so I made no urgent arrangements to see him. As always seems to happen, these things get put off until next year. Peter died on March 1st 2002 and it is one of the very few serious regrets in my life that I did not visit him in his last days. Happily I have since been in semi regular touch with his widow Sara and his son Robert. They have sent me a copy of Peter's own memoirs and it is a privilege to have been included in them. As any reader will by now know that I have borrowed from them to help me cover our period at Lossiemouth and Canada. Happily, we see Syd Guthrie and his good wife Norma, almost bi-annually when they come over from Australia on a fairly regular basis now and who knows we may get to visit them in Aussie some time?

We had several other friends from Spartans that were both that and often customer/clients as well. As is the case even today my place of business always seems to generate a sort of enthusiasts social club element as well, particularly at tea time! Among these ongoing friends were people like Barry Bremner and his wife Ruth. Barry was a brilliant radio and electrical man and was constantly being put upon by Spartans to go off to the remotest places to sort out other peoples' problems and faults. Prue and I put ourselves out to entertain Ruth as often as possible when Barry was away particularly since they lived over on the Quebec side of the Ottawa River (houses were considerably less expensive over there and taxes were lower too) but who had largely rather anti-social French neighbours. Their two year old daughter was just like a chocolate box doll and always dressed accordingly and with lots of ribbons. Another couple were the Kings. He worked for Spartan as an accountant and his wife was a nurse. Prue's greatest friend throughout was still Jean Plottier and her husband Tim and I still socialised, even after the epic rally together! Prue kept in touch with Jean for many years after we returned from Canada by which time I believe she had divorced Tim at some stage. Initially, however we found, to us a strange phenomenon in that when we met someone we liked and invited to visit us any time, was the fact that not one of the Canadians ever did so. We thought this a bit strange and felt a bit slighted until a good Canadian friend told us that no one took such an invitation seriously unless it was for a specific time and place. Such general invitations were just regarded as insincere chitchat. Same language but different customs and interpretations, it appeared, again. We Brits are certainly separated from North Americans by a supposed common language

Some of these friends/customers more than proved their worth as winter was closing in that second winter. In those days Montreal as a seaport closed down and was frozen up for some months. The huge St. Laurence seaway project was completed finally in 1959 so our mass car collection before the port froze over for the winter that we had had to indulge in during the winters of 57/58 and 58/59 would become a thing of the past. This would be much more convenient and save quite a lot of interest payments on the value of all the cars tied up financially, sometimes until even early spring. Therefore, at that time, our possible winter car sales all had to be in stock for these months. We were suddenly stuck with the situation where we had over fifty cars sitting at the docks in Montreal that all had to be collected and brought back to Ottawa at quite short notice. We could not arrange road transporters in time or even expensive rail trucks either. The only solution was to drive them all back! We accomplished this by rounding up all available friends and associates as drivers, packing them up to six in a car (we should have borrowed a bus?) and driving up to Montreal.

When we got to the docks we split ourselves into five or six separate convoys with one of the existing licensed cars in the lead of each group having taken off the rear number plate and fitting it to the rear of the last car in each group. The cars in the sandwich having no plates at all! Each group would stay in tight formation so that at say, traffic light or other stops no one would be able to see that they were plate-less! It was all a bit nerve racking but worked a treat and we got away with it, twice. Even Prue with her very limited driving experience drove a Hillman Husky estate, one of our ferry escort vehicles that she was already used to. Of course it had to start snowing on our illicit way back. She also had no experience whatsoever of driving in snowy conditions. She just bravely followed me having been told to stick strictly to my snow tracks which I made as smooth and steady through the corners as possible and at speeds that she could cope with. She did wonderfully well and I was so proud of her faith, commitment and actual bravery in such circumstances. Well it worked on each occasion and we got away with it (from a legal repercussions point of view) and saved a fortune in transportation and a lot of inconvenience.

After one of these occasions and as a thank-you to such good friends I booked several tables at a Greek restaurant which was owned by the parents of the then up and coming singing star/composer by the name of Paul Anka. We met him on a couple of occasions and Michael Holt had been at the same school as him and also knew the girl *Laura* that Paul produced a hit song about. I am not sure but that is maybe where Prue first started to consider the name Laura as a name for our second baby, a girl born nearly a year later. The young Paul Anka himself of course went on to be world famous. Involved musically in a couple of dozen Hollywood films, making several Top of the Chart songs such as *My Way* with Frank Sinatra, *Diana*, which topped the charts for something like 9 weeks. Plus many others while working with Buddy Holly, Celine Dion and others. Remarkable for a young lad who started off working in the musically converted basement of his parent's home just off the Island Park Driveway, Ottawa. The only other gastronomic story concerns a very pleasantly situated restaurant located on one of the islands (not far from Paul's home) that acted as stepping stones across the RCMP patrolled bridge (called Champlain I think?) to the Quebec side, up river a bit from Ottawa's twin city of Hull. The owner of this quite posh restaurant was a leading member of the city's food quality committee. They were responsible for dishing out whatever stars or rosettes each establishment was thought to warrant. His place was quite high in the ratings until it was discovered that he was catching and serving seagulls as chicken and other meats. When curried I doubt if anyone would have been the wiser?

149. Eric Liebman

The next person to be introduced was probably the single biggest influence on my future life, long term. His name was Eric Leibman and again some will argue as to whether it was sheer chance, luck or predestined! Again, one evening while we were still working at Carling Av. this larger than life character called in as he was in effect entering the city having come from the direction of Toronto. He enquired as to where the VW dealership was that was run by the Morton family. We directed him and struck up a conversation when he saw that we were car enthusiasts and not just a gas garage cum service station. He told us he had, what appeared to be an almost miracle (not his words) carburettor which would fit almost everything and produce up to 20% more power and save about the same in fuel consumption. Normally I would have been almost rudely sceptical with comments like, "what, another one" or "we've heard it all before". On this occasion perhaps because I immediately liked the old man I was polite and he showed constructive interest in my questions to him. He then responded by demonstration with an exhaust gas analyser on his own Buick car how lean the exhaust gases were. I was visibly impressed, as far as I knew, with that leanness the engine should have starved and died!? After a long chat and a hot drink he thanked us and headed off to the Morton's VW dealership.

Less than an hour later he returned having been very rudely received by the Mortons themselves and virtually shown the door! He now felt entirely clear of any sort of obligation to them and offered us the sole franchise for the whole of the Ottawa Valley! He then changed his clothes and set about converting several of our cars with our help. About five hours later all the new installations were finished. At about midnight we were driving up and down the road with cars that seemed to have a new life in them. I was frankly amazed and now took this old man very seriously. He then finally left us with several more stock carburettors and a selection of adapters and linkages and said "just play about with them and I'll come and see how you got in about a months time". Off he went into the night leaving quite a large amount of value with us and did not want a penny deposit or even a receipt in the meantime. Such trust. This same trust was to mark our mutual worldwide dealings in the years to come. Basically all because we had been polite and helpful to a complete stranger even though initially we though of him as just another nutty salesman. My father's frequent comment about "it being the easiest thing in the world to be rude and that courtesy cost nothing", came back to me once again, forcefully and gratefully.

Every chance we got between our more routine work we tried out these carburettors on every thing we could from, 850cc Renault Dauphines to Yank Tanks like Buick, Oldsmobile, Plymouth, Dodge and a Ford/Mercury, up to 6 litres! In all cases the results were all but unbelievable. I was hooked and regretted that I could not spare more time playing with them myself. Little did I ever imagine that they would change my life to the extent that they did, even to me, later getting accused of being Fish carburettor missionary! This activity partly tied in with more and more sporting and modification work to customer's cars for competition. Several club members were now going down to New York State to a fairly new circuit called Watkins Glen to race and they had also opened up a smaller race track near Montreal at St. Jovite. I would love to have got more involved personally but business and family precluded such selfishness.

150. Ice racing fun

Things were however a little slower in the winter so I was able to find a bit of time to do some ice racing usually on the frozen Ottawa River and on frozen lakes in the Quebec ski areas such as at places like St.Agathe, where The L.A.C.(Laurentian Auto Club) held the Laurentian (as in local mountain range) Ice Races on Lac des Sables. There, they just snowploughed the snow down to the ice and left it as a continuous snow bank all round the circuit making it very safe to go off and with very little damage to the cars. Studded tyres were not allowed so the skill levels were therefore much higher than the European equivalent events. I would drive anything I could as well as the Jag, of course. In fact on one occasion I got the officials to allow me to take some of the plug leads off, on the Jag until the still running cylinders came within the smaller class limits. On one occasion I was actually faster on four cylinders than the original six because with the lower power output my relative heavy right foot did not produce so much wheel spin. Another lesson I was to absorb for successful motor racing in the wet some years later. My biggest rival in the unlimited class was a rather spoilt brat who was the son of a very wealthy Montreal builder. His name was McRoberts and his daddy had bought him one of the very rare Jaguar XK SS models which were in reality the Le Mans racing and winning 'D' types, with road windscreen and trim. McRoberts was a very poor loser and complained that his wide bodywork was catching on the snow banks and slowing him down. Ridiculous, but he was so mad at being beaten by me that he then kicked and hammered the car's wings in to supposedly reduce drag. Sacrilege. I still beat him in the run-offs so he then protested and accused me of having wire bits or studs in my tyres. He was so thick that he imagined that the steel bracing of the Michelin X tyres stuck out and gave me an unfair cat's claw advantage. His protest was laughingly rejected which did not help his ego either. My clearest memory of St.Agathe was the Ice Palace cum Castle. This was made up out of fairly large ice blocks cut with chain saws out of the lake. The final building must have been nearly thirty feet high and about fifty feet wide and they then illuminate it with red and green flares from the inside so that the diffused coloured lights filtered through the ice in a spectacular fashion. The French could do some things well! The weather was usually bright up there but very cold. So much so, that one morning when I started the Jaguar up and revved it up too quickly the excessive thick oil pressure blew out the gasket between the oil filter head and the block spilling some oil onto the ice before I realised what had happened. Another lesson; warm up the oil thoroughly before revving up. A lesson I should have remembered from my aircraft experience up in the Hudson Bay area. I finished up jacking the car up on the ice and lying on my back for half an hour under the car on bare ice to replace the gasket with a bit of, hopefully suitable paper and using Prue's nail scissors to cut and trim a new gasket to fit. This make-do gasket was to remain on the engine for the next forty years!

I should also remember the event because I was well and truly beaten in the final, having won all my heats easily. No not by the irate McRoberts still seeking revenge but as a result of my ongoing battle with him and us both sliding about a bit wildly and very wide I (we) failed to notice a little Renault 4cv who with his superior traction and not enough power to spin his wheels creep up on our inside passing us on rails as we were still spinning wheels too much and sliding about in a repeat battle of the Goliaths. Little David crept past us on the inside of a long corner and I had left it too late to get past him again. McRoberts I thought was going to cry because of the ignominy of it all! Being beaten by such a lowly vehicle with an engine a quarter of the size of ours! I thought it hilarious and was more than pleased for the chap. My pleasure at seeing McRoberts's pouting distress, more than made up for my not winning the final and main Trophy Race. In memory of the salient lesson to us both I have also retained my SECOND place shield from the final of that Laurentian Trophy Race, another of the very few trophies I have bothered to keep over the years.

Back in Ottawa we had two good winters of ice racing on the frozen Ottawa River out at Britannia Bay (another colonial hangover?) which was up river from the city and close to where the other western main road, Richmond Road runs out of the city to meet our own Carling Avenue. Richmond Road was an extension of Wellington Street, as in police station and armed hitch-hikers! At these ice races we, as a company, would enter up to two or three of each of the car models that we were selling as well as doing the serious bit with the Jaguar XK120. Our main rivals for the Renault Dauphine were the Morton's VW Beetles, which had a good reputation for traction with the weight over the rear driving wheels, as of course did our Dauphines. The Mortons were also the local agents for the Porche, which are only glorified VW's in the first place but with bigger engines! Porsche, even today are best and most aptly described as the company that, has, "the world's best automobile engineers who for FIFTY years have continued to try to overcome the world's worst basic design, ever?" Later, from the design and basic handling point of view the diabolical dynamics of the De Lorean probably runs them close! It will therefore be easy to imagine their chagrin when we thrashed both their VWBeetles and Porches on almost every occasion to such an extent they stopped competing before their inferior reputation got about and affected their sales!? Despite the good traction that their cars had they had great difficulty in turning round a bend at any speed, as with so little weight upfront the brakes locked up with the slightest excuse and then straight on into the snow bank they went! They just could not believe how well the Dauphine (that should have suffered in the same way) appeared not to and had no problems turning into corners. In fact it turned into the corners just as well as heavy front engined cars did which appeared to defy the laws of physics! This coupled with the good rear engined traction like the VW and Porsche and with less power to spin the wheels by the heavy booted brigade meant that the Renault Dauphines appeared to run on rails by comparison.

 Our industrial secret of success never got out into enemy hands. The secret? Easy, we simply filled up the front boot or generous luggage compartment with water the night before and left the car outside which froze the water solid into a block of ice which then had the effect of several sand bags but without the mess and possible damage to the well painted inside surface. At the end of a racing day we just drove into our service bays, raised the cars on the hoist opened the luggage compartment, removed the large rubber drain plug and turned on the high powered hot air heaters which overnight thawed out the massive block of ice in the boot so returning the compartment to its usual duties. Simple my dear Watson! On one particularly cold and windy day when Prue and baby Laird were spectating up on the cleared snow banks and obviously freezing but refusing to admit it or give in and sit and wait in a car - hardy, these Hendersons. I finally persuaded them to get into one of our competing Peugeot 403s and out of the wind. Then, when I was ready to race with it in its class and about to disgorge them again for a short while, at least, the friendly marshal said "you can't do that to your wife and baby, take them with you, it will be a lot warmer for them!" So they stayed in the back seat of the car for the whole race, in which I won my class as the 403 was very good with its very stable long wheelbase. In fact it was probably the most stable saloon car on ice, regardless of class although not as fast as our Volvos were. I was never actually able to prove it as I could hardly race myself in different cars in the same race, could I? Race times were not always comparable due to often dramatically different sets of circumstances pertaining to each individual race. Can anyone imagine all that being allowed today with our pathetic, out of control culture of petty and intrusive health and safety? Wonderful stuff, wonderful days and I'm not sure if, even today, my son Laird realises that as a result of all this he won his first motor event when barely one year old!?

151. Inferior Merlins

More correctly to my mind and experience, the inferior Packard version of the Rolls Royce Merlin engines should not have shared the illustrious name of Merlin at all! They were clearly made to a lower standard of both materials and tolerances. On one cylinder block I was horrified to see the name Thor cast on it! That is the Thor washing machine company. Then when torque-ing up nuts and studs correctly some would shear off or even break open the casting showing their porous nature. A bit like *Aero* chocolate in some cases! The worst weekend I remember was ELEVEN engine changes in three days! That speaks for itself, sufficiently, I think. I never wanted to see, let alone work on a Packard version, ever again! Apart from the amount of work on a Lanc aircraft one is also operating quite high up on scaffolding trestles which is quite dodgy in itself and also a bit of a chore to have to climb up and down from that height repeatedly. Working on proper Merlins and in the case of Mosquitoes trestles are still required but only about six feet up. Which suddenly brings to mind a freak and unique accident for which I was initially and falsely blamed. I was sitting in the cockpit going through a series of electrical checks when one of the mechanics outside and standing on his trestle beside the propeller of the starboard engine asked me to push the prop feathering button so be could check for operation and leaks etc. This I duly did, only for the engine to start to turn instead and the mechanic to be swept off his feet by the turning prop. and then down onto the floor. He was badly bruised but it could have been so much worse.

As can be imagined I was the subject of communal abuse and criticism. I protested my innocence, as I was absolutely sure I had not lifted the wrong switch guard flaps before pressing the button, apart from the fact that the feathering buttons are nowhere near the guarded starter buttons. I climbed out of the cockpit to face the situation, which from all logical points of view pointed to me alone as the incompetent culprit. Instinctively I went round to the rear and outside of the starboard engine to find the engine cover off and an electrician working near the starter and feathering solenoids, which are beside each other. He was looking confused and holding a large screwdriver in his hand with a great burnt hunk missing from the side of the blade! He claimed that he had no idea how it could possible have happened? I'm afraid I rather rudely told him in no uncertain terms. He had been using this un-insulated screwdriver as a lever to move the starter cable into position, as he was about to tighten up the terminal on it. In the process he had bridged across and also touched the heavy duty and high amperage cable to the feathering solenoid right next to the starter one. So when I had energised the feathering solenoid his screwdriver had shorted across to the starter terminal and energised that as well, so turning the engine and knocking the hapless mechanic off his feet and onto the concrete floor. I was clearly exonerated but very, very angry and took the opportunity to lay into several people who I was not entirely satisfied with, at least where their conscientious dedication was concerned! Even to this day I still remain overly sensitive to and more inclined to overreact when being falsely accused, than to almost anything else.

152. Selling cars

I think that does finally wrap up my Spartan and aircraft experience and returns us to the ever growing car business and some less than savoury characters there too. One day a large American car that was pulling a fair sized trailer filled with household goods and furniture pulled up at the pumps. Out got a very large swarthy man of what I imagined was South American stock. He introduced himself as one, Ed Ensenga an experienced car salesman who had worked for the John Green Corporation in California who were the first in North America to sell Renault Dauphines, we were only the first in Canada. He certainly knew the car well so he was not just spinning a line where that was concerned, at least. I was generally a bit suspicious of him but he talked me into taking him on as a salesman but on a commission only basis. He and his wife found themselves a house to rent not too far away from the garage and he reported back for work the next day. I organised a almost new yellow Dauphine for him as a demonstrator and agreed to have it sign written so he could use it as a mobile advert and be seen wherever it was parked as well. A good idea and not one we had considered before. It worked quite well but quite a few of Ed's potential buyers turned out to be not credit worthy, when checking up on them with Dunn and Bradstreet (internationally known as D.& B.).

Ed worked with us for several months including a period when we exhibited at the central Canadian Exhibition based in Lansdowne Park close to the stock car racing stadium. For a man of his size he displayed an immense amount of energy. He never seemed to stop and was in his element at the show almost dragging in potential customers and arranging demonstrations and extracting names and addresses that he could follow up later as well. One of his party pieces was to drive his Dauphine up a ramp so it was only on three wheels and then defy anyone to rock or bounce it over. No one could but whether anyone wanted to buy a car on that basis I don't know but it certainly held the crowds and proved that Ed. was a showman. The other thing that we did which no one could believe was to turn one of our Michelin 'X' tyres in on itself into a sort of figure 8 so demonstrating the flexibility of the tyre's construction and quality. In those days, largely before radial tyres were even heard of, most tyres had very stiff and almost rigid walls and could only be bent a few degrees for the fitting onto their rims and certainly not flexed as the Michelin could be.

Almost next to us were our arch rivals the Mortons with several varieties of the Beetles including the first of the more attractive Karman Ghia fixed head coupes which were certainly a more stylish car. The odd cabriolet convertible and a selection of the ubiquitous camper and other vans. The Mortons had their crowd pullers as well and the most popular was the demonstration that they would do a complete engine change from start to finish with three mechanics and drive off in twenty minutes. One quiet old man watched this for while, went off and returned later with an invoice in his hand and demanded that the Mortons should refund him some money as he had been charged for seven man hours of labour the previous week for his engine change! They had a very hard time trying to justify the charges in the circumstances. The old man got quite angry and claimed that they were in effect selling the Beetle under false pretences and he would never ever deal with such a deceitful outfit again. Naturally, we found the Mortons embarrassment and visible discomfort highly amusing. They did not and suspended that particular demonstration for the rest of the day as some of the crowd were joining in and backing the old man and it had the makings of a newspaper report! I do not know if the old man got any money back in an effort to shut him up and get rid of him, or not.

Ed had worked for us for about six months when, with the approach of a holiday weekend he asked if he could have a few days off to visit some friends and use the sign written demo car for the journey as he might even manage to sell the odd car while away on the trip. I was a bit hesitant but could not come up with a strong reason why not. And further, could I advance him some of the commission he would be due on couple of sales that were booked. This was against normal practice but the good salesman that he was managed to talked me into agreeing and giving him the money. As a thank you gesture he gave me a very good SNAP ON compression tester set as security! I should have smelled a rat as he was just too ingratiating. A few days later we had a visit from the RCMP who asked if we knew that he had crossed the border back into the USA! It appeared that originally he was wanted by the FBI who had asked the RCMP to trace him after he had crossed over into Canada all those months before and had come to work for us. Ed had got wind of the approaching arrest when they had visited his wife who had obviously lied and stalled them off temporarily. The Ensengas had crossed back into the States with his American convertible car and trailer and she was driving a yellow Dauphine registered and plated in her name! It took a while to figure out how they had pulled the biggest con against me ever! It appeared that Ed while in my office alone for only a very short time had found the dealer car licensing application forms, filled one in and used our official stamp to enable him to register another yellow car in his wife's name. He then used the new plates on the demonstrator having removed the sign writing before leaving the city to escape back over the border in a hurry. So big Ed had got away with our demonstrator car with new plates that we did not yet realised had been issued in our name! Plus some cash from me which turned out to be an advance against false sales names. Plus of course, a full tank of petrol on his account. We also now had a problem with the authorities as to how we could now sell and register for a second time the same car? We could hardly use the abandoned demo plates on a new unused car, which would not tie up with chassis or engine numbers. In the same way Ed might at some later date have to explain that the car he was using had number plates that did not tie in with his engine and chassis numbers. Well, we had to write it all off to experience and the learning curve of life's rich tapestry! In practice the profit on the sales Ed had made more than covered the losses involved if not the inconvenience and wasted time and effort. I still have the SNAP ON compression tester today as a constant reminder that none of us are always that smart or clever as we may think we are! We never heard whether the FBI finally caught up with Eddie, the thieving but remarkably plausible rogue.

153. Moving house

The power situation at our new site for our home out on the farm at RR1 Stittsville was not satisfactory and we eventually made the move well before the winter set in, having had a very pleasant summer in the country with Prue and Laird scooting about and in and out of town in her almost favourite vehicle, the Hillman Husky estate car. She liked the size and ease of driving compared to the much larger Volvo estates. Bob Potter's roguish builder brother came up with a good idea and alternate solution. Not quite so far out of the city and on slightly higher ground was a district called City View and out on one of its dirt roads known as RR2 (Rural postal Route no.2) were some fairly cheap building plots including one where someone had started building a bungalow and then abandoned the project. This seems to be quite a regular situation both in USA and Canada. The abandoned site can then be bought from the local authorities for just the price of the back taxes due (the equivalent to our Rates). Well we arranged to pay off the back taxes and moved our mobile home onto the site and parked it in the lee but also the sunny side of the unfinished house which conveniently was where the well had been drilled and close to where the power line came into the house from the road.

The electrical connection was very easy and it did not take long to rig up a pump to bring up the water from the well below. The only extra modification was to wrap the pipe from below ground level and up into the mobile home with heated cable to stop the water freezing up at that point during the winter, then to insulate and box it all in. The bungalow was excellent storage space as it had all its walls and roof intact but a bit short of windows, doors, any interior panelling and some floor boards, just the odd planks. We thought that in due course when we had nothing else to do we might even complete the self-build and turn it into a very pleasantly situated bungalow. But for the moment we were more than happy in our small but luxury home as it was. That building project would have to be for future years. Our new address was now RR2 City View.

About the time we moved out to RR2 City View and at a crossroads about halfway home there was a place by the name of either, Smith's Corners or Stanley's Corners. I always got them mixed up then so it is no surprise that I still cannot remember which it was now. It seemed to be the local county custom to name many remote crossroads after the local farmer whose land they might dissect. Anyway very close to this particular crossroads, the road on and in towards Ottawa was dissected by the main railway line from Toronto with fairly rudimentary warning lights and simple barrier. One night a very large truck and trailer was hit by a freight train and dragged along the line for about half a mile distributing its load into the fields as it was shunted like a bulldozer by the still moving train. The truck's cargo had been many thousands of very small tins of Gerber (a make I had not heard of until then) baby food, which became well distributed over a very wide area. Reputedly the farmer and many gleaners were mining odd tins for a considerable period afterwards and I imagine when the fields were ploughed again and again that there might have been a fresh crop of tins surfacing for several seasons to come.

About this time another large influence entered my life but I was not to be fully aware of it until several years later. The local radio station in Ottawa was called C.K.O.Y, "the voice of this great nation's capital" was what they claimed to be and how, I think they introduced themselves. I'm not entirely sure if it was on their airwaves that I first heard what I thought of as just another of those dreary American religious salesmen. Except this one, if I could concentrate beyond my inbuilt prejudice, actually talked a lot of good sense, much to my surprise. I could not fault anything he said and unlike any others he challenged any listener to check up on what he said or claimed and not just accept his word alone. This was a new departure and coupled with the fact he was not asking for money either! The man's name was Herbert W. Armstrong and was assisted by an even better presenter, his son, Garner Ted Armstrong. Their words stayed with me in an almost haunting manner at the back of my brain until I heard them again a few years later, very late at night when driving up to Scotland with Laird and Laura on our frequent visits to 'our' island castle on Loch Awe. The broadcasts were by then coming from the pirate radio station Caroline and from Radio Luxemburg as well.

154. French idiosyncrasies

All this was rather different from the situation on the other side of the Ottawa River and in the Province of Quebec where if the husband died the wife could remain in their house but not then own it! It appeared that a wife could not own inherited property. Still Napoleonic Law I was told. While I appreciated the slightly higher speed limit in Quebec compared to Ontario there was a huge potential drawback as there was a law still in force that supposedly restricted speeds to 20 mph past junctions and even side roads so theoretically if a farmer pulled out of a side road at the last minute into a fast main road with his tractor and hay trailer and caused an accident it would be your fault, not his, since you should not be doing more than 20mph to have caused it. Even dafter, than the, "give way to the right", rules in France itself. The other potential hazard of using an Ontario licensed car to and from Montreal in the second half of any month was the problem of the corrupt Quebec Provincial Police stopping Ontario licensed cars for the slightest of flimsy excuses, from dirty tail lights onwards. Ostensibly to reach their quota but in reality to help pay their monthly wages, the same perverted laws and justice we see here now with the pretence that some speed cameras and limits are for safety not for collecting revenue?.

The Roman Catholic church in Quebec Province was very corrupt and powerful in politics as well as where the general population were concerned. No one could start up in business without the blessing of the local church. The congregations would be openly and blatantly told to boycott the un-blessed. As in France still today the small farmers were protected as it was illegal to sell margarine in Quebec because it would reduce the demand for the more expensive butter. So, after a financial deal with the church, exactly the same product sold as margarine in Ontario was in a differently labelled container and then sold as an alternative, cooking fat! Two faced as well as crooked. My friend and erstwhile navigator Tim Plottier had a managerial job with a Simpson Sears Store (a Canadian version of the huge American conglomerate,

Sears Roebuck). Most of Tim's junior staff were, supposedly French speaking from Hull, across the river. The problem was that their French was a sort of native patois and Tim could not understand them nor they him a lot of the time. He therefore reverted to English, which was more successful in practice but resented by the so-called French element. There was still a lot of them and us attitude between the so-called French element and the wider majority of English speakers. During the Second World War, I was told that the central government could not bring in conscription because the majority of the French and particularly the Catholic church were Vichy-ites or in other words they favoured the larger part of France that was not occupied fully by the Germans and often brutally run by the majority French Nazi party headed by the evil traitor, Marshal Petain. This is not to denigrate the thousands of other very brave French Canadians that did fight and lay down their lives to free France of both French and German Nazis. The cowards that stayed at home often joined the church for the duration to help hide their traitorous instincts with hypocrisy too. The English speaking majority sarcastically referred to these now long robed (or skirted) parasites as the Quebec Highlanders! Or even Bull Nuns! The Catholic church thinking they had chosen the winning side and as in the case of the Vatican were believed to have assisted in the smuggling out of Nazi war criminals with the lubrication of some of their stolen gold and art treasures.

155. The ever-growing business

The Carling Avenue base continued to expand and grow as if by magic with next to no advertising but largely by the much lower overhead of word of mouth. The inventory of spare parts was widening all the time but it was only Volvo who were insistent, on the percentage of spares reflecting the rate of sales. Their strong wooden crates just arrived like clockwork along with their latest selection of Swedish publicity gals. In practice the Volvos were the most reliable of all the cars we handled and most of the Volvo bits that we used were on other makes of car. Things like Timken wheel bearings, carburettors (S.U.s) and even door handles (Wilmot Breeden) were common to many other vehicles. Some English Ford bits took 8 to 10 months to arrive so much so that some of the multi Ford outlets refused to carry or sell the English versions at all! The German Ford Taunas cars from Cologne had not got under way at that time. Vauxhall were struggling a bit with their latest effort, the Victor and were desperate enough to ask me to drive one of them in a local driving skill test and rally just to get some publicity. I tried but it was hopeless really but we managed to put up a better than deserved result having almost rolled it at least twice and removed most of the rubber from the tyres before they got the car back. Despite all this they were pleased! My theory was that I had managed to make the car look less of a disaster than it really was.

The mundane servicing of cars did not interest me at all even though our reputation was partly built on it. Honest back up was something totally lacking with imported cars with the exception of the VW Beetle, of course. We therefore had the reputation and the moral duty to do the best we could and stop the almost British mentality or habit of sell and forget. Hence the employment of the best mechanics available, like Eddie and his team. They enjoyed their jobs! I did quite enjoy doing the tuning and road tests on some of the brisker machines such as the Jaguars, Aston Martins, Alfa Romeos and A.C.s etc.. They, usually being driven about town by the average driver, tended to coke up a bit and not run as smoothly as they should. A spark plug change was not a total cure either as the carbon had built up due to lack of revs. due in part, on the automatic transmissions which were the majority in the North American market. This was because they never ever got the chance to be revved up. Many years later I was to find that the cars with an automatic transmission are better running on hotter plugs which burn off the carbon better and never break down at sustained high revs., what I would call thermally elastic. Often our procedure in Ottawa was for the car to be fully serviced first, then I would drive it a few miles out of the city on a good back road with little traffic and careful checking behind advertising bill boards and other likely hiding places for the speed cops. Then turn round and drive flat out in third gear at up to ninety miles an hour, often blowing clouds of smoke and carbon coke out of the exhaust behind me. Back at the garage a small adjustment to the now smooth idle speed and that was that. The trade secret of the great job we were so often complimented on, even by women drivers never got out. The smooth results were also appreciated by even snooty passengers in the back! KISS (keep it simple stupid), was often the answer.

156. The showroom

In all the circumstances, when it came to building the showroom/parts department beside, almost flush and in character with the existing blue and white lubrication bays a serious decision had to be made. It would have been churlish not to have let Bob Potter's rogue builder brother do the work despite my reservations about his reliability, workmanship and continued need to be subsidised with his neverending ploys and excuses. We went ahead and got the planning permission but the planners would not let us have the windows (for extra natural light in the car display area) on the side-wall immediately facing our recently acquired bee-keeping plot next door. This was despite being prepared to give myself written permission to do so. Daft, to say the least but they would allow any sort of blocks or bricks however ugly which could offend any theoretical neighbour much more than windows ever would. The foundations were dug out and the concrete footings were laid, then one morning I came in to find that the dwarf block walls were supposedly finished. I could see that they were not level but the Potter brother (I still cannot remember his name) was insistent that they were. I was adamant and refused to pay anymore money out for the next materials or wages until it was checked properly. Very reluctantly (perhaps he saw his golden goose about to fly away?) he plodded all round the four outer walls of the foundations with a tatty looking spirit level and a rather warped wooden board. Taking probably twenty to thirty step by step measurements before he got right round again he announced that nowhere was more than half an inch out, so there. It was clear that at each short measurement he was just adding error to error and compounding the problem without either seeing or understanding what he was doing. I became very peeved and insisted that I would be the judge not him so he threw the level and board at me and suggested if I was so smart I could check it myself.

This I did, but not by his method. I got a length of car wash hose out and fixed each end to opposite corners of the potential building and proceeded to laboriously fill it up with the bright red Prestone antifreeze we used. Finally when I had filled it at my end to the level of the top of the blocks the level at the other end was about five inches lower! Game, set and match as far as I was concerned but the Potter brother would have none of it and insisted that it was not a proven or an approved method. I had to be very insistent and tell him, "my daddy told me that water will always find its own level and I still believe him, so there. You work to my levels in future or I'll find someone who will". He very reluctantly agreed but muttered to the effect, that it would all be my fault and responsibility when it went wrong later. The work went ahead quite quickly after that. The big steel lintel for the top of the show room windows arrived on schedule and the big windows followed soon after. The roof steel work and sheets went on easily and all fitted well. We then knocked a hole through to the existing lube bays and ducted some of the excessive hot air heating system into the showroom, which, in effect we heated for nothing.

The only potential but luckily short term problem was that when the city planning department came to visit and inspect the finished building they discovered that although I had not flouted their ban on windows on the side wall facing the bee keepers plot I had made a larger part of the wall in glass bricks so letting almost the amount of light I wanted. They tried to argue that I had broken the rules since glass constituted windows in their book. I argued that since the trade description specifically called them glass bricks I had not. After a lot of muttering they said no more and decided not to make a legal issue of it. Pat Faithful was delighted with his parts den at the back of the new building and we found we could get up to four cars in the showroom area with a bit of juggling and with the aid of jacks. Three was a better compromise, particularly on opening night which was on Thursday the 27th of November 1958 just three days before Laird's second birthday and about a month after Laura, "Daddy's Darling Daughter" was born. This with the aid of one of our doctor customer/clients who was very good and in whom Prue had developed great confidence. We had taken out full-page adverts in both the leading newspapers that morning and were surprised at the support we got. The police arrived to complain about some double parking, a quarter of a mile away on a main road! We bribed them with goodies and refreshments and no more arguments or possible charges were then forthcoming.

157. Second thoughts

Car sales continued to rise, plus more and more servicing and mechanical work arrived, to an almost embarrassing level. We were all kept so busy that I for one got to the stage of not stopping for meals. It reached the point where I was living on mushroom omelettes (often cold) and coffee. I ignored the signs of impending health problems and felt I had to keep going, having started it all. I somehow felt I had the moral responsibility to keep running with it for the sake of the others as well as myself. Foolish in retrospect as my drive and enthusiasm was starting to wane anyway. I first became aware of this one day when I passed two Dauphines and did not recognise either driver. I suddenly woke up to the fact that we were now quite a big business and no longer a strictly personal one either, which was what it was really meant to be all about for me initially. I just did not want to get any bigger under these new circumstances. So I had thoughts about leaving the loyal and faithful boys to run an Ottawa branch and I might move out to Calgary and start a new one, all over again, almost from scratch. I liked Calgary, its proximity to the Rocky Mountains and found the view looking down into the city from above at night very attractive. I was also of the opinion that the discovery of shale oil deposits out west, that were at that stage uneconomical to extract would in due course lead to a boom when the price of oil climbed to a more realistic level? Today, I believe that about one third of the USA's oil comes from Canada and presume that part of it is from those oil shale deposits.

However all that was not to be as I was receiving more and more information indicating that my father was dying of cancer and I became determined that he should see his only grandchildren before he died. Somehow I knew that if I did not make the break early in the spring (1959) I would be so bogged down with business that I'd never get away at all. As it was I had to send Prue off with the children on the booked flight on 24th April 1959 and I followed a week or so later when I'd sorted out some, what at the time seemed relatively important problems. Dear little Laura was so small they put her into a mini hammock and hung her from the luggage rack for the flight. The cost of her flight was C$25.20 (no seat reserved!) exactly one tenth of Prue's and with Laird's at half the cost of Prue's. On our arrival back in the UK we all stayed with my parents at Court Echo, which, with my father being so ill could only be a short-term option. When we first arrived it had been a stimulus for my father and for him to make a last valiant effort to walk about hand in hand with a young Laird. They would walk round the garden very slowly and identify the different plants and flowers, including Hi-D(R)angers.

Prue and our Canadian born children, Laura and Laird with the insidious and interfering mother-in-law. Back in the UK 1959

158. U.K. Home sweet home?

I had brought back a few Fish carburettors for my motoring friends to sample and test extensively. They, like me initially, were very sceptical but this changed to amazement after extensive testing. The UK appeared to have finally got its morale into gear after the war and there was some general enthusiasm and drive among the populace. There were rumours of some really new, interesting and worthwhile cars to be announced later in the year instead of stopgap and improved pre-war efforts. The only thing that was showing no sign of improving was the availability of decent housing either to buy or to rent. This was to prove a real problem, in several ways later, as will become clear. As a result of the very favourable testing of the Fish carburettors I contacted Eric Liebman to tell him that he had a huge potential market for his carburettors in UK and possibly Europe too. His immediate comment was, "you are the only one on that side of the pond who knows and understands the Fish Carburettor, so you should stay over there and take on the task yourself. I know, even if you do not realise it yet, that is where your heart lies and where you will be happiest. Further I will grant you exclusive rights for the whole of Europe and the UK for free! That's how much faith and trust I have in you". Needless to say I was flabbergasted at his proposal and generosity. I was stunned and needed to get a whole new brain into gear, there was so much at stake and to consider. It would not be an exaggeration to say that it was potentially the most monumental turning point in our lives. My oldest friend Barry Davison was very keen to help in any way he could and offered the full use of his own family workshop and yard at Soho Mills, Hackbridge near Wallington and Croydon in Surrey as a starting off point and was happy to be a co-director of the enterprise and his family's accountant, a man by the name of Burtenshaw would take on the task of company secretary and accountant for us. Eric Liebman would supply the latest sleeved down American carburettor models in an effort to suit our smaller engined cars.

At that time I was also in a bit of a quandary as I really did not want children of ours to be brought up, or at least educated in the American, almighty dollar, environment. I was getting more and more intolerant of the common comment to the effect, "if he is so clever (or smart) why is he not rich?" Everything seemed to revolve round money and the almost sole measure of success was based on it. If, for instance some brilliant scientist decided he would rather teach at a university, putting something back into education, for much less money that he could earn in industry, then he was regarded as a mug and certainly not to be admired for it! I found a lot of well meaning Canadians kidded or deluded themselves that they were taking only the best of American and Britain cultures and rejecting the rest. I fear that very often they finished up as poor imitators of mostly the worst of American habits and attitudes! But, to be entirely fair and if one had the determination it was possible to break out of such a common mould and pursue your own dreams, culture, values and habits. This was mostly true in the blue-collar trades but was much, much more difficult in the white collar field!

My future fears and apprehensions about the direction that Canada was heading I think have been more than borne out by recent history. This deterioration I would dare to suggest is due in part to the fact that they have largely only had a far too liberal Liberal Govt. ever since and that it has sunk lower and lower when it came to pandering to the screaming lower echelons and minorities of a perverted society. To even consider legalising so called marriages between perverts and allowing the false concept and justification by even using the term, like so many other countries do now, of an alternate life style, which in truth is only a distorted way of trying to justify crime, perversion and the undermining of decent and civilised society. This, in an effort for the powers-that/to-be continue to get the minority votes in the selfish interests of retaining greedy and corrupt political power. All this despite the fact that history clearly shows that once any form of perversion is accepted then even worse ones automatically follow. We are already seeing claims that human to animal relationships should also be recognised and accepted.

This will grow in just the same way that the homosexual agitations did! Such pressure for the acceptance of alternative life styles is already showing signs of rape and even murder becoming more acceptable, at least in some forms. We already have the situation of the President of a supposed civilised country refusing to condemn the rape of baby girls as a cure for Aids, which in itself is entirely the result of perverted forms of sex in the first place. It certainly did not just jump from animals to humans without sexual contact and without the exchange of bodily fluids. This is the confirmed scientific method of transferring the disease among the homosexuals first then later from the bi-sexuals into both adulterous and sadly innocent clean living hetrosexual wives. Then on to the even more innocent newborn babies too.

Add all this to the, now millions of entirely unjustified abortions and it would be very difficult, as all these trends grow to claim that our civilisation is not growing ever more tolerant of perversions, rape and murder! But as created individual human beings we still have the free choice and option to be "in this world but not of it"! Back on the Canadian front they had the additional debilitation and destructive influence of the fanatical French elements, which were stirred up further by the biggest French enemy of the British since the days of Napoleon Bonaparte, a certain Charles Andre Joseph Marie de Gaulle! A man that back during the war had to be reluctantly tolerated (the lesser of several evils) by Winston Churchill and the rest of us. In addition to his preventing the UK from joining the European Common Market in 1962 and 67 (actually a good thing in my personal opinion, aside) he was only too happy to be fostering better relations with the so recent enemy, Germany! Not a lot of people seem to realise that. Perhaps he just could not get away from genes that had come on down from the biblical treacherous and unreliable ancestor, Rubin? Typical, I suppose of the French/Gallic phobia and their resentment of the British and white Americans. I have always said that if I was fighting in the trenches I would feel relatively a lot safer with a drunken American armed with a machine gun behind me than a Frenchman with a knife!!

159. A wise decision?

Right, off my high horse and back to our family lives. We (in retrospect probably mostly me but I do not honestly remember Prue's obvious mixed feeling on the subject) made the decision to stay in the UK and make another fresh start from absolute scratch again. A fateful decision where our marriage was concerned as we were back in the range of the evil and poisonous mother in law and Prue's trouble making elder sister Jane. But since I probably thought myself, and our marriage invincible by then and I certainly underestimated the domestic problems that would ensue and arise and how they would play out. When I say start again from scratch, I mean just that as I left the Canadian business intact and did not take a single cent out of it. I left it for the loyal staff (the boys) to run on and as their own. Young Titch Holt had got himself into a situation where he had to marry his equally young girl friend and had nowhere to live so I gave them our mobile home on the site out at RR2 City View with the rather loose arrangement that he could pay me a nominal $1,000, when he/they could afford it. Needless to say I never received a cent! Everything else from the telly to a complete set of encyclopaedias were given away to friends and the Studebaker I just left with our Aussie friend since he had been using it full time for months anyway. The only thing we brought back, needless to say again, was the Jaguar XK120. Once again I was able to, at least philosophically, shut the door on my past with no backward glances and get stuck into making a success of the new carburettor importing and tuning business, which turned out to be no mean task!

160. Forward to the past! (with apologies to "Back to the Future")

Well Kiddiewinks and any other readers that have stuck with me this far, that takes me to a suitable halfway point or chapter in my life (1959-60+/-). Whether I ever get round to writing the second half, which in effect I am still living, nearly fifty years further on I do not know. My life continued to be a bit adventurous, some times dangerous to some minds but rarely dull. I was never to make the money levels I had reached before as it was always ploughed back into the business. But we never went short of anything and being me continued to get, perhaps selfish satisfaction out of doing too much off my own bat, as it were. Getting at least a gallon out of a financial pint pot, metaphorically speaking. As a piece of literature this screed may well be judged a disaster as it had no real plot or even knew where it was going. It all started, as some thumbnail sketches of my early family and wartime life, once I got to Malaya a few more fingernails seemed to get exposed. Then by Indonesia/Borneo, Lossiemouth and Canada it grew into a bit of an uncoordinated handful. I hope that it gives the odd laugh at my own expense and experience, fills in some unknown or forgotten history, meaning and value to the many lost lives that have enabled us all to live the modern relatively free and civilised life, which would not have been the case for most of us had the communists succeeded in taking over. Most of my readers would then probably never have existed in the first place! We have the Americans to thank largely for that relatively happy situation and despite their atrocious behaviour on occasions and monumental international and domestic disastrous policies and decisions, they are, and for the moment remain, the lesser of the two opposing evils! How they now cope with the array of mad Muslim situations and being in effect bankrupt at the same time will be an interesting bit of history.

I am sure history will also bear me out in the fact that godless communism is/was an even worse plague on civilisation than fascism. Many will dispute it but even the statistics support me on this. Stalin killed many more of his own people than Hitler ever did. And just a couple of other examples, think of Pol Pot and the Khymer Rouge in Cambodia who merely added another two and a half million deaths to their worldwide total almost making the Nazi look like amateurs! Do not forget either Mao Tse Tung's very recent murderous reign in China where some reports suggest that the death toll was in the region of 40,000,000!(?) or again the very dangerous ongoing maniacal North Korea. progression! The totally uncalled for ruthlessness of China's behaviour in Tibet, some of their own provinces and to say nothing of their ongoing aggressive behaviour and attitude towards Formosa (Taiwan) which should be enough to remind us all that behind the present commercial financial smoke screen and charade is still the communistic tiger that has not and will never change it's spots.

On the European front a largely communist Russia is still there and must not be underestimated and it will only be the growing right wing Axis between Germany and the Vatican that will hold them back for a while. The now coming largely German dominated United States of Europe or the Federated States of Europe will replace the now fatally wounded USA as the leading world power. Britain will also fall by the wayside in the painful process. History will show that Britain's Prime Minister, Edward Heath to be the most dishonest one ever. He knew all along that Europe was to be much more then just a trading association as he lied to us at the time. In the meantime we have to cope with fanatical Muslims becoming an even greater threat, this century, to our Anglo-Saxon (Western) culture than communism was in the last.

There are many more stories of my youth and wartime life both tragic and funny. I could literally write a book on parts of the Malayan saga that I have only so far picked for examples of the high and low points. On Indonesia, Lossiemouth and Canada I think I've covered most of it already.

CREDITS

Commonwealth War Graves Commission
Major J. C. Rogerson, Regimental Museum
(West Kent Regiment)
Dr. Mahathir Mohamad. Prime Minister Malaysia 1981-2003
Handbook to British Malaya 1927
Malaya by Gerald Hawkins 1952
Taming the Jungle by Pat Barr 1977
Force 136 by Tan Chong Tee 1994
Jungle War in Malaya by Harry Miller
(rife with false information)
Personal Memoires of Peter Nock
Syd Guthrie
Chye Hock Koh of K.L. & Unocol

Enhancement of personal photographs:
Callum Ramsay & Argyll Computer Services,
Lochgilphead, Argyll
Front cover illustration of a CT by:
Graham Nairn Esq, Kingston-on-Spey, Moray
Initial front cover concept:
Derek's (Meredith) Delightful Designs Studio,
Ardrishaig, Argyll
Final front cover layout and design:
Callum Ramsay & Argyll Computer Services.

Front cover depictions:
Painting of Javanese Volcanic activity and fertile countryside
by the Indonesian artist, A. Soderi

The two most relevant machines in the author's life:
A Jaguar XK 120 and the de Havilland Mosquito

Caricature of the Communist Terrorists
by Graham Nairn